1994

W9-BYA-600

Continuous Quality Improvement in Health Care

Theory, Implementation, and Applications

Curtis P. McLaughlin, DBA

Professor of Business Administration
 and Health Policy and Administration
Kenan-Flagler Business School
Associate of the Cecil G. Sheps Center
 for Health Services Research
University of North Carolina
Chapel Hill, North Carolina

Arnold D. Kaluzny, PhD

Professor of Health Policy and Administration
School of Public Health
Associate of the Cecil G. Sheps Center
 for Health Services Research
University of North Carolina
Chapel Hill, North Carolina

AN ASPEN PUBLICATION®
Aspen Publishers, Inc.
Gaithersburg, Maryland
1994

This publication is designed to provide accurate and authoritative information in regard to the Subject Matter covered. It is sold with the understanding that the publisher is not engaged in rendering legal, accounting, or other professional service. If legal advice or other expert assistance is required, the service of a competent professional person should be sought. *(From a Declaration of Principles jointly adopted by a Committee of the American Bar Association and a Committee of Publishers and Associations.)*

Library of Congress Cataloging-in-Publication Data

Continuous quality improvement in health care: Theory, implementation, and applications / edited by Curtis P. McLaughlin, Arnold D. Kaluzny.
p.   cm.
Includes bibliographical references and index.
ISBN 0-8342-0536-X
1. Medical care—Quality control.   2. Total quality management.
I. McLaughlin, Curtis P.   II. Kaluzny, Arnold D.
[DNLM: 1. Total Quality Management.   2. Delivery of Health Care—
organization & administration—United States. W84 AA1 C76 1994]
RA 399.A3C66   1994
362.1'068'5—dc20
DNLM/DLC
for Library of Congress
93-48062
CIP

Copyright © 1994 by Aspen Publishers, Inc.
All rights reserved.

Aspen Publishers, Inc., grants permission for photocopying for limited personal or internal use. This consent does not extend to other kinds of copying, such as copying for general distribution, for advertising or promotional purposes, for creating new collective works, or for resale. For information, address Aspen Publishers, Inc., Permissions Department, 200 Orchard Ridge Drive, Suite 200, Gaithersburg, Maryland 20878.

Editorial Resources: Amy R. Martin

Library of Congress Catalog Card Number: 93-48062
ISBN: 0-8342-0536-X

Printed in the United States of America

1   2   3   4   5

Table of Contents

Chapter 4   **The Outcome Model of Quality** **47**
               Susan DesHarnais and Curtis P. McLaughlin

               Clinical Quality 47
               Politics of Quality Assessment 48
               Framework for Quality Management 53
               Institutional Responses 66
               Authority Patterns 68
               Conclusions 68

Chapter 5   **Measurement and Statistical Analysis in CQI** **70**
               Susan Paul Johnson and Curtis P. McLaughlin

               Variation—What Is it and Why Eliminate it? 70
               Process Capability 71
               How Does CQI Differ from QA? 72
               The Seven Tools 74
               Conclusion 101

Chapter 6   **Measuring Customer Satisfaction** **102**
               Kate Macintyre and Carolyn Cable Kleman

               What Is a Customer? 102
               Expectations and Loyalty 104
               Using Customer Information 105
               The Customer Survey Process: Measuring Customer
                  Satisfaction 106
               Rewards Systems: Translating Satisfaction into
                  Sustained Effort 118
               Conclusion 121
               Appendix 6-A—Outpatient Services: The Patient's
                  Viewpoint 122
               Appendix 6-B—Central Hospital Physician Survey 124

Chapter 7   **Teams at the Core** **127**
               Rebecca La Vallee and Curtis P. McLaughlin

               Organizing Teams 127
               Group Outcomes 128
               Organizational Context 130
               Team Characteristics 132
               Team Member Characteristics 135
               Professional Socialization 137

Contributors

Editors

Curtis P. McLaughlin, DBA
Professor of Business Administration
and Health Policy Administration
Kenan-Flagler Business School
Associate of the Cecil G. Sheps Center
for Health Services Research
University of North Carolina
Chapel Hill, North Carolina

Arnold D. Kaluzny, PhD
Professor of Health Policy and
Administration
School of Public Health
Associate of the Cecil G. Sheps Center
for Health Services Research
University of North Carolina
Chapel Hill, North Carolina

Contributors

Susan DesHarnais, PhD, MPH
Associate Professor of Health Policy and
Administration
School of Public Health
University of North Carolina
Chapel Hill, North Carolina

Sandra K. Evans, MBA, BSN
Assistant Director of Operations
Vice Chair, Nursing Department
Adjunct Assistant Professor in Nursing
School of Nursing
University of North Carolina
Chapel Hill, North Carolina

Walter C. Gramley, MBA
Health Care Management Consultant
Deloitte & Touche
New York, New York

Russell Harris, MD, MPH
Assistant Professor of Medicine
Director, Program on Health Promotion
and Disease Prevention
Department of Medicine
School of Medicine
University of North Carolina
Chapel Hill, North Carolina

Rudolph S. Jackson, DrPH, MBA
Research Fellow, Cancer Prevention
Lineberger Comprehensive Cancer Center
School of Medicine
University of North Carolina
Chapel Hill, North Carolina

B. Jon Jaeger, PHD, MHA
Professor Emeritus
Duke University
Durham, North Carolina
Research Professor
Health Services Administration
University of Florida
Jacksonville, Florida

Susan Paul Johnson, MBA
Doctoral Candidate
Kenan-Flagler Business School
University of North Carolina
Chapel Hill, North Carolina

David C. Kibbe, MD, MBA
CEO and President
Future Healthcare, Inc.
Adjunct Assistant Professor
Health Policy and Administration
School of Public Health
University of North Carolina
Chapel Hill, North Carolina

Carolyn Cable Kleman, RN, MHA
Unit Manager, CCU
MetroHealth Medical Center
Cleveland, Ohio

Rebecca La Vallee, MPH
Doctoral Candidate
Department of Health Policy and
Administration
School of Public Health
University of North Carolina
Chapel Hill, North Carolina

Linda S. Leininger, MD, MPH
Clinical Assistant Professor of Medicine
Division of General Medicine and Clinical
Epidemiology
Department of Medicine
School of Medicine
University of North Carolina
Chapel Hill, North Carolina

Kate Macintyre, MSPH
Graduate Student
Health Policy and Administration
School of Public Health
University of North Carolina
Chapel Hill, North Carolina

Ronald T. Pannesi, PhD, MBA
Assistant Professor
Operations Management
Kenan-Flagler Business School
University of North Carolina
Chapel Hill, North Carolina

Kit N. Simpson, DrPH
Assistant Professor
Department of Health Policy and
Administration
School of Public Health
University of North Carolina
Chapel Hill, North Carolina

Richard P. Scoville, PhD
Vice President
Future Healthcare, Inc.
Chapel Hill, North Carolina

Victor J. Strecher, PhD, MPH
Associate Professor
Department of Health Behavior and Health
Education
University of North Carolina
Chapel Hill, North Carolina

Preface

Quality management has come of age in health care and undoubtedly will be a major component of any health care reform effort. This book presents an interdisciplinary perspective on quality management in health care, taking into account a number of disciplines, including operations management, organizational behavior, and health services research. Graduate students in health services management are the primary audience. This book will also be of interest to those in undergraduate and extended degree programs, executive education, as well as continuing educational activities involving medicine, nursing, and allied health.

Our approach to quality management is integrative. Special attention has been given to the underlying tools and approaches fundamental to Total Quality Management (TQM)/Continuous Quality Improvement (CQI). The challenges of implementation and institutionalization are addressed in a variety of health care organizations, including primary care clinics, hospital laboratories, public health departments, and academic health centers. TQM/CQI is a "body-contact sport," and any real effort to understand the concept and its application requires studying its implementation in a real setting. The book concludes with five case studies that track the development of CQI in a variety of settings and show how these organizations have adapted TQM/CQI concepts to their particular needs and strategies. Each case describes in detail the implementation in that context and is accompanied by a study guide that highlights the important points and links the case back to specific chapters in the text.

Throughout the development of this book, in its design and drafting, we have had the privilege and good fortune of working with many individuals of considerable talent, dedication, and good humor who permitted the chapters to be delivered on target and on time. This group of faculty and student colleagues has brought home to us how fortunate we are to be at a university where interdisciplinary efforts are encouraged and where informal networking is a reality. Specifically, Gordon DeFriese of the Sheps Center for Health Service Research and Kerry Kilpatrick of the Department of Health Policy and Administration, School of Public Health, have helped create the climate that supported this collaboration. It has allowed us to put together a group of clinicians, health services and management researchers, and health services administrators, all of whom have brought a unique set of skills and points of view to the book.

In addition to working with contributing authors, whom some would say "thrive on abuse," we have had extraordinary support from many other individuals, people here in Chapel Hill and elsewhere. The case writing effort was supported in part by a grant from the American College of Healthcare Executives and by the Kenan-Flagler Business School. Dr. Paul Batalden of Hospital Corporation of America (HCA) has been a frequent visitor to our campus and a powerful intellectual model for this effort. Specific thanks must go to Christina Fowler for her overall assistance in the preparation of the bibliography and various drafts of chapters, to Geoff Walton for his contribution in redrafting various efforts, and to Janice Pope and Jerry Oster for their overall editorial assistance throughout this endeavor. Thanks must also be given to Julie Mohr of HCA for helping to gather illustrative materials, to Claudia Haglund and Steve Durbin from the Sisters of Providence system for their early consultation as we formulated various ideas, and to numerous participants in our early joint Duke-UNC seminar on TQM in health care, especially B. Jon Jaeger of Duke, and more recently, the University of Florida, Chip Caldwell of HCA, and UNC colleagues, Mary Beck and Aleda Roth. We also wish to acknowledge the assistance of Sandy Cannon and Amy Martin from Aspen Publishers for their overall guidance and suggestions in the production of this book.

Introduction

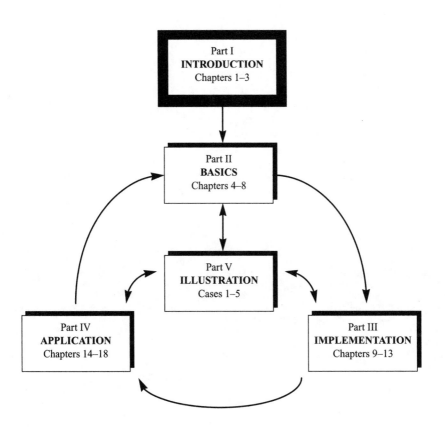

Introduction

Curtis P. McLaughlin
Arnold D. Kaluzny

1

Defining Total Quality Management/Continuous Quality Improvement

Continuous quality improvement in health care comes in a variety of "shapes, colors, and sizes" and is referred to by many names. Don't be confused—whether it is called total quality management (TQM), continuous quality improvement (CQI), or some other term, TQM/CQI is a structured organizational process for involving personnel in planning and executing a continuous stream of improvements in systems in order to provide quality health care that meets or exceeds customer expectations. In this book we will use two terms interchangeably: TQM, referring primarily to industry-based programs, and CQI, referring to clinical settings. We will use the latter term most frequently to encompass all of these efforts and philosophies.

While TQM/CQI has various names, it usually involves a common set of characteristics, including: a quality council made up of the institution's top leadership, training programs for personnel, mechanisms for selecting improvement opportunities, formation of process improvement teams, staff support for process analysis and redesign, and personnel policies that motivate and support staff participation in process improvement. In the course of that process analysis, rigorous techniques of the scientific method, including statistical process control, are typically applied. The purpose of this chapter is to present the distinguishing characteristics and elements of CQI, its underlying philosophy, and an overview of this book's sections and subsequent chapters.

RATIONALE AND DISTINGUISHING CHARACTERISTICS

As health care organizations develop their own CQI approaches, their managements must go through a decision process in which activities are initiated, adapted, and then institutionalized. Organizations embark on CQI for a variety of reasons, including accreditation requirements, cost control, competition for cus-

3

tomers, and pressure from employers and payers. Linder (1991), for example, suggests that there are three basic CQI strategies: conformance to requirements, competitive advantage, and true process improvement. Some institutions genuinely desire to maximize the quality of care provided as defined in customer preference terms. Others wish simply to increase their share of the local health care market. Still others wish to do whatever is necessary to maintain their accreditation status with the Joint Commission on Accreditation of Healthcare Organizations and then return to business as usual. As you might imagine, this book is written for the first group, those who truly wish to give health care customers the quality care that they deserve.

Although CQI comes in a variety of forms and is initiated for a variety of reasons, it does have a set of distinguishing characteristics and functions. These characteristics and functions are often defined as the essence of good management. They include: (1) empowering clinicians and managers to analyze and improve processes; (2) adopting a norm that customer preferences are the primary determinants of quality and that the term "customer" includes both the patients and the providers in the process; (3) developing a multidisciplinary approach that goes beyond conventional departmental and professional lines; and (4) providing the motivation for a rational, data-based, cooperative approach to process analysis and change.

What is perhaps radical vis-à-vis past health care improvement efforts is a willingness to examine existing health care processes and rework these processes using "state-of-the-art" scientific and administrative knowledge and relevant data-gathering and analysis methodologies. Health care processes have developed and expanded in a complex, political, and authoritarian environment, acquiring the patina of science. The application of data-based management principles to the clinical and administrative processes that produce patient care is what CQI is all about.

CQI is simultaneously two things: a management philosophy and a management method. It is distinguished from other philosophies and methods by the recognition that customer requirements are the key to customer quality and that ultimately customer requirements will change over time because of changes in education, economics, technology, and culture. Such changes, in turn, require continuous improvements in the administrative and clinical methods that affect the quality of patient care. This dynamic between changing expectations and continuous efforts to meet these expectations is captured in the Japanese word, *kaizen*, translated as continuous improvement (Imai, 1986). Change is a fundamental of the health care environment, and the organization's systems must have both the will and the way to master such change effectively.

The use of the term *customer* presents a special challenge to many health professionals. It is a term that runs contrary to the professional model of health services and the idea that "the doctor knows best." Some health professionals would prefer terms that connote the more dependent roles of "client" or "patient." In CQI terms, *customer* is a generic term and refers to the end user of a group's output or product. The customer can be external or internal to the system —a patient, a payer, a colleague, or someone from another department. It is user satisfaction that becomes the ultimate test of process and product quality. Consequently, new efforts and new resources must be devoted to ascertaining what the customer does want through consumer surveys, focus groups, interviews, and a wide variety of ways of gathering information on customer preferences, expectations, and perceived experiences. If one encounters resistance and challenges to the use of such words as *customer*, perhaps the best strategy is to demur, since the real issue is the concept and not the words. Although people's perceptions and attitudes represent reality and must be respected, the concept is more important than the labels.

CQI is further distinguished by its emphasis on avoiding personal blame. Issues of personal negligence, poor workmanship, and lack of interest are all avoided, and the focus is on the managerial and professional processes associated with a specific outcome. The initial assumption is that the process needs to be changed and that the person(s) already involved in that process are needed to help identify how to approach a given problem or opportunity.

Therefore CQI moves beyond the ideas of participative management and decentralized organizations. It is participative in that it encourages the involvement of all personnel associated with a particular work process to provide relevant information and become part of the solution. CQI is also decentralized in that it places responsibility for ownership of each process in the hands of its implementers, those most directly involved with it. Yet this level of participation and decentralization does not absolve management of its fundamental responsibility; in fact, it places additional burdens on management. CQI is an approach that calls for significant amounts of management thought, oversight, and responsibility. Management's role is to encourage and support the development of process improvement teams, often multidisciplinary, rather than to impose management's preconceived solutions. Management must be the quintessential teacher and model of the improvement process.

CQI inherently increases the dignity of the employees involved because it not only recognizes the important role of each of the members of the process improvement team, but also involves them as partners and even leaders in the redesign of the process. In some cases, professionals can also serve as consultants to other teams and to management itself. Not surprisingly, organizations using CQI often experience improvements in morale as the operative words become *helpfulness* and *involvement* rather than *avoidance* and *adversarial*. Furthermore, since the level of quality is now being measured, workers are enabled to take more pride in the quality of the work that they are producing.

A further distinguishing feature of CQI is the rigorous belief in fact-based decision making, captured by the saying, "In God we trust. All others send data." Facts do include perceptions, and decisions are not delayed to await the results of scientifically correct, double-blind studies. However, everyone involved in CQI activities is expected to study the multiple causes of events and to explore a wide array of systemwide solutions. It is surprising and rewarding to see a team move away from the table-pounding, "I'm right and you're stupid" position with which so many meetings in health care seem to start. The teams do not start by trying to fix blame, but by trying to gather data, both hard and soft, to see what is actually happening and why. Multiple causation is assumed, and the search is started to identify the factors contributing to less than optimal system performance.

ELEMENTS OF CQI

Together with these distinguishing characteristics, CQI is usually composed of a number of elements. We have divided these elements into three categories: (1) philosophical elements, which for the most part mirror the distinguishing characteristics cited above; (2) structural elements, which are usually associated with both industrial and professional quality improvement programs; and (3) health-care-specific elements, which add the specialized knowledge of health care to the generic CQI approach. The philosophical elements are those aspects of CQI that, at a minimum, have to be present in order to constitute a CQI effort. The structural elements also are usually associated with CQI, but are not defining and might occasionally be omitted for one reason or another. The health-care-specific elements are those that people do not often include in their lists of elements of CQI initiatives, but that are particularly relevant in the health care setting.

Philosophical Elements

The philosophical elements that are representative of continuous quality improvement include:

1. Customer Focus—Emphasis on both customer (patient, provider, payer) satisfaction and health outcomes as performance measures
2. Systems View—Emphasis on analysis of the whole system providing a service or influencing an outcome
3. Data-Driven Analysis—Emphasis on gathering and use of objective data on system operation and system performance

4. Implementer Involvement—Emphasis on involving the owners of all components of the system in seeking a common understanding of its delivery process
5. Multiple Causation—Emphasis on identifying the multiple root causes of a set of system phenomena
6. Solution Identification—Emphasis on seeking a set of solutions that enhance overall system performance through simultaneous improvements in a number of normally independent functions
7. Process Optimization—Emphasis on optimizing a delivery process to meet customer needs regardless of existing precedents and on implementing the system changes regardless of existing territories and fiefdoms. To quote Dr. Deming: "Management's job is to optimize the system."
8. Continuing Improvement—Emphasis on continuing the systems analysis even when a satisfactory solution to the presenting problem is obtained
9. Organizational Learning—Emphasis on organizational learning so that the capacity of the organization to generate process improvement and foster personal growth is enhanced

Structural Elements

Beyond the philosophical elements cited above, a number of highly useful structural elements can be used to structure, organize, and support the continuous improvement process. Almost all CQI initiatives make intensive use of these structural elements, which reflect the operational aspects of CQI and include:

1. Process Improvement Teams—Emphasis on forming and empowering teams of employees to deal with existing problems and opportunities
2. Seven Tools—Use of one or more of the seven quality tools so frequently cited in the industrial *and* the health quality literature: flow charts, cause-and-effect diagrams, checksheets, histograms, Pareto charts, control charts, and correlational analyses
3. Parallel Organization—Development of a separate management structure to set priorities for and monitor CQI strategy and implementation, usually referred to as a quality council
4. Top Management Commitment—Top management leadership to make the process effective and foster its integration into the institutional fabric of the organization
5. Statistical Analysis—Use of statistics, including statistical process control, to identify and minimize variation in processes and practices
6. Customer Satisfaction Measures—Introduction of market research instruments to monitor customer satisfaction at various levels

7. Benchmarking—Use of benchmarking to identify best practices in related and unrelated settings to emulate as processes or use as performance targets
8. Redesign of Processes from Scratch—Making sure that the end product conforms to customer requirements by using techniques of quality function deployment and/or process reengineering

Health-Care-Specific Elements

The use of CQI in health care is often described as a major management innovation, but it also blends with past and ongoing efforts within the health services research community. The health care quality movement has had its own history with its own leadership and values that must be understood and respected. Thus in health care there are a number of additional approaches and techniques that health managers and professionals have successfully added to the philosophical and structural elements associated with CQI, including:

1. Epidemiological studies, coupled with insurance payment and medical records data
2. Involvement of the medical staff governance process, including quality assurance, tissue committees, pharmacy and therapeutics committees, and peer review
3. Use of risk-adjusted outcome measures
4. Use of cost-effectiveness analysis
5. Use of quality assurance data and techniques and risk management data

PLAN FOR THE BOOK

Figure 1–1 presents the basic structure of the book. In this chapter we have outlined the underlying philosophy of TQM/CQI together with its structural elements and its health-care-associated elements. Chapter 2 presents the context within which these elements and the underlying philosophy emerged. Chapter 3 summarizes in a balanced way the theoretical and empirical evidence that CQI can work and can improve health care quality. The remaining chapters are divided into five parts: Part II, Basics (Chapters 4–8), Part III, Implementation (Chapters 9–13), Part IV, Application (Chapters 14–18), and Part V, Illustration (Cases 1–5). As presented in Figure 1–1, the book's structure reflects a continuous process in that the basics lead to implementation, and implementation leads to application. Application of TQM/CQI provides an opportunity for further refinement and

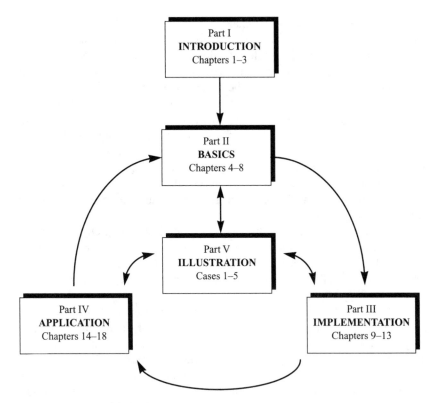

Figure 1–1 Structure of the Book

understanding of the basics through studying illustrative cases and conducting other research.

Part II, The Basics, deals with the underlying tools and approaches fundamental to TQM/CQI. Chapter 4 presents this within an outcomes model. Attention is given here to the existing quality movement within health care and to the specific measurement issues that health care improvement programs must address. Chapter 5 presents the fundamentals of measurement and statistical analysis applied in CQI efforts. Various techniques are presented with specific examples taken from the health care setting. Chapter 6 discusses issues of meeting customer satisfaction requirements together with methods and instrumentation required for assessing satisfaction. Again, specific illustrations are presented. Chapter 7 focuses on the role of teams within the context of CQI. Finally, Chapter 8 examines the role of CQI within the context of health care planning and technology assessment.

Part III, Implementation, presents the challenges associated with the implementation and institutionalization of CQI within a health care setting. The five chapters in this part address the challenges that a manager is likely to face in implementing CQI in the professional environment, including managing a number of transitions during the implementation process, making sure that there is a high level of physician involvement, and providing an appropriate information infrastructure. Chapter 9 outlines the issues of planning, organization, benchmarking, and evaluation in a CQI initiative. Chapter 10 deals with the issues of professional autonomy and administrative authority involved in implementing TQM. Chapter 11 focuses on the transitions required to implement CQI in a health care organization. This chapter assists the manager in dealing with the paradoxes that he or she faces in managing a program based on employee participation. Chapter 12 deals with issues of securing clinician participation in the CQI process. Chapter 13 considers the management information system requirements of CQI and suggests how to set up such a resource.

Part IV, Application, deals with the specific application of CQI to a variety of health service settings, including primary care (Chapter 14), hospital laboratories (Chapter 15), public health departments (Chapter 16), and academic medical centers (Chapter 17). Part IV concludes with a review of challenges facing the research of TQM/CQI (Chapter 18).

Finally, Part V, Illustration, presents a series of five case studies of CQI activities in real settings. All are intended for the purposes of classroom discussion of the philosophy and techniques of CQI as applied in a real context. These case studies both illustrate the applications of the methods and provide a basis for discussing ways of applying the concepts discussed in the earlier chapters. The Family Practice Clinic case shows how a multidisciplinary team can be used to assess and then improve the continuity of care in an academic practice setting. The Holston Valley Medical Center and Hospital case shows the application of a locally developed industrial model to a community hospital's administrative functions. The West Florida Regional Medical Center case outlines parts of the CQI activity followed by a Hospital Corporation of America hospital in response to serious price competition in its community. The University Hospital and Medical Park case outlines the CQI activities of a small, publicly owned community hospital that is part of a multihospital system. The Transportation Services case shows how a TQM effort can be managed in parallel with other management steps to improve services and improve employee responsiveness through increased empowerment.

B. Jon Jaeger
Arnold D. Kaluzny
Curtis P. McLaughlin

TQM/CQI: From Industry to Health Care

2

Quality has been and continues to be a central issue in health care organizations and among health care providers. The works of Avedis Donabedian, Robert Brook, and Len Rosenfeld, to name a few, are legendary and have made major contributions to the definition, measurement, and understanding of quality.

However, the corporatization of health care in the United States (Starr, 1982) and impending health care reform have redefined and will continue to redefine how we manage quality. Specifically, corporatization has forced health services to conform increasingly with organizations in the external environment. Given the increasing proportion of the gross national product being allocated to health services and the redefinition of health care as an "economic good," health care organizations are influenced to a growing extent by organizations in the industrial sector. As part of this process, health care organizations have become more and more isomorphic with the organizations that finance most of the services that they provide. This conformity is reflected by the increasing tendency to refer to hospitals as "corporations"; the development of "product lines" rather than service areas; the replacement of planning by marketing; by the use of titles such as President, Chief Executive Officer, or Chief Operative Officer rather than Administrator; and, in the area of quality, by a nomenclature and perspective known as total quality management (TQM). Although the elements and components of this approach are not antithetical to the way that quality has been defined and managed within health services, neither are the two completely isomorphic. This chapter will trace the development of TQM and then discuss its application as continuous quality improvement (CQI) in health service organizations.

Part of the material in this chapter appeared in B.J. Jaeger, A. Kaluzny and A. Roth, *Management of Continuous Quality Improvement,* Chicago, Ill: American College of Healthcare Executives, 1993, Chapter 1. © Used by permission.

DEFINING QUALITY

Although there are many definitions of quality, there are essentially three levels of quality commonly talked about today. These levels are cumulative, with the difficulty in achieving quality increasing with each one:

1. *Conformance quality*—conforming to specifications; having a product or service that meets predetermined standards.
2. *Requirements quality*—meeting total customer requirements; having perceived attributes of a service or product that meet or exceed customer requirements.
3. *Quality of kind*—quality so extraordinary that it delights the customer; having perceived attributes of a product or service that significantly exceed customer expectations, thereby delighting the customer with its value (Dumas et al., 1987).

CQI is not the same as quality assurance (QA), although at times the concepts overlap. Quality assurance is like the term conformance quality. It implies that a predetermined standard is in place, such as the requirements of a set number of fire hoses for a specific size of hospital, rather than the continuously evolving standard implied by CQI. The confusion that surrounds the use of the two terms *CQI* and *QA* stems in large part from the difference in quality as conceptualized in the work of early leaders in the health care quality movement and the somewhat simplistic popularization of TQM by health care groups and organizations. If one, such as Donabedian, reads carefully the initial quality efforts in health care, there is surprisingly little difference between that conceptualization of quality and what TQM leaders in industry have written.

EMERGENCE OF TQM

The fundamentals of TQM are based on the Scientific Management movement developed at the turn of the century. Emphasis was given to "management based on facts," but with management assumed to be the master of the facts. It was believed to be the responsibility of management to specify one correct method of work for all workers and to see that personnel executed that method to ensure quality. Gradually that perspective has been influenced by the human relations perspective and by the recognition of the importance and ability of the people in the organization. Building on those perspectives, Figure 2–1 presents the major U.S. contributors to the emergence of TQM.

Shewhart

Most histories of TQM credit statistics pioneer Walter Shewhart, at Bell Laboratories, with the first published efforts in this area. His best known contributions

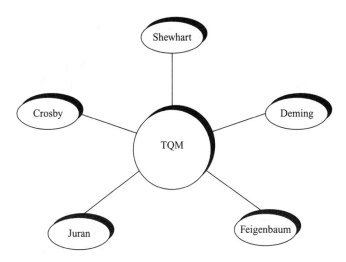

Figure 2–1 Major U.S. Contributors to TQM

are the control chart and the Plan, Do, Check, Act (PDCA) cycle illustrated in Figure 2–2. Although the PDCA cycle is often attributed to Deming, Deming himself attributes it to Shewhart (Deming, 1986).

Shewhart was aware of and promoted the idea that price alone was no indication of value. He wrote that price, without an understanding of quality, was meaningless. Shewart taught that decisions based on price alone were almost certain, in the long run, to be more expensive than necessary and to lead to undesirable results. He also was aware that there were inherent difficulties in defining quality, although he felt that reasonable people could develop operational definitions, that is, standards.

Furthermore, it was Shewhart's idea that statistical control (also called statistical process control) of stable or "in control" processes is the foundation of all empirical CQI activities. If a process exhibited variation, then the cause of that variation had to be discovered and removed. Determining variation and analyzing its causes in order to remove them is the primary function of TQM.

Deming

W. Edwards Deming is the best known of the proponents of TQM. In 1950 he was invited by representatives of Japanese industry to suggest how they might best rebuild their war-ravaged economy. Although he had been advocating his statistical approach to quality for some time, the Japanese were the first to implement his ideas widely.

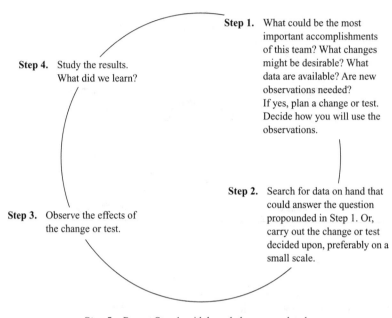

Step 4. Study the results. What did we learn?

Step 1. What could be the most important accomplishments of this team? What changes might be desirable? What data are available? Are new observations needed? If yes, plan a change or test. Decide how you will use the observations.

Step 3. Observe the effects of the change or test.

Step 2. Search for data on hand that could answer the question propounded in Step 1. Or, carry out the change or test decided upon, preferably on a small scale.

Step 5. Repeat Step 1, with knowledge accumulated.
Step 6. Repeat Step 3, and onward.

Figure 2–2 Shewhart's PDCA Cycle. *Source:* Reprinted from *The New Economics for Industry, Government, Education* by W. Edwards Deming by permission of MIT and W. Edwards Deming. Published by MIT, Center for Advanced Engineering Study, Cambridge, MA 02139. Copyright © 1993 by W. Edwards Deming.

Over the intervening years, Deming has made enormous contributions to the development of TQM, but he is perhaps best known for the 14-point program of recommendations that he devised for management to improve quality (see Exhibit 2–1). But his focus has always been on processes (rather than organizational structures), on the ever-continuous cycle of improvement, and on the rigorous statistical analysis of objective data.

Arraying data in various ways to facilitate its analysis, Deming sought to identify two types of sources of improvement in processes. The first was elimination of "special" causes of process variation: variation associated with specific material(s), machine(s), or individual(s). The second was elimination of "common" causes of variation: those associated with aspects of the system itself such as poor design, inadequate training, and improper materials, machines, or working conditions. Special causes of problems can be addressed by those working directly with the process, whereas common causes of problems are the responsibility of management to correct.

Exhibit 2–1 Deming's 14-Point Program

1. Create and publish to all employees a statement of the aims and purposes of the company or other organization. The management must demonstrate constantly their commitment to this statement.
2. Learn the new philosophy, top management and everybody.
3. Understand the purpose of inspection, for improvement of processes and reduction of cost.
4. End the practice of awarding business on the basis of price tag alone.
5. Improve constantly and forever the system of production and service.
6. Institute training.
7. Teach and institute leadership.
8. Drive out fear. Create trust. Create a climate for innovation.
9. Optimize toward the aims and purposes of the company the efforts of teams, groups, staff areas.
10. Eliminate exhortations for the work force.
11a. Eliminate numerical quotas for production. Instead, learn and institute methods for improvement.
11b. Eliminate Management by Objective.
12. Remove barriers that rob people of pride of workmanship.
13. Encourage education and self-improvement for everyone.
14. Take action to accomplish the transformation.

Source: Reprinted from *The New Economics for Industry, Government, Education* by W. Edwards Deming by permission of MIT and W. Edwards Deming. Published by MIT, Center for Advanced Engineering Study, Cambridge, MA 02139. Copyright © 1993 by W. Edwards Deming.

Deming believed that management has the final responsibility for quality. Employees work in the system; management deals with the system itself. He also felt that most quality problems are management controlled rather than worker controlled. This was the basis for his requirement that TQM be based on a top-down, organizationwide commitment.

Feigenbaum

Building on Deming's statistical approach, Armand F. Feigenbaum and Joseph M. Juran provided theoretical constructs for TQM. Feigenbaum coined the phrase "total quality control," which he defined as an effective system for integrating the functions of quality development (conception, planning, design, set-up), quality maintenance (production, distribution, service), and quality improvement (training, data analysis, user feedback). These functions cut across all activities in the organization (including marketing, production, and finance) and involve all system phases (inputs, transformation, outputs, and outcomes). Both suppliers and customers are drawn into the total quality concept. The goal of quality, according to Feigenbaum, is to meet satisfactorily whatever customers believe to be their requirements for the service or product. (Note that factors outside the organization—cultural, attitudinal, and technological changes—can make customers dissatisfied with a once satisfactory outcome, thereby continuously motivating new quality improvement cycles.)

Juran

Joseph M. Juran, like Deming, was involved with the Japanese in the 1950s. He argued that the quality improvement process is a never-ending spiral of progress, or "fitness for use," as defined by customers. He argues that management must focus on two levels within the organization. The first level is the mission (always fitness for use), which is determined by design requirements and by the degree of conformance to the specifications of that design's availability, reliability, and maintainability. The second level is the mission of the individual departments and units within the organization to do their work according to the specifications that have been designed to achieve fitness for use: that is, to go about their work in a way that maximizes the organization's overall attainment of fitness for use. (This may mean that some units must suboptimize their performance in order for the organization as a whole to optimize its performance. This is often a difficult concept for professional personnel to accept.) Juran emphasizes the interdependency of all units in achieving the ultimate outcome.

Juran's writings parallel Deming's concepts of classifying process variations, separating them into "sporadic" and "chronic." Sporadic problems occur when production falls below acceptable standards: chronic problems are inherent in the work setting and require intervention by management. Improvements in chronic problems he calls "breakthroughs."

Furthermore, Juran insists that quality goals be specific. Vague statements like "We are dedicated to improving quality" or "Quality is Job One" are unacceptable. Instead, he insists on a specific goal such as "we will reduce the number of medical records uncompleted after two weeks to 1 percent of total discharges by January 1 of next year."

Juran's followers in health care also emphasize Juran's Quality Trilogy of basic quality processes: (1) quality planning, (2) quality control, and (3) quality improvement. These must be supported by an "infrastructure" of measurement systems, buyer-user-supplier relationships, education and training, and information management. These quality processes must rest on a "foundation" of customer focus, management involvement, and strategic planning that links all quality efforts back to the firm's key business goals.

Crosby

Philip B. Crosby, working in the 1980s, developed a different theoretical perspective on quality improvement based on changing the corporate culture and attitudes. He departed from his predecessors' focus on statistical process control techniques and emphasized the concept of "zero defects." He emphasized organization and management theories rather than the application of statistical tools. Crosby asked two questions: What is quality? What standards and systems are needed to achieve quality? He answered with four "absolutes of quality." The first absolute requirement is "conformance to requirements," often referred to as "Do it right the first time." The second is "defect prevention is the only acceptable approach." The third is that "zero defects" is the only performance standard, and the fourth is that the cost of quality is the only measure of quality. (This led to the often-quoted title of his 1979 book, "Quality is free," meaning that the costs of producing quality (zero defects) are less than the losses associated with nonquality defects.) His approach, like Deming's, is to implement a 14-step process, but a process that stresses changes in the organization's culture and attitudes. Crosby's 14 steps are listed in Exhibit 2–2.

Crosby believed that the quality program should go forward on two fronts. Management needs to master a set of skills, including his 14 steps, and to develop the necessary implementation and support systems. At the same time, individuals will need training in a variety of tools, including process and systems modeling, statistical techniques, experimental design, problem solving, and error prevention.

Crosby's writings emphasize developing an estimate of the "cost of nonconformance," also called the "cost of quality." This involves identifying and assigning values to all of the unnecessary costs associated with waste and wasted effort when work is not done correctly the first time. This includes the costs of identifying errors, correcting them, and making up for the customer dissatisfaction that

---

Exhibit 2–2 Crosby's Fourteen Steps

1. Management commitment
2. Quality improvement team
3. Quality measurement
4. Cost of quality evaluation
5. Quality awareness
6. Corrective action
7. Establish an ad hoc committee for the zero defects program
8. Supervisor training
9. Zero defects day
10. Goal setting
11. Error cause removal
12. Recognition of success
13. Quality councils
14. Do it over again

Source: Adapted from *Quality is Free: The Art of Making Quality Certain* by P.B. Crosby, pp. 135–139, Mentor Books, 1979.

results. Estimates of the cost of quality range from 20 to 40 percent of the total costs of the industry, a range also widely accepted by hospital administrators and other health care experts.

Crosby's concept of the cost of quality is a good one to use when the top management has not yet accepted the philosophical arguments of CQI. They often can be impressed by arguments that show the specific cost items that poor quality generates, especially when the presenter also shows how these faults can be addressed using standard quality improvement techniques.

The Japanese

All the individuals mentioned to this point have been Americans (although their ideas were largely ignored in the United States until about 1980). However, the Japanese have made numerous original contributions to CQI thinking, tools and techniques, especially since the 1960s. The most famous of Japanese experts are Genichi Taguchi and Kaoru Ishikawa. Taguchi emphasized using statistical techniques developed for the design of experiments to quickly identify problematic variations in a service or product, and a focus on what he called "robust" (forgiving) design. He also emphasized evaluating quality from both an end-user and a process approach. Ishikawa and other Japanese quality engineers refined the application of the foundations of CQI and added:

1. total participation by all members of an organization (quality must be companywide)
2. the next step of a process is its "customer" just as the preceding step is its "supplier"
3. communicating with both customer and supplier is necessary (promoting feedback and creating channels of communication throughout the system)
4. a participative team emphasis, starting with "quality circles"
5. an emphasis on education and training
6. quality audits, e.g., the Deming Prize
7. rigorous use of statistics
8. "just in time" processes
9. the "QC Story" idea

New approaches, refinements of older concepts, and different combinations of ideas are occurring almost daily. As more and more organizations adopt CQI, we are seeing increasing innovation and experimentation with CQI thinking and its applications. This is especially true of the health care area, where virtually every organization has had to work hard to develop its own adaptation of CQI to the clinical process.

APPLICATION TO HEALTH CARE ORGANIZATIONS

Around the mid-1980s, CQI was applied in several health care settings. Most notable was the early work done by three physicians: Paul Batalden at HCA, Donald Berwick at Harvard Community Health Center, and Brent James at Intermountain Health System.

Deming (1993) has continued to develop his ideas about TQM. His most recent work argues that management needs to undergo a transformation. In order to respond successfully to the current challenges to our organizations and their environments, the way to accomplish that transformation, which must be deliberately learned and incorporated into management, is by pursuing what he calls "Profound Knowledge." The key elements of his system of profound knowledge are (1) appreciation for a system, (2) knowledge about variation, (3) theory of knowledge, and (4) psychology.

A Deming approach, as adopted by the Hospital Corporation of America (HCA), is illustrated in Figure 2–3. It is referred to by HCA as FOCUS-PDCA and provides the firm's health care workers with a common language and an orderly sequence for implementing the cycle of continuous improvement as adapted by Deming from Shewhart.

For example, the Deming process is especially useful in health care because professionals already have knowledge of the subject matter and have a set of values and disciplines that fit the Deming philosophy. What training in Deming methods adds is knowledge of how to build a new theory using insights about systems, variation, and psychology, and it focuses on the answers given to the following basic questions (Batalden and Stoltz, 1993):

1. What are we trying to accomplish?
2. How will we know when that change is an improvement?
3. What changes can we predict will make an improvement?
4. How shall we pilot test the predicted improvements?
5. What do we expect to learn from the test run?
6. As the data come in, what have we learned?
7. If we get positive results, how do we hold onto the gains? If we get negative results, what needs to be done next?
8. When we review the experience, what can we learn about doing a better job in the future?

In addition, a number of hospitals began to experiment with applications of CQI, some of which began to receive public notice in the late 1980s. Several of those mentioned early in the literature and at professional meetings were Meriter Hospital, Madison, Wisconsin; University of Michigan Hospitals, Ann Arbor, Michigan; Alliant Health System, Louisville, Kentucky; Henry Ford Health Sys-

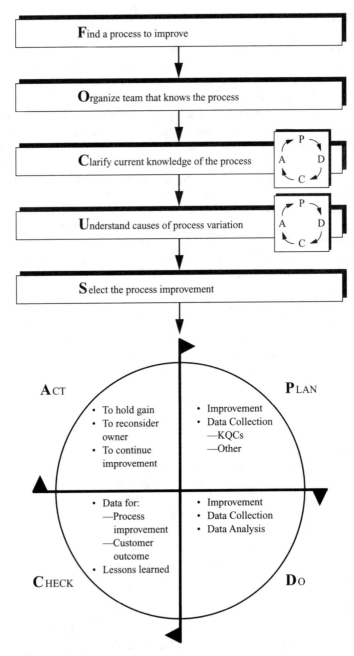

Figure 2–3 The FOCUS-PDCA® Cycle. *Source:* Reprinted with permission of the Hospital Corporation of America, Nashville, Tennessee, © 1988, 1989. Not for further reproduction.

tem, Detroit, Michigan; and West Paces Ferry Hospital, Atlanta, Georgia. The latter, an HCA hospital, hosts formal, monthly orientation programs for interested visitors from all over the country.

As might be expected, the rapidly increasing interest in CQI applications for health care organizations has attracted a growing number of consulting firms able to work with clients to help them get started. These firms range from general consulting firms to TQM/CQI specific consulting firms to health-care-only consulting firms. Their services range from broad and general education, data collection and analysis, assistance with planning and project initiation, personnel training, and statistical process control services. Typically, consultant use is limited to the first two years or so of developing a CQI initiative at a health organization. Today the list of hospitals and other health care organizations involving CQI in their operations is large and growing rapidly, primarily due to its proven benefits and the competitive pressures in the health care environment.

COMPARING INDUSTRIAL AND HEALTH CARE QUALITY

Quality has been a fundamental issue within health services, and therefore some might question the value added by CQI. A comparison of quality from an industrial perspective versus quality from a health care perspective reveals that the two are surprisingly similar and that both have strengths and weaknesses (Donabedian, 1993). The industrial model is limited in that it (1) ignores the complexities of the patient-practitioner relationship; (2) downplays the knowledge, skills, and motivation of the practitioner; (3) treats quality as free, ignoring quality/cost trade-offs; (4) gives more attention to supportive activities and less to clinical ones; and (5) provides less emphasis on influencing professional performance via "education, retraining, supervision, encouragement and censure" (Donabedian, 1993, pp. 1–4). On the other hand, Donabedian suggests that the professional health care model can learn the following from the industrial model:

1. new appreciation of the fundamental soundness of health care quality traditions
2. the need for even greater attention to consumer requirements, values, and expectations
3. the need for greater attention to the design of systems and processes as a means of quality assurance
4. the need to extend the self-monitoring, self-governing tradition of physicians to others in the organization
5. the need for a greater role by management in assuring the quality of clinical care
6. the need to develop appropriate applications of statistical control methods to health care monitoring

7. the need for greater education and training in quality monitoring and assurance for all concerned (1993, pp. 1–4)

In reality, there is a continuum of TQM/CQI activities, with manufacturing at one end of the continuum and professional services at the other (Hart, 1993). The TQM approach should be modified in accordance with its position along this continuum. Manufacturing processes have linear flows, repetitive cycle steps, standardized inputs, high analyzability, and low worker discretion. Professional services, on the other hand, involve nonstandardized and variable inputs, nonrepetitive operations, unpredictable demand peaks, and high worker discretion. Many organizations, including health care organizations, have processes at different points along that continuum that should be analyzed accordingly. The hospital, for example, has laboratory and support operations that are like a factory and diagnostic and treatment activities that are professional services. The objective of the factorylike operations should be to drive out variability to conform to requirements and to produce near-zero defects. At the other end, the objectives of diagnosis and treatment are to do whatever it takes to produce customer satisfaction and maintain the loyalty of customers and employees.

HOW IT WORKS: THE QC STORY

One approach to CQI is called the "QC Story." It emphasizes the problem-solving aspects of CQI. The reader should note, however, that CQI is just as applicable to processes that are operating without apparent problems as it is to problematic areas. An in-depth presentation of this approach, given by Kume (1987), forms the basis for this section.

In terms of the QC Story, a problem is defined as the undesirable result, a performance gap. The solution to the problem is to improve the undesirable result to a level that is acceptable. To accomplish this, seven steps are followed:

1. Problem Identification

Innumerable problems exist; therefore the first thing to be done is to ensure that the problem is the most important of all those that we observe. One's limited resources should be committed only to that problem that the data show will yield the greatest improvement. Importance can be based on cost, frequency, seriousness, or some other factor. One of the tools frequently used to determine importance is the Pareto diagram, an error frequency diagram with types of errors arrayed in order of decreasing frequency. Figure 2–4 is one example of a Pareto diagram applied to a linen supply problem.

Identification of the problem should also lead to identification of the owner(s) of the process(es) involved with the problem so that they may participate in establishing what is to be done. Then the investigators must describe the problem

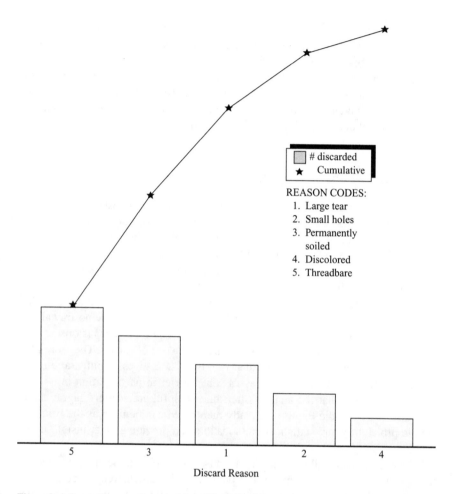

Figure 2–4 Pareto Diagram, Reasons for the Discarding of Linens.

as completely as possible: its history, circumstances, and impact. With knowledge of its impact, management can then establish a goal, a realistic expected achievement. This in turn leads to the establishment of a budget and a schedule of activities.

2. Observation

This is the initial data collection phase of the QC Story approach. It differs from step one, where the problem is being isolated, because here all the features of the problem are observed and recorded: time, type, place, and how common it is in the overall operation. In addition, the problem solvers continue to make direct observations in order to supplement the data with information that can not be readily or appropriately quantified.

Maximum use must be made of factual, reliable data; this is essential to the CQI process. However, intuition and imagination also are important because they can enrich the understanding of the problem and lead to new ways of observing and thinking about the problem. The tools frequently used here are flow charts, control charts, data sheets, and checksheets.

3. Analysis

At this stage, the emphasis is on determining causes and possible remedies of the nonconforming result. To do this, hypotheses are formulated and then verified. Perhaps this is the most important departure from other approaches to management in that the causes of the problem are determined scientifically and not on the basis of subjective reasoning, intuition, or authority. As is the case throughout the CQI process, the question is, "What do the facts reveal?"

A frequent way of beginning this phase is to develop cause-and-effect diagrams, sometimes called "fishbone" or Ishikawa diagrams. These portray all the relevant factors that seem related to the problem. The focus here is on the concrete or known reasons rather than some theoretical set of causes. The more concrete the diagram, the more helpful it is. Figure 2–5 gives an illustration of a cause-and-effect diagram used to assess one barrier to participation in clinical trials. Other tools that the analyst often finds helpful are scatter diagrams and histograms. These and the tools already mentioned can be used as the basis for simple probability and statistical methods that can provide greater insight into a problem.

By using the data collected during the observation phase, the analysts look for those causes that seem to match the pattern of defects, thereby becoming the most plausible causes of defects and thus the ones that receive priority for further investigation. To do this, hypotheses are revised, if necessary, and tested. This testing usually requires a new round of data collection. It is this new data that will determine whether or not the hypotheses are correct and how strong the relationship is. If they are correct, then the QC Story moves into a new phase; if they are incorrect, new hypotheses have to be developed and investigated.

4. Action

Once the cause(s) of the defect have been determined, then the alternative actions have to be defined, and a subset chosen and implemented. Again, the alternative(s) have to be driven by the data, not by preferences, voting, office politics, or other subjective means.

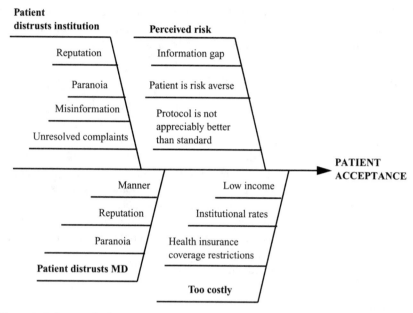

Figure 2–5 Cause-and-Effect Diagram of Causes for Patients Failing to Enroll in Cancer Trial Protocol. *Source:* Hynes et al., 1992.

Here it is important to deal with the cause(s) of the problem in order to eliminate the problem (prevention). Clearly, attention should first be given to that factor that has the most significant impact on the problem, then to the next most significant and so on. However, it is equally important to work on those causes that are controllable. Therefore, one would be smart to defer working on those causes that are not tractable (amenable to change). In fact, early in any CQI program, management must make sure that change efforts succeed, selecting to attack those causes that are sure to yield results easily. We refer to this as part of the early strategy of "small wins" (Weick, 1984).

Before an action is finally taken, it must be thoroughly reviewed to see what impact it is likely to have. Will it cause new problems? Can we get others to cooperate with the new action? Are there any special issues that need to be addressed (such as capital outlays, retraining)? What will be its impact on the overall CQI program, given the current stage of the program's life cycle? Finally, the action decided upon must be taken.

5. Check

With each action that is implemented, data must again be collected to determine the intervention's effect. To what degree does the intervention eliminate the problem—fully, partially, or not at all? Has it caused unexpected problems and, if so, what are the extent and implications of these problems? These questions are asked both before and after the comparison of data and results.

6. Adopt

Once the action is seen to have eliminated the problem, then steps must be taken to implement the action on a permanent basis. In this regard, the "why" of the change is especially important so that people understand the change. This may require rewriting of procedure manuals, educating and training of employees, communication, or other measures in order for the action to be incorporated into the ongoing operations of the organization. Adoption also requires assigning responsibility for the new action so that it can be monitored.

At first, the improvement is likely to work well because there is a tendency to be careful about a change. But then as time passes, people and organizations can tend to slip back into old patterns. Reinforcement of the new action is indicated as soon as any movement toward old patterns occurs.

7. Conclusion

In this final stage, the efforts and result are reviewed to determine the extent of effectiveness achieved, identify any problems that remain and the organizational lessons that have been learned, and establish plans for the future. Then the entire process is repeated. This reiteration is the basis for calling the process "continuous" quality improvement. The QC Story repeats itself endlessly.

ESSENTIAL COMPONENTS OF CQI

Transforming any organization, including a health care organization, into one that practices CQI requires a number of components or conditions to be present. They include a thorough knowledge and understanding of the concept, management and worker commitment, planning, teamwork, communication, education and training, and patience.

Knowledge and Understanding

In the typical organization, responsibility for knowing and understanding the concepts and practices of CQI falls on senior management. Ideally, that person is the CEO. If not, then there must be a person who will help the CEO become knowledgeable. It is through the CEO that the board, and in health care organizations the medical staff, are helped to learn about and understand CQI and what the concept can and cannot do for the organization. Before moving forward with implementation of CQI, as many members of the organization as possible must become knowledgeable. The senior management must have not only the knowledge, but also considerable depth of understanding of the concepts and philosophy of CQI.

Commitment

One of the most difficult steps, but one that must be faced early on, is the need for total commitment to the concept. This commitment must be from the very top, that is the CEO. No matter how committed members of the organization below the CEO are, few effective results can be obtained in an organization where the CEO is uninterested or does not give CQI the highest priority. Indeed, lack of commitment at the top is the most frequently cited reason for failure of CQI initiatives. If the CEO is really committed, others will have little choice but to adopt CQI (or leave the organization).

Strong and widespread commitment is also important because the cost of CQI can be substantial. This cost, however, should be viewed as an investment in the future success of the organization, in the same way that a new hospital building is perceived. The CQI approach is based on a long-term view of the organization and thus requires a well-developed planning process.

Planning

The planning process begins with a clear and well-articulated organizational vision and with mission statements. This vision and mission must be disseminated throughout the organization and to the organization's suppliers and customers. In this sense, strategic planning can no longer be perfunctory. If it is, and a blurry understanding of the vision and mission results, then priorities will also be blurred and the results of CQI will be mixed at best.

Taking the vision and implementing it is known in Japanese as *hoshin* planning and in the United States as policy deployment. Policy deployment is the longer range and higher level counterpart to process improvement. Good strategic planning and its coordinated use and evaluation downward into the organization's departments and units are measures of the effectiveness of the planning process.

Where the organization has an effective strategic plan, it will help clarify priorities and timing. Copies of the plan must be widely available so that everyone understands the "what" and the "why" of the effort. Good strategic plans provide goals and direction and show where resources and effort are to be allocated. Perhaps the severest test of the effectiveness of how well the vision, mission, and strategic plan have been developed and disseminated is whether all employees, all medical staff, and all community leaders can recite (and support) what the organization is attempting to do.

Teamwork

Although there are exceptions based on the nature of the particular process being studied, CQI is based on teams that together approach the problem and its possible resolution. These teams may be permanent, such as the Quality Improvement Council made of up top management, or transitory and designed solely to address a particular problem. Because many of the problems that need to be addressed cross organizational boundaries, these teams tend to be composed of individuals with diverse backgrounds and perspectives. Therefore it is essential to their effectiveness that the teams learn, understand, and use group skills in order to maximize the creativity and potential contribution of the group.

There are other benefits to the use of teams. Teams take on a common culture, and this helps to spread knowledge of the organization's mission and vision. Teams break down barriers to communication as team members cross organizational and professional boundaries. By their nature, teams promote a "we" feeling and commitment in the organization.

Communication

All organizations can improve their ability to communicate, especially internally; few do it particularly well. This is often the reason why there is confusion, dissention, disharmony, and low morale. Health care organizations are no better or no worse than other kinds of organizations. Yet some of these characteristics appear more evident in health care organizations because of their size, their complexity and professional specialization, and the often critical nature of their work. Various means can be implemented to improve an organization's ability to communicate internally—up, down, and laterally—and externally. A discussion of these means can be found elsewhere. But communication is an indicator of the degree of excellence of an organization, and good CQI implementation depends on it.

Education

Next comes education and training. Everyone in the organization must understand CQI and how to apply it to their individual work settings. This means learning not only what it is and how to do it, but learning the basic tools and techniques and associated concepts, such as how to run a meeting and how to make a presentation. Some individuals will need advanced training in many of these areas so that they can serve as internal teachers, trainers, consultants, and mentors. Effective CQI also means that every individual remains up to date and even advances within his or her own specialty. This means that management must commit to even more education and training.

The needed commitment to education and training extends beyond just the understanding and ability to apply CQI. It includes keeping each member of the organization current in the knowledge, tools, and techniques of his or her own job, whether it is professional, technical, clerical, or support. As one employee phrased it, "CQI means that I must do my own job as well as possible and, at the same time, work on how to do it better." With the rapid rate of technological change in health care, it is easy to see why the education and training costs are likely to be quite high. But there is a real payoff in morale when every employee feels that he or she knows how to do his or her job as well as it can be done. Management is therefore able to focus more on planning and process and less on problems.

CQI is not an inexpensive panacea; however, we believe that it delivers the best value. Instilling in all members of the organization the feeling that they are among the best in their specialty and that they have the tools to improve their own efforts for the betterment of the patient is a very powerful contributor to morale and outcome.

Patience

The importance of patience can not be overemphasized. Time and time again, experience has shown that it takes from 6 to 12 months to get enough people knowledgeable to begin planning CQI activities. Another 6 to 12 months is consumed with the first wave of training and the start-up of a few projects to prove CQI's effectiveness to the staff. As a few CQI successes (small wins) are achieved and experience obtained, enthusiasm will slowly spread throughout the organization. The initial projects are likely to focus on issues that are problems and are bothersome to the team members. It takes another year to a year and a half before management can turn its attention to areas that are not seen as problems, but represent major opportunities for improvement anyway. However, it may be five years before everyone in the organization is relatively knowledgeable about CQI concepts and tools, involved in a CQI initiative, and capable of planning and implementing a CQI initiative on his or her own. At that point, gains start to become more apparent. Some experts believe that as many as ten years are necessary before the organization is completely transformed into a "CQI organization." This time frame requires strong management commitment and vision to provide the staying power and the direction for such a lengthy journey.

PROBLEMS, CHALLENGES, AND ISSUES IN HEALTH CARE

As is the case with any new approach to the management of organizations, difficulties and conflicts with prior concepts need to be anticipated.

What Is Quality?

Quality has been an issue in health care for many decades. Quality is inherent in the professional standards, guidelines, and codes of the myriad professions involved in health care, the many associations that represent these professionals, and the health care organizations themselves. A concern for quality is also evident in the many statutes enacted over the years at the local, state, and national levels to "protect" the quality of health care provided to the public. This results in several significant problems. First, conflict can develop between the standards of one group and the standards of another group. Second, there can be conflict between the professionals and the health care organization in which they are working. Third, all these standards can be viewed as "floors" or lowest acceptable limits for quality: as thresholds where quality becomes acceptable but where there is no recognition that some quality levels are better than others. Finally, these standards tend to be static and therefore counter to the "continuous improvement" philosophy of CQI.

Who Defines It?

Akin to the potential differences among the standards set by professional groups is the tendency of health care professionals, particularly physicians, to think of themselves as operating individually, authoritatively, and situationally. In practice professionals are contributing members of a group, each of whose members is empowered to correct the actions of others for the good of the customer. Similar difficulties will be encountered between management and those involved in any participative process.

Will It Help with Malpractice Suits?

There are legal as well as organizational issues involved in CQI. It is not clear whether CQI efforts will be viewed positively or negatively in tort cases, such as malpractice suits. Most states have laws that shield from discovery proceedings in malpractice cases quality assurance studies done on behalf of the institution's board of trustees. Some laws are being amended to cover, under the same principles of law, CQI program data as well. The legal status of practice guidelines and their use is less clear. According to Holzer (1990, p. 78), "Although it is possible that such policies and guidelines could be admitted into evidence to show that a provider breached a legal duty or standard of care owed a patient, it is uncertain whether these risk control standards could ultimately pass the evidentiary rules of relevancy or materiality in a given law suit." Borbas et al. (1990) cite the use of the argument in Minnesota that solid data are more effective for defending physicians' practices than are expert witnesses.

Although many observers express concern about the use of continuous quality improvement data in discovery proceedings associated with malpractice suits, Holzer (1990, p. 78) suggests that it is more likely that "the consensus-based process of creating clinical standards and guidelines specifically for controlling professional liability losses is itself a powerful and emerging standard for health care risk management programs." This would be especially important should the initial data suggest that the quality of care is generally enhanced by the use of health care protocols per se.

How Much Will It Cost?

Another challenge is how to determine the economic impact of quality improvement on health care organizations. Meaningful cost-benefit and cost-effectiveness studies are often difficult to do. Yet, as previously indicated, there are costs associated with implementing quality improvement. Boards, third parties, employer groups, and government entities will want to know what the payoff is for CQI. The costs of quality have typically fallen into four categories, two of which are somewhat easy to determine—the cost of prevention (training, team activities, communication, etc.) and the cost of appraisal (testing and inspection)—and two of which are difficult to determine—the cost of internal failure (waste, rework, downtime, disruption, etc.) and the cost of external failure (patients go elsewhere, litigation, ill will, etc.). There is also the problem of determining when too much is being done.

How Do We Achieve It?

A number of other issues emerge when CQI is superimposed on a traditional organizational approach, some of which are beginning to be investigated by researchers. For example, what can be done to improve the acceptance of TQM/CQI by first line supervisors, the group that seems to have the hardest time adjusting to the changes that CQI calls for?

SUMMARY

CQI is beginning to make a dramatic impact on the way that health care organizations operate. Their management, structure, resource allocation patterns, and the way that we assess their performance are all undergoing a massive rethinking, which is further complicated by the evolving political, economic, and social context in which health care is delivered. One thing that we can be certain of, however, is that the health care manager of the future must understand what CQI is, how it operates, and how it can be used. The cases that follow in Part V of this book give further insight into this process and its effects.

Curtis P. McLaughlin
Kit N. Simpson

Does TQM/CQI Work in Health Care?

3

Despite widespread enthusiasm for total quality management/continuous quality improvement (TQM/CQI), whether and how it works in health care remain legitimate concerns. Health care organizations are paradoxical, large, and complex. Yet at their core they involve a very fundamental relationship between providers and patient. Moreover, if this were not a sufficient challenge, add the uncertainties of health care reform and the difficulty of measuring the impact of any single effort. Although a controlled trial assessing the ability of CQI to promote and maintain the provision of preventive services in private primary care clinics is ongoing (Solberg, 1993) and survey data are beginning to accumulate on its implementation and perceived impact (Shortell et al., 1993), it is likely that concerns about whether and how TQM/CQI works in health care will remain. Therefore let us consider the evidence currently available. This chapter reviews the evidence to date on the effectiveness of TQM/CQI in health care. It presents a discussion of the National Demonstration Project and its findings, and reviews the recent literature on specific examples of TQM/CQI impact in health care organizations.

LESSONS FROM THE NATIONAL DEMONSTRATION PROJECT

The National Demonstration Project in Quality Improvement in Health Care, reported on by Berwick, Godfrey, and Roessner in *Curing Health Care* (1990), was the initial effort to launch quality improvement within health services. Although it did not give evidence on the costs and benefits of CQI, this eight-month demonstration project clearly showed that the quality improvement techniques that succeed in industry could be applied to the health care setting. The Project provided ten key lessons to guide subsequent efforts, namely:

1. Quality improvement tools can work in health care.
2. Cross-functional teams are valuable in improving health care processes.

3. Data useful for quality improvement abound in health care.
4. Quality improvement methods are fun to use.
5. Costs of poor quality are high, and savings are within reach.
6. Involving doctors is difficult.
7. Training needs to arise early.
8. Nonclinical processes draw early attention.
9. Health care organizations may need a broader definition of quality.
10. In health care, as in industry, the fate of quality improvement is first of all in the hands of leaders. (Berwick et al., 1990, pp. 145-157)

In the book's 'afterword' Garvin (1990) suggests that a number of unanswered questions continue to pose problems. These problems include the indirect relationship between input and outputs (and especially outcomes) in health care, the lack of clear quality standards, and the professionally separate organizational structures of the health care institutions. He also suggests some differences between the quality assurance model and the industrial quality model: (1) variation may be viewed differently; (2) prevention is better than successful inspection; (3) the system, not the individual, is the unit of analysis; (4) the focus is on the customer; and (5) the definition of quality extends beyond the technical dimensions.

ADVANTAGES OF CQI APPLICATION IN HEALTH CARE

Health care personnel are likely to focus on the differences between their service sector and other parts of the economy and society. Therefore it is incumbent on advocates of CQI to explain why and how it works in health care. Intelligent and articulate professionals need answers to the question, "What is behind the assumption of 'value added' from a health care organization participating in CQI?"

A number of factors contribute to the sustained interest and enthusiasm for CQI for health care, despite the limited empirical evidence regarding impact and cost. The first argument for CQI is its direct impact on quality, usually a net gain to the customer and to the organization. The second is that systems can often be designed or redesigned to give lower costs at the same time and with the same techniques used for quality improvement. The third argument relates to the set of benefits associated with a plan that empowers employees in health care through participation in decision making.

Although some benefits of participatory programs are well understood, the managerial benefits in health care generally come from five sources, several of which are particularly relevant to CQI: (1) increasing the intrinsic motivation of the workforce; (2) capturing the intellectual capital already developed by the workforce; (3) reducing the managerial overhead necessary to induce managerial change; (4) vastly increasing the capacity of the professionally dominated organization to do process analysis; and (5) creating the lateral linkages across highly specialized organizational units to increase effectiveness and reduce the process irresponsibility inherent in most health care settings. These five benefits are discussed below, with particular emphasis on the provision of health services.

Intrinsic Motivation

The vast majority of health care workers believe in progress and would like to see improvements and take credit for making them happen. Allowing personnel to work on their own processes, permitting them to "do the right thing," and then rewarding them for that behavior is almost sure to increase intrinsic motivation in employees, if done properly. It is a classic case of job enrichment for health care workers.

Capturing the Intellectual Capital of the Workforce

Industrial managers are increasingly recognizing that front line workers know their work processes better than the management does. Therefore management encourages workers to apply that knowledge and insight to the firm's processes. This is especially true in health care, where the professionals employed by or practicing in the institution control the technological core of the organization. Management, which is responsible for coordination and resource allocation, does not have a great deal of knowledge about fundamental clinical processes. Management that does not capitalize on this available pool of professional and specialized knowledge within the organization is naive at best.

Reducing Managerial Overhead

Some companies have been able to remove layers of management as work groups have taken responsibility over their own processes. The redesign work done by the workforce can also lead to less investment in industrial engineers, quality control specialists, and other overhead staff services. Health care organizations are actually already limited in the number of staff positions, mostly because the professionals rather than the corporate staff have the process knowledge.

Increasing Capacity

In health care, the management of the institution lacks in-depth knowledge of the technological core (medicine, nursing, laboratory chemistry, etc.) of most activities. Therefore management representatives, such as industrial engineers, if they are on the staff, are usually restricted to areas where they have full knowledge and legitimacy, namely administrative activities. By imparting many of those skills to professional staff in their respective departments, units, and centers, CQI can vastly increase the effective capacity of the organization to examine its processes and introduce change. This expansion comes both in personnel hours available and in the areas of operation. For example, a management engineer can participate in and facilitate the process, but would not normally presume to study these processes in the normal hospital setting. Figure 3–1 shows this capacity effect in parallel with the quality program effect. This figure shows how quality efforts and process improvement efforts are mutually reinforcing and how the added capacity induced by involving professionals in process improvement also contributes to the support of the quality effort and ultimately can improve both cost and quality in parallel.

Lateral Linkages

Health care organizations are characterized by their many medical specialties, each organized into its own professional fiefdom. Galbraith, for example, sug-

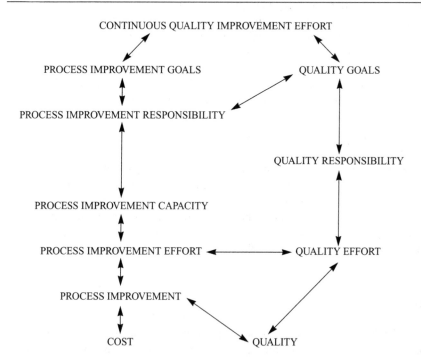

Figure 3–1 Multiple Effects of CQI in Health Care

gests that these units are one response to an information overload in the organization. He suggests that specialization is one way to reduce the need for information-handling capabilities in complex organizations. By specializing, each unit can tend to learn more and more about less and less. One way to offset the effects of this specialization is to provide lateral linkages—coordinators, integrating mechanisms—to get the information moving across the organization as well as up and down the chain of command (Galbraith, 1973; Lawrence and Lorsch, 1967). So far, that has proved very difficult in health care institutions. CQI, however, through its use of interdisciplinary task forces and its focus on a broader definition of process and system as it affects customers rather than professional groups, presents one way to establish linkages. It is clear from the discussions of the technology used that CQI focuses as much on coordination of the change process as on its motivation.

EMPIRICAL EVIDENCE

The preceding section discussed the expected effects from CQI. Empirical studies showing desirable effects within the health organization are just beginning to emerge. The health care literature indicates a number of specific benefits associated with quality improvement and related measures such as customer satisfaction. These benefits include profitability, employee satisfaction, reduced costs, improved patient survival, and better continuity of care.

Profitability

There appears to be a clear relationship between profitability and customer satisfaction in hospitals. Harkey and Vraciu (1992), for example, report on the relationship among the 82 HealthTrust hospitals. They suggest a quality-profitability model that is shown in Figure 3–2. This model shows profitability affected by increased market share and better prices on the market gains side and reduced costs due to productivity improvements and reduced lengths of stay. They reviewed the literature, which had reached varied conclusions on cost/quality relationships. Then they compared the gross margins of the HealthTrust hospitals with the results that were achieved on the company's standardized customer quality surveys in prior years. These surveys were sent to active medical staff, discharged patients, employees, and community members. Each hospital surveyed all of its active medical staff annually by mail with a 60 to 65 percent response rate; 350 discharged patients every six months by mail with a 60 to 65 percent response rate; most employees annually with an 86 percent response rate; and up to 300 randomly selected residents in the hospital's market area annually by telephone survey. Financial performance was defined as the net operating income of

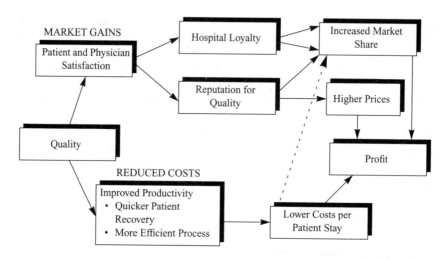

Figure 3–2 Relationship between Costs and Quality. *Source:* Reprinted from Harkey, J., and Vraciu, R., Quality of health care and financial performance: Is there a link?, *Health Care Management Review,* Vol. 17, No. 4, p. 56, Aspen Publishers, Inc., © 1992.

the hospital, excluding interest, depreciation, ESOP expenses, and corporate management fees. The researchers took the results of all these surveys and looked at the relationship between questionnaire values and financial performance.

Factor analysis was used to determine whether a quality factor could be developed from the many quality questions. Two quality factors developed from ten questions. The first seven questions, based on employee, patient, and physician responses, made a very strong factor accounting for 39.4 percent of the variance. The second quality factor was made up of three community responses about the hospital's image and explained 11.1 percent of the variance. The questions used for these two factors were as shown in Table 3–1.

Other factors developed to control for other attributes of the hospitals were wealth of the community and bed size. Given a reliable factor for quality based on the first seven questions above, the researchers then used regression analysis to estimate the relationship between a quality factor score and net operating margin using regression. The reported regression model uses this quality factor and two other variables, Percent Medicare and Percent Managed Care, to explain 29 percent of the variance in net operating income. The quality factor was positively associated with net operating income and significant at the 0.02 level in this model. The other two dependent variables were negatively associated and significant at the 0.01 level. The authors concluded that the perceptions of quality of employees, patients, and physicians were in strong agreement and that the perception of quality, when controlled for payer mix and managed care, added to profitability.

Table 3–1 Questions and Responses

Respondent	Question	Response Used	Mean Value (%)
Employee	"Are you proud of the overall quality of care provided by your hospital?"	Yes (of 5)	34.9
Employee	"Is good service to physicians a high priority for this hospital?"	Yes (of 5)	59.4
Employee	"Do you feel the community views the quality of medicine provided by your medical staff as being generally high?"	Yes (of 5)	24.9
Physician	"My patients typically give positive reports about their experiences at this hospital."	Strongly or somewhat agree (of 5)	78.8
Physician	"The nursing care delivered to my patients is typically good (competent and caring)."	Strongly or somewhat agree (of 5)	79.0
Patient	"How well did our nursing staff do their job (skill, competence, helpfulness, and friendliness)?"	Excellent or very good (of 5)	74.6
Patient	"How would you rate the hospital's overall care?"	Excellent or very good (of 5)	74.2
Community	"HealthTrust has the best physicians." (Yes or No or Don't Know)	Yes	14.1
Community	"HealthTrust has the best care." (Yes or No or Don't Know)	Yes	18.6
Community	"HealthTrust has the most modern technology." (Yes or No or Don't Know)	Yes	12.5

Nelson et al. (1992b) also have reported that patients, employees, and physicians have correlated quality perceptions. They determined that quality ratings by 15,095 patients at 51 Hospital Corporation of America (HCA) hospitals explained 10 to 29 percent of the variation in net operating revenue and return on assets. Both the HCA and the HealthTrust organizations use similar questionnaires, which are described in Chapter 6, to measure customer satisfaction.

The finding of a link between perceived quality and profitability is an important link in justifying CQI. Other research can find other intermediate relationships, but it is this meta-relationship that will be of great interest to boards of trustees and to senior management.

Employee Satisfaction

Rush-Presbyterian-St. Luke's Medical Center in Chicago surveyed 5,174 employees (out of a possible 7,400) in 1990, two years into an extensive TQM program. About half of these employees had participated in that effort. After adjusting for demographic differences in the participating and nonparticipating groups, the hospital found a statistically significant improvement in intrinsic job satisfaction, in the general opinion of the hospital as a place to be a patient and to work, and in a number of positive attitudes toward TQM. Because of the large sample, however, statistical significance was relative easy to achieve. Particularly large changes in scale values (1–5) were achieved in the areas of higher organizational standards, worker and management involvement, and especially TQM awareness (the objective of the program) (Counte et al., 1992).

Cost Effects

The University of Michigan Medical Center in Ann Arbor, Michigan, monitored its savings and its costs from 19 teams between July 1987 and June 1991. Seventeen of the 19 teams showed a positive net cost saving. The implementation costs were estimated at $2.5 million, of which $1.3 million represented programmatic costs. The combined two-year savings and additional revenues attributed to these teams were $17.7 million. Teams focusing on the turnaround of the center's operating rooms led to added revenues of about $13 million. These were direct costs and did not include the time of the team members while in training or carrying out the team efforts. The value of the time spent in training was valued at $1.5 million. Including the training costs, the return was 4.5 times the investment. One might still ask about the cost of employee time in team activities, but the reported return would be highly favorable, even if that cost were included (Gaucher and Coffey, 1993).

Other efforts have also recorded cost savings. Baptist Medical Center in Columbia, South Carolina, found that the suppliers of contrast media solution for radiology were packaging the solution in volumes greater than each patient needed to drink. The team asked the vendor to repackage the material in smaller volumes. The waste avoided came to about $200,000 per year. Yet the bigger part of the saving may be in hundreds of day to day small changes. The West Florida Regional Medical Center case in this book shows a reduction in inpatient antibiotic costs of more than $200,000 per year. Additionally, Bluth et al. (1982) report that one team reduced outpatient "Stat" lab delays by 76 percent, reduced patient waiting time 62 percent, and made a one-time saving of $225,000 and annual recurring savings of $40,000.

Improvements may not come quickly in the beginning, but may occur in spurts as the approach is internalized and then reoriented. Consultant Thomas H. Breedlove, Senior Vice President of Crosby Associates, argues against a time estimate for full implementation of TQM since he sees it as always evolving. However, he does argue that with full consultant experience, the hospital should be getting a three-to-one payback within six months (Burrus, 1993a). Northwest Hospital in Seattle, Washington, found this out when its director decided that CQI was a philosophy and not just a procedure. The director began to develop some 40–45 teams around product lines, representing what he calls "The Molecular Structure," and to emphasize statistical process control. In the first few months of the change, the hospital saved about $3 million and the average length of stay dropped one day. A number of middle management positions have been eliminated, as has the contract management company at a savings of $750,000 annually (Burrus, 1993b).

Other Specific Effects

Reduced costs are not the only outcome of CQI efforts. At the University of Utah, for example, the development of a protocol supported by computer systems to control life support equipment has increased the survival rate of Adult Respiratory Distress Syndrome (ARDS) from 12 percent to 42 percent. A double-blind study was conducted to compare two types of equipment to see which would improve the survival rate. To the researchers' surprise, the improvement occurred with both sets of equipment, indicating that the improvement was the result of the rationalized system, not of the equipment choices (Morris, 1992).

Other effects include increased capacity utilization and improved continuity of care. For example, the Joint Commission on Accreditation of Healthcare Organizations book, *Striving Toward Improvement* (1992), describes the CQI efforts of six hospitals. In the cases the hospitals report improved operating room utilization, a 78 percent reduction in food waste on the pediatric service, increased utilization of transportation orderlies, and reduced admission and discharge waiting times. The cases in this book show increased utilization of capacity, lower supply costs, increased physician continuity, reduced laboratory costs, reduced hospitalization for low back pain, more satisfied obstetric patients, and reduced inpatient antibiotic costs. West Paces Ferry Hospital also reports how empowered employee teams implemented an $83,000 reduction in antibiotic waste. Finally, Kibbe et al. (1993) show how CQI techniques were able to improve continuity of care in an academic medical practice. This report shows how such aspects of health care quality can be measured and used to guide improvement.

Costs of Quality

Crosby (1979) talks about the "cost of quality," meaning the cost of poor quality. Knowledgeable administrators do not hesitate to say that the cost of nonconformance and waste in health care is in the same range—20 to 40 percent of total costs—that has been seen in American industry. As much as 25 percent of the cost of care goes into billing, collections, and handling of claims, and the Florida Health Care Cost Containment Commission warns the public that some 90 percent of hospital bills contain errors. As we will discuss later, there are also the costs of clinical errors and of waste as individual employees and groups of employees act to protect themselves from unpleasant situations due to variation in the system. One can legitimately include in that set of unnecessary costs both malpractice costs and defensive medicine costs. With the costs of health care estimated at about 12 percent of GNP, the size of these unnecessary costs is staggering.

So why then do people often question the investment costs of a CQI program? First, the data cited above indicate potential savings, thus raising the issue of the probabilities of achieving them. Consultants report that the likelihood that hospital CEOs will maintain a CQI effort is probably about 50-50. Moreover, there appears to be a moment of truth about 18 months into the process when the CEO suddenly realizes that the process does not involve simply changing the corporate culture, but involves a fundamental change in the way managers, including the CEO, make decisions. Some CEOs never reach that level of understanding; some do and cannot make the transition.

Another factor limiting the payoff is the fact that only a limited number of quality improvement teams or task forces can be underway at a time. Even though everyone may be trained in the basics of CQI, only a smaller subset are actually practicing CQI at one time, so that the effective increased capacity for change emphasized above is limited by the number of teams that can be maintained at one time: probably five to a dozen teams, depending on the size of the institution. The limit on the number of teams is related to the capacity of the facilitators to fully train and support the teams as well as the number of processes that can be in flux at one time without confusing people. Thus, although the investment in developing the program and doing the awareness training for large numbers of staff occurs early, the returns come later, mostly in the third year and beyond.

Although the savings on the cost side are relatively easy to quantify, the effects of increased competitiveness are harder to document. An increased occupancy rate quickly improves the bottom line, but one usually cannot tell why a patient came to a hospital, and one hears almost nothing about the one who didn't come because a neighbor told him or her that the hospital was unfriendly or poorly run. That is why articles about the relationship between customer satisfaction and financial performance are so important. The competitive effect cannot be justified based on specific events as can the waste avoidance and cost savings effect. Furthermore, any analysis of competition effects can be confounded by the offsetting marketing efforts of competitors. Hospital A may enhance its image in the community by way of continuous improvement, but it may be countered by a heavy advertising campaign by Hospital B or special equipment purchases to attract physicians at Hospital C. Right now we are virtually in the dark about the relative effectiveness of those three strategies or combinations thereof, so it is virtually impossible to compare the impact of a dollar spent on CQI against the impact of a dollar spent on other market-oriented activities.

Because CQI is new, there is little information about how effective such an effort will be after five or ten years. Prior approaches such as quality circles often started with good results but declined over time as motivation waned. Certainly, it is possible in the early years to "pick the low-hanging fruit," to clear up the obvious quality problems, and to show some immediate improvements. However, that is not likely to be the overall rate of return over several years of activity. One may experience diminishing returns, or one may find a learning effect in which teams and management with experience develop sufficient confidence to tackle some major issues with high potentials for payoffs like admissions and discharge. We predict that the program will produce savings immediately, then have a decline in savings or contribution to earnings, and then, as clinicians become more involved and management more assertive in looking for high-potential areas, begin to experience some increasing returns. The Quality-Profitability Model in Figure 3–3 shows how these costs and benefits might interact.

Quality efforts can affect the process directly and lead to improvements and reduced costs. They should also lead to improved physician and patient satisfaction with the institution, leading to more admissions, more patients, more patient days, and an increased share of the market. Improved quality might also lessen the pressure for reduced prices to compete against other institutions. All of these together could be contributing to the observed profitability by both lowering units costs and increasing volume and revenues.

The costs of a CQI program are not trivial. The organization may pay $20,000 to $200,000 for program development, training materials, trainers, and workshops for senior managers, board members, and key clinicians. Then there is the cost of the facilitators and the time lost by employees attending training sessions and engaging in team tasks. In addition to these costs, there are opportunity costs for the resources that went into the program that might have been used for something else. These efforts are not cheap and are not to be undertaken lightly. Much of the opposition to the Joint Commission requirement for a continuous improvement process has been couched in terms of the costs involved and how they might exceed the returns.

CONCLUSION

This chapter has summarized some of the theoretical arguments for and empirical evidence about CQI in the health care environment. There is no certainty that a continuous improvement program at a given institution will enhance quality for the patient and the providers and reduce costs for all concerned. We believe that if

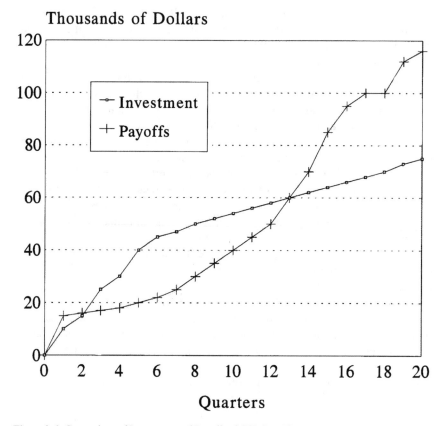

Figure 3–3 Comparison of Investment and Payoffs of CQI Over Time

CQI is managed properly, it can and will provide such benefits. The challenge is to design, implement, and lead a CQI effort that is successful for a given institution. The basics of the successful CQI activity and its implementation are the topic of the remaining sections of this book.

Part II

Basics

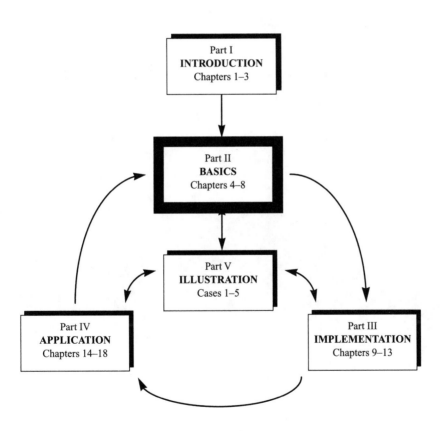

Susan DesHarnais
Curtis P. McLaughlin

4

The Outcome
Model of Quality

A critical question facing most health care continuous quality improvement (CQI) efforts is "Who should evaluate clinical performance, and how?" Controversy often arises over issues of quantity of work performed and its quality. Issues of quantity are relatively easy to address objectively. Issues of quality, however, are much more difficult, both politically and in terms of measurement. The objectives of this chapter are to provide a brief historical assessment of quality measurement in health care, much of which predates the widespread use of CQI; outline a conceptual framework for analysis in health care quality management and procedures for monitoring health outcomes; and, finally, provide an understanding of the institutional responses available for addressing quality issues in health care within the context of patient care, teaching, and research.

CLINICAL QUALITY

Although there is much current interest in using measures of patient outcomes (clinical responses to treatment) to evaluate the quality of clinical care, this focus is not new. In the 1860s, Florence Nightingale developed and used a systematic approach to collecting and analyzing information on differences in mortality rates across hospitals. She evaluated the effects of introducing improvements in cleanliness and nutrition on the death rates of the sick and wounded soldiers treated during the Crimean War. Fifty years later, Dr. E. A. Codman reported on his study of the end results of care in the United States. "This famous study emphasized the same issues that are being discussed today when examining the quality of care, including...the necessity of taking into consideration the severity

Source: Adapted with permission from DesHarnais, S.I., and McLaughlin, C.P., Clinical Quality, Risk-Adjustment, and Outcome Measures in Academic Medical Centers, *Managing in an Academic Health Care Environment,* William F. Minogue, ed., American College of Physician Executives, Tampa, Florida, © 1993.

or stage of the disease; the issue of co-morbidity (two or more illnesses present at one time); the health and illness behavior of the patient, and economic barriers to receiving care" (Graham, 1990, pp. 6–7).

Society did not, however, move in a straight path toward using outcome measures to evaluate the quality of care. Outcome measures were not used more because there were both technical and historical/political problems. The technical problems related to data availability and data processing. In the second half of this century, it became much easier to monitor the outcomes of hospital care using computers and large databases and to develop more sophisticated techniques for modeling risk factors affecting the outcomes of care. Improved access to data will be discussed shortly; however, a more basic issue will be discussed first: the history and politics of quality assessment in the United States.

POLITICS OF QUALITY ASSESSMENT

In 1913, the American College of Surgeons (ACS) was formed to develop minimal essential standards of care for hospitals as a first step toward the provision of quality care in American hospitals. The work of this group led in 1918 to the implementation of the Hospital Standardization Program, which developed into an accreditation process that set minimum standards for medical staff credentialing, privileging, and monitoring functions and for adequate medical records and equipment. At that time, virtually no hospital could meet even those minimal standards, although by 1951 some 3,000 hospitals were accredited by the Hospital Standardization Program. In 1951, the Hospital Standardization Program became the Joint Commission on Accreditation of Hospitals (Joint Commission) . The Joint Commission, created as a private, not-for-profit, voluntary agency, assumed responsibility for the accreditation process, initially using the ACS standards. The Joint Commission standards were later expanded to cover administrative issues. The Joint Commission program gained political acceptance, and accreditation was required for licensure and for Blue Cross participation in many states, and eventually for participation in the federal Medicare and Medicaid programs.

The Joint Commission emphasized establishing a proper *environment* for providing high-quality care, rather than determining whether high-quality care was actually being provided. Over many years, that focus shifted from structure to process. By the 1980s, hospital quality assurance personnel were asked to identify problems, set goals, focus on errors in the process of care, and demonstrate that they had met their own goals. The standards, however, did not indicate how potential problems were to be identified or addressed. As a result, many hospitals and other facilities focused on issues that could be readily resolved, or on problems that did not reflect the major clinical activities of the department or service, (McAninch, 1988).

Because the Joint Commission on Accreditation of Hospitals and its successor the Joint Commission on Accreditation of Healthcare Organizations assumed a central role in the accreditation of hospitals, many hospitals structured and focused their quality assurance activities primarily toward compliance with the Joint Commission quality assurance survey/guidelines. Quality assurance was defined as a function carried out by clinicians within the hospital. The Joint Commission approach to quality assurance largely reflected the values of society. Since the beginning of this century in the United States, society has delegated the establishment of quality standards to the medical profession. As Starr (1982) points out,

> Doctors and other professionals have a distinctive basis of legitimacy that lends strength to their authority. They claim authority, not as individuals, but as members of a community that has objectively validated their competence. The professional offers judgments and advice, not as a personal act based on privately revealed or idiosyncratic criteria, but as a representative of a community of shared standards. The basis of those standards in the modern professions is presumed to be rational inquiry and empirical evidence. (Starr, 1982, p. 12)

Caper (1988) has summarized the effect on the medical profession of this delegation of authority: "Being the perceived custodian of its own standards has distinct advantages for professions such as medicine. First, it has permitted medical professionals to attain, and retain, a very high level of autonomy, both for themselves as a group and for their individual members. Second, it has allowed them largely to determine working conditions and terms of payment. Third, it has helped turn medical decision making into a 'black box,' relatively immune to outside examination" (p. 51).

Much work took place in the mid-1900s in studying quality and in developing criteria, standards, and protocols, as chronicled by Donabedian (1982). In addition, a substantial amount of research occurred documenting variations in medical care practice (Wennberg and Gittelsohn, 1973; Paul-Shaheen et al., 1987), unnecessary surgery (Leape, 1987), and preventable complications (Adams et al., 1973; Brook et al., 1975; Roos et al., 1985). These studies, along with others, demonstrated a need to monitor and improve medical care practice. There has, however, been strong resistance by many members of the profession when it comes to measuring quality, particularly if the evaluations are performed by nonphysicians, even if the evaluators are using explicit protocols that were developed by physicians. In a recent editorial, Chassin (1991, p. 3472) pointed out that "many physicians think about quality of care the way Justice Stewart characterized his ability to recognize pornography: 'I shall not today define the kinds of material I understand to be embraced within that shorthand description [hardcore pornography]; and perhaps I could never succeed in intelligibly doing so.

But I know it when I see it'." Chassin goes on to note that "a growing armamentarium of new quality assessment tools renders this proposition dangerously obsolete" (1991, p. 3473).

By the 1970s and 1980s conditions had changed. As rapid advances took place in medical technology, as the cost of medical care rose in an unprecedented manner, and as evidence began to accumulate about severe quality problems, the government and the public took a growing interest in measuring the quality of care.

During this same period, data on health care use and costs became increasingly available to consumers and regulators, as well as to physicians and hospitals. This change in data availability was significant, making it possible for both professionals and others to compare the performance of various providers.

A variety of factors created a demand for and availability of data on quality, outcomes, and costs of care from hospitals and professionals:

- A 1963 legal case (*Darling v. Charleston Community Memorial Hospital*) established that a hospital governing body is responsible for knowing about problems in patient care and the actions staff has taken to resolve them. This case established the concept of "corporate liability," meaning that the hospital can be held independently liable for its negligence in failing to establish a system of safe practices, as defined by the industry. *Darling* generated demands for information on the part of hospital administrators and board members.

- Corporatization of medicine: HMOs, PPOs, and multisite systems became much more prevalent in the 1970s and 1980s. These types of organizations demanded data on costs, use patterns and practice patterns because such information was crucial in managing care in these systems. It was also essential to evaluate the costs and quality of care given by the providers with whom these organizations contracted.

- A broader concern with quality developed in industry: Many industries in the United States became highly concerned with methods of measuring and controlling the quality of the products and services they produced. There was a growing focus on using scientific methods, harnessing the energy and creativity of all levels of personnel in an organization. Total quality management (TQM) principles were adopted by many U.S. industries. In many communities, industries using TQM were represented on hospital boards as well. TQM concepts were introduced into hospital management and eventually began to change the way certain hospitals approached quality.

- Hospitals wanted information on physician performance for appointment and reappointment decisions. Hospitals often lacked the ability to compare physician performance in terms of outcomes produced or resources utilized. As cost-containment pressures increased alongside of concerns for quality, many hospitals wanted objective information on physician performance as part of decision making on privileges.

- In this more competitive climate, hospitals wanted information on both quality and costs for planning and marketing. If a hospital knows that it is either effective or ineffective in producing certain kinds of services, it can make planning and marketing decisions accordingly.
- Hospitals are developing information systems that integrate medical records, risk management, quality management, and financial management systems as part of a new competitive climate under the Medicare Prospective Payment System. Many hospitals are developing integrated management information systems that provide data on both inputs and outcomes for various types of patients and for individual providers.
- Hospitals have become interested in measuring patient outcomes as a defense against mortality data released by the Health Care Financing Administration (HCFA). In some communities, hospitals have received publicity as having high mortality rates since HCFA began releasing such information to the public in the mid-1980s. Because the methods HCFA used to derive these rates had flaws, in many cases the negative findings were invalid. Hospitals needed to defend themselves against such data releases.
- Specialty societies wanted to set standards for certain procedures and conditions in order to ensure that good care was provided. They wanted information on variations in practice in order to identify areas where there were problems or uncertainties. Such information could then be analyzed in order to promulgate standards for better practice of medicine within the specialty. In addition, some professional societies wanted information on practice patterns for setting standards for board certification.

The increased availability of data on the use, cost, and outcomes of medical services also enabled consumers, insurance companies, and regulatory agencies to analyze independently trends in the use and costs of health care services and to draw their own conclusions. Employers, unions, consumers, and insurance companies began to demand access to such data for several reasons:

- Unions and industry demanded such information as they negotiated contracts. As new benefits were added, it was necessary to analyze whether they were worth what they cost. In some cases, it was necessary to evaluate the performance of providers such as HMOs in order to decide whether to offer certain plans as options to workers.
- Companies that self-insured needed to develop information on use, costs, and outcomes in order to better manage their insurance plans. Local providers that used excessive resources or had consistently poor outcomes could pose a real problem for such plans.
- Preferred Provider Organization (PPO) contracts also required that the contracting agency exercise care when designating preferred providers. If these

providers were producing poor outcomes, marketing of the plan would be impossible, and the PPO could face legal problems.

- Consulting firms that advised insurance companies, labor, industry, or hospitals desired good data on costs and outcomes so that they could analyze choices and provide useful information to their clients.
- Insurance companies needed such information in order to market their products successfully in a more competitive environment.

In order to provide standardized data sets on costs and outcomes, insurance commissioners and state legislators in many parts of the country (California, Florida, Iowa, Maine, Massachusetts, New Hampshire, New York, Vermont, Washington, West Virginia, and others) mandated that hospitals report these data. Several states prescribed the specific data elements that were required. In many cases, new data elements were mandated beyond the common data set used for billing purposes, at considerable cost to hospitals.

Federal regulators (peer review organizations, the Health Care Financing Administration) began to find new uses for data on cost and outcomes of medical care. The federal government used the information for developing changes in payment systems, both for hospitals (Diagnosis Related Groups [DRGs]) and for professionals (relative value scales). It also became clear that the federal and the state programs were paying large amounts of money for treatments and for procedures that might not be the most effective means of caring for patients. By the 1980s, the federal government began to allocate research dollars for "effectiveness research" to learn more about the most effective treatments in areas where great variations in medical practice were discovered.

Also, consumers began to take a much more active role in their own health care. The women's movement in the 1960s and 1970s emerged as a force that was critical of many medical practices. Other consumer interest groups also came forth to question the effectiveness of various practices. Individual consumers, if they had to share costs, get second opinions, select providers from panels in HMOs, and make decisions concerning treatment options, became interested in obtaining accurate and useful data on costs in relationship to the outcomes of care.

Interest in evaluating the quality of care thus moved from the professional domain to the public domain. The medical profession was under attack from the outside as government and consumers sought to measure and evaluate quality. In particular, these groups sought to measure the value received for their money, to evaluate the relative effectiveness of various treatments, and to compare the quality of care provided by different hospitals. This interest led to or paralleled the development of more sophisticated, complex, and useful models of medical decision making, including computerized decision-making systems, complex treatment protocols for various diseases, and risk-adjusted measures of hospital performance.

FRAMEWORK FOR QUALITY MANAGEMENT

Definition of Quality

Quality may be defined in many ways and from many perspectives. The U.S. Office of Technology Assessment (OTA) has defined quality of care as "the degree to which the process of care increases the probability of outcomes desired by the patient, and reduces the probability of undesired outcomes, given the state of medical knowledge" (U.S. Congress, Office of Technology Assessment [OTA], 1988, p. x).

Donabedian (1980, 1982, 1986) has observed that definitions of quality ordinarily reflect the values and goals of the current medical care system and of the larger society of which it is part. He has distinguished several aspects of care that one might choose to measure:

- Structure: Resources available to provide health care.
- Process: Extent to which professionals perform according to accepted standards.
- Outcome: Change in the patient's condition following treatment.

In addition, he has broadened the definition of quality to include not just technical management, but also management of interpersonal relationships, access, and continuity of care.

One can begin to assess and measure quality using Donabedian's concepts and models, presented in the matrix in Exhibit 4–1, as a framework. Within each square of the matrix, one can define aspects of quality for which measures and standards can be developed. For example, in the "Structure/Accessibility" cell, one might measure the scope and nature of services provided, provisions for

---

Exhibit 4–1 Donabedian's Matrix for the Classification of Quality Measures

	Structure	*Process*	*Outcome*
Accessibility			
Technical Management			
Management of Interpersonal Relationships			
Continuity			

Source: Donabedian (1980), pp. 95–99.

emergency care, or geographic factors, such as the distance to the nearest center fully equipped to deal with a given problem. Within "Process/Technical Management," one might measure the adequacy of diagnostic work-up and treatment for a particular condition, using a checklist or "branched" criteria. The value of this matrix is that it helps us to define quality broadly and to identify the components that we might wish to measure throughout the health care system.

Why might one choose to monitor structure, process, *and* outcomes? There are advantages and disadvantages to using each of these approaches. It is relatively simple to monitor structure. In many cases, one can simply do an "inventory" using a checklist. The Joint Commission took this approach in its early days because there was some agreement that certain structural elements were needed as minimal standards to ensure an environment in which good care was possible. It is obvious, however, that adequate inputs alone do not ensure good outcomes.

Process measures take into account professional performance and would seem to be more closely correlated with better outcomes. It should be obvious, however, that outcomes are not determined solely by professional performance. Other factors such as the patient's condition at the time of treatment, patient compliance, patient age, and chance also enter into the equation. Nevertheless, it is often easier to measure provider performance than it is to measure patient outcomes for many diseases. One can use process measures to determine whether the professional has performed adequately for those conditions where (1) there is substantial agreement on what constitutes "acceptable" care and (2) where the technology is reasonably effective.

Health care leaders would also like to monitor the outcomes of care to determine treatment effectiveness, that is, to measure the effect the treatment has had on the patient's condition. It should be noted, however, that it is much more difficult to gather specific outcome data on patients than it is to measure structure or process. Ideally, one would like to obtain data on patient health status before and after treatment for a large national sample of hospitals. Instead, what is in our available databases is information on variations in rates of adverse consequences of treatment across hospitals, under the questionable assumption that hospitals with the lowest rates of adverse events are producing better patient outcomes.

To construct measures of hospital outcomes, two separate but related problems must be solved: how to take into account differences across hospitals in the type of patient treated, and how to take into account differences in the severity of illness in the patients within type treated across hospitals. These issues will be discussed in more detail below.

Procedures for Monitoring Outcomes

Criteria and standards must be developed in order to monitor outcomes. Such standards may be developed in three different ways:

1. Absolute (Normative): determined by clinical trials and/or consensus conferences. Standards developed in this manner by academic health centers reflect the ideal practice of medicine, or the best possible outcomes that can be achieved under optimal circumstances, that is, the most skilled surgeon, the best possible equipment, and the best trained team assisting. Although it is useful to know the theoretical "efficacy" of a treatment, or the best possible result one could achieve, such standards may not be realistic under ordinary circumstances of practice.

2. Empirical: relative to other institutions treating similar patients. Standards developed by comparing oneself to other institutions treating similar patients may be useful to help identify problem areas. If, for example, a hospital is experiencing 20 percent more unanticipated readmissions than other hospitals when treating a specific type of patient, that could be a signal that some correction is needed. On the other hand, it is possible that the "average" care in the community is poor. Such comparisons are only relative to the level of quality in the institutions used for comparison.

3. Institutional: based on self-comparisons over time. Such standards are often used in conjunction with both quality assurance and CQI. One collects observations of the same phenomenon over time to determine if a process is in control (small random variations) or out of control (major fluctuations). This information uses the institution as its own "control," and can be coupled with the goal of continuously raising standards in the institution. Although this approach is useful, some external comparisons are required to understand how to prioritize problems. One needs such external comparisons (benchmarks) to decide which processes to address first.

The Need for Risk Adjustment

Although mortality rates and measures of adverse events are potentially useful to providers and possibly to patients as one way to measure quality of care, such information can be misleading and potentially damaging if misused. This is particularly important when considering how such "report cards" might be used by the government or the public. Such information must be compiled and interpreted correctly. It has been demonstrated in several studies that raw death rates, without adjustment for differences in case mix and case complexity, lead to misleading comparisons among hospitals, with those hospitals that treat "riskier" patients appearing to provide poorer care (Moses and Mosteller, 1968; Wagner et al., 1986; Pollack et al., 1987; Knaus et al., 1986). These findings demonstrate clearly that death rates must be risk adjusted and interpreted carefully along with other indicators of quality. This is especially important to academic health centers, with their tendency to receive the cases with the highest risk and complexity, either through referral networks or through dumping.

Hospital-Level Adjustments

In a general sense, differences in outcomes across hospitals (patients' responses to treatment) can be viewed as a result of several different factors that may influence health outcomes. Figure 4–1 illustrates that this is a complex situation. To measure the effect of provider performance on outcomes with accuracy, it is necessary to control for all the other factors. This is clearly not possible, given the existing data sets and measurement tools. However, because "report cards" on providers are going to be produced, it is essential to try to develop as valid an approach as possible for risk adjustment.

Historically, two different approaches have been used to perform risk adjustment of hospital mortality data: hospital-level variables to adjust crude death rates and indirect standardization of patient-level data. Hospital-level data were used in several early studies. In a 1968 study by Roemer et al. (1968), hospital-level aggregate measures of patient characteristics (e.g., average age, percentage nonwhite, and percentage of cancer deaths), along with hospital characteristics (e.g., control, occupancy rate, and technology level), were modeled in an attempt to understand whether these proxies for case mix and case complexity were related to the observed differences in crude death rates among hospitals. The authors reasoned that if these hospital-level proxy measures were related to the crude death rates, they could be used to adjust the rates more accurately to represent each hospital's performance.

This early risk adjustment, as the authors acknowledged, was rather crude. They justified the approach by pointing out that detailed patient-level data on di-

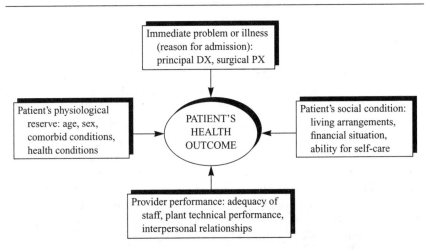

Figure 4–1 Schematic Diagram of Some Factors Related to Health Outcomes. *Source:* Reprinted from DesHarnais, S., et al., The Risk-adjusted Mortality Index: A New Measure of Hospital Performance, *Medical Care,* Vol. 26, No. 12, pp. 1129–1148, with permission of J.B. Lippincott, © 1988.

agnosis and severity of illness were then not available. They adopted hospital-level proxy measures as an indirect approach to estimating case mix and case complexity. The authors stated: "Ideally, one would like to examine the exact diagnosis of each patient admitted and classify it according to a scale of gravity, which might be based on case fatality rates derived from a general literature of clinical investigation.... But it is obvious that such a task of calculating average case severity by such an analytic process could present formidable problems of data collection" (Roemer et al., 1968, p. 98). It certainly would have been difficult in the 1960s, given the limited availability of computers, to model the risks of death for all types of hospital patients using large data sets, even if such information had been available.

Discharge-Level Data

Because hospital-level data are of limited use as proxy measures to account for differences in case mix and case complexity across hospitals, there is no apparent reason to use hospital-level data today. Discharge-level data are now available and are much more sensitive for measuring differences in case mix and case complexity across hospitals. The techniques of using adjusted discharge-level outcome data are documented in early studies, such as the National Halothane Study in the 1960s (Moses and Mosteller, 1968), the Stanford Institutional Differences Study in the 1970s (Flood et al., 1982), and work by Luft and Hunt (1986) on the relationship of surgical volume to mortality. In an article summarizing many of the methodological issues in the risk adjustment of outcome data, Blumberg described indirect standardization, the principle technique used for risk adjustment of discharge-level data:

> Indirect standardization is the method most widely used for risk-adjusted outcome studies. It requires estimates of the expected outcome in a study population, based on the outcome experience of a standard population. To estimate expected outcome, the numbers of cases in the study population with risk-related attributes are multiplied by the probability of the outcome in a standard population with matching attributes. These expected outcomes in the study population are then compared with the observed number having that outcome in the same study population....The first step involves the development and testing of a risk-prediction model, while the second step is a study of the residuals of the observed less the expected outcomes in the study population. (Blumberg, 1986, p. 384)

Severity Adjustment: Concepts and Methods

Vladeck (1988, p. 103) observed that "recent concerns with the quality of health services have focused largely on questions of measurement, comparison, public disclosure, and incentives and disincentives." In order to make valid measurements, and then valid comparisons across institutions, it is essential to take into account the differences in types, severity, and complexities of illnesses among the patients treated at each institution. Otherwise those institutions that treat the less severely ill patients may appear to be the "best," while those institutions treating very sick patients may appear to be the "worst."

As Iezzoni points out:

> The goal of "severity standardization" or "risk adjustment" is to control for the confounding influence of patient severity in comparisons of outcomes that might be related to severity...[T]he major presumption underlying standardization is that severity is connected to outcome in a way beyond the reach of medical therapeutics.... Severity adjustment thus theoretically minimizes the potential for misjudgments about quality due to poor outcomes that are outside the control of the health care provider. (Iezzoni, 1991b, p. 179)

In addition to allowing for better comparisons across institutions, severity adjustments are also needed for making comparisons over time for the same health care provider. For example, a hospital may discover it is producing unacceptably high rates of postobstetrical infections. Using methods based on CQI, the hospital may then redesign the process of caring for these patients. In order to assess whether the process redesign actually resulted in a significant reduction in the infection rate, it is important to determine if the patients served before and after the intervention differed at the time of admission in any way that was related to the probability for such infections to occur. For example, if the proportion of obstetrics patients with diabetes or difficult presentation problems requiring instrumentations was greater in the period after the intervention, then these differences should be explicitly taken into account when evaluating the effect of the process redesign.

One of the difficulties in performing severity adjustments is in defining the concept of "severity" that is relevant to a specific need. The definition that one uses must correspond to the purpose that one is pursuing. The purposes of case-mix and severity classification are many, depending upon who the user of the information is—policymakers, administrators, clinicians, health service customers, or patients—and what question the user is trying to answer.

- *Policymakers* need definitions of severity that are related to decisions in the following areas:
    1. reimbursement formulas that recognize the differences in resources needed to produce different mixes of outputs across hospitals
    2. planning information that is sensitive to changes in the demand for specialized facilities, personnel, and equipment within a service area

3. program evaluations, which require information on the impact of services on the health status of the population served
- *Administrators* need definitions of severity that are related to decisions they must make in the following areas:
  1. quality control, which requires screening criteria that are high in both sensitivity and specificity
  2. institutional planning and budgeting, where information on shifts in case type is needed in order to manage personnel allocations (Hornbrook, 1982)
  3. risk management, which requires a classification of cases according to the potential for adverse events leading to liability
- *Clinicians* need definitions of severity for very different purposes, including:
  1. managing their workload, which requires information for estimating surgical case complexity to predict the time and effort needed
  2. assuring the adequacy of staffing and technology needed to support their activities
  3. judging the effectiveness of their treatments in producing desirable health outcomes for their patients
  4. assessing the adequacy and equitability of reimbursement systems
  5. assessing the difficulty and unpredictability of the clinical management with their patient mix (Kelleher, 1993)
  6. assessing the prognoses for patients, based on comparisons to groups of patients with similar risk factors in terms of clinical and demographic characteristics
- *Groups of customers* (insurers, clinicians, potential patients) need definitions of severity to help them:
  1. make contracting decisions, based on information concerning both costs and patient outcomes
  2. make choices among individual providers at the time that care is needed, using comparative data on outcomes
- In addition, there are various dimensions of severity as viewed from the perspective of *the patient*. Although these severity measures are employed less frequently, they are associated with the patient's satisfaction with the technical aspects of care, which may often be based on information related to:
  1. their subjective assessment of the severity of their illness, and their accompanying expectations regarding pain (degree and duration), stress and anxiety, and the out-of-pocket costs they incur
  2. their subjective assessment of the severity of their illness with respect to the quality of life that they expect following treatment, including residual impairment of senses, loss of independence, and judgment concerning the amount of effort required for rehabilitation.

There are surely other definitions and dimensions of "severity," but the preceding examples do give an idea of the diversity of perspectives and purposes for which one may wish to define and measure "severity."

The challenge, then, is to define one's perspective and purpose first, and then to find a measure that is valid for that particular purpose, that is, a method that has both high predictive validity and explanatory power. These two criteria are valued differently by various people. Clinicians are likely to insist on severity classification methods that have high explanatory power that is consistent with their medical definitions of disease processes. Gonnella (1981, p. 610) states that a disease definition would, ideally, meet the following four criteria:

1. The disease must be defined in terms of the organ(s) involved;
2. The disease must be specified in terms of some pathophysiologic change in the organ(s);
3. An etiological factor or factors hypothesized to be the cause of the disease must be provided; and
4. The severity of the pathophysiological changes must be identified.

Several of the severity classification systems presently in use were developed using a clinical perspective, where panels of physicians worked to define severity measurements. These systems include Horn's Computerized Severity Index (CSI) (Horn and Horn, 1986), Gonnella's Staging (Gonnella, 1981), and Young's PMCs (Young, 1984). Other classification systems started with a clinically based disease classification system, but then focused on further breakdowns within each disease grouping, based on empirical methods for identifying risk factors associated with a particular outcome of care such as mortality, as in DesHarnais' Risk-Adjusted Mortality Index (DesHarnais et al., 1988), or resource consumption by Fetter et al. (1989) using DRGs. Although strictly empirical approaches to severity adjustment are possible and may be reasonably acceptable to many consumer groups and administrators, they are generally *not* acceptable to clinicians. The simple association among variables (predictive power) without adequate clinical relevance (explanatory power) is generally rejected by clinicians.

Any one concept of severity cannot and will not meet the needs of all of the parties mentioned earlier, or even all of the needs of any one of the parties. It should be evident that the same cases that will be relatively high on one of the severity scales will be low on another. For example:

- A normal delivery may be low on severity scales focused on mortality or difficulty of case management, but high on scales focused on pain and discomfort as perceived by the patient.
- An appendicitis case may be somewhat high on a severity scale focused on difficulty of clinical management, but relatively low in terms of the resources used or the probability of readmission.

• A psychiatric patient with alcohol problems may be fairly low on severity scales focused on resource use or probability of death, but fairly high on scales which focus on the probability of readmission.

The difficulty is that many of the severity adjustment methods currently available to researchers, administrators, policymakers, and clinicians are not explicit about what they are supposed to do, and/or have not been validated as to whether they do what they are supposed to do. This makes it very difficult to determine which method of risk adjustment or severity adjustment should be used for a given purpose.

This situation has resulted in much confusion within a very competitive marketplace (Iezzoni, 1991a). The level of understanding about the purposes and details of the many severity systems is very low among many consumers, as well as among many administrators and policymakers. Nevertheless, requirements to use various systems for measuring severity are being mandated by many information users—regulators, insurers, and customers—throughout the health care system. In some geographic areas several different systems are being mandated simultaneously with no clear purposes either stated or pursued.

The good news is that we will gradually gain an understanding of which systems work better for which purposes, and how well each works. Many recent studies have examined the performance of various severity classification systems with respect to specific dependent variables, such as in-hospital mortality, readmission rates, resource use, and complication rates. As we gain a better understanding of these different concepts of severity, and how well various systems work toward helping us with each concept, we will be able to use these methods more effectively to help us accomplish the various purposes discussed earlier in this chapter. Because the severity systems used will have an important impact on patient care, it is essential that the various severity classification systems be evaluated and understood. As Iezzoni (1991a, p. 3007) says, "Opening the black box is only the first step. We need to guarantee that the information generated is valid, and used in a safe and effective way."

Risk-Adjusted Outcome Studies

Eight recent risk-adjusted outcome studies are summarized in Table 4–1. The scope of these studies was limited to very specific types of cases, except for the study by Hebel et al. (1982), which was comprehensive insofar as it included all types of hospitalized patients. However, the database used by Hebel and colleagues for indirect standardization was limited to four hospitals in one community. Large and representative data sources are essential if indirect standardization is to be valid. Each study in Table 4–1 used a different set of variables for risk ad-

Table 4-1 Examples of Recent Outcome Studies Based on Patient-Level Data

Author(s)	Data Source	Scope	Adjustment Variables	Iatrogenic Disease
Pollack et al. (1987)	Prospectively collected from 9 pediatric ICUs in teaching hospitals	Pediatric ICU patients	Age; clinical service; emergency or scheduled; Physiological Stability Index Score	Excluded
Knaus et al. (1986)	Prospectively collected from 13 tertiary ICUs	ICU patients	APACHE II scores	Excluded
Sloan et al. (1986)	CPHA	Seven surgical procedures	Age; sex; LOS; procedure-specific indices of severity; multiple vs. single dx; operation within 6 hours; payer	Included in multiple dxs
Luft and Hunt (1986)	CPHA	Cardiac catheterization	Age (three groups); dysrhythmia (Y,N); heart failure (Y,N); other single secondary dx; multiple secondary dx (Y,N)	Included as any other secondary dxs
Flood et al. (1982)	CPHA and chart reviews and patient and provider interviews from 17 hospitals	15 surgical categories	Physical status apart from principal disease; stage; age; sex; emergency status; cardiovascular status; interaction terms	Excluded
Wennberg et al. (1987)	Medicare claims (Maine) and provincial claims (Manitoba)	Prostatectomy (population approach)	Previous history of hospital/SNF treatment; age; type of operation; secondary cancer; secondary cardiovascular; secondary other	Included as secondary dxs
Kelly and Hellinger (1986)	NCHSR (HCUP)	Four surgical groups	Age (five groups); sex; stage; number of dxs; Medicaid or no insurance (Y,N)	Included as number of dxs
Hebel et al. (1982)	100% of hospital records from four hospitals (all hospitals in one city)	All cases in four hospitals	Age; race; sex; payer; 83 MDCs; any secondary diagnoses (Y,N); any surgery (Y,N)	Included in secondary dxs

Source: Reprinted from DesHarnais, S., et al., The Risk-adjusted Mortality Index: A New Measure of Hospital Performance, *Medical Care*, Vol. 26, No. 12, pp. 1129–1148, with permission of J.B. Lippincott, © 1988.

justment. Age was measured in various ways and was found to be significant in predicting risk of death in all the studies. Other factors, such as emergency status of the patient when admitted, race, sex, and Medicaid status (as a proxy for poverty), were used in some of the studies to predict risk of death.

Patient-Level Data

One of the more difficult problems each of these researchers faced was how to define operationally the severity and the complexity of each case. Several of the studies (Flood et al., 1982; Luft and Hunt, 1986; Sloan et al., 1986; Wennberg et al., 1987; Kelly and Hellinger, 1986) that focused only on a limited number of specific conditions were able to use panels of clinicians to define severity for those conditions and for relevant comorbidities. Some of these investigators adopted various existing instruments for severity measurement, such as APACHE II, Disease Staging, and the Physiologic Stability Index Score (see Table 4–1). However, others used rather simplistic measures of complexity, such as the existence of any secondary diagnosis or the number of other diagnoses. This is an insensitive way to measure complexity because secondary diagnoses can range from minor conditions that do not increase the risk of death at all to major problems such as cardiac arrest. Also, it seems likely that the riskiness of various secondary diagnoses will vary depending on the primary diagnosis.

Condition-Specific Risk Factors

Certain interactions resulting from comorbid conditions are undoubtedly more dangerous than others. Ideally, condition-specific risk factors should be used. Moreover, studies that defined a risk factor simply as the presence of any secondary diagnosis often included iatrogenic events as patient risk factors. This was clearly not intended, because the purpose was to measure the patient's risk factors at the time of admission, not to confound risk factors with hospital performance. Although it is not always possible to separate preexisting comorbidity from complications that occurred during the hospital stay, some attempt should be made to exclude the more obvious complications (e.g., postoperative wound infections or a foreign object left in a surgical wound) when these conditions appear as secondary diagnoses.

Patient-Specific Risk Factors

In order to measure the effect of provider performance on patient outcomes, we must control for all of the factors that may affect patient outcomes to the extent that it is possible to do so. Given our existing data sets and measurement tools, it is clearly not possible to control for all of these other factors, especially those risk factors related to the patient's social condition or health behavior. It is possible, however, to use the information contained in existing databases to develop some reasonable proxies for some of the risk factors, other than provider performance, related to patient outcomes. One can use the information readily available in hospital discharge abstract data to assess the risk of various adverse outcomes associated with patients' diagnoses (principal and secondary), ages, and surgical procedures. Once we control for these risk factors, we can obtain much better (although not perfect) comparisons of hospital performance (DesHarnais et al., 1990, 1991).

A Risk-Adjustment Procedure

It is essential to use risk-adjusted measures for outcome variables to allow valid comparisons across hospitals. The following steps must be followed:

1. In order to ensure consistency in the analysis of risk-adjusted data, it is essential to do a preliminary assessment of data quality, including coding rules, compliance with coding rules, editing for errors, inconsistencies, and uniform rules for exclusions.
2. Collect data.
3. Using the risk-adjustment models, assign the predicted probability of each relevant adverse event to each case.
4. Develop reports for each hospital, comparing predicted frequencies for each category of adverse event to the observed frequencies.
5. As part of these reports, perform statistical tests on the differences between predicted and observed frequencies to determine whether the differences are statistically significant or merely represent random variations.
6. Using these reports, develop systems profiles, comparing hospitals within a defined subset or the system using these multiple risk-adjusted measures.

We can use these profiles for a "first cut." Hospitals with unusual (significant) patterns of adverse occurrences should examine records and perform peer reviews to determine whether there are problems with the process of care and whether administrative actions may be required at a system level.

What Not To Do

Several kinds of things *should not* be done with outcome measures:

• Do not try to rank hospitals as "good" or "bad" simply on the basis of the scores on these indexes. Recognize the limitations of these measures, which are derived from discharge abstracts and billing data. Relevant in-depth clinical information may be missing. We cannot always determine time sequences: for example, whether pneumonia or another upper respiratory infection developed while the patient was in the hospital, or whether the infection was already present at the time of admission. We cannot take into account patient compliance, an obvious factor for predicting readmissions.

- Do not assume that data quality is good or uniform across hospitals. Problems with data quality will definitely affect hospital scores on these measures. Poor coding of comorbidities can make a hospital look worse; good coding of complications can make a hospital look worse.
- Do not assume that a hospital that does well on one measure is necessarily doing well on the other measures. There is no evidence that this is true.

Aggregation of Different Measures of Adverse Events

A valid index of hospital performance must encompass the multiple aspects of hospital care. It may not be possible, either conceptually or technically, to construct a single, all-inclusive index of the quality of hospital care. It is possible, however, to construct several indexes that validly measure important aspects of quality and then to examine the relationships among the various measures to see if they are correlated. If the various indicators are highly correlated, we eventually may be able to construct an overall (unidimensional) quality measure. If they are not correlated, we can conclude that the various components measure distinct dimensions of quality and that the separate measures are all necessary in obtaining a valid impression of a hospital's performance.

A 1991 study by DesHarnais et al., for example, analyzed the relationships among three measures that seem to be "intrinsically valid," in that they clearly are outcomes to be avoided. The three indicators—mortality, unscheduled readmissions, and complications—were adjusted for some of the clinical factors that are predictive of the occurrence of deaths, readmissions, and complications. Risk factors were established empirically within each disease category for each index. The authors demonstrated that hospitals' rankings on the three indexes were not correlated. This result provides some evidence that these different indexes appear to be measuring different dimensions of hospital performance. Thus the three indexes should not be combined into a unidimensional measure of quality, at least not at the hospital level of analysis. Neither should any one measure be used to represent all three aspects of quality.

One cannot simply choose one hospitalwide measure, such as a "death rate," to validly represent a hospital's performance. Neither can one simply add up occurrences of different types of adverse events and then claim to have a unidimensional measure of hospital performance. Those hospitals that rank well in terms of mortality rates do not necessarily do well on the other measures and may have excessive readmissions or complications.

Can these different types of adverse events be weighted in a meaningful way so that they can be combined and used as a tool to rank hospitals? Probably not. Even after careful risk adjustment and data quality control, one is still left with the problem of how to weight a death in importance relative to a return surgery or an unscheduled readmission. Clearly, they are not of the same importance, and it would not make sense to treat them as if they were.

INSTITUTIONAL RESPONSES

Given that the management of a health care organization understands the history and politics of quality of health care, has an appropriate conceptual model of quality, and develops suitable risk-adjusted quality measures, what does it then do about quality? The first step is to make sure that everyone shares a quality strategy. The second step is to see that the strategy is implemented consistently across all the major programs of the institution: delivery of care, research, and education.

Linder (1991) suggests that there are three basic strategies, which she calls "models," that institutions can adopt on quality of care, specifically outcomes measurement. No one is against quality by definition, and no one is about to argue for unreasonable prices. Therefore, all three favor cost control and quality. Linder (1991) describes them as:

- Status quo organizations targeting reasonable quality at a reasonable price. They tend to have medical staff as the dominant group, with individual physicians left to provide quality leadership. Outcomes information in these organizations tends to center on routine compliance-oriented data prepared by medical librarians and nurses.
- Administrative control organizations targeting reasonable quality at an excellent (high) price. Administration tends to take predominant responsibility for quality and focuses on outliers of quality and resource utilization (cost). Nurses tend to constitute the quality assurance staff, and reports tend to focus on identifying outliers.
- Professional network organizations targeting for excellent quality at a reasonable price. These organizations tend to have strong medical leadership and a partnership with the administrative leadership to provide excellent service. The emphasis is on ad hoc studies to inform consensus conferences using the skills of both clinical researchers and information analysts.

About the latter group, Linder (1991) writes:

Twenty percent of the hospitals had begun to take a very different approach. The administrative and medical staffs joined forces to form an organization that held quality as its first purpose. In contrast to Model 2 (Administrative Control), they believed that financial success would follow from medical effectiveness. Their intent was not to manage the external image of quality, but to continuously assess and improve the organization's actual quality. They believed that the way to achieve this goal was through the free and open discussion of medical effectiveness among professionals. In other words, they used an informed, professional peer network, rather than an authority structure, to manage the organization's performance. The network included administrators, nurses, and physicians, and it addressed both financial and clinical issues. (Linder, 1991, pp. 27–28)

It would be foolish to attempt to try to classify an entire health care organization into any one of those three categories. That is one of the handicaps of big institutions in attempting to adapt to environmental pressures. They are loosely coupled organizations that seldom respond as a whole, but rather piece by piece (Weick, 1976). One department, or even a division of a department, may be in the status quo stage while another is in the professional network stage. For example, at a large academic medical center, one teaching hospital may be in the administrative control stage and another working toward professional networking.

We believe that a forward-thinking health care organization is best served by moving toward the professional networking approach as rapidly as its leadership can take it there. The administrative control approach will not be acceptable to patients or to professionals over time. It does not fit with their concepts of professional autonomy or governance or leadership. Sooner or later, it will lead to a revolution on the part of the staff. The status quo approach, however, appears at worst to set the institution's sights too low for long-run survival and at best to become vulnerable to unpleasant regulatory interventions. That leaves the professional network approach as the only viable alternative for the long run. Getting there, however, will take real medical leadership. There are leaders in medicine who argue that the status quo approach is the prevailing set of professional norms (Cotton, 1991).

One fear often expressed by members of the medical profession is that those focusing on health care guidelines are developing protocol-oriented medical automatons or, in other words, promoting "cookbook medicine." Reed and Evans (1987, p. 3280) warn that "as bureaucratic protocols based on cost containment seek to homogenize heterogeneous conditions and events, and the organizational penalties for being wrong or not conforming to the uniformity in the system multiply, there will be a devaluation of concepts such as initiative, innovation, or the utilization of experientially based clinical hunches."

Clinicians need to adapt to the changed environment in several ways:

- They need to overcome some of their resistance to accountability to nonphysicians (administrators, government, consumers) and form working alliances with these powerful groups.
- To cooperate, they need to develop the behavioral skills required to function in interdisciplinary teams.
- They need to develop a reasonable degree of sophistication with the methods and tools used to assess/measure quality and a critical appreciation of their strengths and weaknesses.

If these changes occur, it is even possible that physicians can be empowered to actively participate with others in improving the quality of care (Headrick et al., 1991). There can be a change in role and function, but potentially a gain in the ability of physicians to work with others to produce better results. Reed and Evans (1987) point out that the alternatives are either a situation where professionalism inevitably disappears, as our society follows its course of economic and organizational evolution, or a situation where "physicians can be much less the prisoners of history." Physicians can choose to "either act creatively, quickly, and decisively in the interests of their profession and their society, or acquiesce to changes planned by others" (p. 3282).

AUTHORITY PATTERNS

McLaughlin and Kaluzny (1990) emphasize the autonomy and authority barriers that must be overcome in introducing quality concepts into clinical practice. The debate between Berwick (1990, 1991) and Zusman (1991) shows two contrasting points of view. Berwick (1991, p. 420) emphasizes the TQM approach, with its multidisciplinary emphasis, arguing that clinical care is "a network of deep interdependencies involving other professionals, nonprofessional staff, information systems, policies and procedures, physical systems, and other influences on their own work and on the patients they serve. Sometimes physicians indeed act alone. But usually not." Zusman (1991) argues that quality assurance (QA) is a well-developed, stable approach that deals adequately with clinical quality, but should not consider cost of care as a quality issue, because cost is a responsibility of the utilization management staff. In his ideal hospital, administration "leaves monitoring of the quality of professional care to the QA system (or more strictly, leaves to the QA system that care that falls under the medical staff privileging system) while it monitors the quality of all other services and products that the hospital either purchases or produces" (p. 418).

The current structuring of medical schools and teaching hospitals supports the "traditional" system outlined by Zusman. Yet the results seem to leave much to be desired from a clinical, cost, and patient perspective. It is time for the management of today's health care organizations to take a strong position in this controversial arena.

CONCLUSIONS

Quality is something that all health care providers favor. It is not, as many would like to believe, something that happens without planning and conscientious effort. The outside world is demanding health care organizations of the highest quality at a reasonable price. Information with which to make assessments of outcome performance in health care is becoming widely available. Providers can fight to maintain professional autonomy by pushing the lay assessors back, or they can take the lead by becoming expert on quality assessment and applying those skills to ongoing operations. They can then educate the public in how to interpret the impact of age, comorbidity, and other factors on outcomes measures. The profession can incorporate the measures developed in its research into its teaching and into its delivery of care. It can educate its learners in how to participate in the process of quality improvement, to cooperate with other disciplines and professional groups, to lead the way in analysis and process design, and to help develop consensus about what is currently known and what warrants further study. It can go much further in empowering all its constituents to follow the scientific method at a pragmatic level in all aspects of medicine and in all settings to the benefit of its consumers. It can move from being on the defensive about consumer-oriented quality and how it is measured toward being its primary advocate.

Susan Paul Johnson
Curtis P. McLaughlin

5

Measurement and Statistical Analysis in CQI

A slide that is used in a number of continuous quality improvement (CQI) training programs reads: "In God we trust, all others send data." Measurement is a central element of any CQI effort. Health care institutions are full of data, but they are also full of "factoids," opinions and anecdotes masquerading as facts and data. Using a scientific approach requires using data to evaluate the current situation, analyze and improve processes, and track progress. The methods used to analyze data include both those originally developed for industrial models of quality management and those developed in the specialties of biostatistics, economics, epidemiology, and health services research.

Recently industrial statistical tools have been widely tested on health care models. One conclusion of the National Demonstration Project was that these tools were both transferable and meaningful to quality improvement efforts in health care. The tools are easy to understand and simple to use. They provide information on the consistency (or lack thereof) of the current process, point out sources of errors and variation, and indicate where improvements can be made most effectively.

There is no *one* specified point in the process of implementing CQI where one needs to use given methods of measurement and analysis. They should be used on a continuous basis. In the context of the Plan, Do, Check, Act (PDCA) cycle, data and analytical tools are used throughout. Different tools will be more helpful at different stages of each improvement project, from the initial analysis to the monitoring of changes that have already been instituted. This chapter will assist you in knowing what each statistical tool reveals about the process being improved, when to use it, and how to use it.

VARIATION—WHAT IS IT AND WHY ELIMINATE IT?

In the arena of CQI, variation is the "fat" in the system that needs to be reduced. It is important first to understand variation and how it affects both administrative and clerical processes. Variation is the extent to which a process differs from the norm. It is related to the statistical concepts of variance and standard deviation, familiar to most health care professionals. One can think of variation as a band of outputs around the central measure of a process. If, on average, it takes 10 minutes to complete a test, but it often takes from 8 to 12 minutes, this range gives an indication of the extent of the variation of the process.

Variation exists in every process and always will. This is particularly evident in clinical medical processes since every patient is different and thus the processes used to treat individual patients may vary. This is an important characteristic of the health care environment. Any approach to quality in health care must accept and deal with this variability due to the human condition.

The innate nature of variance in processes allows us to identify two general categories of variance: common cause and special source. Common cause variation is the variance inherent in the process that is a result of how the process is performed. It is often referred to as systemic or internal variation. This type of variation is usually random. Special source (or externally caused) variation is the variance that can be attributed to a particular source. This type of variation is therefore nonrandom.

Another way of understanding variation is to think about the predictability of a process. Can anyone tell a patient entering a health care process what to expect with a high degree of certainty? Can anyone tell the patient how long it will take, whom they are likely to see, and what decisions they may need to make along the way? These are the questions managers would like to be able to answer "yes" to. More than just giving you answers, CQI tools enable you to back them up with facts about the length of time and the potential for errors. The amount of certainty in the answer will depend on the amount of variation that has been observed in a process. The less variation that exists, the more certain management can be about answers. Thus the goal is to decrease variability in the process in order to eliminate uncertainty and the steps that people take to protect themselves against uncertainty. For example, in one hospital where six obstetricians were practicing, some physicians specified one IV solution for a normal delivery and the other physicians specified another type. Since the nurses were uncertain as to which physician would actually do the delivery and therefore which IV would be the "right" one, they protected themselves against uncertainty by hanging both units. The result was increased cost of health care induced by variation.

A process that displays little variation, or variation only under predictable circumstances, is considered under control. Bringing a process under control is often a goal of CQI efforts. Keeping a process under control requires continuous effort as well as the use of simple monitoring techniques.

PROCESS CAPABILITY

Being under control in health care is only a relative term. There is a great deal of variability in the human condition and in the wide variety of activities undertaken by a particular health care organization. Therefore those involved must have a sense of what that inherent variability is. This requires a process capability study. In such a study the variable or attribute to be studied is measured and characterized. One of the first questions would be, "Is the process inherently stable?" Scatter plots and histograms are often used to look at the natural variability of a process before trying to bring it under control.

If a process is chaotic or unstable, probably due to a number of special causes affecting it from moment to moment, those special causes must be dealt with before the underlying process can be understood. Once the process is stable, the investigators can determine its shape (normal or non-normal), its central tendency (true mean), and its standard deviation. This gives those concerned an idea of what is going on and what can be achieved in a quality improvement effort. This type of process knowledge will be useful at all four stages of the PDCA cycle.

During the *Plan* stage, management compares the natural variability with the requirements of the situation to see how good or bad the situation is. During the *Do* stage, the plan is tested on a small scale to see what effect it might have. During the *Check* phase, data is collected on the impact of the change to see whether it brings the process into better alignment with the desired outcomes. During the *Act* phase, the process is monitored to make sure the gains are held.

HOW DOES CQI DIFFER FROM QA?

In order to apply these techniques, it is useful to understand the differing views of CQI and QA with respect to variation. CQI focuses largely on the internal sources of variation in an effort to reduce the random variation in the system. Although the variation is considered to be random, it can often be reduced by streamlining or changing the process so that there are fewer opportunities for random variation to occur.

QA, on the other hand, often emphasizes the special source variation. It looks for the anomalies that occur in the process and cause variation so that it can identify the sources and prevent them from affecting the process any more. The emphasis of QA seems to be on dealing with the outliers rather than changing the process mean or variation. Figure 5–1 illustrates these two points of view. Segment 1 illustrates the quality control view that emphasizes conformance to a standard, namely attempting to bring the process under control. Segment 3 indicates a CQI approach in which the mean has been improved and the process brought under control also (Teboul, 1991).

In general, CQI activities follow a logical sequence of steps. First, the process is described and sources of variation identified. This initial step is followed by indepth analysis of the variation that will help to clarify both the sources and extent of the problems. Then the team weighs the alternatives and makes decisions as to how to reduce variation. Finally, the team will want to try one of the alternatives

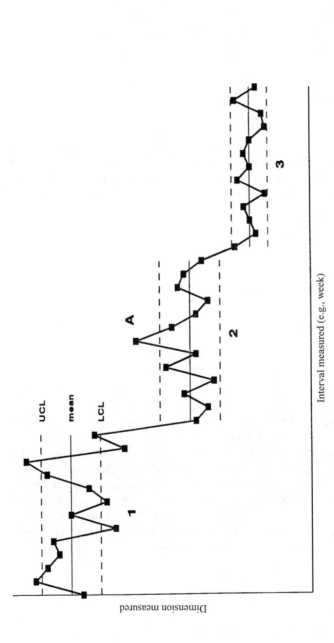

Figure 5-1 Teboul-Type Diagram. This figure illustrates the concept of variation and the results of efforts to reduce variation and improve the process. In Segment 1, we see evidence of a lot of variance in the process as indicated by wide swings. The bands indicate the normal range. Since the process is often outside this normal range, the process at the start would not be considered "under control." When this situation is rectified, as noted where the process tends to stay within the bands, the process has been brought under control. In Segment 2, point A indicates single source variation. Additionally, the overall mean has decreased, signifying improvement (though the variation is still the same). In Segment 3, the mean and variation have both decreased, and the process appears to be under control.

and measure its effect on the process. The team will select the alternative that has the greatest impact in terms of shifting the mean in the desired direction. Once improvements are made, the organization will continue to monitor progress over time to ensure that the process remains in control.

THE SEVEN TOOLS

Most writing on TQM/CQI includes information on "the seven tools" used in process analysis. The seven tools are a set of data analysis tools seen as basic to the application of the approach. Although any pair of writers usually agree on at least six of the seven, eight items are commonly included in this famous set. Therefore we will report on eight statistical methods in this chapter. They are:

1. flow charts or diagrams
2. cause-and-effect diagrams
3. checksheets
4. Pareto diagrams or charts
5. frequency distributions (histograms)
6. run charts
7. regression analyses
8. control charts

We will consider each of these in turn in the context of the stages of CQI. The following sections will take each of these stages and introduce the tools as they might well enter into an analysis. Given a set of objectives, the team starts out on a four-stage journey: (1) describing the process and identifying sources of variation, (2) performing an in-depth analysis of the situation to clarify the team's knowledge and summarize and present its interim findings, (3) weighing alternatives for further investigation and making choices among hypotheses for change, and (4) measuring the improvements as the choices are implemented and monitoring the progress achieved. Table 5–1 also tabulates which tools will be most appropriate during each stage of a CQI effort. Remember, however, that at most stages any one of the previously introduced tools, as well as behavioral strategies like brainstorming and multivoting, may also apply.

Process Stage 1—Describe Process and Identify Sources of Variation

Brainstorming—A Useful Facilitating Technique

Brainstorming is a team process that is useful at the beginning of the CQI process. It will help solidify working relationships with a team while at the same time

Table 5-1 CQI Process Stages and Quality Tools

	CQI Process Stages			
Tools	1. Describe process and identify sources of variation	2. Do in-depth analyses to clarify knowledge and present interim findings	3. Weigh alternatives and make choices	4. Measure improvements and monitor progress
Flow diagrams	Key tool here	Revisit and update		Keep current
Cause-and-effect diagrams	Key tool here, especially after brainstorming	Stratify for detail		
Checksheets		Use to collect process data		Use to collect process data
Pareto diagrams or charts		Key tool here to stratify causes	Key to deciding on vital few	Use to show change
Frequency distributions (histograms)		Helpful in presentation		Helpful in monitoring
Run charts		Important to relate data temporally to changes		Key to knowing whether improvement has been associated with change
Regression analysis			Useful for testing hypotheses	
Control charts				Key to seeing whether the process is or remains under control

revealing useful information. Though useful throughout the project, it is especially helpful during some of the beginning stages when the team is trying to describe the process. Brainstorming is not a statistical tool, but it is a technique that is often useful during continuous improvement projects.

Brainstorming is when a group of individuals gets together and comes up with as many ideas as they can pertaining to a specific task or problem. To employ brainstorming, it is best to bring the whole team together specifically for that purpose. The facilitator must define what the group is going to brainstorm about: for example, the causes of variation, the potential effects of the variation, changes that might be made, or alternative methods for getting something done. It is important to stick to the stated topic (and amazingly easy to get off track!). Additionally, you should split the brainstorming session into different sections, and at certain times the group should offer as many ideas as possible without judging any suggestion. It is valuable to add to the list those ideas that seem the craziest or least feasible. They may contain the kernel of a creative idea that can be modified. Later, the group can go back and evaluate your list and eliminate the inappropriate ones. It is best to use a room with a blackboard or a flip chart for making lists.

Tool 1—Flow Charts

One of the most powerful tools that CQI teams have is the preparation of flow charts of both administrative and clinical processes. Also known as process flow diagrams, these are pictorial representations of how the system works. Simply, they trace the steps that the "object" of a process goes through from start to finish. The object may be a vial of blood in laboratory tests, a piece of paper in a medical record, or a patient in a specialty clinic.

To develop a flow diagram, the group should start by:

1. Defining the basic stages of a process
2. Further defining the process by breaking down each stage into the specific steps needed to complete the process
3. Following the object through the process a number of times, using direct observation to verify the process
4. Discussing the process representation with the project team and coming to consensus on the underlying process

Flow diagrams can be as simple or as complex as you wish. The team should agree on what level of detail is suitable for the specific process and the desired performance shift.

Surprisingly, the continuous improvement team is likely to find that the existing process owners and users do not share a common understanding of how the current system works. Quite heated arguments are likely to ensue until they talk it out. With an accurate, shared representation of how the system works, the team is then able to consider how to improve it.

The first step is to bring together the people involved in all stages of the process being studied so that the information accurately represents current practice. An independent facilitator may need to be present to keep any one group member from having undue influence and to mediate arguments about what is or should be happening. If the group is not used to drawing up such charts, the facilitator can also help explain the notations that are customarily used. Figure 5–2 illustrates these various notations. An activity is represented by a rectangle, a decision node by a diamond, a wait or an inventory by a triangle, a document by a symbol that looks like a rectangle with a curve on the bottom, a file by a large circle, and a continuation of the flow to another sheet by a small circle.

Visibility of the process is very important, even to individuals who are not members of the team. For example, we have used the technique of putting the flow chart on a large posterboard or a wall using Post-it™ notes for both the activities and the decision nodes, and leaving it up in clinical work areas so that everyone has an opportunity to access it. People in the work areas and on the team should have adequate time to consider the current process representation to see whether it is accurate and to think about possible improvements. Where possible the motto is "No surprises!"

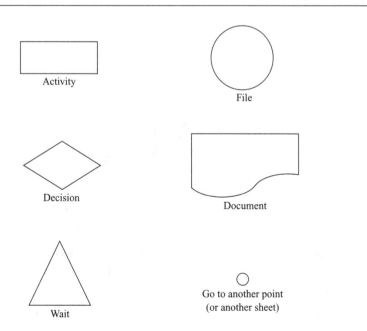

Figure 5–2 Flow Chart Symbols. These symbols are commonly used to create flow charts describing a process. Arrows are used to connect the symbols, indicating the order in which the steps take place.

The posterboard should be available in multiple sheets so that new ramifications and permutations can be added to the permanent records, a requirement that often rules out transparencies or chalkboards. The latter does have the advantage of erasability, which is important early on. Do not let the obsessive members of the committee get caught up in perfecting the artwork. There will always be changes. Save the perfecting until the final presentation.

Information that could be added to the flow chart would be flow rates and flow times. For example, Figure 5–3 shows the flow rates in a university student health service clinic, with data on the average number of patients arriving each day and the percentages flowing to the various providers. Also given are the average waiting times and processing times at each stage of the process. A team is not likely to have this data when the process flow charting is initiated but may choose to collect it and add it later, should it appear useful for further analysis. It can be useful for the team to stop and think about which of these additional measures will be helpful to them as they are creating the flow chart.

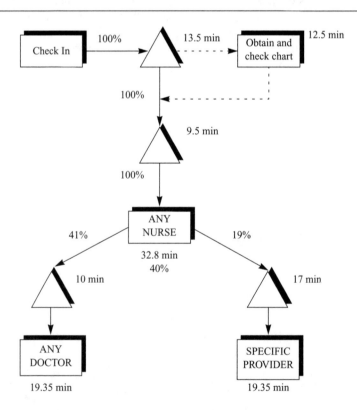

Figure 5–3 Example of a Flow Chart Developed from the Process of Patients Going through a Walk-in Clinic. The average times and patient volumes are noted on this example.

Once agreement is reached on the representation of the current process, the team and the onlookers can begin to ask questions about that process, including:

- Who are the customers? How would they like to be served? How well are they being served now?
- Are there performance gaps or perceived opportunities for improvement driving the selection of this process? What is the data on performance? How good is it? Does it need to be validated?
- Have we identified all the relevant stages of the process? Are the "owners" of each stage represented on our team? If not, what do we do to bring them in?
- What are the inputs required and where do they come from? Are the inputs constraining the process or not? Which ones?
- Are there equipment or regulatory constraints forcing this approach? Is there historical interpersonal or political baggage behind this process choice? This is often the case in health care, where people have been blamed for problems and have set up elaborate and expensive process embellishments so that unpleasant experiences won't ever happen again.
- What measurements are we currently collecting about this process? Are they the right ones for the issues already raised? How might we go about adding the right measures?

Experts warn against asking too many "why" questions at this point because they may be threatening to the professional and personal egos of some participants. Let the whys and wherefores emerge as people loosen up and trust each other rather than forcing the issue immediately. Avoid making the model of discourse like the grand rounds procedure with its inherent power plays.

The potential benefits of flow charting are considerable. Staff gets to know the process much better. The results can be used as a training aid. People begin to take ownership of the process by participating in this activity and, most importantly, the possibilities for improvement become clear almost immediately.

Flow charting should also bring home the need to have internal suppliers, external suppliers, and users (customers) involved in the process. Then one can generate more interest on the part of these individuals in joining the team process when they see the careful and impartial work already underway and their own potential role in it. The visual process analysis is one way to show your customers that you have their concerns at heart and that you are sincerely interested in improving the process in their interests.

Tool 2—Cause-and-Effect Diagrams

These diagrams, also called Ishikawa or fishbone diagrams, are one of the most widely used tools of CQI. This tool was developed by Kaoru Ishikawa (University of Tokyo) for use at Kawasaki Steel Works in 1943 to sort and interrelate the multiple causes of process variation.

Cause-and-effect diagrams are most useful after the team has already described the process and is ready to identify the sources of variation. There is likely to be evidence of variation in the identified problem (either real or anticipated). Additional causes may be revealed through the flow charting process or during brainstorming.

Cause-and-effect diagrams are a schematic means of relating the causes of variation to the effect of variation on the process. If you ignore the words on the diagram, the picture looks like the skeleton of a fish, and thus the name *fishbone* diagrams.

This tool is especially suited for team situations and is quite useful in making sense out of a set of brainstorming session results. It can be taught easily and quickly, allowing the group to sort ideas into useful categories for further investigation.

Sarazen (1990) suggests that there are three types of cause-and-effect diagrams:

1. Cause enumeration
2. Dispersion analysis
3. Process classification

Cause enumeration. The most commonly used type of cause-and-effect diagram is cause enumeration, which starts with a brainstorming session around an identified performance gap. If the group has trouble categorizing and sorting the possible causes into those categories, an affinity diagramming technique can be used to help with the sorting. In the affinity diagramming process, each cause is put on separate cards or Post-it™ notes, and the group moves them around until the groupings (classifications) are satisfactory. Then one can begin the diagramming with the classifications already in hand. Figure 5–4 shows an affinity diagram resulting from a brainstorming session about delays in completing a cardiology evaluation on patients with cardiac problems awaiting noncardiac surgery. The chart shows 17 different identified causes, which have been grouped into four topic areas: scheduling issues, prescreening opportunies missed, process issues, and communications. By classifying items identified in the brainstorming session, the group can identify and focus in on generic problem areas rather than on individual events or complaints.

Figure 5–5 shows the multilayered process of making a fishbone diagram. Step 1 of the diagram starts by putting the identified performance gap in a box at the right and a big arrow leading to it. This big arrow represents the overall causation. Step 2 involves drawing spines from that big arrow to represent main causes, namely major classifications of causes like labor, materials, finances, managerial decisions, and equipment. Step 3 adds the specific causes along each major spine. Specific causes may occur at multiple levels down to two, three, or four levels.

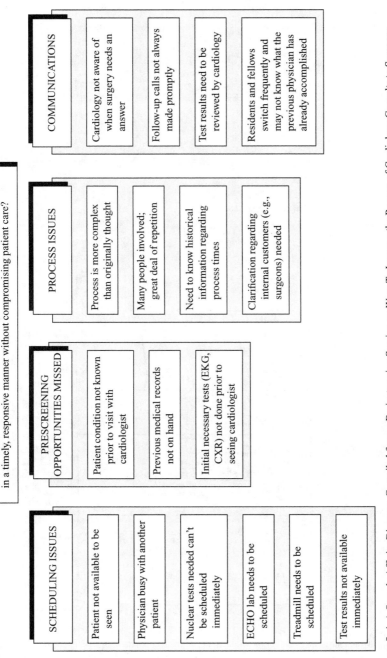

What are the issues involved in completing a request for a cardiology consult in a timely, responsive manner without compromising patient care?

COMMUNICATIONS

Cardiology not aware of when surgery needs an answer

Follow-up calls not always made promptly

Test results need to be reviewed by cardiology

Residents and fellows switch frequently and may not know what the previous physician has already accomplished

PROCESS ISSUES

Process is more complex than originally thought

Many people involved; great deal of repetition

Need to know historical information regarding process times

Clarification regarding internal customers (e.g., surgeons) needed

PRESCREENING OPPORTUNITIES MISSED

Patient condition not known prior to visit with cardiologist

Previous medical records not on hand

Initial necessary tests (EKG, CXR) not done prior to seeing cardiologist

SCHEDULING ISSUES

Patient not available to be seen

Physician busy with another patient

Nuclear tests needed can't be scheduled immediately

ECHO lab needs to be scheduled

Treadmill needs to be scheduled

Test results not available immediately

Figure 5–4 A Sample Affinity Diagram, Compiled from a Brainstorming Session on Ways To Improve the Process of Cardiology Consults to Surgeons

Step 1: Draw spine

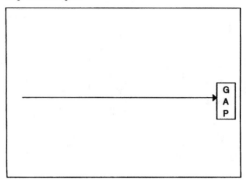

Step 2: Add main causes

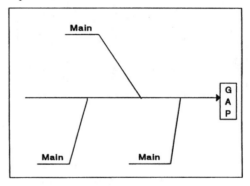

Step 3: Add specific causes

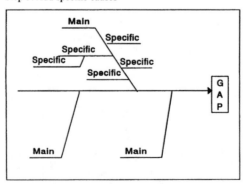

Figure 5–5 Multilayered Process of Developing a Fishbone Chart. First the overall problem is defined, then the main causes of the problem are defined. Often these main causes are segmented into those initiated by methods, materials, machines, or manpower. In the third step, these main causes are detailed with specifics.

Sometimes it is useful to draw the diagram in two stages, first showing the main causes and then making a separate chart with a spine representing the main cause and its associated levels.

Figure 5–6 shows a process flow chart for patients flowing into and completing experimental cancer treatment protocols (Hynes et al., 1992). On the right side are the various possible losses of patients from the protocols group. These losses can be interpreted as quality failures. For each flow loss there is an Ishikawa or fishbone diagram showing the main causes of patient loss and the possible causal components of each main cause. Figures 5–7a and 5–7b illustrate causal analyses of the flow losses resulting from patient suitability and patient acceptance problems. This type of analysis was very useful in specifying research data needs and statistical hypotheses for studying the effectiveness of this process.

The first pass at a fishbone diagram may not be sufficient to understand the specific cause(s) of an error or to quantify it. Therefore it may be necessary to stratify fishbone diagrams further to get at finer gradations of error causes. Increasing the level of detail about causes can help with identifying specific corrective actions.

Dispersion analysis. This approach starts with a known set of unsatisfactory variations and begins immediately to identify the causes of an effect. The problem statement defines the effect, and the team can begin by identifying the main causes and then the multilevel contributors to each gap in process performance. Sometimes brainstorming takes place around the contributing causes to each main cause. It is important in this process to keep relating various causes to each other. Note that various specific causes can appear more than once in association with various main causes. For example, patient ability to pay can affect patient failure to comply as well as the lack of resources to service patients.

Process classification. In the industrial setting it may be effective to identify variation in the various process steps of a given flow. This may be more effective in the manufacturing setting, where process stages are fixed and the need is to identify the causes of a variation in specific process stages and organizational units. In health care, that is essentially what the teams are trying to avoid in order to get collective ownership of processes. One objective is to get health care professionals and administrators to look at bigger systems, ones which go beyond their narrow areas of specialization. Even when the causes are beyond the control or intervention of the team, it is worthwhile to acknowledge their existence and impact. If, however, one cannot get a high degree of group commitment and participation to study the overall process, the process classification approach may be a useful interim alternative. Figure 5–8 shows a process classification diagram developed in some of our research for a cardiology consult process.

Purposes of Cause-and-Effect Exercises

Although the fishbone diagram is a useful tool, it is important to keep in mind that the ultimate goal is to develop a common understanding of a process and to

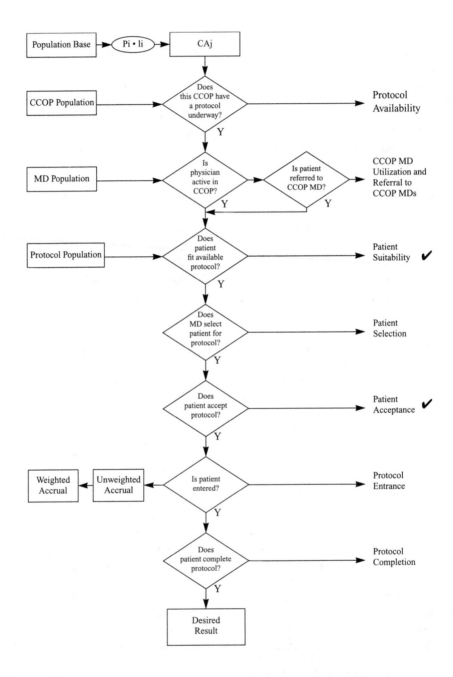

Figure 5–6 Flow Chart of Cancer Clinical Trials. The possible losses are detailed on the flow chart in conjunction with the stages of the process. The two losses noted with a checkmark are detailed in Figures 5–7a and b. *Source:* Hynes et al., 1992, p. 252.

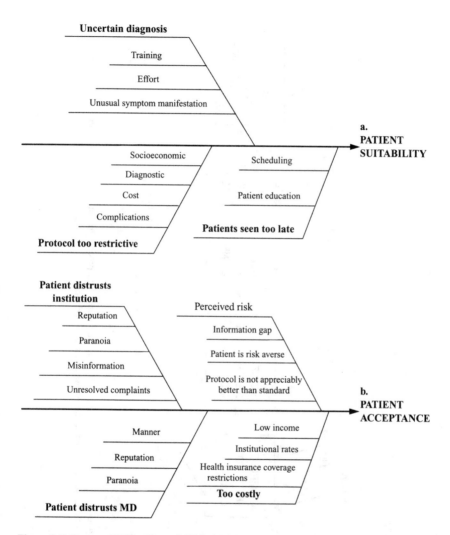

Figure 5–7 Cause-and-Effect Chart of Clinical Trials. Top: Detail of fishbone chart on patients who (a) may not fit the desired protocol and (b) patients who do not accept the desired protocol, and thus do not meet the desired result from the flow chart in Figure 5–6. *Source:* Adapted from Hynes et al., 1992, p. 259.

create a sense of shared ownership of the process. The objective is not to fix blame, but rather to understand the process as it is and how it might be improved. The outcome of this stage of CQI is a decision about what to measure to confirm the team's hypotheses about causation. In addition, the team is also beginning to build a consensus about the relative importance of a particular type of causation, which tends to help indicate where it wishes to put its measurement resources.

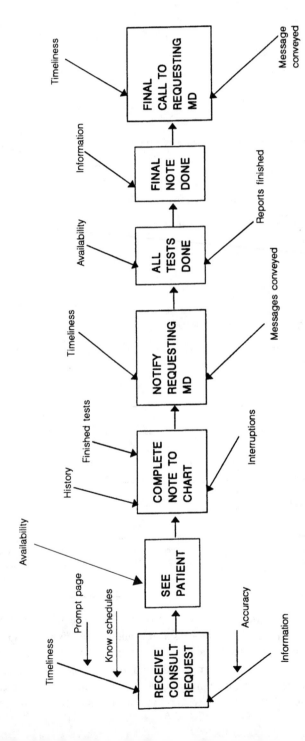

Figure 5-8 A Process Classification Diagram for a Cardiology Consult Process. The main steps of the process are detailed along the main spine of the diagram. The things that might influence the quality of each step are listed on the arrows directed toward them.

Group facilitation is important at this stage of the process. Someone has to deflect the tendency to be judgmental of others and to get the group to withhold judgment and look for data to determine what are special effects and what are normal process variations. Some of that deflection can take place by allowing people time to discuss the work informally and to discuss and review the terminology and categories used. The desired outcome should be a decision as to what actions to take next to confirm these hypotheses about causation, together with a strong common will to implement these measures.

Multivoting

Only a few hypotheses can be tested at one time. Therefore it may be necessary to narrow the options without discouraging specific team members who are wedded to specific hypotheses. Gaucher and Coffey (1993) recommend multivoting as a procedure to reduce the set to a few. They warn against trying to reduce it to a single hypothesis at this stage because of the risk to the team's sense of consensus. They also warn that one has to avoid overaggregating concepts during this weeding-out process.

During multivoting, each team member may at first vote for as many items as he or she wishes. The votes are added up, and those with few votes are eliminated. After the first round, each team member is given a number of votes equal to half the number of alternatives remaining in that round, and the voting is repeated. This process is repeated to reduce the list to between three and five items. Multivoting can be used at any process stage to reach consensus on a reduced set of alternatives.

Process Stage 2—Perform In-Depth Analyses to Clarify Knowledge and Present Interim Findings

At this point the team's findings on causality are essentially the results of the hypothesis-generating exercises. Those hypotheses must then be tested by collecting and analyzing data. As indicated in Table 5–1, checksheets and Pareto diagrams are important tools to use during this stage. Frequency distributions are helpful in presenting the results; run charts help present the data in order of event occurrence and can be used later to monitor improvements.

Tool 3—Checksheets

The simplest form of measurement is to count events, usually the frequency of activities or of outcomes, and to classify the observations using a checksheet. A checksheet is a matrix in which an observer records the number (frequency) of events. In the CQI context this is usually an array in which the anticipated causes of a specific type of defect are in the left-hand boxes and counts of their frequency in the central column. Exhibit 5–1 shows one such checksheet resulting from a study of the reasons that linens are discarded.

Exhibit 5–1 Checksheet for Linen Discards

								Week of _____
Reason for discard	Mon	Tue	Wed	Thu	Fri	Sat	Sun	Total
Large tear	卌	|		||	|||		|	12
Small holes			||||	|	||	|		8
Permanently soiled	||	||	|	卌 ||	|	||	|	16
Discolored	||	|		|				4
Threadbare	卌 |||	卌	||	|||	|		|	20
Total	17	9	7	14	7	3	3	60

An obvious concern of the investigator is making sure that the frequencies are representative of the process being observed. The data must be carefully sampled from the ongoing process to meet this goal. This can be done by randomly selecting the times to observe the process, by systematically sampling at equal intervals, or by making observations on every nth member of a population passing through a process. In some situations it may be desirable to take a stratified random sample, making sure that specific segments of the population are sampled adequately. Once this information has been collected, it needs to be presented to the group to analyze. The simplest form of presentation is the histogram (Tool 5).

Tool 4—Pareto Diagram

A Pareto diagram is a vertical bar chart with the bars arranged from the longest first on the left and moving successively toward the shortest. Each bar represents the frequency of a specific cause of an error. The data comes from a cause-and-effect diagram and a checksheet identifying the frequency of a quality failure due to a specified cause. The causes will have already been developed using the procedure for doing a cause-and-effect diagram. The arrangement of the vertical bars gives a visual indication of the relative frequency of each source of error.

The diagram is named after the seventeenth-century Italian economist Vilfredo Pareto. When he studied the distribution of wealth, he observed that the majority of the wealth had been distributed among a small proportion of the population (Pareto's law). Juran (1988, p. 26) applied this concept to quality causes, observing that the "vital few" causes account for most of the defects and the "useful many" for a much smaller proportion of the defects. He noted that these vital few causes are likely to constitute the areas of highest payback to management. The objective of the Pareto diagram is to highlight these vital few. Concentrating on the high-volume causes should have the largest potential for reducing process variation.

On the same Pareto diagram one also develops a cumulative probability distribution incorporating all the proportions of the observations to the left of and including the bar. It is common to display the frequency scale on the left-hand Y axis and the percentage scale on the right-hand edge. Figure 5–9 shows two Pareto charts developed from data shown in the checklist in Exhibit 5–1. Figure 5–9a shows the cumulative frequency of the event, and Figure 5–9b shows the cumulative percentage of observations. Note that there is no X axis as such because the chart is a bar chart.

Just because a cause is identified as having the greatest frequency does not necessarily mean that it should be worked on first. It must also be tractable and not cost more to change than it is worth. However, it is likely that the first cause to be studied in detail will be among the left-most group. Remember that each Pareto chart focuses on one specific error, making the effect of reducing the frequency identical for each alternative cause. Therefore the choice boils down to significance (frequency) and the cost of modification. Another consideration is to further stratify the main causes, as done for the cause-and-effect diagrams. Segregating the specific causes that have large frequencies can help identify potential improvements.

Tool 5–Histogram

Once information has been collected, it needs to be presented to the group to evaluate. Pareto diagrams can be presented exactly as they are. For checklist data, the simplest form of presentation is the histogram. A histogram is a bar chart representing the frequency distribution of a set of data without the ordering provided by the Pareto diagram. The bars are arrayed on the X axis representing equal and adjacent intervals. The length of the bar against the Y axis represents the number of observations falling into that interval. With the data from a checklist, it is easy to create a histogram using any microcomputer spreadsheet or graphics package.

A histogram presents the measurements in a way that displays the nature of the distribution. Successive histograms indicate whether there has been a change in the variability of a process. Figure 5–10 shows a histogram based on the checksheets in Exhibit 5–1. It too shows that the primary reason for linen discards is wear (threadbare) and permanent soil.

Tool 6–Run Chart

Visual displays of the frequency of causes of error or checksheet values is enlightening, but cannot indicate trends or other characteristics of the observed phenomenon over time. Another way of displaying the variation of a process is to look at its performance over time. This allows the experienced observer to (1) see

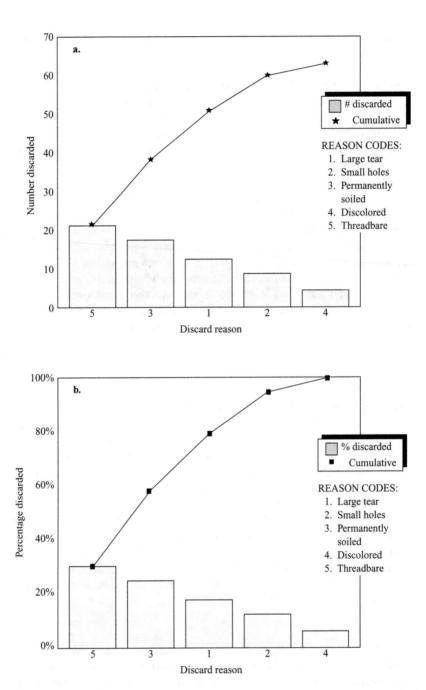

Figure 5–9 Pareto Charts of Data from Checksheet in Exhibit 5–1, in (a) Raw Data Format and (b) Percentage Format

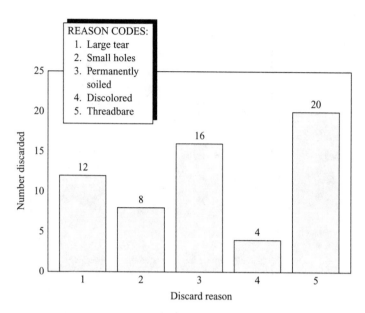

Figure 5–10 Histogram of Data from Checksheet in Exhibit 5–1

what the temporal behavior of the process is and (2) establish the time of process performance changes so that they can be linked to the time of other possibly related events. Figure 5–11 shows a generic series of run charts and some diagnostic interpretations of that data. Chart (a) in Figure 5–11 shows a process that is under control (within upper and lower control limits) and appears to have random variation. Chart (b) shows a process that has too much variability, producing observations outside the control limits in both directions. Chart (c) shows a process that is within control limits, but consistently on the lower side. Since the effects of health care errors tend to be asymmetrical, it is best to look at one-sided rules of thumb for process control. A process is considered under control if most of the observations are near the centerline, if there are few points near the upper or lower control limits (above the mean plus or minus three standard deviations), and there are no runs (more than eight consecutive observations to one side of the mean). Like histograms, run charts are very easy to create on the computer.

Run charts are frequently used late in the quality improvement process to answer the question, "Are we doing better?" To answer that question one must be able to compare where one has been with where one is. The upper and lower control limits are not necessary for the answering of that question. Therefore a run chart does not need to show any control limits. Control charts are used for the purpose of determining whether the process is under control and therefore must contain control limits as described below. There are numerous examples of run charts in this book even though almost all are labeled as control charts. This is be-

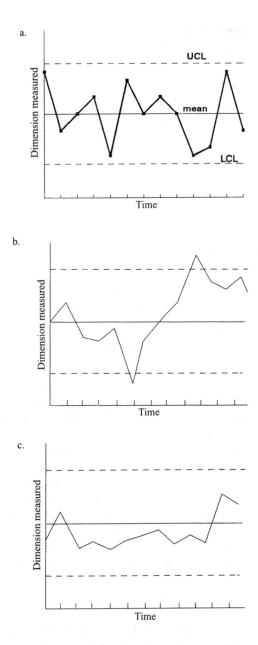

Figure 5–11 Three Examples of Run Charts. In (a), the data is considered to be under control—the points are apparently randomly distributed on either side of the mean, and do not go outside of the control limits. In (b), there are extreme values (outside the control limits), and thus the process is not in control. Another thing to beware is too many observations on one side of the mean. In (c), there are too many values in a row (>8) below the mean.

cause most software packages take a data set and automatically calculate and display the three standard deviation upper and lower limits on the chart. However, very few teams have gotten all the way to controlling the process that they are observing, so the charts are really being used as run charts.

The industrial quality control literature talks about two types of measures that can be used to develop run charts and their cousins, control charts. Measures can be either attributes or variables. "Attribute data arise from (1) classification of items, such as products or services, into categories; from (2) counts of the number of items or the proportion in a given category; and from (3) counts of the number of occurrences per unit.... Important attributes [are]: fraction defective, number of defects, number of defects per unit" (Gitlow et al., 1989, pp. 78–79, 144). Variables are measured directly or based on direct measures only and do not result from a classification scheme. For example, nurses frequently plot the variable of temperature for inpatients. However, the attribute question is often asked, "Is the patient's temperature normal or not? We cannot send her home if she still has a fever." Variable charts are a key part of continuous improvement as the team seeks to reduce variation, come up with a more robust design process, or make the process conform more closely to customer preferences. Charts often present the variable mean (X-bar), the process range (R), and/or standard deviation(s) for a specific process parameter. One might almost go as far as to argue that unless one is following run charts of key parameters, one is not really focused on continuous improvement.

Process Capability Analysis

Given the availability of data at this point, it may be useful to try to characterize the process capability. This method of analysis is not included as one of the seven tools, but it provides a check on the data that has been collected and the underlying assumptions of the statistical tools used. Process capability analysis allows one to determine the process mean and standard deviation and its closeness to the usual normality assumption of much of applied statistics.

The first step is to plot the data. If the plot (histogram) does not appear to support the assumptions of a normal distribution, then a statistical consult is necessary before proceeding further. At this point it is also useful to consider whether you have enough observations to characterize the process and whether they are sufficiently random and representative. The sample sizes needed are surprisingly large. If a variable is to be looked at over time, then the first set of observations should include 50 samples of three to five observations each and in subsequent time periods 25 samples with three to five observations each. If the measure is an attribute rather than a variable, the sample should be even larger. Distinguishing between attributes and variables is often difficult in health care. The proportion of patients admitted due to a single diagnosis and dying from a single cause would be a causal variable in quality improvement terms. The proportion of patients admitted under a DRG and dying of any cause would be an attribute and require roughly ten times more observations in each sample.

Once the stable, natural process has been characterized, it is then important to compare its distribution with the specifications that it is trying to meet. Figures 5–12a and 5–12b show two processes, one within specifications and one with a problem maintaining quality. Figure 5–13 shows the financial losses associated with the ability of a process to hold closeness to a desired value. This model demonstrates the potential cost benefit to reducing process variation.

Process Stage 3—Weigh Alternatives and Make Choices

Now the analysis turns toward collecting data on the chosen causes and on selecting alternative ways of reducing their frequency. In this stage, one is likely to turn first to more detailed flow diagrams. The team begins to look at the process in sufficient depth to begin to find out what part of the process produces the error. At this point, the group is often deciding whether the error being studied is due to common cause or to special cause.

Tool 7—Regression Analysis

At this point one is likely to look at the relationship between specific events and the occurrence that one is focusing on. This can usually be tested statistically by some form of correlational modeling. For example, in 1980, Gardner and McLaughlin developed a regression model to forecast the utilization of perishable blood products in a large hospital. They developed a forecast model that predicted the demand for these products quite effectively based on hospital census and some seasonal patterns. However, the staff reported that one of the attending (faculty) physicians utilized these products much more than the other three. Since the attending physicians rotated through the service, it was possible to assign 0-1 dummy variables to account for which of the attending physicians was on duty. The model indicated that there was not a significant difference in utilization among the four attending physicians. Whatever the staff had to say about that one attending physician was not borne out by the data.

Getting negative findings is not a bad outcome in CQI. That eliminates one alternative and allows the team to focus on other alternatives. It is not unusual either. A significant percentage of teams report that their first impressions of the causes of problems are inappropriate. If they had not conducted analyses or experiments to check out those hypotheses early, they would have continued to work in an unfruitful area. This is one of the advantages of CQI methods. The team is able to use scientific methods of analysis to verify and support any changes that they would like to make, instead of guessing what to do.

Why is it that so many strongly held hypotheses are not borne out? Organizations usually act on their existing hypotheses. If the ones commonly held to be important were the right ones, the performance gap would be narrowing over

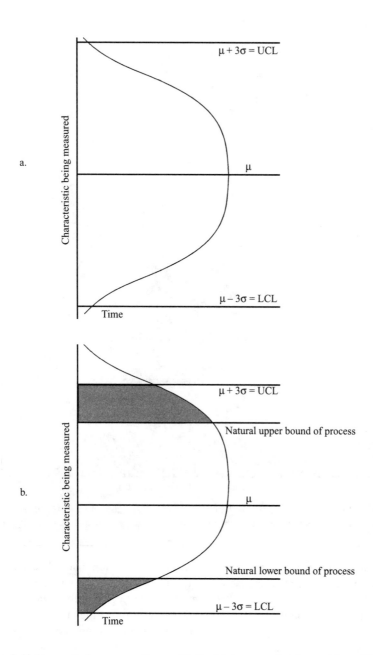

Figure 5–12 Process Performance vs. Process Limits: (a) A process that does not have difficulty maintaining quality will have normally distributed observations over time. (b) A process that has difficulty maintaining quality may still have normally distributed observations over time but may have control limits outside the natural bounds of the process and a mean that is not at the center of the normal curve. The shaded areas in this diagram represent the areas out of specification.

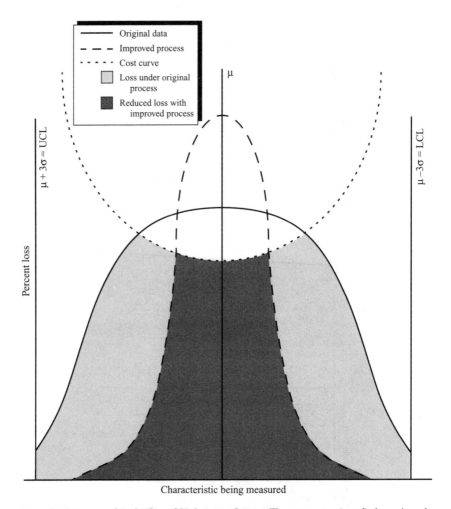

Figure 5–13 Impact of Reduction of Variance on Losses. The cost curve (noted) determines the losses associated with a process. When the variation is reduced, the amount of the losses decreases.

time and that area would not be a prominent candidate for attack. Areas that stay problems tend to linger precisely because management has not been operating with the right hypotheses and has been concentrating its efforts on the wrong ones. Therefore one of the roles of CQI teams is to test the current hypotheses and, when they fail, suggest new, more effective ones. Regression analysis provides one way of looking for unknown or underrated associations.

Dr. Kenichi Taguchi, a Japanese quality expert, strongly recommends using not only regression, but the full science of experimental design to develop and test relationships between various operational factors and quality outcomes. The mathematics of both regression and experimental design are beyond the scope of this book, but such skills, often called Taguchi methods, are frequently used in health services management (Veney and Kaluzny, 1992) and should be considered where appropriate.

Process Stage 4—Measure Improvements and Monitor Progress

Once the experiments have been run and effective ways of avoiding the root causes of variation have been established, the changes will, in all probability, be implemented. Such changes may be effective temporarily, but then the system may slip back into its old ways. A system of measuring and monitoring must be put into place to find out whether these improvements are actually being captured and whether the new process is under control. Control charts, similar to run charts, are the most helpful tool for this stage.

Tool 8—Control Charts

Control charts are a popular form of presentation means for quality improvement teams. Most often, however, these are actually run charts with the addition of notation indicating the control limits of plus or minus three standard deviations (commonly referred to as "3-sigma"). To use a control chart, the team has to be sure that the process is free of special causes of variation at the time the control limits are set and then follow the charts to see whether (1) special causes are again creeping in, or (2) the underlying process has changed. Because these charts are actually run charts, the most common form is X-bar chart. This is a plot of the sample mean (X-bar). In the run chart most often used in health care, the sample size per observation is usually one. This assumes that there is no sampling error and that all observations are accurate. This can become an important issue in health care where observations can vary so much. Taking blood pressure is a good example. A given patient's blood pressure will vary slightly depending on who is taking it. It will vary even more if different cuffs and measuring equipment are used. It will vary even further depending on the emotional state of the patient at the time of the measurement. All these sampling variations would have to be taken into account in a study of the effectiveness of certain hypertension procedures or drugs before the effects of the intervention could be quantified.

Control charts can be configured using almost any of the simple statistics that you calculate for the data collected, such as the mean, standard deviation, and range. One example is the X-bar chart shown in Figure 5–14. The X-bar chart is created by plotting the mean of each group of samples on the Y axis and time or some other indicator of sequencing on the X axis. For the X-bar chart the calculation of control limits is quite simple. The value of X-bar is the mean of the observations taken at that point in time. The standard deviation is taken to be the standard error of the mean (the estimated true standard deviation divided by the square root of the sample size). This allows for the comparison of means from

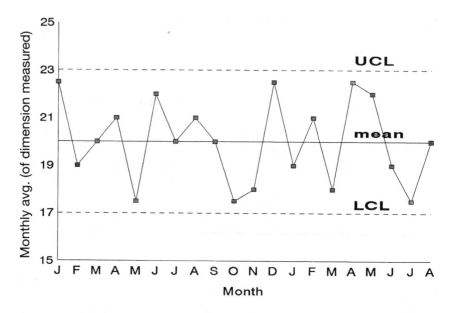

Figure 5–14 *X*-Bar Control Chart. UCL/LCL = avg ± 3 $(sl\sqrt{n})$, where s = standard deviation and n = sample size.

samples of different sizes. When the team is really serious about control charts, they are likely to have charts for both mean and variability.

The charts used to observe and control variability track either standard deviation (S-charts) or range (R-charts). Both of these charts are used to track the amount of dispersion in the data. To create an S-chart, the standard deviation of each group of observations is plotted on the *Y* axis. The standard deviation is adjusted for sample size. The *X* axis is still the same as the *X*-bar chart. S-charts are used when the sample size is larger than ten and the standard error is smaller than the mean. For smaller subgroups, the range is used as an estimate of the standard deviation. The R-chart is created by plotting the range of each group of observations along the *Y* axis. It is common to display either of these types of control charts directly under the *X*-bar control chart so that the means values and the dispersion can be viewed simultaneously. Figure 5–15 displays an S-chart and an R-chart.

The other frequently used control chart is the *p*-chart, an attribute chart that shows the proportion of cases in which a given error or set of errors occurs. A mortality rate would be a natural set of data for a *p*-chart. There are two states: defective and not defective, dead or alive. The distribution of *p*, the proportion defective, is binomial and is easy to use. The corresponding control charts are easy to develop. The standard deviation is equal to the square root of the proportion defective times the proportion not defective divided by the sample size.

a.

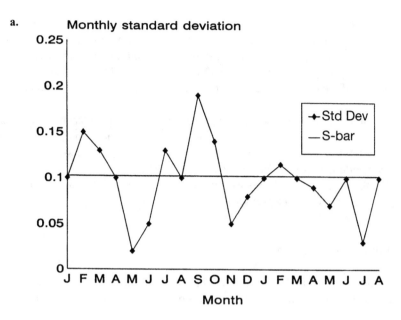

b.

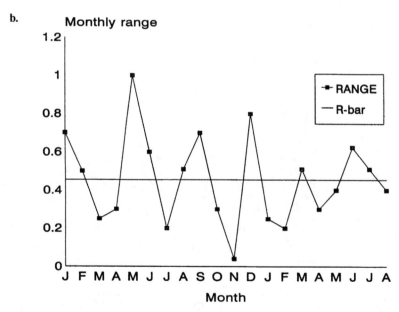

Figure 5–15 (a) S-Chart. The standard deviation for each month is determined by calculating the standard deviation and dividing by the square root of the number of observations in that month. S-bar is the average of these standard variations. (b) R-Chart. The range for each month is determined by subtracting the smallest observation of the month from the largest observation. R-bar is the average of these ranges.

The major difference between the *p*-chart and the others is that the plot is done using attribute data rather than causal variables (and thus simple statistics cannot be calculated, only proportions.) It is important in setting up these charts to start with a historical proportion, such as the previous mortality rates. Then you can keep track of the proportion during and after the intervention period and compare results.

The *p*-chart plots the proportion that you are measuring for each group of observations on the *Y* axis, with a midline indicating the historical proportion. At the very least, the team can monitor that the proportion does not get worse. Then you can conclude that your efforts have improved the process without adversely affecting the outcome of the process, and you may find evidence that it improves. Figure 5–16 shows such a *p*-chart.

Continuing the Improvement

A process that is under control and showing that the latest set of changes has been effective is not the team's final objective. The next step is to return to the

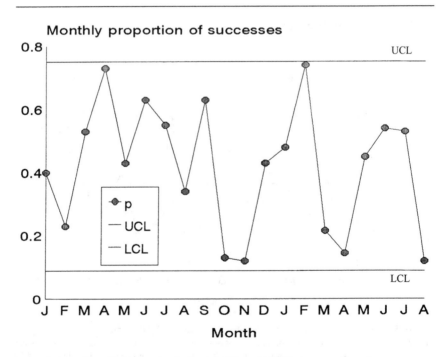

Figure 5–16 *p*-Chart. The proportion is determined by calculating the proportion of successes over the month (*p*). The confidence intervals are calculated as $p \pm 3 \times \sqrt{[p\,(1-p)\,/n]}$.

Plan stage of the PDCA cycle and determine whether it would be worthwhile to try to improve this process further. If so, the team should return to their Pareto analysis and cause-and-effect diagrams to develop further hypotheses for testing and implementation.

CONCLUSION

This chapter has outlined a process that is typical of how the TQM/CQI model is implemented by a team. Many of the seven tools and some others are used to help the team move along with its task. CQI participants often encounter measurement tools very early in their training programs and may assume that they are the essence of the approach. Management must continue to argue that measurement is but one of the core elements of the CQI philosophy, while still remaining flexible about which tools to use and when in the process. These tools are not sophisticated although some team members may be a little put off by their statistical nature. Used appropriately under the guidance of a flexible and skilled facilitator, they will help teams implement the CQI philosophy with a maximum of effectiveness and a minimum of interpersonal conflict. Most of them are illustrated in action in one or more of the case studies in Part V.

6

Kate Macintyre
Carolyn Cable Kleman

Measuring Customer Satisfaction

Health care organizations, like other organizations, are created to serve the needs and expectations of those who use their services; though obvious, this should never be forgotten. So, because the mission of continuous quality improvement (CQI) is to continually improve the organization, its sole function is to achieve and assure customer satisfaction, striving to meet and, when possible, exceed customer expectations.

This chapter provides an introduction to methods of measuring customer satisfaction. It defines "customer" and outlines steps in the measurement of customer satisfaction. Measurement problems are identified, and examples of methods that can be used to ease and enhance the measurement of customer satisfaction are presented.

WHAT IS A CUSTOMER?

As health care managers and clinicians embark upon their quality improvement initiatives, they are asking many questions about the people they serve—their "customers." The first question many ask is usually, who is the "customer"? Is it the patient, the physician, the organization's employees, the insurance companies, or the board of directors? The answer is surprisingly simple.

The term *customer* has two meanings: (1) a person who buys from or regularly patronizes an establishment and (2) a person with whom one has dealings (Webster, 1968). The first, more traditional meaning is associated with business transactions between buyers and sellers. The second meaning is closer to the use of the term *customer* within CQI. Thus, although a patient may be the final customer, the physician is also a customer of the laboratory, who, in turn, is a customer of the laboratory supply firm. Both meanings are relevant since the idea of continuous and regular (customary) relationships is central to the CQI effort. A customer is therefore anyone within the health care system who has dealings with others in the system, either on a temporary basis (e.g., an acutely ill patient) or on a regular basis (e.g., laboratory technicians with nurses, physicians with administrators).

Figure 6–1 illustrates the complex and dynamic network of interactions among customers and suppliers in health care: individuals, groups, departments, and the larger community. Understanding and strengthening these exchanges is a major challenge of CQI.

CQI uses a simple typology to differentiate among customers. Customers are labeled as internal or external. Internal customers include all the professionals, the employees, the managers, and the administrators; external customers comprise the patients, their friends and family, and third-party payers. These two groups are described below.

Who Are the External Customers?

Although patients are usually defined as primary customers, they are also a major group of external customers. Other external customers include third-party payers, the local community, and other groups whose needs may be met by the health care system. Examples of the latter include transport firms, building suppliers and contractors, laundry businesses, flower sellers, and so forth. The friends and families of patients are important external customers. The importance of friends and family as a group is illustrated by the fact that nearly a third of the customer surveys used by many cancer facilities are typically sent to nonpatients (Schweikhart et al., 1993). Recent research has suggested that the friends and family of patients may be a harder group to satisfy than the patients themselves (Strasser and Davis, 1991). The patient may feel dependent upon the caregiver, whereas the friends and family are more assertive on behalf of the patient.

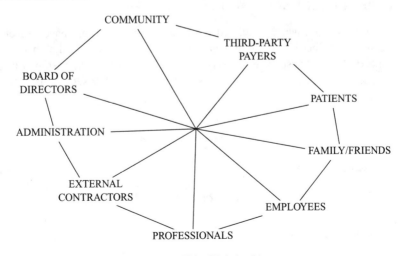

Figure 6–1 Continuous Quality Improvement: A Web of Relationships

Who Are the Internal Customers?

The internal customers are the technical and support staff (e.g., laboratory technicians or housekeeping personnel who function within a health service organization) and professional health providers (specialists, hospital-based physicians, nurses, or physician assistants), all senior and mid-level administrative officers, and support personnel. Within health services, however, the complex nature of the activities challenges simple typologies or mutually exclusive relationships. Community-based physicians, for example, while functioning as external customers, are also internal customers when they are operating within the hospital. They are part of the work flow process within the organization, as illustrated by their use of laboratory data to make clinical decisions.

The concept of internal customers presents the view of the organization as functioning horizontally rather than vertically through predefined departments and hierarchies. The ultimate customers, the patients, move horizontally through the system interacting with many different departments and transcending departmental lines. Moreover, during the process of patient care, the various departments have reciprocal roles as suppliers and customers.

Figure 6–2 illustrates the process and the reciprocal role of suppliers and customers. The example of a medication request demonstrates that there are many different customer and supplier relationships. First, physicians are suppliers to the patient, their customers. In turn, the physicians are customers who request medications from the pharmacy. The pharmacy is a customer of the nursing staff, whose responsibility it is to distribute the requested medications to the ultimate customer, the patient.

EXPECTATIONS AND LOYALTY

All customers, whether defined individually or as a group, have expectations (realistic or otherwise). These expectations are often expressed as needs in the context of CQI. These expectations or needs must be met if the customer is to feel satisfied, so that, from the customer's perspective, quality service has been pro-

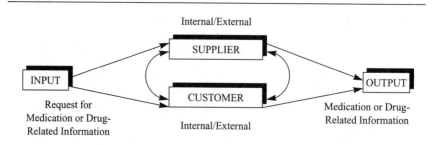

Figure 6–2 Example of a Process: Customer-Supplier Relationship

vided. As described by Deming (1986), an organization must not merely satisfy, "but delight" a customer in order for that customer to return.

CQI goes beyond seeking to satisfy one group's expectations. By highlighting the patient as the primary customer in a complex web of interrelationships, it is reaffirming that health care must be of the highest quality, as perceived by the patient and the provider, that the opinions of the patient are important, and that serving the patient is the primary focus of the organization. CQI therefore seeks to build and strengthen customer commitment to the organization by creating an environment where the needs of patients are understood, where mistakes are recognized or anticipated and prevented, where all errors or complaints are treated as useful sources of knowledge, and where mistakes are redressed sufficiently well to recover customer confidence.

Expectation and loyalty are not without cost or value. For example, the estimated cost to a hospital of recapturing a dissatisfied customer, in terms of future encounters over that customer's lifetime and word-of-mouth effects, can range from a conservative estimate of $8,000 per patient (Strasser and Davis, 1991) to a less conservative estimate (Rosselli et al., 1989) of approximately $400,000. These are only estimates, yet even the most conservative cost estimates of patient loss through dissatisfaction make managing expectations and customer loyalty an essential part of the management process.

USING CUSTOMER INFORMATION

Since the 1960s, Deming has advocated the importance of building customer responses into the design of the product (Deming, 1986). In his words: "consumer research takes the pulse of the consumer's reactions and demands" (p. 177). Companies such as Mitsubishi and Sony have been measuring their customers' satisfaction for a number of years with startlingly and well-publicized beneficial results. Using the Total Quality Management framework, these manufacturers improved the quality of their goods by listening to both actual and potential customers and using this customer feedback to design products to meet and exceed customer expectations. The following are just a few of the reasons why it is beneficial to measure health care customer satisfaction (Davies and Ware, 1988, pp. 40–43):

1. Whatever "quality" means to consumers, their perceptions of quality affect their choices among health care alternatives. Word-of-mouth recommendations are the most important marketing influence on health care buying decisions.
2. Consumers are the best source of data on the interpersonal aspects of care; moreover, consumers can provide data on the technical quality of outpatient care not available from traditional data sources such as claims and records.

3. The costs of obtaining data from consumers are not higher (and are probably lower) than those for obtaining data from more traditional sources such as record audits.
4. Consumers' reports (as distinct from ratings) hold considerable promise as a data source for quality assessment and assurance activities.
5. Consumers' ratings of technical quality do reflect, at least in part, how many services they received.
6. For common problems, consumers can distinguish between the technical aspects of care judged good or less-than-good by physicians.
7. Interpersonal features of care do not obscure consumers' ability to distinguish levels of the technical process for common outpatient problems.
8. Bias from personal characteristics, such as age and gender, does not usually invalidate consumers' ratings of the interpersonal or technical quality of their care.

THE CUSTOMER SURVEY PROCESS: MEASURING CUSTOMER SATISFACTION

Measuring customer satisfaction is the measurement of judgment. It is the scientific process of assigning measurable quantities to the outcomes of individual experiences. This section outlines six essential steps for measuring customer satisfaction. This section also emphasizes the importance of selecting and adapting indicators and provides a framework for assessing the different levels of data-gathering activity (Tenner and DeToro, 1992).

The choice, design, and outcomes of the survey process rest on selecting appropriate indicators for what is to be measured. Indicators are used to measure a particular attribute or activity. Selecting and developing indicators is an iterative process requiring constant attention and flexibility.

In general, the indicators used to measure customer satisfaction can be divided into three categories (Donabedian, 1982): structure, process, and outcome. Structural items include such inputs as equipment, personnel, buildings, and the physical layout of an organization. Process items are the activities that people undertake within the organization to convert the structural items or inputs into outcomes. Examples of processes include a nurse delivering medication or transporting patients from one area of the hospital to another. Outcome items are the result of structure and process and include various indicators of patient mortality and morbidity.

Methods of Measurement

Exhibit 6–1 presents methods commonly used to gather customer information for decision making. Any serious effort to systematically assess customer satisfaction requires an interactive combination of these various methods (Veney and

Exhibit 6–1 Typical Methods Used To Measure Customer Satisfaction

Self-administered questionnaire Direct observation Participant observation Telephone/mail surveys Focus groups Semistructured interviews Structured interviews Open-ended interviews Critical incident interviews Content analysis (letters of complaint or praise)

Kaluzny, 1992). For example, focus groups and direct observation provide an opportunity to identify the issues upon which to design questionnaires and structure interviews, which in turn provide information for further focus group discussion.

Tenner and DeToro (1992) use a two-dimensional framework for determining data-gathering techniques for different desired levels of understanding about the customers. Most importantly, this framework illustrates the relationship between the program's approach (reactive to proactive) to understanding customer needs and expectations and the level of customer understanding attained (high to low). Figure 6–3 illustrates this framework.

- At Level 1, management's approach is reactive and the level of customer understanding is low. Customer complaints are the primary method of gathering information. There is minimal understanding of the customer's expectations, except as negatively recorded. This approach is event based.

- Level 2 involves active listening to the customer. The information-gathering mechanisms at this level are aimed at increasing the communication channels with different customers, heeding and responding to questions and concerns, and initiating additional efforts to counteract problems identified. Examples of this level of approach include hotlines, feedback from customer advocates or labor unions, and unstructured surveys.

- Level 3 implies a search for an in-depth understanding of customer expectations. A systems approach can be used at this level, and methods for gathering information include focus group interviews, specially designed surveys, and personal structured interviews.

Although categorizing appropriate methods by level of customer understanding is useful for different purposes, there are often benefits from utilizing techniques from each level at the same time. Indicators can reinforce and validate each other if used carefully and constructively.

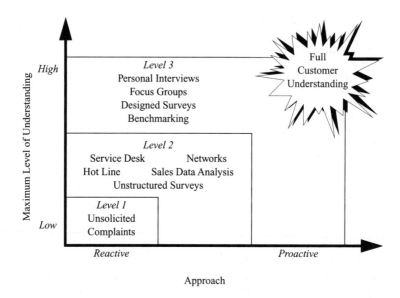

Figure 6–3 Mechanisms for Understanding Customers. *Source:* A.R. Tenner and I.J. DeToro, *Total Quality Management* (p. 84), © 1992 by the Addison-Wesley Publishing Co., Inc. Reprinted by permission of the publisher.

Steps to Measuring Customer Satisfaction

Measuring customer satisfaction involves a series of six steps: goal setting, method selection, data collection, data storage, data analysis and presentation, and translating knowledge into action. Below we present each of these steps (Exhibit 6–2) and discuss their function within CQI.

Step 1: Goal Setting

The first step in designing a customer survey is to decide the purpose that it will serve. Critical questions include: Who is the customer? What is going to be

Exhibit 6–2 Steps to Measuring Customer Satisfaction

Step 1. Goal setting
Step 2. Method selection
Step 3. Designing the data collection tool
Step 4. Data collection and storage
Step 5. Data analysis and presentation
Step 6. Translating the knowledge into action

achieved through this survey? How will the customers benefit from the survey? How will managers and teams interpret and use these data?

In addition, it is important at the outset that a number of logistical issues be resolved. Is the organization merely gathering data for its own sake or because data are required by regulatory agencies? Who will be responsible for converting the data through analysis into information? Who will receive the results of the surveys, and how will these results be used? Will the results be used in performance appraisals?

Step 2: Method Selection

With clear understanding of the survey's purpose, the second step is to select the data-gathering method or methods. Method selection involves learning more about information-gathering techniques and choosing the right technique for the target customer group and for the information to be obtained. A combination of methods may be appropriate for meeting the various needs of the organization. Each method has its advantages and disadvantages.

A focus group method, for example, is frequently employed to gain insight into patient needs or into the conflicts between professional staff. As Nelson et al. (1991a, p. 18) emphasize, "the chief advantage of the focus group is that the group process can stimulate ideas, reactions and comments that would not have surfaced without multiple people sharing insights and experiences."

In a typical focus group, patients, employees, or others from whom you are interested in obtaining information meet with a facilitator. This facilitator is often an organizational representative trained in managing group processes. The group meets to discuss issues related to the organization and the services that are important to them. The facilitator usually has some structured questions that may assist the group in moving through the group process and stimulating new ideas, but the general format is open and unstructured. The questions are there to help the facilitator remember those aspects of the organization that a customer group might omit. These questions can be used as cues to assure that the group addresses issues important to the organization. This process may elicit information on positive and negative perceptions by the customers; it may also help determine how they, as a group, define quality. Other possible outcomes include the identification of unavailable services or services in need of improvement. These flexible methods may also be used to monitor the perceived value of the products and services provided.

The limitations of this method are in the recency and the selectivity of the perceptions of the group. Complaints about recent incidents, rather than more comprehensive problems, may dominate discussion since they are in the customer's most recent memory. Ideally, there should be multiple meetings with different individuals representing the same customer group. This helps assure generalizability of the information.

Focus group meetings ideally take place in comfortable, nonthreatening sur-roundings where everyone can introduce him- or herself, and have an opportunity to contribute. If managed well, focus groups provide important information for identifying expectations of a variety of customers as well as suggested solutions and strategies for meeting these expectations.

Step 3: Designing the Data Collection Tool

A customer-driven organization requires a continuous information-gathering effort. Unfortunately, this is not always feasible or cost effective. Indeed, a brief and pretested questionnaire administered on a regular basis may produce far more interesting and usable data than a hastily written, poorly worded, and long survey that tries to gather all possible information on a particular subject. This need for thoughtful design of the questionnaire and selection of the appropriate data collection period should be obvious, yet such concerns are too frequently dismissed as causing unnecessary delays in the quest for data.

Any survey instrument attempts to avoid errors of measurement. An instrument that has been proven both reliable and valid is a very valuable tool. Indeed, where possible, instruments already tested with their results published in the medical/health administration literature should be reused or adapted. The process of creating new measurement instruments requires special skill and experience, as well as considerable time and money.

Appendix 6–A illustrates a survey instrument specifically designed for use within the CQI context. The 29-item questionnaire was developed by the Hospital Corporation of America to assess patient satisfaction with outpatient services. It is divided into eight sections: getting to the hospital, parking, registration, medical tests, the facilities, overall satisfaction with the hospital, and facts about the patient. The first five sections ask the patients to rate the service they have re-ceived from poor to excellent. The questionnaire was designed to fit on one two-sided card and to be completed in pencil. The use of pencil facilitates automated data entry, thereby reducing the time needed for processing, storing, and analyz-ing the data collected.

Below are some important considerations for designing a measurement tool to collect quality data.

Situational Contaminants. Environmental factors such as room temperature, time of day, and the presence of others may distract the interviewee/customer and produce different answers under different circumstances.

Response-Set Biases. Individuals may have set predispositions. For example, some customers may give the answers that they feel are most desired—("predis-position toward satisfaction" [McMillan, 1987, p. 55])—whereas others may choose the extreme answers to every question or provide only positive feedback on questions. These biases may be influenced by a number of factors, including transitory personal factors such as fatigue, hunger, physical pain, psychological mood, or anxiety level, as well as a variety of method effects such as mode of administration, timing of survey, and response format (Meterko et al., 1990).

In situations where customers are inundated by different surveys from different units, patients, in particular, often express confusion, frustration, and irritation. These feelings will contribute to response biases and affect the quality of the data. To avoid this situation, which also produces needless duplication and over-burdening of the patients (or other customers), coordination at the earliest planning stages is required. Furthermore, no customer should be surveyed more than once by the same method and no more than twice per visit or per year. The survey should always be pilot tested to refine the questions, even if the questionnaire itself has been used a number of times. Lengthy questionnaires frequently result in lower and more biased response rates.

Finally, many organizations use consultants to design and manage the survey and even to implement the CQI team process. Although this may reduce the bias that the organization itself introduces in the desire for positive feedback, the position of outsiders in this situation may also reduce trust and confidence among the managers and clinicians. Any approach is contingent upon the situation and the cost. However, convenience and expected, long-term, beneficial results suggest that the effectiveness of outside consultants may be greatest in the planning stages of the measurement process.

Variations in Administration. Variations in the methods of collecting data or the materials and media used can affect responses. Geriatric patients, for example, are easily distracted by high-technology equipment such as video cameras or computers. Careful thought to the reactions of different customer groups at the design stage or following the pilot stage may save time and money in the long run.

Reliability. Reliability is the degree of consistency with which the instrument measures the attribute it is supposed to be measuring. It is often thought of as the extent to which scores obtained on measures are reproducible. If there are errors in measurement, reliability is compromised.

Validity. Validity refers to the degree to which an instrument measures what it is supposed to be measuring. A measuring device that is not reliable cannot be valid. There are several different types of validity for which any measurement instrument should be checked. *Content validity* refers to how adequately an instrument covers the proposed or substantive content area. *Criterion validity* involves the comparison of results from one questionnaire to a criterion measure or standard. *Construct validity* tests the question, "Does this measure agree with others thought to measure the same thing?" This type of validation requires quantitative analysis, but as yet lacks an identifiable and accepted criterion or standard.

Content and construct validity are of concern to those measuring customer satisfaction since there are few accepted criteria for many of the measures applied in these surveys. When developing a survey for a particular organization, validity and reliability of the instrument should be tested. Four methods are available for boosting reliability and validity (Polit and Hungler, 1985, p. 171):

1. Subtle, indirect, and delicately worded questions
2. A permissive atmosphere
3. Efforts to maintain customer anonymity and encourage frankness
4. Mixing of positively and negatively worded statements

Step 4: Data Collection and Storage

Given a clear survey goal and appropriate data collection methods and tools, the next steps are actual collection and storage. Data collection is not purely mechanical. The timing of the survey (before, during, or after an exchange with the health care system) has a strong effect on patient satisfaction. Major problems may easily arise at this stage without careful planning and communication of intention to the survey respondents. Unfortunately, there is no recovery from a poorly designed form or from poorly executed data collection.

Insufficient time allowed for interviewing customers (i.e., a rushed environment) may create its own response bias, as, of course, non-"user-friendly" questionnaires also do. Self-administered surveys should be attractively laid out with large print and clear and self-explanatory instructions. In the pretesting stage, problems of layout should be diagnosed and solved to the extent possible.

The production, collation, and implementation of survey questionnaires often tend to take longer than planned. A monitoring system is an advantage. This can ensure that the questionnaires are being distributed and completed appropriately and that respondents' time is not being overburdened with the data collection process.

Data Storage. Health care organizations in the process of implementing CQI require an efficient and effective information system in which to store and access information generated from customer surveys. Orme and Parsons (1992), for example, have described a generic customer information system (CIS) as a method for collecting and presenting information about customers that senior managers, the quality council, project team members, and others can use to improve processes. They suggest that customer information be kept in a CIS database. This would contain information about external customers such as the patients, payers, and regulators, as well as the survey results from internal customers (employee groups, physician and administrator work groups). The CIS database would contain information from a variety of sources, including periodical literature, books, conferences, workshops, and government publications. In the context of CQI management, a database for the storing of information should be considered for at least three reasons: (1) to eliminate duplication of research efforts and hence to decrease costs; (2) to ensure that information about the customer groups is properly collected and interpreted throughout the organization; and (3) to provide decision makers with access to better, more reliable, and appropriate information that can then constitute a sound basis for further change. Figure 6–4 demonstrates the role of customer information in the quality improvement process.

Health care organizations that have already initiated a quality improvement system understand the advantages of implementing an efficient and accessible CIS. The transformation to continuous quality improvement is easier if project teams and managers have access to better information on which to base decisions. Health care organizations that can collect, store, and access information more efficiently than their competitors are also more likely to satisfy their customers' changing expectations.

Establishing a CIS is a complex task. If designed correctly, a CIS can be a tremendous asset to any organization's quality improvement efforts. In order to design the most effective system possible, a few specific areas of concern need to be addressed. First, the organization must identify the source of customer information, who is receiving it, and whether it is useful to various departments, thus avoiding redundant data collection. Second, the organization must determine if this collection process is technically acceptable. Is the information reliable and relevant and is the analysis useful? Next, it is important to determine whether automation will be required. If the system is going to be fully automated, what Management Information System (MIS) expertise will be needed to manage the database, who will perform these tasks, and what management protocols will be

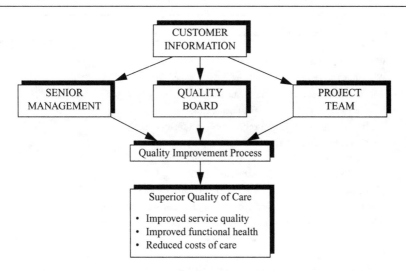

Figure 6–4 The Role of Customer Information in the Quality Improvement Process. *Source:* Reprinted with permission from Orme, C.N., and Parsons, R.J. "Customer Information and the Quality Improvement Process: Developing a Customer Information System." *Hospital & Health Services Administration* 37, no. 2, pages 197–212. Ann Arbor, MI: Health Administration Press. © 1992, Foundation of the American College of Healthcare Executives.

necessary to ensure effective and desired utilization of the information? Orme and Parsons (1992) have highlighted these CIS implementation concerns in the list of questions in Exhibit 6–3.

Step 5: Data Analysis and Presentation

After customers' satisfaction data have been gathered, they are analyzed using statistical or other analytical methods. Cross-tabulations, simple correlations, frequency tables, and a range of summary statistics can provide an overview and basic descriptions of the distribution of the data. Graphic presentations of these basic statistics, distributions, and relationships are frequently and effectively used to communicate the results. Trends over time are easily demonstrated with regular customer surveys, though validity and reliability may be a problem beyond the most general statements. More complex methods using linear and logistic multiple regression techniques to explore the relationships between the variables measured can help to increase understanding of the data (Veney and Kaluzny, 1992).

After the analysis, the next step is communication with the clear, graphic presentation of the results to those who are most affected: the internal or the external customers. Maps, scatter plots and graphs, pie charts, and bar charts are all useful for graphic presentations. It is impossible to overemphasize the need for clarity and precision at this stage.

Who presents the material is also important. Employee and professional relations may be improved and encouraged when senior management display their

---

Exhibit 6–3 CIS Implementation Questions

- Who are our customers?
- What information do we currently have about our customers?
- Who is collecting customer information?
- Is research being duplicated in our organization?
- Are the methods we use to collect customer information reliable?
- Are the results being interpreted correctly?
- Who in our organization qualifies as a research advisor?
- To what degree do we want to automate the CIS?
- Do we have the MIS experience to set up and manage a CIS?
- How much money are we willing to spend to implement and maintain the CIS?
- Who will have access to the CIS?
- What will be the CIS database security protocol?
- Who will manage the CIS database?
- How will we monitor the effectiveness of the CIS?

Source: Reprinted with permission from Orme, C.N., and Parsons, R.J. "Customer Information and the Quality Improvement Process: Developing a Customer Information System." *Hospital & Health Services Administration* 37, no. 2, pages 197–212. Ann Arbor, MI: Health Administration Press. © 1992, Foundation of the American College of Healthcare Executives.

commitment to quality improvement by their physical presence. Presentation of the findings by an outsider or consultant may only heighten feelings of division. CQI involves every member of the organization moving toward a patient-focused, patient-driven approach. By good, personalized presentation of the material, each supplier-customer relationship within health care can be strengthened. Brief written summaries, published through an internal network, may also show internal customers that their voice is heeded. Prearranged public hearings can be more appropriate for community groups and patient families. A mixture of these strategies may be the most potent approach.

Step 6: Translating the Knowledge into Action

Once the data have been collected and analyzed, the information is ready to be utilized in improving specific work processes. Translating data and its analysis into an effective change in operations is among the fundamental challenges of CQI. Speedy response to the concerns raised by the data analysis is crucial to both internal and external customers' perceptions of commitment by the organization to the CQI process. This perception of commitment, in turn, determines the loyalty of the customers to the organization and their support for its quality improvement efforts.

One effective approach to utilizing the information to identify specific work processes for improvement is Quality Function Deployment (QFD). According to Chip Caldwell, CEO of West Paces Ferry Hospital in Atlanta, QFD represents the "purest integration between marketing (customer satisfaction surveys) and operations we had ever seen" (personal communication). The process involves systematically comparing customer expectations (determined through surveys, focus groups, and interviews) against work processes that are supposed to meet these expectations. The information is weighted to identify the areas with the highest relative importance and also to identify areas that have the most significant gaps in quality in comparison to the competitors. Utilizing this information, the organization identifies the work processes it feels would have the most significant impact on operations as the subject of a quality improvement project (Nelson et al., 1991b).

Measuring the Satisfaction of Different Groups

External Customers

The Patient. Although research on patient satisfaction is perhaps the most developed, relative to other customer groups, its collection and management presents significant challenges, including:

• Lack of any norms for satisfaction
• Unclear definitions

- Failure to specify any consistent group to measure satisfaction
- Inconsistent psychometric properties of satisfaction instruments, such as inclusion of items that do not measure satisfaction
- Ambiguity and inconsistent or nonexistent reporting of reliability and validity
- Failure to differentiate dissatisfaction from satisfaction
- Lack of control and monitoring of data collection
- Frequent use of unrepresentative samples
- Poor handling of skewed responses
- Inconsistent data analysis
- Poor presentation, leading to mistrust of the system and a deepening of dissatisfaction with the practice (Lebow, 1984, p. 239)

To minimize or at least to address some of these challenges, surveys of patient satisfaction should take into account several factors that may influence the measurement process, including sociodemographic characteristics (age, race, gender, education, income), physical and psychological status, attitudes and expectations concerning medical care and recovery, the health care setting, and the outcome of treatment. Any of these factors may have a positive or negative influence on satisfaction (Cleary and McNeil, 1991). Patients are aware of whether the care provided met their expectations and whether there was an acceptable outcome, but are less likely to know whether they had reasonable expectations or whether any undesired outcomes were the result of poor care or unusual circumstances. This matching of expectations to outcomes requires further applied research and detailed commentary from administrators, clinicians, and managers within health care, as well as complementary work with patient-focused research.

When should patient satisfaction be measured? The survey's administration can occur before the patient enters the facility, while the patient is in the facility, or after the patient has left the facility. Response cards (questionnaire cards) can be used at the time of discharge (Nelson et al., 1991b), and telephone interviews and mail surveys can be used after the patient has left the facility.

What is the unique contribution of using patient judgment? Various studies have documented that patients are better at judging interpersonal relations than the technical aspects of care. Using experimental and anecdotal evidence, however, Rubin (1990) showed that patients do judge the clinical components of health care quality, and that these judgments may be accurate and may determine whether a patient returns to that provider (see also Davies and Ware, 1988). For example, patients routinely evaluate the pain management aspects of their clinical care (Schweikhart et al., 1993). Similarly, primary care patients are quite discerning as to when they want continuity of care and when they want a rapid episodic response (Kibbe et al., 1993).

Patient satisfaction information has proven useful in many ways. Davies and Ware (1988, p. 40), for example, state that "consumers who hold more favorable attitudes toward the technical and interpersonal features of their care are significantly less likely to change physicians, and. . .more favorable ratings of care also have been linked to various measures of compliance."

Family and Friends. The patient's family is an external customer group that often goes unnoticed. This group may be more difficult to satisfy than the patients themselves (Schweikhart et al., 1993). Even though friends and family often receive support, counseling, and direct training as part of the hospital's total service to the patient, the satisfaction of family and friends is rarely evaluated. Yet they may be blamed for a failure or breakdown in the recovery of the patient. In many cases, such as when a patient is acutely ill or very young, a family member becomes a surrogate patient. The family is a valuable source of information and can be a very influential force in the patient's care and in the perception of quality of care.

The Community. A number of health care organizations have formed focus groups that involve members of the wider community. These focus groups collect information on the expectations of potential *future* patients. This is particularly difficult since individuals who lack any experience with the organization also lack experiential reference points against which to anchor their expectations. This presents one of the problem areas of measuring expectations.

Internal Customers

Physicians. Most managers would quickly identify the physician as an internal customer whose satisfaction is essential to any quality improvement initiative. Physicians are the primary, if not the sole, source of admission to the hospital and thus are a crucial link in hospital operations.

A method for measuring physician satisfaction with hospital services has recently been explored through the use of the Quality Improvement Strategy (QIS). The QIS focuses on physicians as key internal customers whose loyalty can be measured through their satisfaction with services. The purpose of the QIS is to maintain or increase physician satisfaction with the hospital's services, relative to its competitors, in order to increase admissions. Beach and Burns (1993) describe this method as one where hospital managers can link quality improvement efforts directly to physician satisfaction. This is accomplished using two questionnaires that elicit physicians' perceptions and judgments regarding which services need greater attention and which services do not meet expectations or are less satisfactory in comparison with competitors' services. The physicians' perceptions are based on a mixture of the discrepancies between the current and the desired situation at the hospital where they work and at a competing hospital.

QIS employs three strategies to assess physician satisfaction. First, physicians are asked to benchmark the hospital's services relative to its competitors. Second, questions aimed at measuring physician satisfaction with the hospital's services are asked to ascertain the degree to which those services fall short of, meet, or exceed physicians' expectations. Appendix 6–B provides an example of a physician survey. Finally, the method combines these two kinds of information to determine where to invest scarce resources in ongoing service quality improvements.

Employees. The measurement of employee satisfaction is not new or unusual to many organizations. However, the idea of employees as customers is quite new and redefines the function and utility of the employee survey. From this perspective, the purpose of gathering information from the employee is to gain an understanding of what it is like to be a customer in the overall work process. As described by Batalden and Nelson (1991, p. 13), "The aim is to view health work from the customer's perspective. This provides a horizontal view in contrast to a vertical view. By viewing health work from the customer's perspective, it becomes possible to understand better the nature and size of quality gaps that might exist when departments try to work together to meet patient needs."

An example of an employee satisfaction measurement tool was introduced recently at St. Mary's Hospital in Blue Springs, Missouri. Employees at Blue Springs were given a standardized survey to measure their satisfaction with the organization. The responses were entered into a national database so that the employees' responses could be compared with similar institutions. It was found that 46.8 percent of all St. Mary's Hospital employees felt that their current appraisal system did not reflect their true performance. This finding prompted the hospital to form a CQI committee to improve the performance appraisal process. At the time, the hospital had been involved with CQI for over two years (Myers, personal communication, 1993).

The CQI team at St. Mary's selected the appraisal system as their improvement project to reflect their belief in CQI. They have analyzed the current situation and are now in the analysis stage of the process. They are currently defining the root causes of dissatisfaction with the performance appraisal system. They will then progress through the following sequence: generate alternatives, choose among the alternatives, implement a solution, and monitor and evaluate the selected solution.

REWARDS SYSTEMS: TRANSLATING SATISFACTION INTO SUSTAINED EFFORT

The ultimate challenge is to translate customer information into reward systems that sustain continued effort among personnel. Health care organizations have not been particularly creative in this area, even though their very product is one of substance, namely, the health and welfare of people. The advent of CQI has stimulated some health care managers to meet the challenge.

Although the limits of the effort are defined by the creativity within the organization, several principles guide these efforts:

- Financial rewards are only one of the currencies that influence behavior. Although there is no doubt that monetary rewards are important factors affecting individual behavior, they are not the only factor. Increasingly, managers are recognizing that there are other equally important and, under certain conditions, more important factors (Bradford and Cohen, 1990). These include being involved in a task that has larger significance for the unit, organization, or society; having the opportunity to do important things really well; and, perhaps most basic, doing the "right thing" by a higher standard than efficiency.

- Reward systems themselves are the subject of CQI efforts. Like all other systems, the rewards system is created by the organization, and thus it too is subject to the continuous quality improvement process. Although a reward system is usually designed, implemented, and managed in a "top down" administrative manner, a great deal of benefit is likely to occur by simply establishing a quality improvement team to assess the rewards and recognition strategy of the organization (Gaucher and Coffey, 1993). This activity is likely to reveal the rewards and recognition that are truly appreciated, and to develop a forum for creating future strategies.

- Work groups are the unit of analysis. Perhaps the greatest challenge is to transcend the individual within the organization and provide a reward structure that reflects the group effort required in any quality improvement activity. Failure to achieve a reward structure corresponding to group efforts may result in individual efforts, perhaps well intentioned, operating at cross purposes. It is not sufficient to have rewards and recognition targeted solely at individuals. A program corresponding to group efforts is required. This may include explicit recognition of the group's performance and/or remuneration to the group based on the overall performance of the organization.

Below are some examples of financial incentives for group and individual performance and some concerns with their application in health services.

U.S. Healthcare Inc.

U.S. Healthcare Inc., an HMO, surveys its members regularly to see how well they like their doctor and uses the results of patient questionnaires in their incentive-pay program for doctors. The doctors' incentive pay is based in part on the scores their patients give on the surveys. Here are some examples of questions on the questionnaire:

How easy is it to make appointments for checkups?
How long is the waiting time in a doctor's office?
How much personal concern does a doctor show for patients?
How readily can patients obtain follow-up test results?
Would patients recommend their doctor to others? (Anders, 1992)

Although this practice illustrates the use of customer satisfaction and its links to incentive systems, there are some valid concerns about this approach. Does it promote competitive behavior instead of collegial behavior? How reliable and valid is the survey? What are the effects on the clinical outcomes of care?

As Deming (1986) himself pointed out, this reward system runs counter to the CQI philosophy. He argues that anybody's performance results from a combination of forces: some interpersonal; some from coworkers; some within the job, including the material available and the equipment provided; some from customers; some from managers; some from supervisors; and some from environmental conditions.

Parkview Medical Center

Performance appraisal need not be linked to salary. Employees at Parkview Medical Center in Pueblo, Colorado, now call the tool used in performance appraisal an APOP, or "annual piece of paper." This paper belongs to the employee, and it is brought to the coaching sessions the employee has with his or her supervisor. The employee and the supervisor discuss the work processes to which the employee contributes, and these are written on the APOP. They then talk about the training and educational needs the employee has related to those work processes. They also use criteria-based competency testing for performance evaluation. Pay is not connected with performance appraisals. However, there is shared employee compensation. Twenty-five percent of net income above budget is divided among all hospital employees (M. Pugh, personal communication, 1993).

The University of Michigan Hospitals

The University of Michigan Hospitals believes that it has found a way around the traps identified by Deming that allows it to use the strong incentive of financial rewards while actually increasing organizationwide teamwork and commitment to its mission and goals. The Gainshare Program, instituted in 1991, is surprisingly simple (Gaucher and Coffey, 1993). The organization determines a desired margin from operations, taking into account depreciation, interest expenses, interest income, prior year settlements, and contribution to the academic enrichment fund. If this target is exceeded, half of all the excess is distributed to all full-time employees, with each receiving an equal share. Performance measures are shared with employees throughout the year. Information relating to revenues, expenses, admissions, clinic visits, attendance, and other measures is provided by a variety of methods, enabling employees to see the effect they have on the overall operations of the hospital. The Gainshare checks are distributed in October each year, with all due fanfare, no doubt.

CONCLUSION

Health care organizations and health service providers are predisposed to "meet the needs of the patient." This has taken the general form of the "doctor-patient" model, with the patient presenting and the doctor providing. The advent of CQI has changed the rules, broadening the focus beyond the doctor-patient interaction alone to all interactions involved in the process of care and changing the dimensions that need to be considered in all these interactions. The management challenge is to define the relevant interactions, develop systems that will monitor expectations and the character of these expectations, and decide how to use this information to improve the overall operations of the organization.

Outpatient Services: The Patient's Viewpoint

OUTPATIENT SERVICES:
THE PATIENT'S VIEWPOINT

Please rate your hospital visit in each of the areas listed below in terms of whether it was excellent, very good, good, fair, or poor. Please mark only one answer for each statement.

◀ No. 2 pencil only ▯▯▯▶

Correct mark ○ ● ○
Incorrect mark ☑ ☒ ◌

Rating columns: **Excellent** · **Very Good** · **Good** · **Fair** · **Poor** · **Does Not Apply**

GETTING TO THE HOSPITAL

1. DIRECTIONS FROM YOUR DOCTOR'S OFFICE: Clearness and completeness of directions to the hospital you may have gotten from your doctor's office. ➡ ○ ○ ○ ○ ○ ○

2. DIRECTIONS FROM THE HOSPITAL: Clearness and completeness of directions to the hospital you may have gotten from the hospital staff. ➡ ○ ○ ○ ○ ○ ○

3. SIGNS: How clear and correct the signs were that directed you to the hospital. ➡ ○ ○ ○ ○ ○ ○

PARKING

4. PARKING FACILITIES OR SERVICES: How easy they were to use and how well they met your needs. ➡ ○ ○ ○ ○ ○ ○

REGISTRATION

5. WAITING TIME: Length of time you spent waiting to register AFTER you arrived at registration. ➡ ○ ○ ○ ○ ○ ○

6. PERSONAL MANNER: Respect, friendliness, and courtesy shown by registration staff. ➡ ○ ○ ○ ○ ○ ○

7. EFFICIENCY: How smoothly registration procedures ran. ➡ ○ ○ ○ ○ ○ ○

8. INFORMATION: Clearness and completeness of explanations given by registration staff. ➡ ○ ○ ○ ○ ○ ○

YOUR TESTS: Please answer the same questions for EVERY department you went to.

9. WAITING TIME: Length of time you spent waiting for your test.
   in X-RAY ➡ ○ ○ ○ ○ ○ ○
   in LABORATORY ➡ ○ ○ ○ ○ ○ ○
   in NUCLEAR MEDICINE ➡ ○ ○ ○ ○ ○ ○
   in MAMMOGRAPHY ➡ ○ ○ ○ ○ ○ ○
   in EKG ➡ ○ ○ ○ ○ ○ ○
   in OTHER SERVICES ➡ ○ ○ ○ ○ ○ ○

10. Information from your DOCTOR'S OFFICE: How well your doctor's office staff described what it would be like to have these tests.
    in X-RAY ➡ ○ ○ ○ ○ ○ ○
    in LABORATORY ➡ ○ ○ ○ ○ ○ ○
    in NUCLEAR MEDICINE ➡ ○ ○ ○ ○ ○ ○
    in MAMMOGRAPHY ➡ ○ ○ ○ ○ ○ ○
    in EKG ➡ ○ ○ ○ ○ ○ ○
    in OTHER SERVICES ➡ ○ ○ ○ ○ ○ ○

11. Information from HOSPITAL STAFF: Clearness and completeness of explanations given DURING your test.
    in X-RAY ➡ ○ ○ ○ ○ ○ ○
    in LABORATORY ➡ ○ ○ ○ ○ ○ ○
    in NUCLEAR MEDICINE ➡ ○ ○ ○ ○ ○ ○
    in MAMMOGRAPHY ➡ ○ ○ ○ ○ ○ ○
    in EKG ➡ ○ ○ ○ ○ ○ ○
    in OTHER SERVICES ➡ ○ ○ ○ ○ ○ ○

12. PERSONAL MANNER: Respect, friendliness, and courtesy shown by the staff.
    in X-RAY ➡ ○ ○ ○ ○ ○ ○
    in LABORATORY ➡ ○ ○ ○ ○ ○ ○
    in NUCLEAR MEDICINE ➡ ○ ○ ○ ○ ○ ○
    in MAMMOGRAPHY ➡ ○ ○ ○ ○ ○ ○
    in EKG ➡ ○ ○ ○ ○ ○ ○
    in OTHER SERVICES ➡ ○ ○ ○ ○ ○ ○

continues

		Excel-lent	Very Good	Good	Fair	Poor	Does Not Apply
13. EFFICIENCY: How smoothly procedures ran	in X-RAY .... ➡	◯	◯	◯	◯	◯	◯
	in LABORATORY .... ➡	◯	◯	◯	◯	◯	◯
	in NUCLEAR MEDICINE.... ➡	◯	◯	◯	◯	◯	◯
	in MAMMOGRAPHY .... ➡	◯	◯	◯	◯	◯	◯
	in EKG .... ➡	◯	◯	◯	◯	◯	◯
	in OTHER SERVICES ...... ➡	◯	◯	◯	◯	◯	◯
14. YOUR PERSONAL NEEDS:	in X-RAY .... ➡	◯	◯	◯	◯	◯	◯
Courtesy, interest, attention, and support	in LABORATORY .... ➡	◯	◯	◯	◯	◯	◯
shown for your privacy and comfort.	in NUCLEAR MEDICINE.... ➡	◯	◯	◯	◯	◯	◯
	in MAMMOGRAPHY .... ➡	◯	◯	◯	◯	◯	◯
	in EKG .... ➡	◯	◯	◯	◯	◯	◯
	in OTHER SERVICES ...... ➡	◯	◯	◯	◯	◯	◯

THE FACILITIES

15. GETTING AROUND IN THE HOSPITAL: Helpfulness of signs, directions, volunteers. ➡ ◯ ◯ ◯ ◯ ◯ ◯
16. HOSPITAL BUILDING: How would you rate the hospital building overall? ➡ ◯ ◯ ◯ ◯ ◯ ◯
17. EQUIPMENT: Having the latest equipment and technology. ➡ ◯ ◯ ◯ ◯ ◯ ◯

OVERALL SATISFACTION WITH THE HOSPITAL

18. The care I received was so good that I have bragged about it to family and friends.
   ➡ ◯ Strongly agree   ◯ Somewhat disagree
   ➡ ◯ Somewhat agree   ◯ Strongly disagree
19. The prices were reasonable for the care I received.
   ➡ ◯ Strongly agree   ◯ Somewhat disagree
   ➡ ◯ Somewhat agree   ◯ Strongly disagree

YOUR OVERALL HEALTH STATUS

20. In general, would you say your health is...
   ➡ ◯ Excellent   ◯ Good   ◯ Poor
   ➡ ◯ Very Good   ◯ Fair

FACTS ABOUT YOU

21. Please mark all the departments were you were seen today.
   ➡ ◯ Diabetes Treatment Center   ◯ Radiation therapy
   ➡ ◯ EKG   ◯ CT
   ➡ ◯ Heart cath lab   ◯ MRI
   ➡ ◯ Mammography   ◯ Ultrasound
   ➡ ◯ Nuclear Medicine   ◯ X-Ray
   ➡ ◯ Pain clinic   ◯ Respiratory therapy
   ➡ ◯ Physical therapy

22. What time did you arrive at the hospital?
   ➡ ◯ 6 am–9 am   ◯ 12 noon–3 pm
   ➡ ◯ 9 am–12 noon   ◯ 3 pm–6 pm

23. What day of the week was your visit to the hospital?
   ➡ ◯ Mon   ◯ Thurs   Sun
   ➡ ◯ Tues   ◯ Fri
   ➡ ◯ Wed   ◯ Sat

24. Are you (the patient) male or female?   ➡ ◯ Male   ◯ Female

25. In what year were you (the patient) born?
   example: 5 ⑨ ⑩ ⑳ ㉚ ㊵ ● ㉖ ㉗ ㉘ ㉙ ➡
   1958 8 ⓪ ① ② ③ ④ ⑤ ⑥ ⑦ ● ⑨ ➡

   ⑨ ⑩ ⑳ ㉚ ㊵ ㊿ ㉖ ㉗ ㉘ ㉙
   ⓪ ① ② ③ ④ ⑤ ⑥ ⑦ ⑧ ⑨

26. Why did you choose this hospital?
   ➡ ◯ Doctor suggested   ◯ Insurance or employer encouraged
     OR my choice based on...
   ➡ ◯ prior experience   ◯ advertising   ◯ what I've heard

27. Did anything good happen during your visit that you did not expect? If so, please tell us what it was.

28. Did anything unpleasant happen during your visit that you did not expect? If so, please tell us what it was.

29. Why would you return or not return to this hospital? Please give us your honest opinions.

Source: Copyright © 1991, Hospital Corporation of America Hospital Quality Trends[SM]. Not for further reproduction.
THANK YOU FOR YOUR TIME AND ASSISTANCE!

Central Hospital Physician Survey

The format of this survey makes use of a new opinion survey technology that most professionals find easy to use. The aim is to elicit *your* opinion about where CH currently allocates its attention and resources and how those allocations might best be changed.

Your responses will be completely anonymous; only aggregated results will be reported. Thank you for contributing to our effort to improve CH's services to physicians and patients.

INSTRUCTIONS

Column 1: Within each of the five categories described below, please rank-order the listed activities according to the amount of attention you think CH allocates to each (1 = receives the most attention from CH, 5 = receives the least attention from CH). If you think some activities receive the same amount of attention, give them the same rank.

Column 2: Do the same thing to indicate the amount of attention you think *another hospital* to which you admit the largest or second largest number of patients allocates its attention. (Again, 1 = receives the most attention from the other hospital, 5 receives the least attention from the other hospital.)

Name of the other hospital _____

Column 1 *Central* *Now*	*Services*	Column 2 *Other* *Hospital*
	Rank 1 = Receives Most Attention 5 = Receives Least Attention)	
_____	Medical Records	_____
_____	Scheduling (Tests/OR)	_____
_____	Radiology	_____
_____	Emergency/Trauma	_____
_____	Restorative Services (PT/OT, etc.)	_____

Column 1 *Central* *Now*	*Communications*	Column 2 *Other* *Hospital*
	Rank 1 = Receives Most Attention 5 = Receives Least Attention)	
_____	Medical Staff Meetings	_____
_____	Newsletters from Hospital	_____
_____	Computer Access to Lab Results	_____
_____	Liaison/Service Representative for Physicians	_____
_____	Dictation System/Transcription Services/ Hospital Telephone System	_____

Central *Now*	*Nursing*	*Other* *Hospital*
	Rank 1 = Receives Most Attention 5 = Receives Least Attention)	
_____	Nursing Care Management (Nurse/Physician Coordination of Care)	_____
_____	Turnover/Retention	_____
_____	Clinical Competence/Quality of Nurses	_____
_____	Nurses' Attitudes Toward Patients	_____
_____	Nurses' Attitudes Toward Physicians	_____

Central *Now*	*Support/Facilities*	*Other* *Hospital*
	Rank 1 = Receives Most Attention 5 = Receives Least Attention)	
_____	Equipment Maintenance	_____
_____	Continuing Medical Education	_____
_____	Help Physicians Cope with New OSHA Requirements (e.g., Medical Waste)	_____
_____	Help Physicians Handle Red Tape Concerning Insurance Precertification Before Admitting Patients	_____
_____	Central Location for Phoning in All Test Orders	_____

Column 1 *Central* *Now*	*Special Programs*	Column 2 *Other* *Hospital*
	Rank 1 = Receives Most Attention 5 = Receives Least Attention)	
_____	Group Liability Plan	_____
_____	Outpatient Laboratory Services	_____
_____	Homecare Services	_____
_____	Telephone Answering Service for Physicians	_____
_____	Advertising that Addresses Physicians' Concerns and Builds Their Practices	_____

Now, please rank the five categories of activities that are described above in terms of CH's overall attention:

Central *Now*		*Other* *Hospital*
	Rank 1 = Receives Most Attention 5 = Receives Least Attention)	
_____	Services: Records, Scheduling, Radiology, Emergency/Trauma, Restorative Services	_____
_____	Communications: Meetings, Newsletters, Computer Access to Lab, Telephones, Dictation	_____
_____	Nursing: Case Management, Turnover, Competence, Attitudes toward Patients/Physicians	_____
_____	Support/Facilities: Maintenance, Education, Help with OSHA, Insurance Red Tape, Central Phone Location for Test Orders	_____
_____	Special Programs: Group Liability, Lab Services Homecare, Answering Service, Advertising Relevant to Physician Needs	_____

Rebecca LaVallee
Curtis P. McLaughlin

Teams at the Core

7

"A team is a small number of people with complementary skills who are committed to a common purpose, set of performance goals, and approach for which they hold themselves mutually accountable" (Katzenbach and Smith, 1993, p. 112). Team members share leadership roles, measure their performance directly by the quality of their collective work products, and encourage open discussion and active problem solving. Teams need to focus on performance goals associated with some urgency and spend adequate time together to develop collective values, develop work rules and norms, and interpret their own behavior. Top management has a great deal of influence over the teams' effectiveness by the way that they signal the significance of the effort, provide feedback and stimuli to the members, evaluate team performance, and provide recognitions and rewards (Zmud and McLaughlin, 1989). Finally, teams can make a difference, outperforming other types of work units, including individuals. As described by Katzenbach and Smith (1993, p. 9), "Teams outperform individuals acting alone or in larger organizational groupings, especially when performance requires multiple skills, judgements, and experiences. Most people recognize the capabilities of teams; most have the common sense to make teams work. Nevertheless, most people overlook team opportunities for themselves."

This chapter focuses on total quality management (TQM) teams, especially teams "cutting across" departments, examining delivery systems and attempting to improve organizational and caregiving processes. Forming and motivating these teams is a core management process in setting up the parallel organization that implements continuous quality improvement (CQI).

ORGANIZING TEAMS

The teams studying the organization's processes are a key to CQI success, whether they are operating within a function or across functions. This section will focus mainly on the attributes of these task-oriented teams, but with the understanding that the concepts involved are also applicable to the performance of the quality steering committee and the design teams. The model in Figure 7–1 identifies many of the variables and relationships that may affect the level of quality improvement that these teams achieve. The variables are grouped under (1) antecedent variables, (2) moderating variables, and (3) outcomes representing a process in and of itself. The antecedent variables deal with the organizational context, the nature of the team, the characteristics of the team members, and the impact of professional socialization upon their behavior. The moderating variables relate to the group processes and the task to which they are applied, and the outcomes relate to how the customers feel about the process and its results. Critical to these variables is the management process and the overall management climate that controls antecedent variables such as the selection of tasks, the agenda and assignments given to teams, and the selection, training, and motivation of team members. Gaucher and Coffey (1993), however, report that teams can be productive only when the organizational climate is right.

> This means that teams should have adequate resources, the ability to implement decisions, the sponsorship of managers, and an effective reward and recognition system. The appropriate training materials and time for skill building must be available during team formation. A standard problem-solving process is also required to help the team stay on track. Finally, leadership commitment to support the team effort is essential for success. (Gaucher and Coffey, 1993, p. 219)

GROUP OUTCOMES

On the right of Figure 7–1 are the group outcomes that appear to be influenced by the team effort and by team characteristics. These outcomes affect and are evaluated by a wide array of constituencies, including the patients, the providers, the team members, and the administration of the health care organization. Although "there seems to be agreement that something happens during group interaction that affects group performance" (Watson and Michaelsen, 1988), there is no general agreement on what types of outcome measures best define effective group performance. Most experienced managers know when a group is working and when it is not. When it is not working, they need to use the CQI approach to turn it around.

Gaucher and Coffey (1993, pp. 241–242) report the use of cause-and-effect analysis on unsuccessful teams at the University of Michigan Medical Center and report a wide range of causes for lack of success, including:

- Lack of effective training, the main reason for failure
- Unskilled leadership

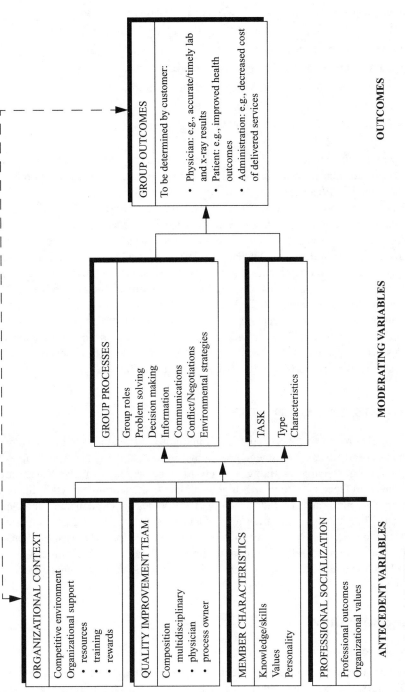

Figure 7–1 Groups in the TQM Process

- Unclear goals, including lack of adequate customer definition
- Unsupportive environment or one in which systems are unstable
- Lack of reward and recognition
- Lack of urgency or a champion for the project
- Jumping to a desired solution before studying root causes
- Selecting a system and not a process to improve
- Dysfunctional behavior by individual team members

They report that some teams can be put back on track by doing a CQI root cause analysis and then developing and implementing part of a series of options to address the identified causes of poor team performance.

Outcome measures associated with productivity are variously defined in terms of output, performance, motivation, efficiency, effectiveness, production, profitability, cost/effectiveness, competitiveness, and work quality (Pritchard and Karasick, 1973; Watson and Michaelsen, 1988), as well as Donabedian's (1990) seven items. Group effectiveness has also been defined in such terms as a quantitative measure of productivity, satisfaction of group members, and ability of the group to survive (Ancona, 1985). The CQI philosophy would call for leaving the definition of group effectiveness up to the judgment of the "end users" or customers of the product or services provided by the group, as well as to group members themselves. Inasmuch as CQI teams are ad hoc groups, long-term survival is not an issue. However, short-term effectiveness, including survival, is.

ORGANIZATIONAL CONTEXT

The first group of variables considered in Figure 7–1 relate to the organization: namely, competitive environment, group environment, and organizational support in the form of resources, training, and rewards. The degree to which a health care organization feels itself to be in a highly competitive environment will influence the urgency and intensity with which the CQI process is implemented and supported. This urgency may translate into increased resources, thus increasing chances for success. On the other hand, it may translate into increased time pressures that can impede effective program implementation, impairing orderly team development and jeopardizing the creativity and factual underpinnings of project activities.

Antecedent Variables

Competive Environment

External (competitive) environmental factors can have a profound impact on a CQI effort. For example, a hospital that is the only hospital in town can be less concerned about physicians' negative reactions to involvement in the CQI effort than one where there is a major competitor nearby at which the same set of physicians also practice. At a less global level, internal environmental features can be as simple as the availability of settings for group meetings that are conducive to social interaction, or perceived management needs to control those interactions (Paulus and Nagar, 1985) through influences over group membership (Ancona, 1985). Other features of supportive environments include (1) recognition, (2) responsiveness to the group's requests for information, resources, and action, (3) legitimization of group's task and process, and (4) expectations of group success (Ancona, 1985; Shea and Guzzo, 1987; Zmud and McLaughlin, 1989).

Organizational Support

A second component of the organizational context outlined in Figure 7–1 is organizational support. Support includes the involvement of organizational leaders through a regular role of participation or monitoring of results, a clear statement of missions and tasks, team-contingent rewards, team performance feedback (Bettenhausen, 1991; Kaluzny and McLaughlin, 1992; Melum, 1990), and organizational learning that continuously improves the program. This is sometimes referred to as providing the necessary infrastructure to support the CQI teams, and includes resources, training, and rewards.

Resources. The organization must provide adequate resources for the group effort. The organization pays for the work time, while the group members contribute their individual knowledge and skills. The organization also provides technical information (data) to the group through facilitators, team members, and information systems, and mentors both from within the organization and through outside resources. The organization must also define meaningful and tractable tasks that are of value to the participants and to the organization. Early in the effort, these tasks should present an opportunity for team members to reduce discomfort in their units.

Training. Much group skill and knowledge is gained or enhanced through training programs provided by the organization. Training needs for TQM vary for different levels of the organization and by functional group. Organizational leaders need an understanding of fundamental concepts, strategic planning needs, and technical methods associated with team efforts. Middle managers need training to help them guide and facilitate the TQM implementation. TQM teams need training to provide proficiency in the use of statistical tools and an understanding of group processes. Local experts/ facilitators/ coaches need an understanding of technical aspects of TQM principles as well as a firm grounding in organizational development (OD) concepts and practices in order to facilitate organizational change through group processes. Chapter 10 discusses the training matrix that management needs to see developed to make sure that the right training takes place in the right sequence.

Organizational development interventions are directed toward increasing "organizational effectiveness through initiation of planned change within the organization" (Young et al., 1988, p. 69). They are targeted toward behavioral change in individuals or changes in organizational processes. In a sense, TQM projects are OD interventions, as are the team-building and meeting skills training programs provided for TQM group members. Porras and Hoffer (1986) report the behaviors commonly listed by OD experts as hoped-for results of OD efforts: communicating openly, collaborating, taking responsibility, maintaining a shared vision, solving problems effectively, respecting/supporting, processing/facilitating, inquiring, and experimenting. These same behaviors influence the success of TQM project groups markedly.

Rewards. Team member behavior and group outcomes can be influenced by reward systems. Successful project outcomes depend on interdependent effort by team members. If rewards are not provided or are provided on a competitive basis, the usual response is for team members to see individual success as more important than group success. Both the objectives of a quality improvement effort and any associated outcome rewards should support group effort and cooperation. Group rewards include financial incentives such as bonuses, which are not usually associated with CQI, and informal incentives, such as a recognition dinner or feature write-up in the organization's newsletter. Informal incentives tend to be used more in CQI because of the fear of setting up competition for rewards and because many members of the team members' work units also contribute by collecting data, providing data, and covering for the team members when they are in team meetings. It is important to recognize that those not on a team also contribute to the team effort.

TEAM CHARACTERISTICS

The second set of variables in Figure 7–1 relates to the quality teams themselves and includes consideration of the type of team, composition of the team (particularly the use of a multidisciplinary membership and physician participation), and a sense of ownership.

A quality improvement team is formed only when an opportunity for improvement is identified that is important to customers *and* is selected as a priority issue by management. In most settings it is not possible or practical to constitute groups based on "demographics, need, personality, or ability for particular problems, and then re-sort them for new problems" (Wanous and Yautz, 1986) in order to provide diversity and improve the range of possible solutions. But CQI attempts to do precisely this by selecting individuals on the basis of their professional/ technical knowledge of the process being examined and their ability to contribute to its improvement, regardless of their department of origin or normal hierarchical status. Therefore these teams represent temporary, secondary task assignments for most employees. Zmud and McLaughlin (1989) define secondary tasks as tasks that are not considered part of one's permanent job description and are not likely to be used as a component of promotion decisions. Thus a CQI organization might overcome the secondary role and its problems by adding "contributes to process improvement" to everyone's job description and by adding that area of performance to his or her evaluation procedure.

Multidisciplinary Membership

To succeed, CQI requires a kind of "shadow" organization to operate. The process in question may have suppliers in other units of the "regular" (formal) organization, and the customers of the process may be in yet a different set of units. Thus a team that comes together to work on a process that is causing trouble may be multidisciplinary (sometimes referred to as cross-functional) and be composed of individuals from a variety of formal organizational units or professional backgrounds. Indeed, the suppliers and/or the customers involved may even be outside the formal organization. It is the transient nature of these teams that makes them work and prevents their interference with the ongoing activities of the formal organization.

Berwick (1989a, p. 55), for example, states that "teams must be created, trained and competently led to tackle complex processes that cross customary department boundaries." Professionals must come out of their individual departments and professional orientations to form multidisciplinary groups and collectively take responsibility for patient care and organizational processes. Members of multidisciplinary teams must develop common goals, engage in cooperative and coordinated activities, and take advantage of a mix of professional skills and orientations to fully utilize the CQI process. These heterogeneous groups have the potential to provide a breadth of ideas and prevent the limited mind sets that inhibit creative problem solving.

However, multidisciplinary groups bring their own set of problems and limitations. Bettenhausen (1991, p. 356) remarks that "most studies have found that diversity hinders group and organizational performance, especially in times of crisis or rapid change." Malfunctions can arise from a complex of individual member characteristics and group dynamics such as territoriality (by department or profession), role confusion, or lack of experience/training in group processes.

Gaucher and Coffey (1993, pp. 235–240) observe that multidepartmental teams go through four stages, which they describe as:

1. Form—the new group members wait for their roles to be clarified before addressing the issue at hand. The focus is on the team leader and on domineering team members.
2. Storm—There is an interchange of ideas, but they are one-way, critical, and conflictful. The leader becomes less of a focus.

3. Norm—Conflict is addressed and reduced as objectives are clarified, people become comfortable with the ground rules for group behavior, and trust and common interests are developed. At this point the leadership must challenge the group to set and reach new goals and try new techniques and approaches to spur group development.

4. Perform—Team members make contributions of data, facts, and logic and are motivated by the results. Team members share leadership according to their knowledge and skills, and the task gets accomplished effectively and efficiently.

Selection as a quality improvement team member is based on the individual's professional and technical knowledge of the process being examined and ability to contribute to its improvement, but the role that each individual represents may be unclear. Was the team member selected as a representative of a particular department, particular profession, or position in the organizational hierarchy? These representative roles differ from the group process roles associated with effective group work, and may influence the perspective from which the team member contributes and the motivation to continue participating in quality improvement team tasks. Although the representation role is played down in the literature on the CQI process, the likely case is that the individual is selected to fulfill multiple roles, some representational and some problem solving. Therefore one of the secrets of success may lie in individuals' ability to juggle multiple roles and to signal to other team members which hat (role) they are wearing each time they offer a contribution during the flow of the meeting.

Multidisciplinary teams can be avoided early in the CQI process, but they cannot be avoided long under the CQI philosophy. In health care, multidisciplinary teams are likely to have the highest impact on process quality, on costs, and on patient quality perceptions. One should not avoid them because of their inherent risks, especially the problems presented by the need to use physicians as team members.

Be prepared to see team membership change. There can be a number of causes for this. The first is that as the definition of the task is clarified, so is the ownership. New members may have to be added to represent areas newly found to be critical to the process. They should not be left out, however. Internal duties, responsibilities, and workloads change rapidly in an institution. These should be reflected in team composition where relevant. In health care, people come and go all the time.

Physician Participation

As Berwick (1989a, p. 56) so well describes, "In hospitals, physicians both rely on and help shape almost every process pertaining to patients' experience, from support services (such as dietary and housekeeping functions) to clinical care services (such as laboratories and nursing). Few can improve without help of the medical staff." Yet physicians have not been exposed by training or experience to the type of teamwork necessary for QI team success. In addition, "physicians' sense of time urgency" is often incompatible with the time-consuming group and statistical analysis process involved in participating on a TQM team. Yet experience (Merry, 1990) suggests that it is possible to gain physician participation by appealing to their

1. desire for greater control over economic stability
2. desire to maintain sufficient clinical freedom to cope with the uncertainties of patient care
3. sense of participation and influence in institutional development
4. need for improving the diminished social value of physicians' work

In other words, appealing to the classic Maslovian hierarchy of needs can also influence this powerful group of individuals. This topic is discussed further in Chapter 12.

Process Owners

Important team members are the "process owners" who at the end will understand the whole process as it crosses functional areas or departments and who will assume the responsibility to hinder or support improvement and quality efforts or at least be candidates for that role. A process owner may reside in any department or level of the organizational hierarchy. This person becomes a group member because of knowledge of how the customer(s) experience of the process, but also must possess the task-related knowledge and group skills necessary to gain the other group members' participation in analyzing and improving processes. Task-related knowledge and skills include the ability to assign and coordinate group member tasks and activities, facilitate group processes to reach objectives, and maintain connections with the rest of the organization and/or environment. In addition, there must be sensitivity to socioemotional responsibilities shared among group members. This is necessary to build group cohesion, maintain morale, and reduce interpersonal conflict throughout the process. Other roles include the responsibility for follow-up and implementation—the "A" of the PCDA cycle (Plan, Check, Do, Act).

TEAM MEMBER CHARACTERISTICS

The third set of antecedent variables in Figure 7–1 affecting quality improvement team outcomes is team member characteristics: skills/knowledge, values, and personality.

Skills/Knowledge

As discussed previously, "each group member's knowledge structure repre-sent[s] a fundamental element in a group's collective knowledge structure" (Walsh et al., 1988, p. 195). The knowledge base of the group and the skills of group members, especially those skills related to process characteristics, infor-mation management, and data manipulation, are important to the problem-solv-ing and decision-making processes of the group.

Values

Competing value systems influence group processes. Value sets important to CQI include flexibility versus operational control, attention to internal group is-sues versus external conditions, and an emphasis on means (processes/proce-dures) versus ends (outcomes/objectives). Values are also shaped by the interests of the team members' professions and by the work group they represent, in addi-tion to group values developed through the CQI process (Reagan & Rohrbaugh, 1990).

Personality

Personality, when defined as how a person is viewed and reacted to by society, that is, as "social reputation," can provide both positive and negative influences on group performance. Various authors suggest that we may operationalize per-sonality by measuring such aspects as:

- Intellect—Although there is little research relating it to group performance, whether an individual is bright or dull is believed to be associated with group leadership.
- Adjustment—Emotional stability is positively related to group performance, especially in situations requiring creative problem solving.
- Prudence—A concrete (conforming) cognitive style has a mixed association with group performance except under conditions of time constraints where outcomes are likely to be poor.
- Ambition—An achievement orientation provides the best performance in sit-uations that are task oriented. However, self-serving behavior is likely to be identified and rejected by the well-trained CQI team.
- Sociability—Extroversion improves group performance on creative and problem-solving tasks.
- Likability—The impact of likability on overall group performance has been mixed, but it does appear to be related to satisfaction with group interaction.

PROFESSIONAL SOCIALIZATION

The final set of antecedent variables in Figure 7–1 refers to professional socialization. The socialization process can be very powerful. The socialization of physicians is undertaken "through the intermediacy of education, training. . . . [During this process of] socialization professional properties are transformed into individual attributes—traits so deeply rooted in each physician that they seem features of personality," (Palmer, et al., 1991, p. 85). For these reasons, professional socialization must be considered as an antecedent variable in any model in health care TQM.

Occupational socialization is a form of developmental socialization. The student is acquiring an adult role and self being resocialized from a layperson into a professional. The first phase is formal academic preparation, generally conducted within a university or other formal academic setting. The second is apprenticeship or clinical training conducted within the context of a clinical setting. The last phase occurs at the time of first entry into the work setting and is in response to the demands of the institutional practice setting.

Professional Outcomes

In addition to the general outcomes of the socialization process discussed above, there are some specific outcomes tied to the profession, such as:

1. Argot—the private language of the profession, the technical jargon that defines the body of knowledge and sets the boundaries between one profession and all the others.
2. Heritage—the historical dimension of the profession, the legends, myths, cultural symbols, and ceremonies associated with that profession. Ouchi (1969), in fact, refers to this as "clan" control that operates alongside reward systems and bureaucratic controls and is based on the rites, rituals, and totems of professional socialization, namely the professional school.
3. Professional Etiquette—an understanding of how one member behaves toward another, the order of rank and status, and how one defends one's peers against external threats.
4. Network— access to marketplace information, formal and informal connection to other members of the profession.
5. Occupational Title—the appropriate professional title, indicating an area of expertise and responsibility that implies status in society.
6. Occupation-Associated Ideology—the norms, values, beliefs of the profession regarding such things as the ethics, qualities, interests, and capabilities of members, also work norms and procedures.
7. Commitment to Task—a commitment to professionally defined standards of quality performance for specific tasks and application of "special knowledge." The Hippocratic Oath is one such statement of commitment.

Table 7-1 Subcultures in Health Care: Empirical Findings

Basic Assumptions	Subculture		
	Medical	*Nursing*	*Managerial*
Relationships to Environment			
Basic identity	Experts, specialists	Helpers, supporters	Public authorities
Relevant environments	Scientific, technical	Socio-cultural	Economic, political
Position vis-a-vis environment	Dominant	Harmonious and symbiotic	Dominant
Nature of Reality and Truth			
Basic orientation	Physical, external criteria	Physical, social	Physical
Criteria of verifiability	Scientific test, authorities	Traditional, moral dogma	Authorities, rational-legal
Time orientation	Past and present	Past and present	Past and present
Essence of Human Nature			
Basic nature	Neutral	Neutral	Neutral
Mutability	Own group members mutable, doubting others	Same	Same
Nature of Human Activity	Proactive, oriented toward doing	Harmonizing, being-in-becoming	Proactive, but to some extent being oriented
Nature of Human Relationships			
Relationships between people	Individuality, competition	Collaterality, group consensus	Collaterality, autocratic
Relationships between organizations	Paternalism, collegial	Participation, delegation	Paternalism, consultation

Source: Reprinted from Kinnunen, J., The Importance of Organizational Culture on Development Activities in a Primary Health Care Organization, *International Journal of Health Planning and Management,* Vol. 5, pp. 65–71, with permission of John Wiley & Sons, Ltd., © 1990.

8. Commitment to Institutions—exhibiting a preference for a particular institution or type of institution as a practice site. This may relate more to the particular clinical training experience of an individual, than to a broad professional generalization.

Organizational Values

Because multiple socialization agents are involved during the period of entry into the organization, the newcomers to an organization sometimes have to make choices among competing sets of values and beliefs. Competent professionals within organizations come up against two other pressures: (1) to conform to organizational expectations, and (2) to advance. The latter often requires additional professional or skill-based competencies. The less able the individual is to leave the organization, the greater the pressure to conform. Advancement will require continual acquisition of new skills, technical knowledge, *and* appropriate social behaviors.

Kinnunen (1990) conducted a study of three professional subcultures (medical, nursing, and managerial) in a primary health care organization employing 700 individuals and serving the needs of 80,000 clients. His results (Table 7–1) point out the possible end results of the professional socialization process. Three different orientations to the environment, discovery of truth, and human relationships were found.

MODERATING VARIABLES

Group Process Skills

Group process or interaction "is the way group members pool their abilities in a collaborative context in order to reach the best decision" (Watson and Michaelsen, 1988, p. 495). These processes form the set of moderating variables presented in Figure 7–1.

A quality improvement team comes together to analyze a process and develop solutions or alternatives for improvement. As they work interdependently, they exchange information, coordinate activities, and form interpersonal impressions of each other. The basic group process skills required include meeting skills, ability to generate ideas and reduce data to a useable form, and the interpersonal skills of listening, participation, and conflict resolution. The problem-solving nature of CQI team tasks requires individual and group procedures that address three phases and eleven procedural functions summarized below:

Phase	*Function*
Orientation	establishment of operating procedures
	sharing of problem-related information
	presentation of specialized/technical information
Evaluation	analysis of problem
	generation of alternatives
	establishment of evaluation criteria
	evaluation of alternatives
	reconciliation of interests to achieve consensus
Control	position group values/solutions within those acceptable to environmental powers
	recommendation of alternatives
	implementation of plan

The group processes included in the model in Figure 7–1 are those relating to group roles, problem solving, decision-making schemes, information sharing, communication, conflict/negotiation, and environmental linkage strategies.

Organizations that have introduced TQM/CQI report that the meeting skills and the interpersonal skills of listening and responding to others have a high payoff both inside and outside the organization. Managers often report instances of workers expressing profound thanks after practicing those skills in personal relationships at home with spouses and teenage children. Meeting skills in and of themselves also have a high payoff in productivity when meetings begin on time and end on time, when there is an agenda ahead of time, and when people stick to a process that they all understand, such as the storyboard.

Group Roles

Accomplishing group tasks requires that certain group functions be performed and that group roles support them. These group roles are of three types: group task roles, group building and maintenance roles, and individual roles. Group task roles can be assumed by any group member and are focused on problem-related tasks. These roles include:

* initiator-contributor
* information seeker
* opinion seeker
* information giver
* opinion giver
* elaborator
* coordinator
* orienter
* evaluator-critic
* energizer

- procedural technician
- recorder

Not all roles are task related. The group itself has to be developed. Therefore, group building and maintenance roles are required of individuals concerned with the effectiveness and survival of the team. Again, roles should not be restricted to any one individual. These roles are:

- encourager
- harmonizer
- compromiser
- gatekeeper and expediter
- standard setter
- group-observer and commentator
- follower

Furthermore, each individual has some potential roles to play that satisfy personal needs unrelated to group tasks and unconcerned with group development or continuity. These roles can include:

- aggressor
- blocker
- recognition seeker
- self-confessor
- player
- dominator
- help seeker
- special interest pleader

Needless to say, fulfilling some ego needs is important for motivation, but their expression has to be constrained by members fulfilling group norms and attending to group building and maintenance needs, including their own.

Successful groups require different roles depending on the current stage of the task cycle or the level of maturity the group has reached. A high level of individual-centered role taking, as opposed to group-centered role taking, generally indicates a need for group self-assessment and further group-process training (Benne and Sheats, 1948). What the group wants to avoid has been described as the garbage can decision process (Cohen et al., 1972), in which people come in and dump onto the table whatever is on top of their minds, ignoring the task for most of the meeting, and approaching it only when there is not enough time left to move it ahead sufficiently. The smart group members understand that individuals may come in with a need to ventilate about something, but are prepared then to focus them quickly on the task at hand.

Problem Solving

To take advantage of an opportunity for quality improvement or to solve a problem requires that the team have access to and the ability to collect information and assess the following:

1. the problem situation—nature, seriousness, possible causes, and consequences of ineffective action
2. requirements for acceptable alternatives—objectives that need to be met
3. positive qualities of alternatives
4. negative qualities of alternatives

In general, the greater the number and diversity of alternatives proposed and evaluated, the greater the opportunity for selection of effective solutions. However, solution diversity can work against successful problem solving if it leads to interpersonal conflict or decision paralysis because of lack of consensus.

Group dynamics and interpersonal relations can also influence, interfere with, or inhibit problem solving. Some of the causes outlined by Van de Ven (1974) are:

- focus effect: in a rut, group think, tunnel vision
- self-weighting effect: group members participate only to the level where they feel equally competent with other group members (called social comparison: see Turner et al.,1989)
- judgment effect: judgments are made, but not expressed for fear that they will be perceived as criticisms
- status inhibition effect: opinions are not expressed because they are not in agreement with those of higher status group members
- group pressure for conformity through implied sanctions
- influence of strong personalities on group
- overemphasis on group maintenance functions
- pressure for speedy decisions

Successful problem solving also requires the ability of the group to reach decisions.

Decision Making

Efficient closure requires that the group be able to make a final recommendation effectively. Hirokawa (1988) found a positive relationship between group decision performance and the group's ability to (1) accurately understand the problem, and (2) accurately assess the negative consequences of alternate choices. But individuals can arrive at different conclusions hearing the same information if their decision rule orientations are different (Beatty, 1989). An illustration of the potential complexity of decision schemes is Reagan & Rohrbaugh's (1990, p. 28) four-perspective scheme provided below:

FOUR PERSPECTIVES CONCERNING EFFECTIVE DECISION PROCESSES

FLEXIBILITY

CONSENSUAL PERSPECTIVE	*POLITICAL PERSPECTIVE*
(participatory process;	(adaptable process; legitimacy
supportability of decision)	of decision)

INTERNAL - **EXTERNAL**

EMPIRICAL PERSPECTIVE	*RATIONAL PERSPECTIVE*
(data-based processes;	(goal-centered processes;
accountability of decision)	efficiency of decision)

CONTROL

No matter what decision, rule, schema, or orientation is applied, a group must go through four phases of a process to arrive at a decision:

1. Orientation—Tally the group resources, establish pleasant interpersonal relations, define boundaries of the task.
2. Formation—Define norms, assess member decision orientation, develop work strategy.
3. Coordination—During the work period, seek and exchange information, resolve conflicting views, build consensus.
4. Formalization—Formalize decision, develop commitment, communicate conclusions and recommendations.

Information

Decisions cannot be made, problems solved, or quality improved without information. Unfortunately, many researchers "are pessimistic about managers' abilities to accurately read complex information environments" because individuals "are thought to suffer from selective perception" (Walsh et al., 1988, p. 197). One way to surmount this problem is information pooling from all group members.

Although Stasser (1992) admits that there is little empirical evidence that his recommendations work, he feels they are theoretically sound. They are:

1. Establish the expectation that the available information leads to a demonstrably correct answer.
2. Keep information loads low or develop procedures for high recall (TQM's use of seven statistical summary and graphic techniques helps accomplish this).

3. Make each member aware of the unique information he or she has to contribute.

Communication

Hirokawa (1988) suggests that the relationship between the quality of decisions made and the communication process employed is based on three assumptions:

1. Decision-making tasks are bound by critical requirements.
2. Successful decision making is enhanced by meeting these requirements.
3. Group communication is the mechanism groups employ to met these requirements (Hirokawa, 1988, p. 489)

Conflict/Negotiation

Conflict is a natural element in any group that is attempting problem solving and decision making. With respect to conflict, group leaders and members must come to understand the distinction between situational conflict and interpersonal conflict. Beckhard (1969) suggests that the successful, adaptive organization has a high level of situational conflict and a low level of interpersonal conflict. Scarce resources and organizationally challenging targets lead to situational conflict. One can think of the analogy of Brownian movement. As the environment heats up, the molecules begin to ping off each other and the pressure builds. Situational conflict is an existential problem. The trick is to keep professionals, who normally have trouble differentiating between their professional persona and their personal one, aware that what is happening is situational and should not be taken personally. If people start taking situational conflict personally, the organization loses its effectiveness rapidly. Note that it is inherent in the nature of CQI to create or at least bring to light situational conflicts that team leadership must be ready to manage.

Before conflict can be managed or resolved it is important to understand "the dimensions of differentiation, clarity, and centrality." Here differentiation is the group's ability to identify distinct types (clarity) and strengths or relative importance (centrality) of points of view (Pace, 1990, p. 83). Unfortunately, the process of differentiation tends to tag specific positions to individual group members and creates the "potential for differentiation to escalate into uncontrollable conflict" (Pace, 1990, p. 82). There are four basic dimensions of group conflict: personalized/depersonalized and competitive/cooperative (Pace, 1990, pp. 80–81). A description of these is presented below:

1. Personalized—connected with interpersonal relationships, emotions or personalities, becomes tied to individuals or subgroups
2. Depersonalized—connected with ideas and issues and not tied to individuals, but viewed as a group phenomenon

3. Competitive—conflict is viewed as a win/lose situation; characterized by defensiveness, hostility and escalation

4. Cooperation—conflict in promotion of mutual benefit; characterized as positive, supportive; solutions are by integrative consensus

Pace suggests that the best decisions come out of depersonalized cooperative or depersonalized competitive mixes because these dimensions allow the group as a whole to make the most effective use of the specialized knowledge of individual group members. This approach is recommended strongly by Deming in his new book, *The New Economics* (1993), in which he notes that

> we have grown up in a climate of competition between people, teams, departments, divisions, pupils, schools, universities. We have been taught by economists that competition will solve our problems. Actually, competition, we see now, is destructive. It would be better if everyone would work together as a system, with the aim for everybody to win. What we need is cooperation and transformation to a new style of management. (Deming, 1993, p. xi)

Conflict resolution through negotiation and bargaining may take one of seven forms.

1. Simple disputes—limited to two people, each with full authority to reach an agreement
2. Horizontal bargaining—each side has a designated formal authority figure, but negotiations can not be completed without consultation of the present informal authority figures
3. Constituency bargaining—negotiating individuals are serving as representatives of constituency groups
4. Vested interests—an individual has hidden authority to allow or disallow agreement
5. Unilateral bargaining—cross-table agreements that may leave negotiators at odds with their respective teams
6. Bilateral bargaining—formal problem solving.
7. Multilateral disputes—multiple negotiators or teams, each with multiple special interest perspectives (Gill, 1987; McLaughlin, 1991, 1992)

Quality improvement teams will find the negotiation process complex, even when confined to conflict resolution within the team, because of the multiple perspectives and representative roles held by the individual members. However, negotiations have a good chance for successful agreements if a personal relationship built on mutual trust has been developed. Agreements will stand up to implementation if (1) each party has had some needs met, (2) the agreement was formalized in writing, and (3) each party recognizes that circumstances are going to change. Cooperative negotiation requires each side to present clear goals accurately stated with full disclosure of all facts. Bargaining is restricted to major issues that remain open until all issues are settled to the mutual advantage of both parties.

Environmental Strategies

Groups like organizations are in contact with and interact with their environments. By controlling who becomes a group member and whether group members spend time in other parts of the organization, groups can define or change their group boundaries. Three environmental management strategies proposed by Ancona (1990) may be applicable to quality improvement teams. They are expressed as team types:

- *Informing teams* remain isolated from the environment during problem assessment and reengage only when ready to present recommendations.
- *Parading teams* are passive observers of the environment and process under study, yet spend extensive amounts of time and energy building the team and maintain a high visibility with organization and department constituents.
- *Probing teams* are constantly interacting with environmental constituents to collect information and relevant data and to assess customer(s) needs. Problem solutions or process changes are field tested and modified for a good fit. (Acona, 1990, pp. 344–345)

The last type of team has the best match with the team function within the TQM philosophy of total involvement.

Task

Another set of moderating variables in the model in Figure 7–1 relate to the task to be performed by the quality improvement team. Deming (1986, p. 90) believes that "a team should have an aim, a job, a goal" or a task defined by a problem statement, but not stated so specifically as to stifle initiative.

Type of Task

The selection of the task is important. Quality improvement can be achieved through team effort by systematically selecting well-defined projects and assigning them to teams whose members have the knowledge of the process and the skills necessary to contribute to a successful outcome (Sahney and Warden, 1991; Jackson, 1992). Appropriate CQI team projects in health care organizations include patient care, administration, management processes, improved service designs, creation of new services and processes, and investigation of specific problems (Ebel, 1991). At first, the tasks will represent areas of obvious poor performance, but after initial successes, new teams will be chartered to address important processes that may not be current sources of distress, but have high potential for a high payoff.

Task Characteristics

The approach used by a team will also change with the nature of the assigned task. Relevant task characteristics (Latham, 1987, p. 61) for CQI include:

- difficulty: the amount of effort required to complete the task
- solution multiplicity: the likelihood of more than one solution
- intrinsic interest: the degree to which the task will engage and motivate group members
- cooperative requirements: level of coordination/cooperation required to complete the task
- population familiarity: the likelihood of finding individuals with experience with the task in the pool of potential group members
- benefit/cost potential: the degree to which the benefits will in all likelihood exceed the costs of the team effort and the costs of implementing the changes recommended.

To this we would added causal complexity, something often overlooked by health care personnel, who often tend to assume simple causation.

CONCLUSIONS

Teams are an integral part of CQI. They are a means and not an end, but they are generally a very effective means. CQI management must study what is known about teams and apply that to their individual processes. Management must be concerned about team composition, team roles, team development, and team performance. Flexibility in the management of teams is also an important learning area for CQI management. The literature on teams is extensive, but does not necessarily offer practical advice. The health care environment is used to teams as a way of dealing with emergencies, but not as a generalized mode of addressing day-to-day issues. The primary emphasis in health care organizations is on individualism. Therefore management must sell the use of teams and provide their members with both basic and advanced training in how to make them effective. Facilitators must be available to help with the team process, even after training has been given. Often teams are as much a way of getting people to talk with each other and to understand each other in highly compartmentalized organizations as they are agents of change. Management remains the primary agent of change, with teams available as their collaborators and colleagues.

Kit N. Simpson
Curtis P. McLaughlin

8

Strategic Decision Making, Economic Analysis, and TQM

Total quality management/continuous quality improvement (TQM/CQI) is a process that does not occur in a vacuum, but is part of a larger and unrelenting process of change within the organization. The objective of this chapter is to examine TQM/CQI in the context of planning and technology assessment as parallel, ongoing processes of continuous improvement, but ones that also involve different levels of abstraction and often different sources of data. This chapter will describe the major steps in the planning and technology assessment processes of a hospital, discuss how these process steps are operationalized, and identify where and how quality managers can forge linkages between TQM/CQI and these two processes. Although the linkages are described here for a hospital, the approaches can be applied with modifications to most other health care organizations.

THE ECONOMIC CONTEXT OF TQM

The TQM process must link closely with broader, more abstract change processes that transfer new ideas and new capital goods into the hospital setting. Donabedian (1990), for example, identifies seven pillars of quality: efficacy, effectiveness, efficiency, optimality, acceptability, legitimacy, and equity. These seven should be aligned consistently in all change processes. To maximize the organization's ability to integrate important aspects of these seven concepts into its strategic management decisions, TQM/CQI must be linked to the organization's other existing methods for supporting strategic management decisions (Sahney and Warden, 1993; Durbin et al., 1993). Linkages with two specific processes are especially important: the planning process and the technology assessment process. This is because strategic decision making in any organization requires the answer to the question: Which steps do we take to reach our goals? To answer this question top managers must integrate four distinct types of organizational information. They need information relating to (1) corporate vision (a topic discussed in an earlier chapter), (2) research and development, (3) operations, and (4) planning. All are needed to make informed strategic choices.

The research and development function for a typical hospital is embedded in medical technology assessment—the evaluation of technology developed elsewhere. Most hospitals do not conduct significant amounts of research and buy their technology in the form of equipment or of personnel trained and educated elsewhere. Planning data provide directional input and benchmarks for strategic choices; the CQI hospital also receives essential data on the current status of operating procedures from the CQI process. The information integration required for making strategic choices in hospitals is depicted in Figure 8–1.

Note the definition of a strategic decision used here. A decision is strategic if it is intended to be permanent (that is, good for more than a couple of years) and if it commits the hospital to pursue a specific strategy or policy that thus excludes other desirable options. Often such decisions require long-term (three- to five-year) commitments of scarce resources, such as personnel, space, money, or management attention.

Planning

Planning is done for many different purposes, and numerous models have been designed to achieve these purposes (Blum, 1974). Health planning models may

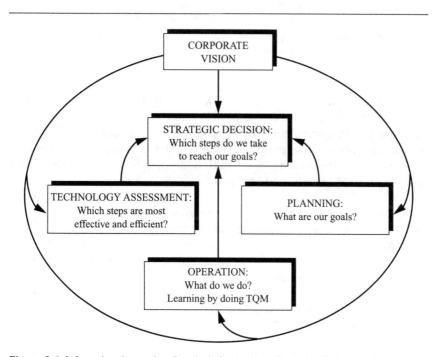

Figure 8–1 Information Integration Required for Making Strategic Choices in Health Care Organizations

be categorized by their aim. Public policy level plans guide the design of health systems toward the achievement of a healthier society and specify health goals. Institutionwide (also called strategic or comprehensive) plans define the strategies and interventions that will be used to achieve given health goals. Operational or program plans specify how, when, and where resources will be deployed to implement the interventions specified in the higher level plans (Reinke, 1988).

Comprehensive and strategic planning models can be differentiated on whether a model approaches the planning process from a normative (synoptic) or incremental (reactive) perspective (Nutt, 1984; Webber and Peters, 1983). Comprehensive planning models are generally normative in that they identify what *should* be done to achieve a specific mission and goals. Strategic planning models are most often incremental in that they identify limits imposed by the organization's strengths and weaknesses and the threats and opportunities present in the environment, and then chart a course towards the goals that will maximize the fit between the organization's strengths and environmental opportunities.

Hospital strategic planning is a cyclic process. Indeed, it is very similar to the TQM process in that its aim is to manage change rationally and continuously. Its objectives are to assess the organization's purpose, formulate and clarify management's vision of what the organization should become, specify the hospital's unique mission given environmental forces, and develop goals and objectives that will serve as markers to chart its course towards maximal alignment between environmental demands and opportunities and organizational strengths (Simpson et al., 1992; Henderson and Thomas, 1992).

The Planning Process

The hospital strategic planning model described by Peters and Tseng (1984) is used here to illustrate the hospital planning process because it is based on an open systems perspective that is highly consistent with TQM. It would involve in the planning process two groups essential to TQM planning: individuals from outside the organization and medical staff. It identifies the following tasks that a strategic planning process must accomplish:

1. Current position assessment that identifies the organization's vision, mission, goals, objectives, and policies based on what it is currently doing
2. Analysis of the environment that identifies competitors and collaborators and tries to assess current and future threats and opportunities, using a three- to five-year planning horizon
3. Conduct of an internal audit that inventories resources and identifies internal values, strengths, and weaknesses. CQI teams would probably be effective contributors to such audits.
4. Identification of relevant strategies through analysis of internal and external data to find a set of strategies that could be used to reach goals, given the available resources

5. Comparison of strategies and the selection of one or more that provides a maximal fit between goals, values, and resources

6. Gaining acceptance for that selection by communicating the strategic choice to important groups whom it was not possible to involve in the planning process, and gaining their support, endorsement, or acceptance

7. Preparation of a plan documenting the objectives and actions required, specifying resources and any changes required, and specifying time frame for actions and changes

8. Implementation and evaluation, using the objectives, actions, and time specifications contained in the strategic plan as the basis for the preparation of operational plans and budgets and as the benchmarks for evaluating progress toward organizational goals and the accomplishment of the overall organizational mission

The concepts of markets and marketing inform most successful hospital strategic planning efforts. Marketing may be defined in its broadest terms as a process for facilitating voluntary exchange of items of value between equals. Marketing is not advertising, nor is it sales. It is a systematic analysis of the four key factors that may influence the success of the exchange process: product, place, promotion, and price (Clarke and Kotler, 1987). Marketing embraces the customer focus of CQI and provides a set of data-gathering and analytical tools that may be used to improve the hospital's ability to identify those customers upon whom to concentrate the majority of its efforts, what new products should be considered, and what modifications to existing offerings are required to increase customer satisfaction.

Employment of a marketing perspective during a strategic planning process leads the hospital to ask questions such as:

- From which sections of the county do most of our current obstetrical patients come, and what types of care and amenities do most of these patients want?

- Which members of our medical staff admit the greatest proportion of our obstetrical patients, and what do these physicians value about practicing at this hospital?

- How can we improve patient and physician satisfaction with the obstetrical process and facilitate better birth outcomes?

In CQI terms, the successful application of a marketing perspective involves the hospital in listening to the voice of the customer. A marketing perspective does not necessarily mean that the hospital will focus solely on advertising, promotion, or fundraising programs. The choice to use these tactics to improve a hospital's market position is a strategic choice driven by specific information on current strengths and weaknesses of hospital products and their community image, and threats and opportunities in the hospital's environment. The application of a marketing perspective to the management of quality does not mean that the hospital starts an advertising campaign aimed at communicating the idea that it provides care of superior quality. Indeed, this approach may be quite counterproductive in that it can raise the public's expectations about the quality of care that they will receive and result in a greater gap between the expected quality and the experienced quality (DesHarnais and McLaughlin, 1992).

Marketing tools, such as satisfaction surveys, the use of focus groups to define service advantages and disadvantages, and the use of population demand models to predict total demand for a service and the hospital's contribution towards meeting this demand for care, are common to most hospital strategic planning efforts, whether they are for CQI purposes as outlined in Chapter 6 or whether they serve some other end.

Strategic concerns should also govern a hospital's decision to use CQI. For example, a strategic market decision is made when a hospital chooses to differentiate its product based on quality in a given environment: for example, to offer family-centered birthing if the "voice of the customer" indicates that this modification to the obstetric care process will improve quality of care and patient satisfaction. In this case, the hospital is creating a unique image of its definition of quality care in comparison to the care delivered by its competitors.

However, strategic planning and marketing strategy are rarely mentioned in the CQI literature. This is because most authors take it for granted that the organization has already chosen to differentiate itself from its competition on the basis of superior quality. However, some markets demand differentiation based on other product characteristics, such as price. When this occurs, management in other markets may simply elect to move their efforts into other market sectors. This is not possible for most hospitals because hospitals are not geographically mobile. They are inextricably linked to their geographic service area because their customers are part of the production process. However, hospitals cannot usually choose the market in which they will locate because they have responsibilities for providing comprehensive care to a defined population area. In such cases, the hospital must find other bases for differentiation to ensure healthy survival. This does not mean that CQI is of little use to the hospital; it just means that the major effort of CQI groups is likely to focus on reducing waste and improving the efficiency of core processes, while improving or holding quality constant.

In addition to the customers who are the focus of hospital marketing efforts, hospitals have to pay attention to other groups. Any group that influences the hospital's ability to achieve its goals is an institutional stakeholder. Stakeholders may be internal or external to the organization. They may be perceived as powerful or powerless; they may be permanently organized; they may have leaders who have formal authority to speak for the group; or they may be an informal group bound together only by a common issue. Examples of stakeholders are county commissioners, community leaders, hospital employees, advocacy groups such as pro-choice and pro-life groups, medical and other professional associations, hospital associations, and major insurers. These groups must also be considered and/or involved in the planning process and should also be informed of and perhaps involved in process improvement efforts.

Linking CQI to Planning

When CQI is linked to a hospital's strategic planning process, the insights that may be gained from planning may be sharpened, that is, focused more on the true voice of the customer. It is important that CQI goals and objectives be included explicitly in the strategic plan because this inclusion may have symbolic importance and can assist in facilitating the movement of the organization's culture towards a customer perspective. The linkage of CQI to planning may also have an important allocational impact. Goals and objectives that are specifically included in a strategic plan may be allocated additional financial and other resources for completion and be included among the goals reviewed at intervals by the board and top management. For example, the fact that a process has been studied by the CQI effort may increase its likelihood of getting the requested capital improvement budget that the team recommends.

Quality managers may have to initiate several actions to ensure the linkages of the CQI process to hospital strategic planning. The first step is to identify the group of individuals who have operational responsibility for the strategic planning process: the actual planning staff. This sounds simple, but may not be. Although many hospitals have planning departments, these often focus on space planning and regulatory responses to constraints such as certificates of need. Actual strategic planning functions may be located elsewhere. Some institutions give major planning responsibilities to staff in fiscal services or staff personnel that assist the president, whereas others delegate the essence of planning support to marketing departments or to external consultants.

Once the key planning staff members are identified, the quality manager should determine the length of the normal planning cycle for the hospital, the stage of the planning cycle that the organization is currently in, and the steps that occur in the planning cycle. This information may not be readily available. It may be necessary to take some time talking to staff, listening to their descriptions of planning work, and integrating this information into a synopsis of planning, such as that outlined by Peters and Tseng (1984).

Once this indigenous organizational planning model has been identified, and once planning staff, customers, stakeholder involvement, and data contributions have been defined, then the quality manager has a framework for assuring that data and insights generated by the CQI process may contribute maximally to the strategic planning process. CQI data can supplement strategic planning data and contribute insights at every step of the planning process. Some examples of how CQI may be used to supplement planning data to enrich insight into customer or stakeholder perspectives are provided in Exhibit 8–1.

Exhibit 8–1 Examples of TQM Contributions to Health Care Strategic Planning

Planning Task and Results	TQM Contribution to Data or Insights on Customers/Stakeholders
1. Identification of Current Position: One objective is to increase the hospitals' share of paid deliveries to assure that indigent high-risk clinic services may continue.	**TQM Contribution:** A TQM team has identified the essential steps in the normal delivery process and how the process may be made more efficient allowing improvement in capacity at no increase in cost.
2. Analysis of the Environment: Projected need for normal deliveries increases based on influx of young working couples to market area.	**TQM Contribution:** The TQM process analysis identified key factors that influence the satisfaction of two types of customers of the normal delivery process: mothers and obstetricians.
3. Internal Audit: Obstetrical floor has excellent high technology equipment but is very "cold and institutional," and many patients have long waits in the ER.	**TQM Contribution:** A TQM team found that the Emergency Room's admission process and ER staff's assessment of patients has a major impact on the outcomes of premature deliveries. The analysis of the high-risk delivery process revealed that only 18% of "premie" babies had the benefit of antenatal steroid treatment because of late or no assessment of their mothers in the emergency room.
4. Identification of Strategies: The hospital could: 1) improve Medicaid coverage of indigent deliveries; 2) limit the use of the hospital to insured families; 3) implement policy that transfers of indigent deliveries from counties that do not contribute to the indigent care fund will not be accepted; or 4) institute a cost control program.	**TQM Contribution:** Process analysis indicates that slight changes in the admission process and some additional ER staff could decrease ER waits for normal deliveries and assure that women in premature labor are assessed for treatment to improve the baby's lung maturity. This would decrease the rate of Respiratory Distress Syndrome in babies and save the cost of intensive care and surfactant treatment.
5. Selection of Alternatives: The alternatives are compared based on criteria of: a) impact on net annual revenues from obstetrics; b) feasibility of implementation, given budget, staff, and political constraints; and c) effect on the quality of obstetric services.	**TQM Contribution:** The TQM process analysis described in #4 above identified the fact that a fourth important criterion for assessing the value of a strategy is marginal cost effectiveness, that is the increase in resources used by each strategy compared to the improvement in health outcomes effected by a change.

continues

continued

6. Gain Acceptance:
Staff provides summary reports of the analyses of the obstetric strategy options.

TQM Contribution: The TQM-generated criteria of cost effectiveness resulted in an analysis that indicated that both improvement in outcomes and overall reduction in unreimbursed use of neonatal intensive care and surfactant would result if the hospital made minor improvements in emergency room staffing patterns. This has high acceptance by all stakeholders.

7. Prepare Plan:
Staff documents the improvement in outcomes and resource use expected from process changes.

TQM Contribution: The TQM process has identified baseline data for the current process and external sources of data that serve as benchmarks for the process improvement. These data provide realistic values for defining measurable objectives for a plan.

8. Implement and Evaluate:
The implementation of the plan is dependent on the commitment of the operational staff to an objective. Planning staff can only communicate and try to "sell" the final plan and hope that someone will assess the impact of implementation.

TQM Contribution: Since the TQM process involves the process "owner" in the generation and selection of solutions, the commitment to the plan is greatly improved and the evaluation of the impact of the improvement is "built into" the TQM process.

The plan set down on paper serves to communicate the organization's mission and goals. However, the more important contribution of organizational planning is its ability to clarify issues, develop consensus, and achieve momentum for change. More insight may be gained from the process of planning than from reminders provided by the written plan. The linkage of CQI, with its insights and consensus building, and hospital planning is essential if well-informed strategic choices are to be made.

Technology Assessment

The research and development (R&D) information that hospital management must integrate into strategic decisions is usually produced outside the organization and covers a multitude of technological areas (Mosteller and Burdick, 1989). The R&D process in health care has a special name, *medical technology assessment* (TA). TA is often considered the purview of public agencies, such as the Office of Technology Assessment in the Public Health Service, but it actually is regularly performed in many settings, including hospitals. However, hospital decision makers may not clearly recognize when they are performing a technology assessment and therefore, may not get maximal benefit from the process. The first step in good medical TA is to define the technology appropriately. Buxton (1987), for example, reviews several classifications and issues that must be considered in the assessment of the technology of health care. He draws attention to the fact that decision makers who limit the definition of hospital technology to "hardware" items or "programs" that require extensive and costly capital investments may be allowing unnoticed, but very costly, technological expansion in low-ticket items. These can add heavily to hospital costs while adding very little to patient benefits. Thus it is important to define technology as broadly as possible. The comprehensive process focus of CQI provides a natural framework for doing this.

In broadest terms, the technology used in a care process is a specific combination of the expert knowledge, equipment, and supplies that are utilized. Each process has its own unique technology, and this technology may change if any component of the process changes. Three major components of medical technology need to be distinguished: (1) large-scale physical items, such as pieces of equipment or specially configured space that requires capital investment; (2) small-scale consumables, such as drugs, disposables, or data collection/management processes that constitute low unit cost items, but are used at high volume; and (3) specific human capital, such as highly skilled/trained personnel with specific knowledge or experience (Buxton, 1987, p. 244). Most hospitals decentralize the TA task by giving committees of physicians or other technical experts the responsibility for assessing new developments in drugs, devices, or surgical procedures; giving financial experts the role of assessing new programs or equipment that requires capital investment; and giving clinical staff and administrative personnel joint responsibility for assessing the need for employing or attracting highly trained or experienced workers. This decentralized process has the advantage that those with the greatest technical knowledge do the assessment, but it has the disadvantage that the assessment of the value of a change most often is based on very limited technical criteria. Thus the total impact of a change of the technology on processes often may not be considered. A formal TA may be required to produce answers to the questions that decision makers need to ask in cases where a technology change is being considered. Such an assessment may be patterned on TAs undertaken for national health policy decisions and may indeed draw both data and insights from published studies that describe a technology's impact on outcomes and costs, as well as other issues.

From time to time, CQI teams may also have to undertake technology assessments when an alternative is spotted that calls for adopting new methods or equipment that is unfamiliar to the institution. Several examples exist in the cases in Part V where new birthing procedures and two-way radios were identified and considered.

The key questions to be answered when a new technology is considered are: What is the usefulness of this technology for patients? Should we pursue its implementation? What is its economic and social cost? (Durand-Zaleski and Jolly, 1990). Information must be gathered on the benefits of using the new technology compared to current practice. The economic implications of a change must be considered and any ethical and legal implications assessed (Feinberg and Hiatt, 1979).

An issue analysis, combined with economic and financial studies as needed, should be performed in order to assure that the information is comprehensive as possible. Issue analysis is a structured approach to finding, organizing, and reporting qualitative information about a technology and how it fits a care delivery system's structure, process, and values. Simpson and Snyder (1991) describe the analysis in detail and identify five categories of issues that are useful for summarizing information on health care technology. These categories are payment, risk, quality, professional practice, and competing technology. For TAs performed at the hospital level, the categories of legal and ethical issues should be added. An issue analysis recognizes the validity of both sides of an issue and presents the issue in a dispassionate manner supported by scientific references. Thus in some cases an issue analysis may serve to decrease organizational conflict by modifying polarization between groups with different stands and values related to a volatile issue, much as a CQI team would seek to do. It may also serve to limit bias injected by the testimony of advocates of a specific technology.

Technology assessments are usually based on the assumption that there is an underlying "truth" or "value" that differentiates a new intervention from the one currently in use (Deber, 1992). This means integrating what is known about a technology and summarizing its benefits and costs in an unbiased manner in terms that are relevant for informing decisions about adoption. A family of economic studies is often used for this type of integration (Weinstein, 1990). The type of study selected depends on the assumptions that can reasonably be made about the impact that a new technology may have on current health outcomes and costs. If outcomes are expected to be the same but costs differ, a cost-comparison study is undertaken. If both outcomes and costs differ, a cost effectiveness, cost utility, or cost benefit study design is used. These three types of studies differ mainly in how the health benefits are summarized. Each type of study uses one common measure of impact and expresses the value of an intervention in terms of the cost of achieving an additional unit of benefit. Cost effectiveness studies use natural outcome units, such as deaths averted or sick days avoided. Cost utility studies "translate" the length of time of illness and the level of morbidity of the illness into one common metric (Guyatt et al., 1989), for example, a quality adjusted life year (QALY) (Torrance and Feeny, 1989). Cost benefit studies translate health and possibly other benefits into monetary values and express the value of an intervention in net dollars gained. This latter method is rarely used in medical TA because most decision makers dislike having to value life and health in monetary terms. A final type of TA involves interventions where costs are assumed to be equal and only benefits differ. The cases where this condition is assumed to hold are rare, and assessment is performed by comparing only key outcome measures (Eddy, 1992).

The most common and most relevant method of economic assessment for use in informing strategic decision choices that relate to quality assessment and process improvement is cost effectiveness analysis (CEA). This method is described below and used in the examples given in this chapter because the approach can also be used by CQI teams on occasion.

Cost Effectiveness Analysis

Understanding of the complex cost and effectiveness relationships involved when medical and economic issues interact can be facilitated by CEA. Questions such as "Is this particular expenditure of health resources worthwhile, given the alternative uses to which it might be put?" (Weinstein and Feinberg, 1980, p. 229) must be asked increasingly by decision makers about a number of interesting initiatives, including CQI. The results from such analyses provide a "yardstick" that can be used, in principle, to guide decisions about resource allocation and priority setting. These types of analyses are therefore increasingly used in evaluations of diagnostic, preventive, and treatment interventions.

Cost effectiveness is the relationship between resources consumed and health outcomes achieved and is often reported in terms of net cost per unit of health outcome, for example, cost per year of life saved (LY). This linkage of costs to units of health outcomes that are common to many different treatments allows the comparison of costs for different types of treatments for the same disease, or indeed for different types of treatments for different diseases. In other words, it allows us to assess the comparative value of interventions competing for scarce health care resources (Freund and Dittus, 1992).

Measuring Benefits. The first two tasks in a CEA are (1) to define the most relevant current treatment for comparison with a new technology, and (2) to select the units in which benefits will be measured. It is critical for the validity of an analysis that these two tasks be performed carefully (Luce and Simpson, 1993).

The practice to which any new hospital technology should be compared is the average practice that currently prevails in the hospital or the community. This means that the analyst must first define average current practice to the satisfaction of the practice community. This may be defined based on the analysis of recent descriptive treatment data sets, such as discharge data tapes, or may be defined by expert panels who describe the clinical treatment paths and resources currently used. Each approach has its advantages and disadvantages. The analysis of discharge data is quick and inexpensive, but it will not capture clinical process details, and the results are subject to biases injected by coding errors and shifts in practice over time. The use of expert panels assures that the most current practice is defined, but it is time consuming and expensive; it also requires careful use of structured decision methods in order to minimize biases due to experts' tendency to identify with the ideal practice instead of average practice and biases related to recall, status differences, and interpersonal process problems. The best specification of current practice is probably done in studies that combine the two methods.

Once the appropriate comparison treatment has been defined, the analyst may proceed to the selection of outcome measures. This step requires the integration of data from many sources. Two major sources of data are epidemiological studies and the reports of clinical trial results. The first may provide data on the frequency, severity, and natural history of the condition of interest; the second may provide data on efficacy and effectiveness of specific treatments.

Randomized clinical trials are usually considered the "gold standard" for the measurement of effectiveness (Jaeschke and Sackett, 1989), but the best choice of outcomes measurements for clinical trials and for CEA may differ. This is because even though intermediate measures, such as CD4 counts for AIDS patients or decreases in blood pressure for heart disease patients, may serve as adequate proxies for the desired patient outcome in a clinical trial, these types of measures are not useful for CEA by themselves. They must be translated into actual morbidity measures, such as the rate of opportunistic disease for AIDS patients or the rate of strokes or myocardial infarctions for heart disease patients, in order for the outcome measures and resource use measures to correspond in the analysis.

Many different methods may be used to integrate data on health outcomes (Wortman and Yeaton, 1987). The choice of a method of integration depends on the data sources available. If all data are from randomized clinical trials, they may be summarized by using a meta-analysis approach (Kassirer, 1992). If some data sources are from studies with a different design, it may be better to use a graphical integration method, such as the Odd-Man-Out method (Walker et al., 1988; Sullivan, 1989). The integration of data from several types of sources, such as database analysis, case study series, and clinical trials, is best done by using either evidence tables (Eddy, 1992) or cross design synthesis (Droitcour et al., 1993). The use of different types of studies to estimate benefits may increase the external validity of a CEA study's results because study designs have different strengths and weaknesses, and the analyst has a greater chance of coming close to measuring effectiveness rather than efficacy if the results of studies with different types of design are integrated.

The different methods that may be used to integrate data and knowledge about a technology's benefits are listed in Table 8–1, together with key references that discuss their use. Studies that base the comparison solely on the results of clinical trials rarely measure effectiveness (the impact of an intervention under average practice conditions). Rather, they measure efficacy (the impact of a treatment under optimal conditions) and should be labeled as cost efficacy studies. These types of studies are quite common, but their results may be of only limited relevance for informing strategic choices at the hospital level. This is because the

Table 8-1 Methods for Selecting and Combining Evidence of Benefits of Medical Technology

Method	Reference
Classical meta-analysis	Kassirer, 1992
Pooling of results	Hunter and Schmidt, 1990
Variance weighting	Wortman and Yeaton, 1987
Peto	Lau et al., 1992
Dersimonian and Laird	Chalmers et al., 1987
Cumulative meta-analysis	Chalmers et al., 1989
	Antman et al., 1992
Effect size estimation	Hunter and Schmidt, 1990
Probability of gain (Mann-Whitney statistic)	Colditz et al., 1988
Confidence profile method	Hunter and Schmidt, 1990
Odd-Man-Out graphical analysis	Walker et al., 1988, Sullivan, 1989
Cross design synthesis	U.S. General Accounting Office, 1992
Evidence tables	Eddy, 1992
Voting	Eddy, 1992
Global subjective judgment	Eddy, 1992
Pick one	Eddy, 1992

practice patterns that they depict are very different from most community practice, and because they do not include factors that may modify the use of a technology at the community level (Bennett et al, 1985; Hanson, 1992).

Costing. The next two steps in a CEA are the identification of resources used in the care process and the costing of these resources (Luce and Elixhauser, 1990). Skills at cost analysis are also important for those leading and facilitating CQI efforts, and the team will probably need to get special assistance from fiscal and management engineering personnel. Gaucher and Coffey (1993) point out that at some point a team is likely to do a "cost benefit" analysis of its recommendations to determine their financial impact. They also point out that there will often be skeptics who want to know whether the expenses of the CQI effort are worth it. A case study of TQM at Paul Revere Insurance reports that the management tended to fall into two groups, the "bean counters" and the "humanists," when it came to assessing TQM. Both groups will probably exist in any organization, requiring the CQI effort to collect and present data on the financial impacts of its works to satisfy the "bean counters."

It may seem tempting to proceed directly to the identification of cost, but if careful resource specification is not undertaken, the analyst may easily select the wrong cost measures for the analysis. This is because costs for a CEA must be defined as opportunity costs (Russell,1992), and these types of costs may be very different from the usual ways we measure costs in hospitals (Finkler, 1990). The types of cost measures needed for good CEA studies are quite similar to cost information required for hospital product line management (Cooper and Suver, 1988) or for the assessment of activity-based costs (O'Guin, 1991). Such analyses are very sensitive to the way overhead costs are handled. Hlatky et al. (1990) illustrate this phenomenon in their analysis of the cost effectiveness of coronary angioplasty versus bypass surgery for a teaching hospital under different accounting assumptions. Luce and Elixhauser (1990) provide clear guidelines for the process used to identify resource use and costs for CEA studies.

The last three steps in a CEA are (1) the discounting of costs and benefits (2) the calculation of the cost effectiveness (CE) ratio and (3) the examination of the sensitivity of the results to the assumptions made in the specification of the benefits and costs of the technologies that are being compared.

Discounting is an attempt to translate the streams of costs and benefits that occur over time into present value measures. Discounting of costs is not a means of adjusting for inflation; rather it is an attempt to capture societal "time preference" for using funds for purposes that have immediate benefits. The discounting of benefits at the same rate as costs may seem controversial to clinicians, but it is accepted practice, and is essential in order to avoid results that are counterintuitive (Keeler and Cretin, 1983). The selection of a discount rate is difficult because there is no "right" rate or method that is useful in all circumstances. Five percent discounting seems to be the most common in U.S. studies (Luce and Simpson, 1993).

The calculation of the CE ratio is easy: it is simply the difference in the total costs of the new process minus the total cost of the current care process. This dollar figure is then divided by the improvement in outcomes, giving the average cost per unit of benefit. Weinstein and Stason (1977) provide a comprehensive formula for calculating the CE ratio.

There is usually considerable uncertainty about the "true value" of many of the probabilities and measures on which a CEA is based. In order to examine the potential impact of uncertainty on the CEA results, analysts perform a sensitivity analysis: a series of recalculations of the CE ratio where one or more key measures or assumptions are varied. The measures that should be varied in the sensitivity analysis are those that have the greater uncertainty. Two types of uncertainty are usually involved: (1) random variation in the results of studies, and (2) lack of knowledge about important factors that influence disease paths or costs.

To test the impact of random variation on the CE ratio, study variables may be changed to reflect values at the upper and lower bound of their 95 percent confidence interval. For measures where uncertainty is due to lack of knowledge, the analyst often selects an upper and a lower bound that reflect the maximal reasonable variation in a specific measure. If the basic study conclusions still hold after these manipulations, confidence in the results is greatly increased. If, however, the basic conclusions are sensitive to the variations tested in the sensitivity analysis, then there is less confidence in the CE ratio, and decision makers may want to weigh other types of information more heavily than the CEA result.

The cost-effectiveness ratio has little meaning unless it is compared to similar figures for competing interventions (Weinstein and Stason, 1985). This comparison, also called *league table analysis*, is the most important feature of any cost effectiveness analysis. New treatments may cost more to provide than older ones, but only when they are compared on costs over time for the health outcomes achieved is it possible to judge which treatment gives the best value for the money.

Some new treatments result in overall savings. These, however, are few. An example is some vaccines. Most new treatments are considered to be giving good value for the money if they improve outcomes at only a moderate cost increase. It has been suggested that any medical intervention that improves health outcomes at a cost of less than $20,000 (1990 Canadian) per QALY saved provides good value compared to treatments that are already provided routinely (Laupacis et al., 1992).

It is important that decision makers recognize the limitations of CEA. This type of analysis is meant to provide data on only one aspect of quality—efficiency. However, by careful design of CEAs it is possible to incorporate most of Donabedian's (1990) seven pillars of quality into the assumptions that guide the analysis.

A CEA may be designed to accommodate comprehensive quality dimensions as follows. The relative weights of efficacy and effectiveness may be adjusted for quality when the outcome measures for the analysis are selected. The dimensions of acceptability of technologies to patients and their families may be incorporated into a CEA by the use of measures that include the value of different process changes to patients (utilities). The legitimacy of a process change to the community can be incorporated into the CEA by performing the analysis from the perspective of society. The most difficult dimension to include in an analysis is equity. This is because CEA usually values costs and benefits equally no matter to whom they occur, and all cost and benefits are also discounted the same. This standardization of measures is at once both a strength and a weakness of CEA. It may improve equity for specific groups under some assumptions and decrease equity under other assumptions (Sabatini, 1985). It is therefore important that the results of a CEA be used only to advise decision makers and that these results be presented in a format that is as transparent as possible and accompanied by a thorough issue analysis that includes the discussion of ethical and equity concerns.

Using CEA in a CQI Hospital. The undertaking of a CEA is obviously a major task that requires considerable expertise. For that reason it is only practical to use this type of analysis to inform important strategic decisions. The performance of

CEA by the hospital management or by a CQI team may be worthwhile, however, in several specific circumstances: (1) when the streams of cost and outcomes generated by competing alternatives clearly differ over time; (2) when the results of financial analysis that relate to the "affordability" of a change indicate that several types of changes are affordable, and there is a clear difference of opinion between clinicians and administrators on what constitutes the "best" choice; and (3) when the economic interests of the hospital and the interests of the practice community or specific patient populations seem to diverge. Under each of these conditions, CEA may contribute insights and help focus and clarify the assumptions that relate to the different choices. Finkler and Wirtschafter (1991) provide examples of how the use of CEA with risk-adjusted outcome measures at the hospital level may help inform decisions related to the improvement of obstetric services, and Hlatky et al. (1990) discuss the use of CEA for informing choices related to the process of care for cardiac patients.

The performance of a CEA requires the analyst to specify and model the complex relationship between clinical treatment and patient outcomes and to capture the opportunity costs that are related to different clinical paths. Special skills are required in order to accomplish this feat successfully. Often these skills are not available among current hospital employees. The hospital must then seek help from consultants. When choosing a consultant for a CEA, decision makers should look to organizations that specialize in technology assessment rather than those with specialization in financial analysis. Among candidates that fall in this category, it is best to choose one that (1) has documented experience in analyses that relate to the technologies or outcomes under consideration; (2) can provide a lead analyst who understands enough about health care to have credibility with both clinicians and administrators; and (3) can provide an analyst who has a basic understanding and knowledge of CQI and its use in health care quality improvement.

These characteristics are important because the analyst must work closely with the CQI teams, medical staff, and finance personnel in order to design a valid CEA model, and must select outcome and economic measures that are relevant to the hospital's choice situation. An analyst who also understands CQI may be able to build on existing team efforts, for example, to translate process measures that are available from CQI teams into valid measures for the CEA. This type of translation can help keep down the cost of the undertaking, increase the speed with which the results are available, and increase the relevance of the results and the insights that the CEA contributes to the strategic choice facing the organization.

It may, however, not be necessary to undertake a complete CEA *de novo*. It may be possible to gain information and insights from CEAs published in the literature. Where there are multiple CEAs, they may be in conflict. This is because economic analysis of medical technology is a young, still evolving science, and some of the methods used for CEA are under debate in the scientific community (Luce and Simpson, 1993). It is quite common for competent, reputable scientists in this field to approach the same tasks using different models and assumptions (Blades et al., 1987). Several authors do, however, provide sound and easy-to-understand instructions on how to judge and use CEAs, as well as information on other issues and questions to consider in using TAs done by others.

Drummond and Stoddart (1984a) identify the questions that should be answered prior to an economic analysis and clearly outline the different types of analyses. In a follow-up paper (1984b), they give a ten-point, detailed reader's guide for judging efficiency studies. Evans (1990) discusses the societal issues that are relevant to most cases of TA and CEA in health care. Drummond (1987) outlines issues in the contribution of technology assessment to policy decisions, and the methods that may be used to influence technology diffusion. Luce and Simpson (1993) summarize the practice community's agreement on methodological issues for economic analysis and identify current areas of debate.

Quality managers should realize that the results of technology assessment in general and of CEA in particular may not be received with unquestioned acceptance by all organizational stakeholders. CEA results especially may be questioned by clinicians. Indeed, these data may generate considerable hostility if they have not been derived with adequate involvement of clinical leaders or if they are used with little attention to the differences in perspectives and values that exist between those who have responsibility for maximizing effectiveness for the individual patient and those who are responsible for managing the resources used for a whole patient population (Detsky and Naglie 1990). The CQI coordinator can do much to prevent such hostility from forming by making sure that any CEA provides results and discusses issues from the perspectives of the individual patient, the hospital, and society. He or she should also carefully prepare decision makers for using CEA by educating them as to the strengths and weaknesses of this type of analysis and by involving clinical experts in the assessment and interpretation of any published CEA studies that will be used. The use of cost effectiveness ratios to inform medical decisions is still new and may seem (and be) threatening to decision makers. Maynard (1990) expresses the potential power of these data when he says that they may be used (1) to prioritize expenditures and thus to determine decisions that influence who will die and who will live, and in what degree of pain and discomfort, and (2) to inform medical audit so that efficient decision makers can be identified and inefficient ones can be reformed or dismissed. It is the job of the quality coordinator to assure that TA and CEA are incorporated into the strategic decision-making process in a CQI hospital in such a way that their use reflects the values of TQM and focuses on improving the process. These powerful tools should not be used to identify "sinners" who are then singled out for the retributions implied in Maynard's assessment.

The issue has been raised by critics of economic analysis that the use of CEA to allocate or "ration" health care resources is unethical and incompatible with good medical practice. Several authors have discussed this issue in depth (Williams, 1992; Mooney, 1980). One of the key points in their responses is that economic analysis assumes a state of limited resources. In a world of limited resources, "health care costs" means sacrificing doing something else for another patient, be it prevention, early cure, or alleviation of pain, and it may be unethical *not* to use CEA to inform decisions (Mooney, 1980). However, the issues involved are complex, and it is important that these types of ethical questions or concerns be thoroughly discussed by decision makers.

CONCLUSIONS

Quality coordinators and other decision makers in hospitals should cooperate to integrate organizational planning, technology assessment, and quality management efforts. Only institutions that manage to accomplish such integration will truly be able to maximize the quality of the care that they offer their customers.

Hospitals who do not plan may survive, but the planning effort provides decision makers with two important advantages that may help them move their objective from survival to excellence. The plan provides decision makers with reasoned reasons to say no, and with guidance on how to respond to the flow of crises with which complex health care organizations must deal continuously (Wilson and McLaughlin, 1992).

The strength of the institution is manifest in its ability to respond flexibly to unanticipated problems and its ability to turn a problem into an opportunity. Good strategic planning can provide the basis for more effective problem-solving by providing a framework for anticipating problems and by generating alternative solutions to issues that may lend themselves to resolution of unexpected obstacles. (Wilson and McLaughlin, 1984, p. 159)

The importance of the recognition, incorporation, and use of research and development, that is, technology assessment, into hospital strategic decisions seems obvious. Yet few hospitals recognize that the TA currently performed in a decentralized manner may be limited in perspective, and only a handful of hospitals have the organizational structure and personnel capacity to perform the analysis in-house (examples are Latter Day Saints Hospital in Salt Lake City, Utah, and Johns Hopkins Medical Institutions in Baltimore, Maryland).

A thorough TA effort may help define and integrate into the organization's choice structure the seven dimensions of quality described by Donabedian. It does this by comprehensively describing the comparative value of strategic choices from the very different perspectives held by hospital customer and stakeholder groups, and it may help manage the inevitable conflicts that arise when scarce resources must be allocated and, as a result, some worthy, worthwhile projects are not funded.

One effort that will have to withstand the scrutiny of technology assessment is TQM/CQI itself. Teams must be able to assess the benefits and costs of what they are doing so that the effort can be evaluated just the same as any other innovation. To do this, teams must be able to differentiate between relevant costs affected by the team's efforts and costs that are not so affected, and to measure team impact currently and over time.

The CQI manager must work diligently to integrate the quality management system with these two processes—planning and technology assessment—as they feed information into the hospital's strategic choice decisions. Only when such integration is complete will the hospital be able to reap the full benefits possible from total quality management.

Part III

Implementation

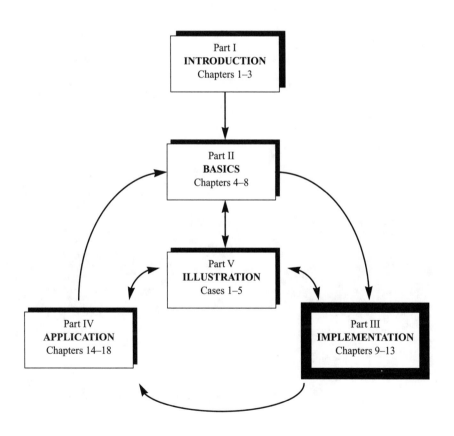

Kit N. Simpson
Curtis P. McLaughlin
Arnold D. Kaluzny

Planning, Organizing, and Leading Continuous Improvement

9

The application of total quality management (TQM) and continuous quality improvement (CQI) is underway in many health care organizations. A few have moved well along in the process; others are stuck, and many are just beginning. The performance of three key management tasks—planning, organizing, and leading—clearly affects the success of TQM/CQI in an organization. The objective of this chapter is to provide a diagnostic model and an overview of how aspects of these three tasks relate to and influence an organization's TQM/CQI effort.

Consider two forms of TQM implementation: the first, Model A, is the model of implementation often recommended by experts, and the second, Model B, is what we have observed in many of the organizations that we have visited. Comparison of these two models illustrates some of the strategic choices that managers must make about their own involvement that may serve to delay or enhance the role of TQM/CQI in the organization.

MODEL A

The ideal application of TQM to health care operates with the characteristics outlined in Exhibit 9–1. There is strong support for beginning with the Board of Trustees. All of the top management team is actively involved and visible in implementing the approach. The planning horizon for the effort is five to seven years. There is a transformation that the organization and its supporting systems must undertake to support TQM and assure an adequate commitment of resources for training and implementation of each team's recommendations. The philosophy of the program is clearly one of maximal employee empowerment and customer responsiveness. It is expected that the effective implementation of the program will have a major impact on the various cultures that the professional

Exhibit 9–1 The Recommended Model—A

Initiation:	CEO initiation with strong board support and/or push.
Time horizon:	Long-term (five to seven years) focus.
Focus:	Change aimed at organizational cultures.
Leadership:	CEO in a mentor/teacher role for team leaders and facilitators.
Structure:	Organizational structure changes, including realignment of traditional management and committee structures with an active Quality Council and/or Vice President for Quality.
Planning:	TQM/CQI is a guiding framework in strategic planning, with clear linkages between that strategic planning process and operational planning, budgeting, and human resources management.
Training:	Heavy investment in internal training system with links to community training institutions.
Customer linkage:	Continuous monitoring of both external and internal customers' satisfaction with responses throughout strategic team deployment.
Information systems:	Modification to clinical and financial reporting systems to meet the needs of process improvement.
Human resource management:	Prior TQM training/experience recognized as an asset for new hires. Plans/explorations of way to modify evaluation and reward systems to support the TQM/CQI culture.
Scope of application:	Application of process management to both administrative and clinical opportunities for improvement based on a management vision and strategy.
Physician involvement:	Strong, formal medical staff involvement on teams and in Quality Council.

groups bring into the organization as well as on the administrative climate and on management's roles.

MODEL B

Exhibit 9–2 outlines the characteristics of implementation that appear to be occurring in many organizations. In most situations the board is a relatively passive participant, and the CEO has seen TQM/CQI as simply another program among many and/or a requirement of the Joint Commission on Accreditation of Healthcare Organizations that must be complied with. Once that conclusion has been reached, the CEO delegates the leadership of the process to a middle manager or to a group of middle managers to implement, while supplying some symbolic support at obvious key junctures. The time perspective of the effort is limited to the current planning horizon, which is usually either three or five years.

Exhibit 9–2 The Reality Model—B (What Is Often Seen)

Initiation:	CEO decision to implement with board acquiescence.
Time horizon:	Medium-term (three or five years) focus.
Focus:	Change aimed at skills and processes.
Leadership:	Primary leadership delegated to staff personnel in line or in QA.
Structure:	TQM is added as an overlay on the existing management structure. It is treated as one of a number of programs being tried.
Planning:	The linkages between TQM teams and processes and the planning process is very tenuous.
Training:	Use of consultants and "packaged programs" to train educational staff and departmental managers.
Customer linkage:	Patient and medical staff satisfaction surveys available to teams if needed for specific team activities.
Information systems:	Special study data collected by teams is primary data source. Heavy reliance on QA data rather than on outcome or financial reporting.
Human resource management:	Search for and use of inexpensive rewards that may be used as staff incentives.
Scope of application:	TQM is used as a method for quality management and/or cost avoidance focused primarily on administrative opportunities.
Physician involvement:	Individual physicians involved (with varying success) on teams.

CQI MANAGEMENT TASKS

Whether Model A or Model B currently prevails, implementation of CQI/TQM represents a process involving a number of managed activities, all of which are affected by management's choices and leadership. Although teams are the core capacity of the CQI process, management must plan and organize a number of organizational changes to support the work of teams and fulfill a number of leadership roles during this change process. We have listed these management responsibilities below under the headings of planning, organizing, and leading to improve the organization of the material. In reality, these management responsibilities often merge seamlessly into one management process. The key tasks are as follows:

- Planning/Evaluation:
  1. Forming the vision of the new CQI organization
  2. Defining the quality deployment policy
  3. Staging the organization for CQI implementation

4. Evaluating improvements by comparison to benchmarks
5. Monitoring and evaluating the adoption and implementation of changes
- Organizing:
    1. Developing a formal quality management structure
    2. Modifying existing organizational structures to facilitate networking
    3. Assuring training for skills change
    4. Identifying champions
- Leading:
    1. Creating the climate and culture; justifying the CQI effort
    2. Creating/recharging champions
    3. Mentoring teams

Planning and Evaluating the CQI Process

CQI cannot just be layered onto existing organizational activities. It must be planned and then led and must become an integral part of a planning process that involves forming a vision, defining policy, staging implementations, and evaluating results in comparison to benchmarks (Godfrey, 1993).

Vision

As with any soft capital investment, the effectiveness of CQI starts with its role in achieving management's vision for the organization. Management has to be able to show how TQM/CQI is expected to contribute to the survival and growth of the organization. Without that link, it is not worth undertaking organizationally or individually. This vision is then the focus of the quality policy deployment process that has to take place.

Quality Policy Deployment

Quality programs do not take place in isolation. They are there to serve the objectives of the organization, and they should reflect a vision of where the organization is going. The planning process that tries to make sure that things happen that way is called *quality policy deployment* in the United States and *hoshin* planning in Japan. In the industrial model of quality policy deployment,

- Top management is responsible for developing and communicating a vision, then building organizationwide commitment to its achievement.
- The vision is "deployed" through the development and execution of annual policy statements (annual plans).
- All levels of employees actively participate in generating a strategy and action plans to attain the vision.

- At each level, progressively more detailed and concrete means to accomplish the annual plans are determined; that is, there should be a clear link to common goals in activities from the shop floor to the top floor. The plans are hierarchical, cascading downward from top management's plans.
- The Pareto principle is used at each organizational level to set priorities, to focus on areas needing significant levels of improvement, and to concentrate on activities that are the most highly related to the vision.
- Implementation responsibilities, timetables, and progress measures are determined.
- Frequent evaluation and modification based on feedback from regularly scheduled audits of the process are provided.
- Plans and actions based on analysis of the root causes of a problem/situation, rather than on the symptoms, are developed.
- Planning has a high degree of detail, including the anticipation of possible problems during implementation.
- Emphasis is on the improvement of the process, as opposed to a results-only orientation. (Huge, 1990, pp. 40–41)

Now, this sounds very mechanistic and a lot like the old Management-by-Objectives (MBO) approach, except for the last item. Gaucher and Coffey (1993) differentiate MBO as being objectives driven, whereas CQI focuses on the processes leading to those objectives. Imai (1986, p. 145) in his book *Kaizen* describes it as being more decentralized since "policy deployment calls for everyone to interpret policy in the light of his own responsibilities and for everyone to work out criteria to check his success in carrying out that policy." Huge (1990) suggests that quality policy deployment does differ philosophically from the MBO system in that (1) the emphasis is on organizational improvement rather than individual evaluation and reward, (2) the unit goals derive from overall institutional improvement goals, (3) the system is more participatory and less oriented toward control, and (4) the system emphasizes much more frequent and timely feedback on progress. Health care organizations are much more loosely federated than most industrial organizations. Some actors are employees and some are not. Each group closely values its own professional autonomy and may even resist accountability. However, that does not mean that management should not carry the policy deployment process as far as it seems feasible.

King (1989, pp. 1-2 and 1-3) has provided a definition for the Japanese concept of *hoshin* planning:

Hoshin kanri is the Japanese name for *hoshin* planning. In Japanese, these words mean "shining metal" and "pointing direction." Hoshin planning is a system that points the organization in the right direction. The more common translation of *hoshin kanri* is "policy deployment."

The word *hoshin* can be translated as "policy" or "target and means." The word *kanri* is translated as "planning" but also means "management" and "control." So sometimes you'll see "policy management," sometimes you'll see "policy control." A literal translation that would seem to make sense to people is "target and means management." Another name is "Management by Policy (MBP)," which is used in Japan to distinguish it from "Management by Objectives (MBO)."

The use of the word *policy* in this definition does not mean a broad-brush approach. The tools of *hoshin* planning are concrete and highly detailed, involving affinity diagrams and many other forms of charts and matrices to define the interrelatedness of activities and to hold them in close strategic alignment. Management must trade off the value to be gained from such detailed planning versus the cost of the effort in time, money, and the propensity of those health professionals who are involved to engage in more action-oriented activities.

Staging Implementation

Not all parts of the organization will be at the same state at the same time with respect to TQM/CQI. Therefore management must be prepared to stage its implementation. Staged implementation can use the existing but limited resources to demonstrate the impact of the approach and show enough successes to sustain interest. It is also possible to use the staging approach to bypass areas of major resistance or apathy or poor leadership until the overall organization gains a sense of momentum. These concepts of managing transitions over the life cycle of the CQI effort are presented in more detail in Chapter 11.

Benchmarking

Benchmarking is an important adjunct to managerial planning. Benchmarking is not only finding out what the best performance is in an area, but also how it is achieved. That function may or may not be performed best in your industry. Statistically, it is unlikely that it is, so one should go outside to see what is being done.

For example, an acknowledged leader in handling waiting lines is Disney; for order-entry processes the leader is WalMart, and for quick changeovers it may be Indy 500 pit crews. Practices in one's own industry are easiest to understand and probably the most comparable, but other industries may be more sensitive to the customer's needs or have tried different and innovative approaches that you have not heard about.

Health care professionals have used the benchmarking of clinical performance for many years. They are very conscious of what their peers are doing. They follow the professional literature and like to keep up with what is happening at the famous teaching centers. They want to know what is the leading edge of technology. Yet the institutions in which they work are quite insular in terms of following "best practice" in health care delivery systems.

> When *Healthcare Forum Journal* faxed out the question "Are you benchmarking?" the replies showed that many institutions wanted to compare themselves with organizations that were conveniently close by, familiar, in their own system, or in their own associations. Besides using large proprietary databases in clinical benchmarking, few organizations have cast far afield for ideas. (Flower, 1993, p. 14)

Yet health care has tolerated some process flows that would never be tolerated in other industries.

> Many practices considered normal in healthcare would get you fired in other industries. If a hotel woke up all its guests in the middle of the night to vacuum or fix the TV—as many hospitals wake up the sick to perform routine functions— that hotel would not last long. If any other business routinely kept its customers waiting half an hour or an hour past appointment times, it would die a quick death. If a legislator, judge, or regulator was discovered to have a financial interest in the outcome of a decision that critically affected many people's lives—as doctors routinely do when they order tests or recommend surgery— they would be brought to trial on criminal charges. If a restaurant jacked up the price of one person's meal because the guy two tables down had ordered pate and a magnum of Mumm's but had no money, the first person wouldn't pay. (Flower, 1993, p. 16)

Why benchmark? Benchmarking can identify the potential areas for breakthroughs in performance. One prestigious teaching hospital found that it was taking two or three days more to do a presurgical cardiology work-up that a community hospital in their area was doing in 24 hours. When Arthur Andersen & Co. studied best practices in ambulatory surgery, they found that the average time from arrival to surgery was 98 minutes. The top 20 performers in that process averaged 56 minutes, and the top individual performer averaged 40 minutes (Cattalini, 1993). Furthermore, benchmarking by looking for the breakthroughs also stimulates breakthrough thinking internally. Instead of looking for marginal improvements, personnel are motivated to look for order-of-magnitude improvements.

The benchmarking process has four stages:

- Planning the study by deciding which process to study, identifying who does it well inside and outside the health care industry, studying your own process intensively before you go to the field, and formulating intelligent questions to ask about the process used at the sites visited.

• Visiting the selected sites and gathering data on process performance and on how those performances have been achieved.

• Analyzing what the performance leaders have done to see how far they are from you and how their system might fit the health care setting.

• Interpreting, adapting, and improving on what you have seen to find a fit with your setting. This may include some prototyping of the new approach that you come up with to make sure that it is workable. (Olmstead, 1993, p. 27)

Benchmarking can also be used to alleviate burnout in the current high pressure environment. Instead of stewing about how to do things better, personnel go outside and see that it can be done better and how. The pace of improvement is rapidly increased by benchmarking since the staff does not have to reinvent improvements found elsewhere. One condition is that the staff is open to ideas from elsewhere and does not have the NIH (not-invented-here) syndrome.

Good benchmarking visits open up the individual's eyes to what customer service is all about. It shows what can be accomplished when the individual is rigorous in keeping the needs of the customer foremost. The quote just above shows how far-reaching such attitudes can be in health care.

Good benchmarking must be done by a team that already has a relationship and a commitment to improvement. The benchmarking process then leads to the development of consensus among the team members about what the process at home should look like. This means that the team doing benchmarking must know in considerable depth how the process is done at home before looking outside. Perhaps as much as 50 percent of their effort should go into characterizing the existing process before they go out and look at the best practices. Then the team can see the "enablers" in the outside process. Enablers may be methods and procedures, or equipment or information systems or new methods of treatment. Although comparison is stressful, it is much less stressful when the enablers are also evident (Heidbreder, 1993). The departments' decision to use two-way radios for patient transport (see Part V) was influenced greatly by their finding and visiting a local competitor who was benefiting from such a system. It may be significant that the resistance came from the department's supervisor, who had not been included on the benchmark visit.

In the clinical area, benchmarking may already be well integrated into the organization's armamentarium of methods. In a sense, quality assurance has been using a kind of clinical benchmarking when comparing the providers in an institution with each other and with available outside norms. However, the outliers do not account for most of the opportunities for improvement, so hospitals have formed consortia to look at best practices across hospitals in clinical areas. An example is provided by the Borgess Medical Center in Kalamazoo, Michigan, which under heavy pressure to cut costs began to look at its performance against other hospitals using MediQual Systems data on its 650 open-heart cases annually. In the first stage of searching for variations from the norm, the hospital reduced the standard battery of tests to save $780 per case; fine-tuned pharmacy utilization to save $525 per case; shortened average length of stay by two days; and changed a number of other procedures and methods. The results were a net saving of $4,000 per case, sufficiently reduced variation so that a package price could be offered for the procedure, and, best of all, a drop in mortality rates from 3.2 to 2.1 (34 percent), mostly accomplished in the low-risk groups. The next target of scrutiny there is the high-risk patient. Thus the result was higher clinical quality and a saving of over $2 million. Columbia-Presbyterian Hospital, working with Baxter Healthcare Corporation, evaluated its procedures for Coronary Artery Bypass Grafts (CABG, DRG 106-7) by comparing its procedures and clinical paths with those of five other large hospitals. After a three-month study, the cost per case had dropped from $22,000 to $15,000 and outcomes had improved. The savings were over $2 million annually.

Numerous benchmarking networks, both for operational and clinical topics, are available in health care today. Savings of the type reported by Borgess Medical Center and Columbia-Presbyterian are hard to achieve without participation in clinical networks and without the consulting services associated with them.

Benchmarking your customers may also be useful. Some writers suggest going to the world-class achievers in each topic area or to one of the winners of the Malcolm Baldridge Award. However, remember that employers in your area, who are paying much of your patients' health care bills, are also candidates. They have a special reason for wanting to help you and are likely to be very cooperative. Being asked advice is always a boost to the customer's ego and is likely to improve the hospital's image in their eyes. Furthermore, what better way is there to advertise to these customers that you are serious about TQM?

Monitoring and Evaluation

The final managerial planning/evaluation function is monitoring the CQI effort, especially the adoption and implementation of changes as needed. One thing that is likely to happen after the first few teams have succeeded is a an increase in the level of CQI activities. Yet everyone is busy already. Therefore management must keep the quality effort focused on key organizational objectives. With other committee and team activities continuing and the new CQI efforts increasing, managers can become like "dogs on bungee cords." The planning process must continue and perhaps even intensify once CQI has been accepted as an instrument of change. The vision must be refined so that each organizational unit and each team has its own operational set of targets and so that the available support resources are allocated effectively (Godfrey, 1993).

Second, management must articulate a realistic timetable for change. If it is going to take a year to get results, then management must make sure that this is understood and yet is not used as an excuse for lack of urgency in execution. There-fore management must state what is perceived as a reasonable time horizon and hold people to it. If that period is long, say over six months, management must be sensitive to its own tendency to lose interest and take special steps to sustain that interest. One way to do that is with periodic reviews of the status of the effort so that everyone is reminded that it is still there and that there are potential benefits at the end point.

Organizing for TQM/CQI

CQI requires that the health service institution itself organize for continuous change. It must develop a formal quality management structure, modify its or-ganizational structure to assure networking, assure a change in knowledge and skills by providing training and reinforcement through practice and incentives, and identify champions who will work for and support these changes.

Developing a Formal Quality Management Structure

Organizing for CQI requires a variety of teams at different organizational lev-els with a variety of specific functions. There is almost always a steering commit-tee or quality council made up of senior managers and charged with managing the ongoing quality effort within the organization through the setting of policy and direction of the quality process. The next level team is the quality improve-ment team (QIT). This is composed of professional and other personnel assem-bled to address a specified process improvement opportunity across functional areas. The QIT is the team examined in most CQI literature. The corrective action team is usually formed to solve a specific problem (usually within a specific func-tional area) and then disbanded. Some programs use a fourth type of team, the design team, to look at aspects of the program itself, such as how to charter the teams or how to reward participation.

The Quality Council. The quality council or quality steering committee is made up of the top management team, who meet to carry out the planning that must precede and then govern the implementation of CQI. They normally meet as a group around other issues, so one might well question the need for the quality council. First, their act of setting aside a specific time to deal only with quality, rather than the welter of other issues circulating in the institution, emphasizes the organization's commitment to CQI. Second, they are then the source of critical components of the program, such as a quality mission statement, quality objec-tives, and a quality plan. The quality council also becomes a role model for the participants in the program and the place where the teams are expected to present their findings on a regular basis.

Design Teams. Design teams allow wider participation in the development of the details of the CQI program, increasing organizational commitment and allowing the introduction of specialized skills and viewpoints that would not be represented on the quality council. The design teams can also reduce the workload of senior managers by developing the detailed implementation of the program.

Design teams are especially important where there is not full top management involvement. If management does not own the process, those involved in the effort must have a high degree of ownership of the approach and the way that it is implemented. Design teams are one way of building that interest.

Quality Improvement and Corrective Action Teams. These are the basic structural building blocks of CQI. They were discussed at length in Chapter 7, which emphasized that management has a major role in chartering, selecting, and motivating these teams and in monitoring their progress.

Modifying the Structure for Networking

The TQM/CQI approach requires the health service institution to organize itself for continuous change. Because the organization does not know where the process of change is going to take it, its response must be highly flexible. It essentially consists of a network of individuals and groups who come together to exploit the opportunities that are there and then go their separate ways after the work is done. Each brings knowledge of the process to be studied and a set of competencies, access to data, and insights to share with the other participants. Therefore a highly important structural factor involved with CQI is the organization's ability to support networking. In a sense it is an internal parallel to what industrial managers call the "virtual corporation," a process in which successful managers perform the following:

- Define objectives: Ask the question "What is in it for me?"
- Marry well: Choose the right partners, because they have to have the right knowledge and skills at the right time.
- Play fair: There must be a win-win opportunity for everyone involved.
- Offer the brightest and the best: People will judge your commitment by the quality of the people you assign to the project.
- Build a common infrastructure: Set up common information systems that facilitate interaction. (Byrne et al., 1993, p. 102)

Networking should be extended to involve the hospital board and medical staff. These two very important constituencies must be involved early and often in the CQI process, yet they need not participate in every aspect of the process equally. Certainly, both should be informed of what is being undertaken and the results reported as they become available to the usual forums: board meetings, medical staff retreats, and so forth. Moreover, the organization should also consider inviting appropriate members of both groups to participate on teams from time to time, with particular emphasis on clinician involvement on clinical teams. Board members may already have experience with TQM in their usual work setting and may even be willing to contribute resources from that setting to the health care organization if the opportunity is presented properly. Do not forget either of these two groups at any period over the life cycle of your CQI efforts.

One study of the impact of outcome measures on hospitals concluded that it was important to change the organizational structure before or as the system was implemented. This is one means of showing the importance attached by management. It also may be necessary if the skills required for the new system are different from the old. For example, an outcome measurement system requires data interpretation skills as well as data entry and manipulation ones. Higher status and skilled people may be necessary to establish credibility for a new system and to figure out how to use it effectively (Linder, 1992). Management must have the will to change the structure promptly as new requirements become evident or as symbolic acts are called for.

Structural organizational efforts may also be required to assure that new knowledge and insights are transferred rapidly. Some organizations—HCA, for example—bring each of the teams working on quality problems at a specific worksite together periodically to participate in presentations and then in open discussions of their progress with an employee and management audience. Such presentations are often supported with "storyboards," overheads, posters, and other display media, much of which are also kept on display in the work area. The purpose is to give the teams recognition, new ideas, and feedback and to expand their base of knowledge about the problem and possible solutions. It is also a powerful educational technique. Some institutions use this meeting effectively as an orientation device for new employees. Multisite organizations may have CQI "fairs" at which representatives of teams from the various sites get together to share their successes, essentially transferring technology from site to site or at least establishing benchmarks for other sites to try to achieve and perhaps surpass.

Assuring Training for Skills Change

Questions that all managers face are what to include in which training programs for which employee groups and when. Actually the when is easier to choose than the what. It is inefficient to undertake extensive training of all employees. The organization is only going to have a limited number of teams operating, so most individuals will not be using these new concepts for quite some period of time. By then they are likely to remember only dimly what was presented earlier. It is much better to have most of the training take place within two weeks of when individuals are beginning a team activity or are already involved in it. Then the learning is reinforced by being applied to a task. Most adults learn best by doing. That is why much training should be experiential and involve the group in an application as they learn the concepts.

One way of getting effective "just-in-time" training to work groups is to have the knowledge move down through the organization by having the managers and supervisors learn the concepts and do the bulk of the training. They are much more likely than staff trainers to know what quality activities their personnel are involved in. They can either do the training themselves or call in the staff trainers to offer the concepts when they are needed. Furthermore, employees are more likely to use the quality improvement tools when they know that their managers expect to see them. They can dismiss the concepts when they come from trainers, but it is harder to do so when concepts come from managers who obviously believe they should be applied to everyday work.

Therefore training starts with those at the top and proceeds down through the organization. However, at some point most organizations provide a "music appreciation" training session on CQI for a large number of its employees. The objective of such an effort is to prepare the ground for the cultural changes that will come with the further implementation of CQI. Such introductory training is designed to

- Let people know what is going on and why
- Encourage individuals to participate when opportunities occur
- Understand the current importance attached to quality by management
- Stimulate thinking about ways to implement the process
- Motivate greater involvement in just-in-time training as it occurs
- Raise individuals' consciousness about quality in their daily work
- Emphasize the importance of the customer in the activities of the health care organization

A design team or committee can be set up to develop the training plan and perhaps to oversee the development of the training materials. They are going to have to decide who to train and about what. One purpose of using a design team rather than having top management or outside experts select the topics is to promote more widely commitment to the training and its objective. Members can go back to their respective work units and tell their peers how carefully the program was planned and how good it is going to be.

Another approach is to develop a quality education matrix (Huge, 1990). Table 9–1 gives an example of such a matrix adapted for the health care organization. In this illustration, it is assumed that training is going to be given to all levels of management, to key board members, and to key professional and nonprofessional staff. Being considered key would be related to one's status as an opinion leader or one's level of activity in ongoing continuous improvement activities. Just who is trained and in what would be a function of the organization's strategy for implementing CQI. The matrix would reflect

- The philosophy of the training, e.g., train everyone or do just-in-time training of specific groups

Table 9–1 A Health Care Quality Education Matrix

Topic for	Executives	Middle Managers	Supervisors	Key Professional Staff	Key Board Members	Key Nonprofessional Staff
Quality improvement philosophy	X	X	X	X	X	X
Basic problem-solving skills	X	X	X	X	X	X
Statistical thinking	X	X	X	X	X	X
Basic statistical process control	X	X	X	X		X
Employee involvement	X	X	X	X	X	X
Team building	X	X	X	X		
Leadership/facilitation	X	X	X	X		
Outcomes measurement	X	X	X	X	X	
Competitive benchmarking	X	X		X		X
Robust design		X		X		X
Becoming a trainer	X	X	X			
Quality policy deployment	X	X	X		X	
Experimental design		X		X		X

Source: Huge (1990), p. 110.

- The structure of the program, e.g., whether full-time staff are assigned to it
- The organizational development objectives of the program, e.g., the development of more independence and initiative among first-line supervisors
- The educational philosophy of the organization, e.g., professionals are responsible for their own development or the organization is responsible for leading such development
- The training strategy of the organization, e.g., use of outside experts versus developing in-house experts to motivate greater learning
- The quality history of the organization, e.g., whether prior quality efforts have left a bad taste in clinicians' mouths
- The nature of the current quality plan, e.g., whether the management wants to involve clinicians in the early activities

- The normal peer interaction and evaluation approaches of the groups involved, e.g., whether the groups involved are used to treating each other as peers

Any quality education matrix must be flexible to reflect those transitions and to change as the organization's status changes. Each program goes through its own life cycle, and many of the issues to be addressed will be handled differently depending on where the organization is in that cycle. For example, at the early stages of a program the teams may tend to be more within one department than across departments. In the early phases, then, supervisors could easily lead and facilitate the teams. Later, however, as the issues become cross-disciplinary, "neutral" facilitators may have to be available as the teams address turf issues or if one party believes that the analysis and discussion may be biased by the presence of the supervisor or manager from one of the departments involved.

Physician Training in TQM. Managers often ask when and how physicians should be trained in TQM. The time when training is most likely to be effective is during residency programs. Then the learners are interacting with the system with great intensity. Some residents and fellows, especially the chief residents, are coming into contact with the governance process, sitting on committees such as Pharmacy and Therapeutics. Their education should include the results of team studies in their field so that they can recognize TQM as a legitimate form of clinical research.

Identifying Champions

Change does not take place in any area without an effective champion. The implementation champion must either be in top management or be able to maintain contact with top management. With respect to a specific outcomes measurement system,

> [w]hether through formal structure or informal advocacy, effective implementers found system champions. These individuals were boundary-spanners, bridging departments and specialties within the hospital. They were tough and relentless in their pursuit of quality and in their insistence on measurement. Through their backgrounds, relationships, or personal styles, they crossed factional barriers and enabled the hospital to move beyond parochial disputes. (Linder, 1992, p. 157)

Leading the CQI Process

Leadership, as Figure 9–1 indicates, is at the core of successful CQI implementation. It provides the influential increment over time over and above mechanical compliance with routine directives. As described by Bennis and Nanus (1985,

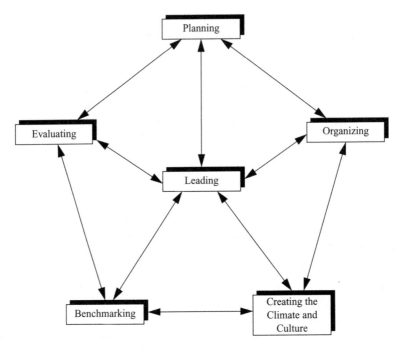

Figure 9–1 Planning, Organizing, and Leading Tasks

---

p. 21), management involves "doing things right," whereas leadership involves "doing the right things." Critical to leadership in CQI are creating the climate and culture, and creating and recharging the champions.

Creating the Climate and Culture

It is management's responsibility to create the climate and culture that support CQI. Much of this has been mentioned in other chapters, but it is reemphasized here because of its importance as a management responsibility. The index of Gaucher and Coffey's (1993) book on the University of Michigan Medical Center experience lists "aspects of creating culture, pp. 97–315." As a symbolic leader, the manager must tailor his or her own responses to every situation to support the philosophy and behaviors of CQI. That is called "walking the talk," since people look for ways to deny management commitment to the level of cultural change that CQI requires. The management must communicate continuously the positive vision of CQI: that it is a route to success; that people will be energized by the empowerment and the learning that come with it; that it will lead to improved care; that the effort will not be a threat to people's jobs, but an opportunity for personal growth and increased job security; and that it will consciously be made to be not life-and-death serious, but fun. On the other hand, management must reinforce the understanding that with CQI comes the requirement for high commitment and the expectation of high standards of performance. With this effort, management must interject the element of celebration. This often runs counter to the expectation that a good professional always does his or her job, and the less said the better.

One part of leadership is dealing with conflict, and one place where conflict will arise is with those who are resistant to change. There will be resistance to any paradigm shift in the quality area. Linder (1992) has outlined the resistance to an outcome measurement system such as MedisGroups in 31 hospitals. One of her findings was that the degree of implementation was related to the degree of resistance as well as the degree of advocacy.

If there is resistance, that will slow down the implementation. However, in dealing with resistance management can become more deeply aware of the philosophy and process that they are implementing. It is even possible that during the argument and discourse some opponents will be converted to advocates due to their deepening knowledge base (Linder, 1992).

Creating/Recharging Champions

Champions have to stay in that role for a long time for the implementation to succeed. That is one of the problems in an industry where executive turnover is high and promotions are rapid and linked to job changes. There is even a risk that being a champion, while giving a positive image, may lead to a slowing down of career advancement.

In CQI, managers function to support problem-solving teams, not to impose their own ideas. This sometimes creates unusual role-reversing situations, but if everyone understands that the purpose is to get the problem resolved as quickly and as effectively as possible, there is no incongruity. As CQI develops across the organization, some teams will become self-managing of both the process and themselves. The evolution of such "super teams" is an indication that CQI is well embedded in the organization's culture. The organization must provide resources for and support the legitimacy of those who will mentor both management and teams in the implementation of CQI.

Mentoring

Mentoring can take place by example as well as by hands-on leadership. Top management has both symbolic and operational roles. Not only does management have to use the language of quality and reducing variation and data-based decisions, and to "walk the talk," but there have to be occasions where its CQI performance is made visible to the participants.

The implementation of CQI can proceed rapidly or slowly depending on how it is staged and supported. Top management must create a sense of urgency about it, a sense that it is important and that results are time dependent. One way to do this is to identify a perceived threat or time deadline, such as the risk of lawsuits, or meeting an accreditation deadline, or damage to image and reputation that could ensue. Management can use external threats or internal opportunities to motivate that sense of urgency.

SUMMARY

This chapter has introduced Part III on implementation with an emphasis on the role of management in CQI. It has focused on three key management tasks: planning, organizing, and leading. Managers report that CQI has them working both smarter and harder. There is much less wasted time, but they also have to put effort into the tasks of managing CQI. They must already have or develop a comprehensive plan that can be communicated to others to guide the planning of the CQI effort. They must put time into the efforts of the quality council and the process of quality policy deployment. They may choose to go on benchmarking site visits to learn more about improvements that can be made from ideas near at hand or in other types of businesses. They have to be flexible in planning to respond to the skill availability, champions' efforts, and opportunities as well as to the problems that present themselves over the life cycle of CQI.

Management must continually adjust the organizational structure to be responsive to the needs of the CQI effort. Teams must be chartered and supported. Compensation and reward systems and employee evaluation systems must be modified as the CQI process proceeds. Resources must be made available to help train the managers and facilitators and then to train potential and actual team members, including board members and medical staff, as the information is needed. Both the organizational structure and climate must be changed to facilitate networking and knowledge transfer and exchange, to support the philosophy and behaviors of CQI, and to make the CQI experience one of success, learning, improved care, personal growth, high commitment, high performance, fun, and celebration.

Leadership creates such a climate by communicating the philosophy and objectives of CQI; by mentoring managers, champions, and team members; and by presenting a shared vision that creates a sense of urgency. Asking for all of these, plus the other tasks of managing a health care organization, is a tall order, but also the order of the day.

Curtis P. McLaughlin
Arnold D. Kaluzny

Managing with TQM in a Professional Organization

10

Interest in total quality management (TQM), a major managerial innovation, is running high, and a growing number of health service organizations are implementing TQM. Some will succeed; many will fail. TQM represents a fundamental paradigm shift in health care management. This chapter explores a series of potential conflicts between TQM and the way that health care institutions normally are managed. A number of action guidelines are suggested to better ensure that TQM fulfills its potential and functions effectively within health service organizations.

TQM AS A PARADIGM SHIFT

Total quality management is a conceptual approach different from quality assurance (QA) and quality inspection and runs counter to many underlying assumptions of professional bureaucracies. It calls for continuous and relentless improvement in the total process that provides care, not simply in the improved actions of individual professionals. Improvement is thus based on changing both outcome and process.

Batalden et al. (1989, p. 580) outline what the health leadership must learn in order to implement TQM successfully.

- Management must learn the meaning of quality: they must especially understand the importance of the customer and the fact that there are multiple customers of the health care production process.

- Top management must sponsor and encourage continuous improvement of quality, including the wise use of teams that can work together effectively to

Source: Adapted from McLaughlin, C.P., and Kaluzny, A.D., Total Quality Management in Healthcare: Making It Work, *Health Care Management Review*, Vol. 15, No. 3, pp. 7–14, Aspen Publishers, Inc., © 1990.

improve systems, and of other processes, including group processes and organizational and system change skills.

- Management must learn the meaning of statistical thinking: how to look at variation as a generator of errors and costs; how to speak with data and manage with facts; how to take the guesswork out of decision making; how to reduce variation and unnecessary complexity through the use of the seven standard tools of data analysis and display (cause-and-effect diagram, Pareto chart, histogram, scatter diagram, flow chart, run or trend chart, and control chart); and how to link the results of the use of these tools with appropriate management action.

TQM demands that change be based on the needs of the customer, not the values of the providers. It requires the meaningful participation of all personnel and a rapid and thoughtful response from top management to suggestions made by participating personnel. Management is no longer able to stifle the suggestions of personnel by requiring additional study or by requiring that all decisions be reviewed by several layers of management. The teams must report to management before undertaking changes. However, management must be prepared to veto such proposals only rarely and only when the negative consequences are important. Otherwise, staff motivation will quickly wither.

TQM is more than a change in values and responsiveness by top management. It requires rigorous process flow and statistical analysis, evaluation of many ongoing activities, and the recognition and application of a number of underlying psychological principles affecting individuals and groups within an organization. It requires accepting the fundamental assumption that most problems encountered in a health care organization are the result not of errors by administrative or clinical professionals, but of the inability of the structure—within which all personnel function—to perform adequately.

In problem characterization, TQM places primary emphasis on the functioning of the system rather than on the individual. Deming (1986) estimates that 85 percent of errors introduced into a process are the result of problems with the system rather than random errors and mistakes introduced by individuals. This runs counter to the prevailing assumption in health services that a problem is a result of one individual's error rather than of the larger structure or system within which the individual functions. The following incident illustrates this assumption.

Mr. Smith was hospitalized briefly and experienced a number of scheduling and coordination difficulties that unnecessarily complicated the stay. In an effort to provide constructive feedback to the management of the hospital, Mr. Smith described his experience and displeasure to a senior staff member with whom he was personally acquainted, suggesting that these problems could be improved, if not eliminated. A few weeks later at a social occasion, the supervisor of one of the departments involved approached him and started asking questions such as, "What did the person look like? Was the employee short or tall? I checked the records the day you were in, and the person who was on duty was the one least likely to do that." Unfortunately, the normal response to complaints is to "take names and kick butts."

Finally, TQM challenges the prevailing model of who the customer is. The customer in TQM is not only the patient, but also every user of a department's output. Here again, the criterion is not whether the work meets professional standards but whether the user, often a member of a different profession, is satisfied with its timeliness and utility.

IMPLEMENTING TQM IN A PROFESSIONAL ORGANIZATION

TQM/CQI within health services does not function in a vacuum, but within a rich tradition and culture emphasizing the role of the professional in the way the organization functions. This tradition and culture is characterized by a set of norms and values, including individual responsibility, professional autonomy, and professional authority. Although these traditions and the TQM philosophy are a priori neither mutually exclusive nor in conflict, Exhibit 10–1 outlines several areas of potential friction between the two.

Conflicts

Although the observed points of conflict will vary between organizations, each of the potential areas of conflict requires explicit recognition.

Individual Versus Collective Responsibility

The professional approach to work places the responsibility for performance squarely on the individual professional. As described by Mintzberg, "the Profes-

---

Exhibit 10–1 Areas of Potential Conflict between Culture and TQM Philosophy

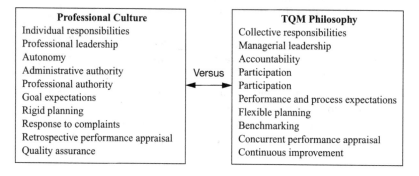

Professional Culture	TQM Philosophy
Individual responsibilities	Collective responsibilities
Professional leadership	Managerial leadership
Autonomy	Accountability
Administrative authority	Participation
Professional authority	Participation
Goal expectations	Performance and process expectations
Rigid planning	Flexible planning
Response to complaints	Benchmarking
Retrospective performance appraisal	Concurrent performance appraisal
Quality assurance	Continuous improvement

Versus

sional Bureaucracy. . . hires duly trained and indoctrinated specialists—professionals—and then gives them control over their own work" (1979, p. 349). He goes on to state that such control means that the professional works independently of colleagues but closely with clients. If the professional makes a mistake, then that professional is primarily liable for damages. If the error is blatant, a quality assurance (QA) committee, and in the very worst cases the professional society, sanctions the individual. Only in the most grievous cases is the organization itself at risk for damages.

The TQM approach focuses on the system. If system errors or problems occur (e.g., if individuals were not properly trained, key information was not transferred, or procedures were not adequate to the variety of possible situations), the TQM approach focuses on the process, not the individual provider. To correct problems and errors, a group—usually interdisciplinary—of individuals in the organization is asked to assume ownership of each process and share joint responsibility for its improvement.

Clinical Versus Managerial Leadership

In the health service organization, a continuing source of conflict is the relationship between the various levels of administrative management and the clinical professional leadership. At a time when management is trying to gain more control over the clinical professional in the face of pressures for cost containment, TQM comes along and demands that management take a more participative approach. Managers are required to involve clinical professionals in the decision-making process, leaving it up to them to solve quality problems as they arise. Yet, although this is a participative program, it is clearly a managerial initiative. Paradoxically, participation may be perceived as a threat to professional autonomy even as it contributes to individual and group autonomy.

Autonomy Versus Accountability

Autonomy is central to the role of the professional. Under this approach, clinical professionals have the special privilege of freedom from the control of outsiders. This privilege is justified by three claims:

1. Unusual degrees of skill and knowledge are involved in clinical professional work, and administrative professionals are not equipped to evaluate or regulate it.
2. Clinicians are responsible, and they may be trusted to work conscientiously without supervision.
3. Clinical professionals themselves may be trusted to undertake the proper regulatory action on those rare occasions where an individual does not perform work competently or ethically.

Clinical professionals are thus suspicious of managerial actions in the areas of cost control and QA. To them, TQM may look like another in a progression of management steps designed to reduce their professional autonomy. Although TQM is an approach that is likely to increase personal autonomy in undertaking task-oriented change, it does not respect professional autonomy as much as it respects personal autonomy. At the same time, it demands that clinical professionals hold themselves accountable for both outcome and process performance on a continuous basis.

Administrative Authority Versus Participation

TQM, through the use of quality circles and interdepartmental teams, puts responsibility for quality control in the province of the front line managers and employees. Quality circles are small groups of employees from the same area who work on a range of problems, including increasing productivity and efficiency. TQM also relies heavily on interdisciplinary teams to study bigger processes. Maintaining quality no longer means taking names and booting bottoms; it means training employees and empowering them to monitor their own performance and take corrective action.

Professional Authority Versus Participation

The TQM approach diffuses responsibility for quality among the members of the team responsible for the delivery of care. The criteria selected by the teams are not necessarily those that would have been selected by physicians and other professional groups. TQM emphasizes that criteria are to be selected by the users of the output. It was best described by the director of a major teaching hospital, who defined his objective in a TQM initiative as wanting to "make this a customer-driven instead of a doctor-dominated hospital." Teams are likely to be multidisciplinary, and the creativity and worth of every team member must be respected equally. This has been reported frequently as a perceived threat to the status of middle managers. The same is quite likely to be the case with some high-status professionals.

Goal Versus Process and Performance Expectations

The usual expectation in health care is that one has an objective goal for every act—that there is a "gold standard" for care. This means that each activity has a protocol for behavior and an expected outcome, and that the protocol remains in effect until a technological change makes it obsolete. That is not the case with TQM. The objective for TQM is one of continuous improvement. Although this idea is not totally foreign to health care (e.g., the history of organ transplants has been one of continuous improvement), hospitals have not typically measured the success ratios of many of their basic procedures, such as getting the discharged patient out the door more quickly.

Rigid Versus Flexible Planning

A major teaching hospital tried forming quality circles that successfully developed a series of major cost-saving actions. As might be expected, these proposals often had associated capital requirements. However, the hospital administration had already planned its capital investment for three or more years. Therefore the proposals were not implemented quickly, and the quality circles lost interest.

TQM requires that management be responsive to quality improvement suggestions. New priorities are necessary, and they must be addressed aggressively through flexible, ongoing planning rather than through rigid, preprogrammed activities.

TQM includes a concept called *benchmarking* of products and processes. This involves comparing current activities and performance against the best of the competition, the idea being to develop a product and process that significantly betters the competition. This implies several changes to existing approaches in health care, where the primary stimulus for change is the recognition of a problem vis-à-vis the established norm. First, TQM explicitly acknowledges that there is a competition to be studied and surpassed. Second, it recognizes the customer's experience as the basis of comparison. Third, it expects that the organization and its processes should be improving all the time, regardless of whether a complaint is registered or a problem identified. It means that the accepted way of doing things does not last long. Such an effort requires continuous growth and learning on the part of everyone, no matter how old or how well educated.

Retrospective Versus Concurrent Performance Appraisal Systems

Most performance appraisal systems are based on setting goals and then meeting them. TQM appraisals focus on gaining skills to contribute to the process of quality improvement. Therefore the reward system is based on contribution to a team effort to improve outcomes rather than on meeting of specific set objectives. If TQM is in effect, the objectives will be changing almost daily: as some are achieved, new ones are immediately set. The following case illustrates the concept of TQM.

A European company won a contract to deliver headlamps to a Japanese car manufacturer. The initial contract allowed 50 defective lamps per 100,000. The lamp manufacturer modified its process to meet that standard painlessly. The next contract called for 20 defective lamps per 100,000. The lamp manufacturer managed to meet that too, so the next contract called for 5 per 100,000. Once again, the supplier struggled and met the new requirement. The next contract called for 10 per 1,000,000. This time the lamp manufacturer complained, "Why didn't you ask for that standard the first time?" "We didn't know what you could do when we started," the Japanese replied.

The concept of *kaizen*, or "continuous improvement," is what drives a TQM program. No matter how well one does, one should be preparing and attempting to do better (Imai, 1986).

Quality Assurance Versus Continuous Improvement

The underlying premise of QA has been to identify human errors in the process, to follow established protocols, and to search for failures to meet the gold standard. This had been the traditional approach of the Joint Commission on Accreditation of Healthcare Organizations (Joint Commission): either the standard is met or it is not. TQM emphasizes reducing variations, correcting system errors, and continuous improvement. Moreover, it requires that improvement becomes the responsibility of all personnel, not just those designated as QA personnel. Fortunately, the new Joint Commission standards are planned to reflect the TQM approach, emphasizing a process for continuous improvement rather than a go versus no-go measure (Ente, 1989).

Preparing for Change

The implementation of TQM requires that administrative and medical managers mediate these areas of conflict. How well management functions during the transition will depend on its ability to follow the action guidelines presented below.

Action 1: Redefine the Role of the Professional

Most health care organizations have hired professionals on the basis of their possession of technical skills and standards certified by the training programs from which they were credentialed and hired. Management has claimed relatively little control over professionals once they are hired, so they must bring the right work habits, standards, and methods. It has been assumed that the possession of this training and these work habits would lead to decision making that would meet the gold standard for an extended period of time.

The new set of decision-making skills required by TQM will have to include not only technical skills but also the ability and flexibility to be guided by a quest for continuous improvement. This requires fundamental skills for statistical analysis of professional procedures and the ability to work with and in multidisciplinary teams. In essence, the basic training of the physician, the nurse, and other providers will have to include basic epidemiology, statistics, and a variety of group process skills.

Action 2: Redefine the Corporate Culture

Americans tend to look for the quick fix, the home run, and the Nobel Prize. Although TQM may yield a home run early on, the basic philosophy is one of incessant change, hitting lots of singles, and the tortoise over the hare. Imai observes that Westerners are concerned with performance, whereas Easterners are concerned with both performance and process. The Eastern philosophy calls for continuous employee training to assist with continuous improvement. This means that there must be a change in what Kilmann (1989) refers to as culture, management skills, team-building strategy, structure, and reward system. Failure to address each systematically will greatly limit the implementation of TQM. When visiting a site, one of our favorite questions is whether every job description includes "Is responsible for recommending methods for continuous improvement of all work processes." We have yet to get an unequivocal yes.

Action 3: Redefine the Role of Management

In TQM, the manager becomes a symphony conductor, orchestrating the independent actions of a variety of professionals and project-oriented teams. This change greatly modifies current leadership roles at the top, middle, and bottom of the management hierarchy. Top managers will do less of the decision making, leaving it to lower and middle levels of management to make the majority of the decisions, often on a consensual basis among the departments involved. The role of top management, then, is to manage the culture and to allocate resources to support the change process. Top management will have to establish a planning process that is flexible enough to adapt to the proposals that the TQM process develops. Top management will have to be the spokespersons for the clients who are not well represented in the system, especially patients. Middle management has responsibility for monitoring the process of TQM and authorizing the implementation of the process changes that are identified for improvement of both quality and cost. Front line management acquires the key role in TQM. The first-line manager has to lead the process and at the same time give people enough room to make it work. All levels of management must be evaluated as role models for TQM, and top managers have especially important roles in modeling, teaching, and providing feedback as part of the TQM process.

Action 4: Empower the Staff to Analyze and Solve Problems

The most important challenge for management is to empower the staff to gather data, analyze it, and make recommendations. This involves convincing the staff that it is safe to collect data and do something with the results. This means that management must overcome status barriers; must be diligent in convincing people to try out statistical quality control techniques, making sure that people get rapid feedback to their proposals; and must be diplomatic. They must implement Deming's point that management should drive out fear. Supervisors also have to act as liaisons if problems turn out to have multiple causation (as they so often do). They have to be able to see the system in a systems way, not focusing on their own unit alone, but seeing their unit as a component in a complex system. Most of all, they must all be supporters of the massive social changes that TQM can require.

Action 5: Change Organizational Objectives

The organization's objectives need to be expressed in terms of both performance objectives and process objectives. This means that programs will have to set their own quality objectives period by period as they develop the capacity to measure, follow, and modify their own processes.

Action 6: Develop Mentoring Capacity

The professionals and the managers will both perceive these changes as risky to implement and threatening to their professional identity. They will need models of behavior to follow and mentors with whom they can discuss their plans and their concerns about the risks involved. Senior executives who are convinced of the importance of TQM are going to provide advice and support. In fact, in one industrial organization, a criterion for promotion among mid- and upper-level managers is how subordinates judge their boss's ability to function as a TQM role model.

Action 7: Drive the Benchmarking Process from the Top

One of the hardest steps will be the benchmarking process, a process that must be led from the top of the organization. Top management is the group responsible for assessing the outside environment. They have the capacity to identify the best performance of competitive organizations and compare internal operations with these high-performance organizations. This will not happen effectively without strong leadership at the top.

The unit of analysis for benchmarking is critical. It is not just "Do we have the best radiology department in the country?" It is also "Do we give our patients the best experience? Do we serve the attending physicians better than anyone else? Are we making fewer processing errors and fewer delayed reports than last month? Are we working to make this the best unit in the world?"

Action 8: Modify the Reward System

The reward system of health care is constrained to a high degree by concerns about professional status and professional prerogatives. The health care institution, however, must generate rewards for those who cooperate wholeheartedly and effectively with TQM. These rewards are most likely to be psychic rather than financial payments. They can effectively include travel, entertainment, employee recognition (best used for teams), and vacation time. For example, one major U.S. company that is very successful at TQM has eliminated all financial awards in its suggestion system. It now gives books on how to improve job performance and trips to continuing education programs instead. The ideal reward system should reward both outcome performance and process development.

Action 9: Go Outside the Health Industry for Models

Xerox Corporation of Stamford, Connecticut, has been one of the most successful adherents of TQM. TQM has helped the company to thrive in the highly competitive copier market and to compete well enough to recover some of its market from the Japanese. David T. Kearns, retired chairman and chief executive officer of Xerox, has suggested that the next benchmark for Xerox copiers after Japanese copiers should be the telephone, with its attributes of both high reliability and low cost. Health managers should not hesitate to go outside of the health industry for its models of consumer-driven quality. The obvious future targets are highly successful consumer service organizations such as Walt Disney, American Airlines, Marriott, and American Express.

Action 10: Set Realistic Time Expectations

The process of adopting and institutionalizing TQM, like all organizational change processes, takes time under the best of circumstances, most likely three to five years. It is likely to take longer in a large, complex organization like a teaching hospital. People will have to start with realistic estimates of the time required. Two types of time are required—hours of input by already busy managers and professionals, and calendar time required to implement the program. The latter is illustrated even in the case of a very tightly controlled organization such as Xerox, where new issues concerning TQM institutionalization continue to surface five years after the initial implementation. For example, employee evaluation systems were not changed to include management commitment and role modeling for TQM, and college employment recruiters were not using TQM-related selection criteria until shortly before the firm received the Malcolm Baldridge Prize in 1989 in recognition of its successful implementation of TQM.

Action 11: Make the TQM Program Itself a Model for Continuous Improvement

The cases cited above highlight possibilities for using the TQM program to model a continuous improvement orientation for the total organization. Those who are responsible for program oversight must consciously challenge the TQM staff to suggest improvements in the program and respond rapidly and effectively. Other professionals will be especially sensitive to any gaps between what is preached and what is practiced by those associated with this program. They have already seen many programs come and go in recent years, and they must be convinced that management is serious about TQM. Here actions will truly speak louder than words.

Health service organizations are facing new challenges, challenges that require a new look at how and why resources are organized and managed. The expectations are high for TQM. A recent survey by Peat, Marwick, Main & Co. (1988) of Chicago reports that 69 percent of institutional providers and 78 percent of physicians, purchasers, and third-party payers believe that the cost of poor quality is so great that quality improvement should pay for itself. Industrial organizations have reduced their operating expenses by 20 percent to 40 percent. If health care organizations can do half as well, quality improvement programs will have a major impact on the field.

CONCLUSIONS

TQM represents an approach with a great deal of potential, yet it presents some basic conflicts with underlying norms and expectations that guide professional bureaucracies. Although the conflict exists, the problems are not intractable and, if recognized, represent opportunities not only to improve quality of care but also to improve the systems designed to provide quality care.

Arnold D. Kaluzny
Curtis P. McLaughlin

11

Managing Transitions: Assuring the Adoption and Impact of TQM

Total quality management (TQM) presents new challenges to health care managers. Often seen as a panacea to many of the problems facing health service organizations, TQM nevertheless presents a number of contradictions:

- TQM is a participatory, decentralized approach to quality and productivity improvement—yet it must be managed from the top, intensively and in detail.

- TQM as a managerial innovation is a paradigm shift that affects the whole organization, with the greatest payoffs derived in rationalizing multidisciplinary and interdisciplinary systems—yet it is most easily adopted one work unit at a time.

- TQM requires an environment of low threat and implied job security and takes time to implement and institutionalize—yet health care organizations are under siege by the realities of the marketplace, operating under severe time constraints to contain costs and improve quality.

- TQM depends on the strength of apparent outcomes—yet the strength of outcomes is likely to depend on the extent of adoption.

How well managers accommodate these contradictions and, more importantly, manage their effects will ultimately determine whether TQM is truly adopted and integrated into the ongoing activities of the organization and whether it improves performance. This chapter presents some of the challenges managers face as they accommodate and manage these contradictions during the adoption process, especially those that involve the interaction of individuals, work groups, and the organization as a whole.

Source: Copyright 1992 by the Joint Commission on Accreditation of Healthcare Organizations, Oakbrook Terrace, Illinois. Adapted with permission from the November 1992 *Quality Review Bulletin.*

TQM AS A MANAGERIAL INNOVATION

TQM represents a "new order of things" in the provision of health care. It involves continuous improvement in the processes that deliver care and uses interdisciplinary teams to rigorously analyze processes, to apply statistical methods to ongoing activities, and to reduce unnecessary variance in delivery activities by application of scientific methods and psychosocial principles. With adoption of TQM, the institutional emphasis on quality changes from after-the-fact inspection and outlier identification (quality assurance) to process variance reduction (continuous improvement).

The adoption of TQM in health care organizations will deeply affect the objectives, policies, and procedures of those organizations. In essence, TQM is a management innovation that represents a significant departure from the status quo and affects the nature, location, quality, and quantity of information available in the decision-making process.

ORGANIZATIONAL COMPLEXITY AND TQM

The adoption and impact of TQM require a fundamental understanding of the complexity of health care organizations. Health care organizations are not unitary entities but multistructures; they represent an amalgamation of individuals, work groups, and various coalitions of professionals, especially physicians, who enjoy considerable autonomy yet have great influence on activities occurring within the organization. Moreover, the total of these individuals, work groups, and coalitions is greater than the sum of its parts. The organization itself represents an entity that functions within a larger environment that greatly influences the adoption and impact of TQM.

TQM requires a locus of change within the organization. Particular attention must be given to various work groups and to the differential effect of TQM among these groups. The shift from intermittent to continuous improvement calls for changes in the way group activities are conducted within the organization; however, the adoption and impact will vary depending on the tasks and character of the work group. For example, TQM requires that work groups solve problems using statistical and behavioral approaches, with considerable emphasis on customer perceptions of quality. Yet health care providers, and particularly physicians, who are experts in only one segment of the total care process, do not always accept with equanimity the perceptions of other professionals. Consider the tension generated when a pharmacist identifies a potential drug interaction as the result of a new prescription written by an attending physician. And how often have physicians asked nurses, "How may we help you do your job better?" Moreover, the very nature of the work group's task can greatly influence the reaction to TQM. For example, personnel working in psychiatric care may find it difficult to see their patients—whom they assess as fundamentally impaired—as competent judges of quality, and may fear that their own professionalism could be inappropriately influenced by such a "customer" evaluation.

Furthermore, the role of work groups within the larger organization is demonstrated by the varying degrees of compliance and adoption among these groups. Even with strong top-down management, individual groups exhibit considerable variation in their rate of TQM adoption. The conventional wisdom is that the chief executive officer (CEO) must lead the process and that all units within the organization will follow. Yet as Beer et al. (1990) point out, effective change may also occur one work unit at a time. Thus, among work groups, there may be considerable variance in the level at which and manner in which adoption occurs. Some units may choose to become involved early in the transformation, and others may choose not to participate. A number of factors may contribute to this variation. For example, the leadership style of some managers may predispose them to TQM. Moreover, the relevant unit may not even exist since the formation of work groups are a function of, first, a fundamental understanding of the process, and, second, an integrating of the members' expertise to resolve the problem. For example, improving a hospital discharge process would require at the minimum a work group composed of representatives from nursing, housekeeping, finance, and transportation: a work unit that neither exists nor is easily convened in most hospitals.

TRANSITIONAL CHALLENGES

A fundamental understanding of organizational complexity is necessary for implementation of TQM, but it is not sufficient to assure adoption and impact. Equally important is the recognition that the process of adoption faces significant challenges at various stages that involve units of the organization and the organization as a whole, particularly design issues related to a number of transitions that management must make.

Although researchers do not agree on the number of stages involved in the process, they generally agree that TQM adoption requires multiple decisions and actions over time involving various individuals and work units within the organization. Figure 11-1 presents the basic process: awareness of a problem, identification of a solution, decision, and institutionalization and impact. Institutionalization and impact—the two end points—are highly interdependent. Impact is the difference that TQM makes in organizational or work group performance; institutionalization is the extent to which TQM is integrated into ongoing activities of the organization. Impact cannot occur without institutionalization, and institutionalization is unlikely to take place without some observed positive impact. The following are the stages of the adoption process, along with specific transition challenges that management faces during each stage.

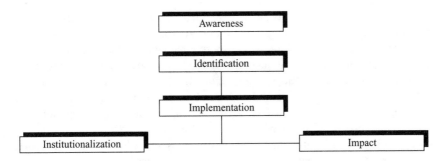

Figure 11–1 Basic Process of Adopting Total Quality Management

Awareness

Awareness is the first stage in the process of adoption of TQM, and includes three transitional challenges. As presented in Figure 11–2, the first is the identification of a performance gap: the organization moves from acceptance of the status quo to a recognition that there is a discrepancy between how the organization is currently performing and how it could or should perform. This awareness may be sparked internally by the expectations of employees or externally by community or regulatory pressures. For example, a hospital may launch a study of its postmyocardial infarction work-up procedures to reduce the length of stay because of similar actions by a competing facility.

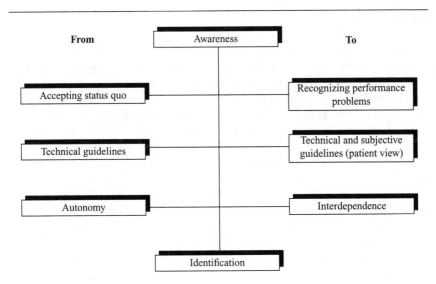

Figure 11–2 Transitional Challenges Presented by the Awareness Stage of the Process of Adopting TQM

A second challenge occurs when management realizes that the existing definition of quality is no longer appropriate nor adequate. The transition involves a shift from a technical definition of quality to a recognition that effective care requires a subjective as well as technical evaluation. Specifically, a definition of health care quality is inadequate if it does not include the customer. Comparisons of health care quality by citizens' groups or by professionals using more than one institution may trigger dissatisfaction at the hospital work unit level. An ophthalmic surgeon, for example, who has used a free-standing "surgicenter" may inform hospital administration that future cataract cases will be treated at the center rather than at the hospital because at the surgicenter patients receive greater attention, are never rescheduled, and seem (with their families) to be much more relaxed there, where the staff are more concerned and cooperative than in the hospital operating room. Such a comparison may cause hospital operating room staff to survey its other surgeons and find that they are similarly disaffected, thereby confirming a performance problem.

A third challenge involves the transition from an emphasis on the autonomy of the provider to the recognition of interdependence of all personnel involved in providing quality of care. Thus it is no longer appropriate to artificially partition issues of cost and quality, relegating cost to management and quality to quality assurance (QA) professionals. Instead, clinical care must be seen as a network of professionals, information systems, policies and procedures, and physical systems (Berwick, 1990).

Identification

The second stage of the adoption process is the recognition that TQM is the appropriate solution to the performance problem. This awareness may come through passive activities such as quality seminars or more painful realizations such as the superior performance of competing institutions. Several transition challenges are presented in Figure 11–3. Take, for example, the transition from strong managerial leadership to employee initiatives within the organization. Although employees within departments have the expertise, information, and interpersonal contacts with patients and families with which to assess perceived quality, management has the symbolic function of legitimizing this search and facilitating the adoption process. For example, at one large teaching hospital it sometimes took hours to move a discharged ambulatory patient from the fifth floor to the front door. When a group of nurses and middle management personnel at this hospital were asked to analyze this problem, they easily outlined the steps necessary to speed up the process. When asked, "If you know what to do, why don't you do something about it?" they replied, "Management hasn't asked us!" Management must ask, and personnel have to be made aware that they are sufficiently empowered to respond to the challenge.

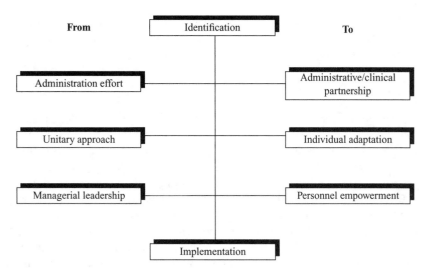

Figure 11–3 Transitional Challenges Presented by the Identification Stage of the Process of Adopting TQM

A second transition involves the development and adaptation of a guiding philosophy. TQM is more than a program of activities; it is a philosophical perspective about how organizations function. Many organizations initially adopt a unitary approach to TQM and subsequently allow the organization to develop its own version, one that meets the social and cognitive needs of its personnel. For example, hospitals at the onset may use an existing industrial philosophy developed by Deming ("top down"), Juran ("fitness for use"), or Crosby (emphasizing the cost of poor quality). Other health care organizations have adapted the quality program of a local industry, using a major local employer as a source of legitimacy and expertise. In either case, the transitional challenge is to adapt the approach to the organization and its employees. Moreover, management must give different work unit supervisors ownership of the initiative. For example, two Hospital Corporation of America hospitals, both equally successful in implementing TQM, had completely different approaches to the use of storyboards. One hospital used storyboards extensively, and staff at the other hospital allowed supervisors to develop their own individual approaches.

It is critical at this stage to include board members and physicians in the process. The question is not if but when to include them. Clearly, the factors of competition and the payers' concern about cost and clinical quality mean that clinical issues must ultimately be a focus of the TQM initiative. The transition challenge comes when TQM moves from being solely an administrative activity to one that involves administrative and clinical quality issues. Experience suggests that the process is highly idiosyncratic and that it involves a continuous transition depending upon the readiness of various groups. Most likely, the transition begins with focusing predominantly on administrative activities and moves incrementally to clinical issues.

Implementation

Implementation refers to the presence of TQM activity within the organization or among relevant groups within the organization. Institutionalization and impact occurs, however, when these activities are truly integrated into the operations of the organization and substantively affect performance. During institutionalization, employees at all levels use certain key words and, most importantly, are comfortable with the underlying concepts. Problems are described in terms of contributing factors, and attention is given to the concept of and measurement of variance. Various work units interact easily and frequently, and run charts and storyboards are visible throughout the organization. Employees gather and use data to solve problems, rather than blaming others for their problems, and this is reflected in improved performance.

As presented in Figure 11–4, the transitional challenges here focus on assuring institutionalization and impact within the organization. A critical challenge is the transition from a voluntary, participatory, problem-oriented initial phase to one that focuses on major opportunities for change, requiring greater probabilities for conflict, and that is driven by external competitive forces, requiring a sense of

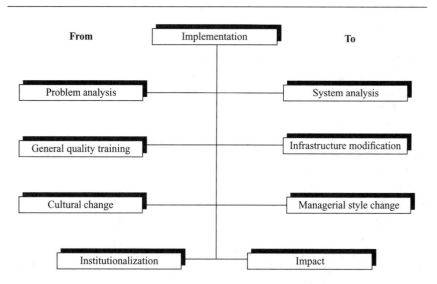

Figure 11–4 Transitional Challenges Presented by the Implementation Stage of the Process of Adopting TQM. These challenges, if met successfully, lead to institutionalization and impact throughout the organization.

competitive urgency. Employees must shift from targets of interest such as scheduling problems or equipment shortages to a systematic assessment of the key success factors that will ensure organizational survival. That transition, however, must evolve over time. For example, although significant payoffs in health care quality could be achieved through multidisciplinary efforts that focus on the total system delivering care to the patient, with special attention on integrating the work of various components involved in the overall system, any attempt to deal with a problem of this size and scope would clearly overwhelm even the most enthusiastic group attempting to apply TQM. Experience suggests that it is easier to implement TQM within a more limited work group and then methodically expand it to systemwide problems. Initiating activity involving teams from multiple units leads to the risk of one or more team members' being threatened by the assertiveness or sophistication of others, thereby threatening the entire approach. Management must thus be prepared to guide the transitions from a focus on work units to a focus on more complex multidisciplinary issues as employees gain confidence and experience.

Another critical transition is training and mentoring to ensure the growth and development of work groups. This requires that a series of compromises be made to facilitate training and confidence building. The challenge is to modify the training program to meet the needs of various groups as they move through the adoption process. Management must ensure that work groups and various ad hoc groups are receiving the necessary skills and receiving "just-in-time" support to improve overall group effectiveness. For example, if months elapse between the time a group's members learn about control charts and the time they first try to use them, they will probably need reorientation when a control chart is needed. Training is not a single task but a process to be managed throughout the adoption process.

A final challenge involves a transition in the infrastructure of the organization as well as in cognitive structure at the level of top management. Given the complexity of TQM, as well as that of the adopting organization, other changes occur in administrative systems, many of them subtle, with profound consequences for both the process and the ultimate impact of TQM adoption. Perhaps most critical is the recruitment, selection, and hiring of employees since it is through this process that the long-term institutionalization of TQM can be assured. Current employees may be reluctant to change and may have to be replaced. Experience from industry suggests that participatory programs of all types are generally accepted well by workers, but that there is significant voluntary and involuntary turnover among first-line supervisors, often exceeding 50 percent.

Other infrastructure challenges include modifications in job descriptions, reward systems, and existing performance appraisal systems. Moreover, information systems must be modified not only to focus on vertical reporting relationships, but also to get information to move laterally among groups within the organization. The role of existing QA personnel will also have to be redefined.

Health care organizations are experimenting with alternative approaches, with some hospitals retaining QA as an independent activity that adopts TQM to deal with clinical issues. Other organizations have merged QA into a larger quality management function. Finally, institutionalization and impact cannot be successful unless top management realizes that what is required is not the simple manipulation of a cultural change within the organization, but a fundamental change in management style. Specifically, managers must "walk the talk"; that is, they must change the way they use facts, delegate decisions, respond to recommendations, and view people. Consultants report that it is at this juncture that managers either provide true leadership or simply become part of the problem. This realization will facilitate the institutionalization of TQM and prevent the "solution of the month" syndrome that has characterized so much of management in general and health services management in particular.

CONCLUSION

As health care organizations confront increasing competition and tighter cost-containment measures, issues of TQM adoption and impact become more than an academic exercise. The ability of TQM to reduce cost and enhance quality requires that management recognizes a need for, plans for, and negotiates the transitions that must be made to take into account the complexity of health service organizations. Only when this occurs is it possible to assure the adoption and impact of TQM.

Arnold D. Kaluzny
Curtis P. McLaughlin
David C. Kibbe

Involving Clinicians: The Challenge of CQI

12

Although continuous quality improvement (CQI) may be sweeping the country, critics and supporters alike frequently express concern about what they consider a critical test: will physicians participate? They report using a number of strategies with respect to clinical activities, including

- Seduction: Phased implementation focusing only on administrative and support activities, in the hope that physicians will be enticed by intellectual curiosity.
- Procrastination: Phased implementation involving all units of the organization on a schedule, usually with an outside consulting firm providing initial leadership training, including the board and senior medical staff, but leaving clinical activities until late in the process.
- Grafting: Adding CQI activities to existing quality assurance (QA) activities.
- Benign neglect: Advocates or "champions" for CQI, including physicians, within the organization develop CQI projects clandestinely or without formal management approval or support.

Physician reactions have ranged from resistance to tolerance to acceptance and support, and, in a few cases, to leadership and advocacy. Many factors influence the effectiveness of each approach, including the prevailing attitudes of physicians; the skill, commitment, and sensitivity of administrative personnel; and a range of environmental and competitive factors in the organization's community. Critical, yet often overlooked, is the fundamental character of the professional community: its structure, its relationship to the larger organizational setting, and the processes by which change and adoption occur within the organization and

Source: Based on Kaluzny, A.D., McLaughlin, C.P., and Kibbe, D.C., Continuous Quality Improvement in the Clinical Setting: Enhancing Adoption, *Quality Management in Health Care*, Vol. 1, No. 1, pp. 37–44, Aspen Publishers, Inc., © 1992.

within the profession itself. This chapter examines the influence of these organizational and professional factors on the adoption of CQI activities and suggests directions for designing and implementing more effective adoption strategies.

THE CHANGING CHARACTER OF MEDICAL PRACTICE

Medicine, together with the ministry and the law, has long been considered the prototype of "a profession." Medicine fits the following accepted criteria for a profession:

- a systematic body of theory that is socially valuable
- a professional authority recognized by the client
- the sanction of the community and support for that authority
- a regulative code of ethics
- a professional culture with values, norms, and symbols

Medicine, however, is not practiced in a vacuum. It is part of a complex network of organizational arrangements that influence physician behavior and increasingly challenge the status of the profession. These challenges have taken on significant proportions. For example, professional autonomy is challenged by the expanding presence of managed care, and the very knowledge base and standards heretofore unchallenged are increasingly being questioned by evidence of untested medical theory and inappropriate application.

Such challenges have made physicians cautious if not suspicious of governmental and managerial initiatives. QA requirements, whether payer or management initiated, are often seen as regulatory and legal intrusions that threaten physician autonomy and control. Many physicians view these efforts primarily as cost-containment strategies that do not address the substantive issue of quality. In any case, these efforts clearly do not take into account the complexity of medical practice. CQI is construed as just another round in the continuing struggle to maintain the autonomy and control over the workplace. As described by one clinician (Jaffe, 1992), "What will they think of next?"

OTHER BARRIERS

Autonomy, heavy time commitments, and a perceived threat toward and need to protect one's professional identity are other barriers to be considered. One type of barrier is fear of failure at using the CQI process or of the possible exposure of professional failures. Some other barriers may be perceptual, such as not seeing the applicability of the CQI process to health care or finding the structure and discipline of CQI too constraining, especially in that it limits physicians' use of intuitive solutions that appear to save time and energy. Others who are by nature given to the intuitive reasoning process may find the CQI approach too linear and reductionist for their comfort. This often manifests itself in complaints like "Well! We got to a solution, but we could have done it in half the time, if we had just listened to _____."

Individuals need to make transitions at various points in the adoption process (see Chapter 9) such as recognizing a performance gap or acknowledging the interdependency of the clinical process rather than focusing on its individuality. Failure to comprehend one of these key transitions, like accepting the customer's point of view as legitimate data, can become a barrier to clinician involvement, even though there have been signs and actions implying initial acceptance.

Another barrier is that clinicians are reluctant to get involved with CQI because they do not feel prepared to participate in the process. For example,

- Their concepts of team roles (always being in charge) conflict with the proposed team process.

- They may fear the uncertainty of the process, including statistical thinking and the less structured process of CQI as compared to grand rounds and randomized clinical trials.

- They may resent the learning and student role required by CQI, feeling that their student role ended with their boards and the few hours a year devoted to continuing education activity under relatively unthreatening and unchallenging conditions.

- They may see the CQI process as requiring an unwelcome change in their decision-making styles because of its emphasis on blame-free analysis, setting up win-win situations, and analyzing causes and effects one at a time, as opposed to jumping into large-scale actions.

The organizations composed mostly of "smart people" may encounter the greatest challenge (Argyris, 1991). Such individuals may (1) define situations too narrowly as mere "problem solving" focused on the external environment, and (2) fail to reflect critically on their own processes, on how they might have contributed inadvertently to the problems or failed to define the problem properly. One of the ironies cited is that highly successful people have little experience with failure, giving them little understanding of how to learn from it. Consequently, smart people tend to become defensive, to blame others and not themselves, and not to reflect on or critique the thought processes that guide their performance. Professionals embody a learning dilemma, often being enthusiastic about CQI but often being the biggest obstacle to its success. Questioning of the reasoning process has to start at the top, with senior managers analyzing their own defensiveness, and then proceed to establishing a culture in which questioning each other's reasoning is seen not as a sign of mistrust but as a valuable opportunity for learning how to learn.

Perceived political barriers may also be a problem. At academic medical centers CQI leadership seems to emerge among the hard-charging elite in their late thirties and early forties. If, however, the formal leadership, who are somewhat older, fail to exhibit the same enthusiasm, other faculty and staff may attribute some disapproval and fear the political consequences. If some groups of clinicians see CQI as a challenge to their autonomy and technical knowledge base, not so subtle messages about "whose side are you on" or other evidence of we/they thinking can chill the enthusiasm of some. This is especially true if some people believe that the impact will be felt through the referral network and that others who do not participate enthusiastically in CQI will be more likely to get cases.

Despite these challenges, the fundamental role of the clinician remains the same. In medicine, supervision and control are carried out by those who perform the work. Although the importance of administrative personnel has obviously increased, it is unlikely that administration will gain legitimate authority to formulate standards and supervise and control the provision of care.

FORCES FAVORING PARTICIPATION IN CQI

Given the changing character of medical practice, the ability to assure physician participation in continuous quality improvement activities must be based on (1) a fundamental understanding of how the quality of professional work is controlled in professional organizations, (2) an understanding of how the larger organizational structure and process function vis-à-vis the structure and operations of the profession itself, and (3) an understanding of how organizational innovations such as CQI initiatives are adopted by professional organizations, especially physicians, over time.

Understanding Professional Practice

From afar the medical profession appears to be a homogenous group that shares a sense of identity, values, definition of roles, and interests. Although there is obvious variation, individuals interested in affecting physician behavior are often overwhelmed by the mechanics of cohesiveness and the image of solidarity. In reality, the practicing profession is a loose amalgamation of specialty groups, each pursuing different and sometimes conflicting objectives, that is delicately held together under a common name at a particular point in time. Different groups of clinicians, including groups within the same organization, can have a different sense of mission and different work activity, methods, techniques, and clientele—all of which can have profound implications for the ultimate adoption of CQI activities.

No single mechanism or set of rules can account for the complexity of clinical work. The search for and exchange of information and decision making in a clinical setting are much more idiosyncratic than one would first assume. Much of what goes on in daily practice is unobserved and not easily controlled or managed by hierarchical structure or even collegial processes. Moreover, the process works slowly in that information about individual clinicians is a function of the information system. Even when available, any effort to intervene requires that clinicians be responsible to professional norms except in the most grievous errors. As described by Freidson,

> The system is quite helpless in the face of a man who did not depend upon the esteem and trust of his colleagues and who did not respond to the symbolic values of professionalism. Confronted by a man who is not so incompetent or unethical as to be grossly and obviously dismissable and who fails to show any respect for his colleagues' opinions, the administration and the colleague group are helpless. He cannot be flattered, shamed, or insulated and so cannot be persuaded to mend his ways or resign: all that can be done is to seal him off and try to minimize whatever damage he is believed to do. (Freidson, 1972, p. 53)

Physicians practice in a dynamic environment where events often seem more temporally than logically related, and they experience a scarcity of time and psychic energy. Problems are in search of solutions, and people with solutions are searching for problems. People move in and out of the decision-making process almost at random. What may be top priority at one point in time may be quickly and temporarily replaced by another top priority a day or two later, making it difficult to sustain a course of action.

One factor favoring physician participation is a fundamental value favoring quality of care. Although the cynics might equate the use of the word *quality* as a code word for money, clinicians talk about and defend staunchly the need for quality care. Physicians also care about patient outcomes. Therefore an effort to improve patient outcomes, especially with the threat of the reporting of negative outcomes, clearly is in the clinicians' best interest as well as the patients'. Improvement of outcomes should be a major selling point of any CQI program involving professionals. As outcome indicators become a part of the Joint Commission on Accreditation of Healthcare Organizations accreditation process by the mid-1990s, they will be a powerful weapon in getting clinicians interested in continuous improvement.

Organizational Structure and Processes Affecting Practice

Understanding the mechanisms and diversity of control within the profession is a necessary but not sufficient condition for developing successful adoption strategies. Equally important is an understanding of the ongoing activities within which the clinician functions, particularly given the ascendence of larger organizations in the delivery of health services.

Just as clinicians project an image of homogeneity, health organizations project an image of coordination and integration and the pursuit of a common set of goals. In reality, these organizations (e.g., hospitals and health maintenance organizations [HMOs]) are perhaps better characterized by "organized anarchy." They are characterized by a number of fundamental ambiguities pervading all segments of the organization and greatly influencing their management. Ambiguities include serious questions about organizational goals, the allocation of power within the organization, and, perhaps most importantly, how to assess success. These ambiguities present a number of managerial challenges. For example, most issues most of the time for most people have low salience. There are high levels of inertia, weak information systems, and decision outcomes that are often separate from the ongoing processes, partly because these processes of choice and the information systems that support them are easily subject to overload.

Moreover, the very ambiguity pervasive within the organization and the resulting challenges enhance confusion about who is responsible for what process. Although hospital-based physicians such as pathologists and radiologists tend to get involved in clinical CQI activities, there often is considerable confusion among clinicians and administrators as to who will assume the leadership role. Administrators are reluctant to provide leadership, given the technical nature of clinical decision making. Clinicians, though willing to participate, will do so only if the administration provides the leadership.

Adoption As An Organizational Process

The introduction and effective use of CQI within a clinical setting represent a substantive organizational innovation. Although many of the techniques that characterize approaches such as CQI are not new in absolute terms, their application within health service organizations is new, and use in a clinical setting is rare. The challenge is developing a means to ensure a more systematic way of introducing these procedures and activities. As described by Greer, "There are no magic signatories or formats which will cause knowledge to jump off the page and into practice" (1988, p. 23).

Although there may be no magic signatories or formats, there is general agreement that adoption involves an interactive process having multiple decision points (Figure 12–1). Moreover, any adoption strategy must be appropriate to each stage of that process. Most models begin with a recognition stage, followed by identification, implementation, and finally institutionalization. Specifically, for organizations and personnel within the organization to adopt a new activity, they must first *recognize* that the organization is not fully meeting expectations. *Identification* implies that key decision makers have recognized a problem and have

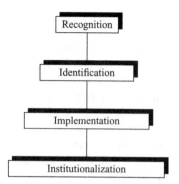

Figure 12–1 Decision Points for Adopting Innovations

begun searching for a solution. *Implementation* involves the very presence of CQI activity within relevant clinical groups within the organization. The final stage, *institutionalization*, occurs when these CQI activities are truly integrated into the operations of the organization and substantively affect performance. Personnel at all levels, particularly clinicians, are using the terminology and tools, and most importantly, are comfortable with the underlying concepts.

The process of adoption therefore involves moving from recognition to identification, from identification to implementation, and from implementation to institutionalization. The management of that process involves a number of challenges based on the unique characteristics of professional practice and the organizational context within which that practice occurs.

Recognition and the Physician

The first step in the adoption process is the recognition among clinicians that there is a discrepancy or gap between what the organization is currently doing and what it should, could, or must do. Recognition must take place without alienating physicians and assaulting the legitimacy of the professional knowledge base and standards. Recognition can be achieved in several ways:

- Select initial problems that have already been identified by a group of physicians as problems or as opportunity areas.
- Survey physicians about areas needing improvement and use their responses as the justification for selecting the topic.
- Support clinicians who are well respected and who believe that things should be better.
- Offer educational programs that challenge physicians to think about what might be done better, including data about benchmark studies and service improvements at other institutions.

Recognizing performance problems is only one challenge in the process of moving from recognition to identification. Others include recognition that outcomes are not just technical but are a combination of technical performance and patient or client perceptions about the quality of their experiences, and recognition that although autonomy is important, the physician's clinical success is often dependent on processes that he or she does not control directly. Developing awareness of these issues is important to identifying CQI as an approach to improving clinical processes. Data from patient and personnel surveys provide an opportunity for clinicians to incorporate these factors into their decision-making process.

Awareness of the need for change is unlikely to take place in the medical staff as a whole at any one time. Because the medical staff is an amalgamation, the recognition of problems will vary by specialty groups. For example, surgeons and obstetrician-gynecologists might be dissatisfied with the timeliness of the anesthesiology services, something of little interest to internists and family practitioners. This allows and requires customization of the approach to physicians, but makes it possible to involve the medical staff a few individuals at a time.

This recommendation should not imply that one should not try to reach as many clinicians as possible as early as possible. Strong administrative and professional support from the beginning is likely to have a strong favorable effect on the rate at which individuals listen to and ultimately adopt the CQI philosophy. The elites that guide the professionals should be showing their support early and often.

Identification and the Physician

Once physicians have recognized a problem, the challenge is to link CQI to the resolution of the problem. Key physicians and administrators need to gather and evaluate information from other institutions likely to have similar problems. The more the organization knows about activities elsewhere, the more likely linkage will occur.

A critical transition at this stage of adoption is to adapt approaches used in other settings to the unique challenges recognized by the physician. Specifically identifying CQI as a possible resolution to recognized problems provides an opportunity to understand clinical work as "a process and system," an opportunity for curious physicians to think differently about their daily work.

Effective communication between administration and physicians will be likely to facilitate the linkage. Communication should emphasize potential uses of CQI for solving priority problems for physicians and their patients, thereby increasing the effectiveness of clinical practice. This can be encouraged by several strategies (see the box entitled "Strategies to Link CQI with Problem Solving"). These strategies include:

- presenting CQI as similar to a paradigm with which physicians are already familiar, such as epidemiology, preventive medicine, or systems analysis

- presenting numerous examples of how physicians at similar institutions have resolved problems through CQI
- illustrating how other physicians have enhanced the productivity or volume (or both) of their clinical practices by adapting to patient perceptions and by securing the cooperation of nursing and ancillary or support departments through participation in such efforts
- indicating how participation on CQI teams can provide access to decision-making areas that are not normally open to physicians (e.g., nursing staffing decisions)

Strategies to Link CQI with Problem Solving

- Present CQI as a familiar paradigm
- Give numerous examples
- Illustrate positive impacts on clinical practice
- Emphasize increased decision-making potential

Implementation and the Physician

Implementation involves the actual use of CQI by physicians and involves a number of challenges. They include (1) moving from a solely administrative initiative to a partnership between management and clinicians; (2) moving from a unitary, organizationwide, lock-step approach to an approach adapted to individuals and units; and (3) moving from a management-driven program to a program in which administrative and clinical personnel feel empowered to act.

Capitalizing on the variability among clinicians and clinical specialties provides an opportunity to collaborate with those groups that are more receptive to the fundamentals of CQI and postpone collaboration with the others. Early involvement with such physicians can help with the challenges of an administrative-clinician partnership and can help physicians feel empowered to act. There is no need to implement CQI with a uniform lock-step approach in the clinical area. Given the fundamental characteristics of various specialty groups in terms of values, interests, and role definitions, each has a different level of receptivity that needs to be acknowledged and taken into account in the adoption strategy.

Moreover, even within groups, there is likely to be considerable variance among individual clinicians in terms of their attitudes, both positive and negative, and their differential power base within the organization. Thus one of the critical challenges is to create working alliances within these groups, thereby enhancing the ability to integrate CQI within ongoing work processes.

One approach, called *stakeholder mapping* (Gilmore, 1967), attempts to provide a systematic assessment of the variance among clinicians as stakeholders. The process involves three key steps: (1) identifying relevant stakeholders (i.e., clinicians who are affected or may be affected by CQI); (2) ranking each stakeholder or clinician based on attitudes toward CQI, favorable or opposed; and (3) assessing each stakeholder's power within the organization to shape and affect its ultimate utilization. With this information, relevant clinicians are identified and strategies are developed appropriate to each one. Those clinicians who are found to be in favor and clearly in a strong position within the organization should be mobilized to ensure support of this endeavor. It is critical that they be kept informed continuously of developments and planned activities in order to facilitate support of the activity.

Those individuals who are found to favor the CQI approach but are in a weak position within the power structure can be empowered and thereby given an opportunity to influence events relative to the development of CQI studies. For example, physicians favoring the activity but marginal to decision making can be appointed to various advisory panels to ongoing activities in the organization.

Individuals who oppose the idea but are weak may be co-opted into a larger ongoing effort. More difficult, however, are those stakeholders who oppose and are in a strong position within the organization. Gilmore suggests "reframing" or redefining the issue so that they may see it in a different light. If someone is opposed to CQI, one can frame it as a research process consistent with the larger goals of the organization. For example, Strong Memorial Hospital, a teaching and research institution in Rochester, New York, has framed its CQI program in terms of research on clinical processes. In each such case, the challenge to CQI is to translate the methodology and the approach into terms that are relevant to clinicians and clearly demonstrate its effectiveness by solving problems important to these individuals.

Another strategy is to acknowledge the ambiguity involved in management processes and to devise strategies that capitalize on the fact that much of what goes on in organizations involves an almost random process of solutions looking for problems, problems looking for solutions, and individuals involved in both processes looking for each other. For example, at a major medical school the administration of the teaching hospital is trying to adopt CQI as part of a formalized systematic sequence of planned activities. At the same time various clinicians throughout the facility are already involved with improvement efforts independent of the formalized effort. The hospital CQI effort is very likely to fail if administration limits itself to a formalized sequence of planned activities. Management may be better served if it applies available resources to a set of "small wins" and capitalizes on the emergent interest and activities. On the other hand, any evidence of senior professional involvement and support may help. For example, an invitation to participate in training or teams signed by the chief of staff or the chair can dispel any political uncertainties about support from the professional hierarchy.

The strategy of small wins (Weick, 1984) emphasizes concrete, quickly implementable interventions of moderate importance. Such an approach, when complete, can provide building blocks and visible accomplishments that will serve as a model and a source of encouragement to others who try to implement the approach. The ability to accomplish small wins gives visibility to the CQI innovation, thereby providing an opportunity to attract the attention of people who have short time perspectives or information overload. A good example is the focus in many hospitals on improving operating room turnaround. Physicians often complain about the lack of operating room capacity, yet the causes for lost capacity are easily identified and resolved compared to many other systems problems in a hospital. Surgeons, for example, are likely to respond to positive results in this area. Assured initial wins make it possible for the staff to gain the satisfaction of real progress early. The small wins approach provides hope to supporters, attracts new allies from among the clinicians, lowers resistance to future steps, and changes the framework within which clinicians experience the activity.

Because the lack of and the value of time are important to clinicians, any effort to involve clinicians must take time into account. For example, training for physicians must be available when they are available. It should be scheduled in short blocks, not in multiday seminars, and perhaps offered on weekends to some of the medical staff. The training should be condensed, emphasize reading matter as a component, and be concrete and fast paced. It can also be blended into existing staff activities such as annual retreats, reducing the incremental time investment and at the same time making it clear that this is part of the current way of doing things.

The timing of meetings must fit the time values of the professionals involved. If one wants to involve surgeons, one does not schedule meetings in the early or mid-morning when the bulk of the staff would be losing premium value operating room time. In the Neumann Hospital program described in Part V of this book, meetings for staff were held on weekends so as to minimize interference with normal work schedules.

The top management can also emphasize the value of time spent in these activities. One can point to the example of what happened when clinicians ignored the QA process in past years. A strong argument is that participation empowers the clinicians and pre-empts the likelihood that other interested parties will take over the process to the detriment of the clinicians. Although there may be a short-run loss of income, the failure to participate could lead to drastic income shifts in the future.

Similarly, flexibility is critical when involving physicians in team and group activity. For teams improving administrative processes such as admissions and discharge planning, a physician can serve as a consultant rather than stay with the team process. Management may also create miniteams within the ongoing larger teams. The miniteams can assess aspects of the process of particular interest to physicians over a shorter period, thus maintaining the interest of participating physicians. If a clinician misses a session or arrives late, the group does not have to sanction that individual, but can be appreciative of the effort. However, the key is not to hold back the process waiting for a clinician who may or may not arrive.

Other strategies to facilitate implementation are presented in the box entitled "Strategies to Facilitate Implementation." These include

- inviting interested physicians to lead improvement teams that assess clinical processes
- integrating CQI into all administrative processes of the institution that have a clinical component, such as QA and tissue committees
- providing substantial facilitator support to clinical teams because physicians have less experience with group processes and participative approaches
- assigning support personnel to do data gathering, data analysis, flow chart specification, and other tasks that might otherwise fall on clinicians directly, allowing them to review the data rather than spending time collecting it
- providing high visibility to project results, especially those of interest to clinicians
- empowering those who support continuous quality improvement

---

Strategies to Facilitate Implementation
- Physicians as team leaders
- CQI integrated into administrative processes
- Facilitator support to clinical teams
- Empowerment of supportive individuals

Institutionalization and the Physician

The final stage of the adoption process is the integration of CQI into the ongoing activities of clinical practice. This stage involves a number of challenges, including moving from problem-based analyses to system-based analyses and moving from general quality training toward fundamental modifications of the hospital's infrastructure (i.e., personnel and clinician evaluations, rewards, personnel selection, personnel evaluation, information systems, and basic organizational structure).

The initial emphasis on activities that will attract individuals to participate on improvement teams at some point becomes a conscious effort to deal with opportunities for change that are of high potential, but not necessarily problems. Processes may be working well, but there is always the potential for improvement, or processes may be part of large systems where no one has ownership or has been empowered to improve. It is here that a collegial relationship among clinicians and administrators is critical in deciding what should be changed. This relationship can occur if both clinicians and managers have come to understand the impacts of unnecessary variation on cost and outcomes, so that process analysis is not seen as violation of professional autonomy.

Some organizations use direct *quid pro quo* benefits for clinicians that are involved. These are often controversial. For example, a chief of staff may tell a physician who has been complaining for several years about being on the tissue committee that he can get off by participating in this team that needs representation from his department. Some community hospitals even pay community physicians for the time that they spend in scheduled team activities. The rationale is that the nurses and other hospital salaried staff are being paid to be there but that the private physician is not and at the same time is losing money. Therefore a flat hourly fee is paid in recognition of that fact.

Finally, although infrastructure modifications can facilitate institutionalization, they are less likely to affect physicians directly because physicians usually are not subject to hiring, evaluation, and personnel systems of the institution. Clinicians, however, will encounter changes in the methods and procedures used in the hospital, and their concerns will have to be addressed in any modifications. Given physician interest and sensitivity to changes in QA, clinicians need to be involved in the total process of restructuring the organization. The ultimate structure of the CQI effort, however, will vary with the strategic perspective that management has toward quality improvement and the demands of a changing environment.

CONCLUSION

The design of strategies to increase the utilization and application of CQI to clinical issues requires understanding of the professional culture, of the organizational context within which the profession functions, and of the process by which adoption occurs. Based on this understanding, there are a number of guidelines that may help to increase and assure physician participation in CQI. These guidelines include the following:

- Involve clinicians in CQI in ways that do not imply that clinicians are providing poor quality care.
- Capitalize on the variability among clinicians and clinical specialists by initially collaborating with those groups that are most receptive to the philosophy of CQI; delay collaboration with others.
- Take special care to conserve the time of participating clinicians by involving them as consultants to improvement teams and by appointing them to miniteams that address segments of the process analysis and change but not necessarily the entire process.
- Assure that physician representatives are involved early in the CQI process so that individual physicians feel empowered to participate in the process within their time constraints.
- Use the early education process to "nurture the curious" by identifying physician champions and encouraging them to lead clinical teams.

- Maintain flexible implementation plans to allow improvement efforts to emerge spontaneously as physicians become advocates for the process.
- Diagnose the stage of adoption in specific units and groups and design appropriate change strategies for moving the group and relevant individuals to the next stage in the adoption process.
- Acknowledge the ambiguities involved and devise appropriate management strategies to capitalize on the fact that much of what goes on involves a random process of solutions looking for problems and problems looking for solutions among those who want to participate.
- Accept adaptation of the adoption process to meet the professional and personal needs of the clinicians and their work settings.
- Accept the fact that clinician involvement will be episodic, stimulus related, and hard to maintain at a consistent level. Respect clinicians' need to maintain professional autonomy without compromising the CQI initiative.

David C. Kibbe
Richard P. Scoville

Information Systems and Health Care CQI

13

As health care organizations advance from a few early successes with pilot projects to institutionwide continuous quality improvement (CQI), their leaders must anticipate the need for a strategy to manage the emerging data. This chapter is intended to help health care leaders visualize the role of personal computer technology in their CQI implementation strategy. The chapter discusses data management requirements for CQI and describes how recent advances in PC hardware and software make it possible to facilitate and enhance health care CQI projects with desktop computing at an affordable cost.

One of the major misconceptions about CQI is that it is complicated and requires sophisticated statistical software programs. In fact, a number of popular general purpose PC applications can meet the needs of most CQI teams. Here we review the commonly available software packages and offer advice on how to select the right software. Then we show how a single software platform, Microsoft Excel 4.0, can be used to meet a broad range of typical CQI team needs.

CENTRALIZED VERSUS DECENTRALIZED DATA MANAGEMENT

Data Management under QA and CQI

CQI challenges many of the assumptions held by both traditional quality assurance (QA) and health care information services (IS) bureaucracies regarding information and its uses. There are important differences between QA and CQI regarding the kind and scope of data to be collected, who collects them, and where

Source: Based on Kibbe, D.C., and Scoville, R.P., Computer Software for Health Care CQI, and Tutorial: Using Microsoft Excel for CQI, *Quality Management in Health Care*, Vol. 1, No. 4, pp. 50–58, and Vol. 2, No. 1, pp. 63–71, Aspen Publishers, Inc., © 1993.

they are used to make improvements in quality. Because of these differences, the shift from QA to CQI calls for an entirely new approach to the management of health care quality-related data.

In a typical hospital's clinical QA program, data flow in a convergent path from patient charts located on the hospital wards, through staff reviewers from the QA department, to centralized peer review committees. QA data are usually collected by hand, and analysis is limited to simple counts and percentages. Reviewers screen cases for adverse occurrences, tally events, and report summary information. The data are seldom displayed, nor are they widely disseminated. In fact, clinicians receive feedback from this process only when their performance is unacceptable. Finally, any action to address problems or make improvements must originate from the central peer review committees (see Figure 13–1). Utilization review data are often collected by the same reviewers for another set of peer review committees.

Most patient-related hospital data never enter the QA process at all. Data management systems in hospitals are driven by the requirements of administrative and financial functions, such as billing, purchasing, payroll, and accounting. Typically, a central IS department staffed by systems analysts and information managers maintains the mainframe computers and data systems serving these functions. IS-supported hospital data management systems are not linked to QA data collection efforts except to supply QA analysts with patient identification information, diagnostic codes, and length of stay data. In effect, administrative data management and clinical quality assurance have remained separate domains, with distinct information needs and uses. The common thread, however, is that they both exhibit a convergent flow of data whose endpoint is leadership. Convergent data flow, storage, analysis, and usage are the *sine qua non* of what we refer to as centralized data management.

CQI Calls for Decentralized Computation

In contrast, one requirement of CQI is that cross-disciplinary teams of front line employees collect and analyze process- and outcome-related data. The scope of the information that could be relevant to such teams is very broad: it routinely includes both clinical and administrative data captured from multiple sources inside and outside the organization. For example, a CQI team charged with improving emergency room evaluation of patients with chest pain would gather information directly from patients and other customers; from the current medical literature; from suppliers of medical and diagnostic equipment; from data systems containing financial, scheduling, and demographic information; and from patient charts, among other sources. Furthermore, CQI team members commonly analyze the data and take action at the local level and share data with others. This combination of activities performed by improvement teams is what we mean by the term *decentralized data management.*

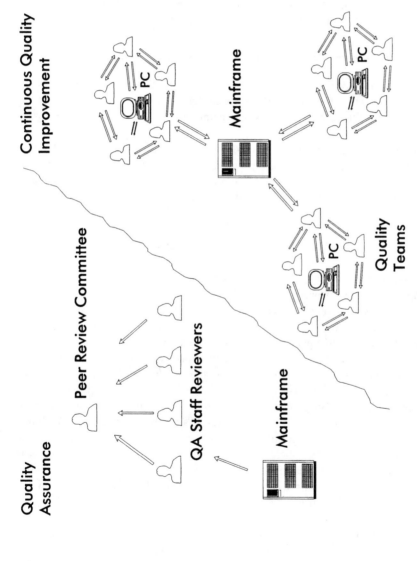

Figure 13–1 In contrast to quality assurance, CQI information flow is decentralized, which calls for computer skills.

Dispersed and decentralized data traffic of this sort lends itself to personal computing. In fact, health care organizations implementing CQI find that quality teams spontaneously reach for PCs in order to handle their data management needs. By and large, teams that do so are on their own: the majority of health care organizations are so busy "rolling out" CQI philosophy and skills that they have little time to think through the computing needs of their CQI teams or to implement the software training necessary to support them.

Decentralization of Computation Demands Software Standards

If CQI is to succeed, then quality teams must manage their own data. Personal computers provide a natural platform for this activity. However, an approach that allows each CQI team to select its own computer software can lead to chaos, as the following vignette illustrates.

Two years into the adoption of a CQI program, the leadership at Alpha Medical Center felt optimistic about their progress. Every employee had received basic training in the principles and methods of quality improvement. A quality management department had been established to coordinate CQI activities. Most importantly, they had initiated over 30 CQI projects, ranging from improvements in the hospital paging system to benchmarking the preoperative cardiology consultation process. A number of significant cost savings and quality improvements could be documented.

Unfortunately, the hospital CQI program had rapidly acquired almost as many computer software packages as it had CQI teams. Several teams chose special purpose, personal computer-based quality control software to help them draw graphs and charts, but used other software to gather and analyze data. Most teams chose IBM-compatible personal computers, but a few preferred Apple computers and software. Some teams used software that was based in a departmental mainframe computer and required special programming to use. A few teams farmed out all their graphical display work to the hospital medical arts department while sending their data management problems to IS staff. Still others opted to hand-draw most of the charts and graphs. The result after two years: a Tower of Babel consisting of many languages used for presenting CQI data and results. Software incompatibility caused duplication of effort when teams tried to share data sets and had to re-enter information, made training and support by IS staff almost impossible, and left everyone wishing they had planned this aspect of the CQI initiative more carefully from the start. Now the center is about to launch a CQI project team to improve the support of CQI itself.

The solution is to start with organizationwide standards for CQI software. There are many advantages to be gained from setting software standards. These standards are associated with reduced training costs. They encourage the organization's community of users to share tips and techniques, form user groups, disseminate program updates, and find new ways to apply the shared technology.

Users of the same software can develop a common repertoire for collecting, storing, and analyzing data and producing graphs and charts and linking them to text in order to produce reports.

As an institution moves to adopt CQI, improvement teams can combine CQI training and software skills training synergistically. Teams learn CQI-related analytical skills in the context of specific software procedures. As they begin their first projects, they collect their data and produce their first charts and graphs using the software. When team members learn to use computers and software as an integral part of their basic training in CQI, they both enrich their understanding of improvement methods and gain a practical tool that they can apply in their daily work.

Software standardization also makes the IS department a much more productive resource for the organization. In a decentralized computing environment with explicit software standards, IS technologists can arrange for access to central databases, provide help with specific problems, and develop applications to automate complex routines for front line users. The IS department will not be able to provide such comprehensive assistance if it receives too many calls from users of diverse hardware and software products and applications scattered idiosyncratically around the organization.

Decentralized CQI Computation Entails a New Role for IS

It is important to recognize that neither the information system bureaucracies organized for QA nor the data systems that serve hospital administrative functions are well suited to the kind of PC literacy and decentralized control over information required by CQI. For one thing, in most hospitals the software skills needed to acquire, manage, and present data remain sequestered in the IS, management engineering, and the medical arts departments, where they are the "property" of nonclinical specialists. It is not feasible for CQI teams to simply delegate their data management tasks to IS personnel. The inevitable delays and procedural formalities inherent in traditional centralized data processing run counter to the main purposes of CQI initiatives, namely to empower the people on the front lines to "talk with the data," manage with facts, and make process changes that improve quality.

For their part, IS personnel may already be overextended by the daily requirements of handling financial and operational data and are often reluctant to assume the additional task of helping to collect, analyze, and report data for a host of new CQI projects. It is entirely understandable if they become frustrated with calls from CQI teams for data that are not captured by existing information systems and with requests that vary widely across CQI teams.

Instead of assuming the burden themselves, the IS personnel can leverage their skills by supporting CQI teams engaged in decentralized computation. They must play a prominent role in evaluating and implementing software standards, training CQI teams to use hardware and software, developing procedures and application to ensure the accuracy of data, and supporting end users.

IS expertise is essential to help ensure that health care teams understand the sources, meaning, and relative accuracy of data gathered both by the teams themselves and from outside the teams' domain (e.g., through downloads from mainframe systems). IS experts have rightly pointed out that CQI teams following independent initiatives run the risk of collecting inaccurate data and developing their own, sometimes incorrect, interpretations of data meaning and utility. The costs of correcting poor quality can be substantial and even prohibitive (personal communication from John Glaser, February 1993).

In the experience of the authors, IS department personnel are quite willing to help with software technical problems and with training nonexpert users, provided they are approached early on in the development of software support for CQI and can participate in a systematic analysis of users' needs.

All these considerations indicate the need for a new model for health care quality data management based upon decentralized collection and analysis of data related to patient care processes and outcomes. Key features of this model include (1) decentralized data analysis by teams using PC software; (2) an institution-wide plan for standardizing PC data management; and (3) coordination of CQI activity with centrally stored data systems. In each part of this model, IS expert leadership and participation are imperative. The structure of information systems in health care organizations will eventually change in the direction we have outlined above, because fundamentally this change is needed and, if given a fair test, it will work.

Computer Industry Trends

Recent developments in personal computer technology and growing computer literacy among health professionals have made it possible for health care organizations to offer their CQI teams powerful desktop and mobile computer software tools. These advances make it feasible for the first time to use a single software program as a platform for CQI activities. Just a few years ago, prudent, computer-knowledgeable readers would have dismissed the suggestion that a single software program could perform all of the tasks required of health care CQI. Several programs would have been necessary: a graphics package like Harvard Graphics for charts and presentations, a spreadsheet for calculations, a database for data storage and application programming, and a statistics program like Statgraphics or SAS for statistical tests. However, recent developments in the PC industry make the ideal of a single software platform for CQI a practical reality. Computing power grows cheaper even as the speed and capacity of the hardware increases. Each new wave of programs is easier to use than the last, yet enables more and more sophisticated operations. The paragraphs below elaborate on some of the relevant current trends in the PC industry.

Hardware Trends

Declining Cost. The personal computers that routinely appear on most health care organizations' purchase requisitions are immensely powerful by the standards of only a year ago. They typically incorporate advanced processors, large data storage and memory capacity, high resolution color displays, and high-speed communications devices. Paradoxically, though computing power has increased dramatically, prices of high-end systems have declined precipitously in recent years. For example, the cost of one advanced desktop system (an Intel 80486 32-bit processor with 33-MHz internal clock speed) from a major national vendor declined from $2,995 to $1,995 between December 1991 and December 1992. As of this writing, a notebook-sized PC capable of running Windows can be purchased for less than $1,500.

Notebook PCs. Health care employees have hectic schedules. They may find time for CQI tasks late at night, in the library or cafeteria, or at home. The recent appearance of notebook-sized computers with virtually the same storage and processing capacity as desktop models promises to facilitate CQI by letting employees take the computer with them. In addition, a notebook PC may allow a CQI team member to use the computer for direct data collection, thus eliminating the need for pencil-and-paper data entry. Paired with an equally portable overhead projection pad, it can serve as a valuable aid during team meetings as members view the data and start to discuss, theorize, and construct a common set of notes.

Local Area Networks. Networks allow many personal computer users to share common data storage and printing resources and make it easier to support software standards. Many organizations have already linked their PCs together and have come to depend on this increasingly reliable technology to handle their most critical tasks. Equipped with electronic mail software, networks greatly facilitate communication and data sharing among CQI team members. For example, team members can easily exchange draft documents and charts, schedule meetings, and even forego meetings altogether in favor of an ongoing electronic dialogue.

Software Trends

Graphical User Interface. A new generation of software, modeled on the Apple Macintosh's graphical user interface (GUI) has become available for IBM-compatible computers. Running under Microsoft Windows or IBM's OS/2 operating systems, these programs are radically easier for nonspecialists to learn and use. Of course, they require more powerful hardware, but, as noted above, appropriate hardware is becoming more accessible to organizations even on relatively tight budgets.

GUI software offers two significant advances. First, basic commands and procedures are standardized across programs. For example, saving a document in the word processing program WordPerfect for Windows involves exactly the same steps as in the spreadsheet program Excel or the graphics program Freelance Graphics for Windows. Such standards mean that users need not relearn the basics for each new program; they can manipulate a new program immediately and rapidly move on to learn more substantive procedures. Second, GUI software is increasingly object oriented. In an object-oriented program, the traditional command prompts and menus give way to a "work space" filled with "objects" that the user can manipulate, using either the keyboard or a mouse or other pointing device. For example, to change the width of a spreadsheet column in the original Lotus 1-2-3, the user had to execute a five-step sequence of menu choices; in the Windows spreadsheet program Excel, one simply uses the mouse to "drag" the border of the column to the desired position.

Standard Data Formats. It is becoming easier to transfer information from one program to another. For instance, a Freelance Graphics for Windows user can simply "copy" and "paste" a diagram or chart into an Excel spreadsheet. In addition, competitive pressures have led most software vendors to recognize certain standard data storage formats—notably those defined by Lotus 1-2-3 and the database program dBASE III. This means, for instance, that it is a simple matter to transfer data from a Paradox database to Excel by using the Lotus 1-2-3 format as an intermediary.

Client-Server Databases. In many health care organizations, information needed by CQI teams already exists in computer databases, but the data are scattered across disconnected mainframes, minicomputers, and personal computers and thus remain relatively inaccessible. Meanwhile, the plunging cost and increasing power of personal computers are driving many organizations to replace their old, expensive mainframe databases with modular, networked client-server systems. In a client-server database, data are stored in one or more server PCs that communicate with client PCs running spreadsheets or other application programs. With careful database planning and implementation, client-server systems promise quick, organizationwide data access for authorized CQI team members.

In summary, the growing power of PC hardware and software has made computer support increasingly available to health care CQI team members. The current generation of spreadsheet software makes possible a single software platform for the full range of common CQI tasks.

Selecting PC Software to Support CQI

A first step in planning for decentralization of quality data management and support of CQI teams should be the choice of software standards. There are literally hundreds of PC-based software programs that could be used to support CQI activities. Which ones are best suited to decentralize CQI computing? How many different programs will be required? Which programs can be linked to central data systems most easily? What will these systems cost? In the next section of this chapter, we examine specific requirements that organizational leaders should consider when choosing PC software for CQI teams and review some of the currently available alternatives.

The Ideal: A Single Software Platform

The same factors mentioned above that compel the setting of organizational standards also make it preferable to employ a single program instead of several, provided the program is easy to use and flexible enough to handle all of the tasks required by CQI teams (Figure 13–2). Busy health care professionals do not have the time to learn and stay familiar with several new software packages. A single software package would greatly simplify both the learning required of CQI team members and the support role of IS personnel.

Even readers well versed in computer technology may be surprised to learn that all of the major CQI activities, from drawing flow charts through displaying regression analyses, can be carried out with any one of several widely available PC software programs (Table 13–1). As of this writing, Excel 4.0, a spreadsheet program published by Microsoft Corporation, provides an almost ideal platform for CQI. It consists of a rich set of tools for collecting, storing, and manipulating data, statistical analysis, graphical display, and even drawing diagrams.

The use of a single software platform to support CQI may not suit the needs of all health care organizations, but health care quality managers should be aware of the availability of such support.

Current Software Alternatives

Of the many software programs that could support CQI, we will compare just a few that are widely available. Readers should bear in mind that software vendors continually upgrade their programs. The comparisons below are based on the revision numbers cited below:

- **Excel revision 4.0 and Q+E.** Microsoft's flagship Windows spreadsheet program, which includes Pioneer Software's Q+E, is the leading contender for a single platform for CQI activities.
- **Quattro Pro 4.0 and Paradox 4.0.** These programs, both from Borland International, are not Windows based, so they can often run acceptably on an organization's existing hardware. Quattro Pro is a spreadsheet program; Paradox is a database manager. They are designed to work closely together, and they provide an excellent alternative for non-Windows shops.

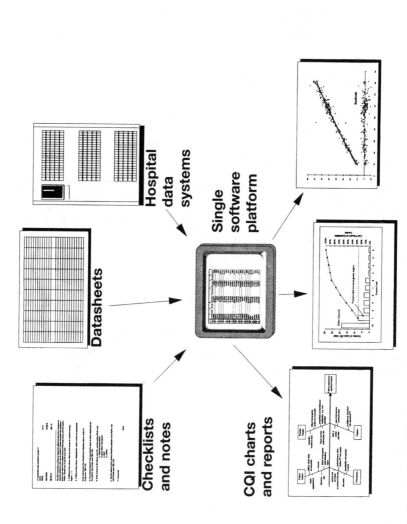

Figure 13–2 CQI Software Platform. A single CQI software platform, such as Excel 4.0, can combine data entered by users with data from host computers, perform necessary statistical analyses, and produce the essential CQI displays.

Table 13–1 CQI Software Trade-offs

Key					
●● = Excellent ● = Good ○ = Deficient ✖ = Missing					

Characteristics	Excel 4.0 and Q+E	Quattro 4.0 and Paradox 4.0	Lotus 1-2-3 v. 3.4	SAS/QC	Epi-Info 5.0
Easy to Use	●	●	○	✖	○
Flexible	●●	●	●	●	✖
Features					
Pareto & control charts	●	●	●	●●	✖
Diagrams	●	●	✖	○	✖
Statistics	●	○	○	●●	●
Presentations	●	●●	✖	✖	✖
Data base management					
Data entry	●	●	○	●●	●
Value checks	✖	●	✖	●	●
Relational database support	●	●●	○	●	●
External database access	●	○	●	●	✖
Programmable	●	●	●	●	✖
Portable	●	●	●	○	●
Network compatible	●	●	●	●	✖
Support					
Vendor	●	●	●	●	✖
Public classes available	●	●	●	○	✖
Widely known	●	●	●	✖	✖

- **Lotus 1-2-3.4.** This spreadsheet program, the most recent from Lotus Development corporation, provides broad capability and built-in external database access.
- **SAS/QC.** Published by the SAS Institute, this program comprises a set of specialized tools that operates as part of the extensive SAS software system. SAS is traditionally a mainframe computer program, though current versions

also run on high-performance PCs. It is primarily used for statistical analysis, but it can also serve as a central environment for the full range of enterprise data management functions.

- **Epi-Info 5.0.** This program, published by the Centers for Disease Control in Atlanta, is in the public domain and is available free of charge. It offers essential database, statistical, and graphics capabilities, but it is not easy to use and does not provide CQI-specific tools such as Pareto and control charts.

The ideal CQI software should enable front line workers and CQI team members to perform statistical tests and ad hoc database manipulations, collect data, and generate routine charts with a minimum of training. Clearly, no single software program will suit the needs of every organization. Budgetary constraints, existing computing standards, and long-term plans vary from hospital to hospital. However, based on the experience of the authors, it is possible to identify specific requirements for a CQI software platform and to assess the degree to which the above programs fulfill them.

Ease of Learning and Use

If CQI projects impose a significant new burden of data management, there is a serious danger that quality improvement will languish while CQI team members attend to more urgent needs. The software must be capable of functioning in the hands of end users at all levels of the organization, from staff in the transportation department to nurses in the intensive care units. Ease of use frees the team from dependence on IS support.

For ease of learning, Excel with Q+E, which takes advantage of the Windows graphical interface, is clearly the best choice, with Quattro/Paradox and Lotus 1-2-3 running a close second.

Flexibility

However, "ease" is not the only criterion. The software provided for teams must be flexible enough to accommodate a diverse range of CQI activities and users. Software programs that "lock in" the end user to a particular sequence of CQI displays will squelch creativity and cause frustration. Dedicated software products, which are designed to do one or a few jobs only, will quickly have their capabilities outgrown. You can educate your software or educate your people; in the end, successful CQI organizations are the ones that educate their people.

Excel, with its broad range of functions and other analytical tools, database features, and graphical capabilities, scores high on flexibility, as do SAS and Quattro/Paradox. Lotus 1-2-3 is a general-purpose spreadsheet program, but its drawing and presentation capabilities trail behind those of the other spreadsheets, Excel and Quattro. Epi-Info, by contrast, is specialized for database and statistical operations.

Analytical and Graphical Capabilities

In addition to being flexible, the software should provide the following specific tools required by CQI teams.

CQI Charts. Teams routinely need to use the seven standard tools of data analysis and display (histogram, cause-and-effect diagram, Pareto chart, scatter diagram, flow chart, run chart, and control chart). It is not necessary that the program provide specific commands and procedures for these CQI displays, but its charting features should make it quick and easy to produce them.

SAS/QC provides extensive, highly automated support for all types of CQI charts except process flow diagrams. Quattro, Excel, and Lotus can easily produce needed data graphs, including control charts, scatter diagrams, and Pareto charts. Only Excel and Quattro can also double as drawing programs to produce process flow diagrams.

Statistics. The program should provide a broad set of tools for performing all kinds of calculations, including basic descriptive statistics like means and standard deviations and date arithmetic (e.g., subtracting one date from another to calculate the duration of a patient's hospital stay). On occasion, CQI teams may need to perform statistical analyses, such as analysis of variance or regression; the software should be capable of such analyses.

SAS/QC, as a part of the SAS system, offers the broadest selection of advanced statistical tools available anywhere. Excel's spreadsheet-based analysis tools, though minuscule by comparison, are adequate for the vast majority of health care CQI activities. Epi-Info also offers significant statistical capabilities.

Presentations. Team members will need to present the results of their work to one another and, periodically, to management, so the ideal CQI program should provide for attractive output, on-screen slide shows, and flexible, hassle-free printing.

Excel provides wide flexibility for annotating and enhancing the appearance of reports and graphs, and its printing system is notably easy to use. Quattro and Lotus 1-2-3 provide similar capabilities, but their nongraphical interfaces make formatting and layout a bit more troublesome. Both programs offer on-screen slide shows.

Database Management. The program should provide at least rudimentary database capabilities. That is, CQI team members should be able to enter data from quality studies, verify their accuracy, sort the records, and query the data by selecting records with specified characteristics. The program should provide mechanisms for verifying the accuracy of the data entered (e.g., by rejecting values that fall outside permitted ranges).

In addition, the software should provide for basic relational database operations. In a relational database, facts pertaining to different entities (e.g., patient visits for each entity) are stored in separate tables or files in order to reduce re-dundancy and errors. Later, the information from the separate tables can be combined for analysis. The software should readily permit users to perform frequency counts and group subtotals.

To avoid re-entering data into the PC software, the program should be able to extract existing records that reside in PC, minicomputer, and mainframe data-bases. The ideal CQI software would serve as a "universal database can opener" that would allow team members to log into the host system via a modem or network gateway, open the required database, compose queries, download the result-ing data to the PC, and combine them with data entered locally.

Considered in combination, Quattro Pro and Paradox provide advanced rela-tional database capabilities: Paradox allows for customized data entry screens, value checking, and sophisticated queries. The results of queries can be trans-ferred seamlessly to Quattro for analysis and display. On the other hand, these Borland products are not adept at accessing external databases.

Excel and Q+E together provide basic relational capabilities and advanced que-ries; they fall short in the area of data verification but allow for good external da-tabase access. Lotus 1-2-3's external database access is powerful but difficult to maneuver. Epi-Info provides excellent general database services at the level needed by CQI practitioners, and SAS, though immensely powerful, requires a specialist to fully exploit its database capabilities.

Programmability. When a CQI project enters the "check" phase of Deming's PDCA cycle, staff members will need to monitor the ongoing process, regularly entering data and viewing control charts or other reports. This procedure can best be optimized by providing an "application," with customized data entry screens and menus, that reduces routine operations to a few keystrokes or mouse clicks. Thus the software should allow IS specialists to develop dedicated applications for data entry and standard charts and reports.

Excel, through its macrolanguage, is a fully capable development environment, as is Quattro/Paradox. SAS includes a complete programming language that can be used to design enterprisewide data management systems.

Portability. In order to gain ready acceptance, the software should be able to run on diverse hardware platforms. Ideally, it will work on both PC and Apple Macintosh systems and be used on a notebook-size computer as easily as on a desktop.

All of the programs under consideration except SAS can be used on both large and small IBM-compatible PCs. Only Excel currently runs on both PC and Mac-intosh computers.

Network Compatibility. Local area networks allow CQI team members sepa-rated by their busy schedules to work together, sharing files, documents, spread-sheets, and databases and exchanging electronic mail messages. The software they use should be "network aware." For example, it should provide "locking" mechanisms that prevent two users from opening the same file at once and making their own changes. Were this to happen, the last user to save the file would obliterate the changes made by the other.

Epi-Info is not network compatible; the other programs under discussion all provide locking mechanisms required for simultaneous data access by multiple users.

Affordability. Because many copies of the software will be distributed throughout the organization, the software must not be too expensive. Readers should note, however, that the cost of licensing is only a small part of the total cost of software. Over time, the cost of training and the cost represented by time lost during the learning period far exceed the initial outlays. Nevertheless, one argument for a single software platform is to avoid the expense of licensing many copies of many different programs. In addition, many vendors offer special site licenses that further reduce costs.

Because it is in the public domain and available free, Epi-Info is the most inexpensive alternative (see Table 13–2).

Dependable Support. Support means help in using the software. Support comes from extramural sources (e.g., the software vendor, community college courses, commercial training vendors, and training consultants) and from intramural ones (e.g., the organization's IS staff and other users). Selecting a popular software product from a large, stable company helps ensure that extramural support will be readily available, and it also increases the likelihood of locating candidates for IS positions who are already familiar with the program. Selecting a single CQI software standard means that intramural support networks will develop as users acquire and share skills.

Table 13–2 Software Costs: The Cost of Personal Computer Software for CQI

Program	Price[*]
Excel 4.0 (includes Q+E)	$299
Quattro Pro 4.0	299
Paradox 4.0	529
Lotus 1-2-3 v. 3.4	399
SAS/QC	369
Epi-Info	0

[*]Typical street price for a single-user license.

Support for popular PC programs from established vendors, such as Excel, Quattro, and Lotus 1-2-3, is obtainable in a wide range of forms, from public courses to toll-free telephone services provided by the vendors. Support for SAS is often excellent in university environments but may be expensive or hard to find elsewhere. Epi-Info offers no support beyond the published documentation.

PREPARING FOR CHANGE

Decision makers in health care organizations must recognize that CQI demands a basic change from centralized to decentralized management of quality information. Above all, front line staff must have the research tools and the skills necessary to turn group process into local action for improvement.

CQI teams, functioning at the periphery of the organization, require computer software that is easy to use, PC based, and portable. The software must provide for graphical display and database management, and it must be able to access data stored in mainframe databases for use when and where they are needed.

Fortunately, recent advances in PC hardware and software technology have made it possible to realize the following significant benefits of standardizing hardware and software for CQI data management:

- reduced software and training costs
- synergistic skills acquisition by staff
- focused IS support for CQI teams
- the opportunity to facilitate training in CQI concepts and methods by means of specific software techniques

At the time of this writing, Microsoft Excel 4.0 for Windows and Borland's Quattro Pro for DOS are the leading candidates for a single software platform for CQI. Appendix 13–A illustrates the use of this software to support CQI efforts. This information has been placed in an appendix to emphasize the fact that such applications are subject to change at any time with the advance of technology. This appendix is for the reader who has little or no experience with personal computers, but illustrates the learning that one must go through to begin to be able to use such systems.

Guidelines for Management Action

Successful transition from QA to CQI depends on management's ability to follow the information action guidelines presented below.

1. Invest in planning for infrastructure and organizational change. CQI is not a technology or management style that can simply be grafted onto existing

quality management activities. In CQI the manager becomes less of a decision maker and more like a symphony conductor who orchestrates professionals in project teams. In order to empower their staffs to analyze and solve problems, managers must act as liaisons between the IS professionals and the project team leaders. They must guide software use by teams under their jurisdiction. Not everyone in the organization needs to have extensive software skills, nor does software training have to be done in lock-step fashion. In fact, it is more likely to be successful if it is provided on a "just-in-time" basis to teams that have a need for it and can develop their skills with a specific use immediately in front of them.

2. Redefine the role of the information manager. Most health care organizations have hired information managers to work in IS departments on the basis of their technical skills and professional certifications. But the new priorities for data analysis and usage under CQI demand a broader set of skills. Information management staff must now support multidisciplinary teams of health care workers—including physicians, nurses, middle managers, telephone operators, and many more—as they design and execute CQI studies. That role requires, in addition to software skills, an understanding of the philosophy and methods of CQI and the ability to communicate effectively with this broad range of colleagues. Adopting a single platform and involving them closely in the CQI training effort will help information management staff learn how to fulfill these obligations.

3. Adopt standard, institutionwide software for CQI teams to use. Leaving each team to make its own software choices can cause confusion and fragmented efforts. A single institutionwide standard allows for focused training and support and fosters a broad culture of skilled users throughout the organization, while at the same time reducing costs.

4. Train your people to do CQI using that software. Training people in the methods of CQI and training them in computer software to perform the analytical tasks demanded by CQI are parallel processes that should be integrated. The computer and its software as an integrated tool can enrich the experience of trainees as they learn about process analysis and process design, about the causes of variation, and about how to apply basic statistical methods to process data.

Examples of CQI Applications Using Microsoft Excel

This tutorial discusses advances in PC hardware and software technology that have made possible revolutionary changes in health care quality data management. It then presents several detailed examples of how to use Microsoft Excel 4.0 for Windows to support commonly used CQI tools and analyses.

It is not possible in a short tutorial to provide a complete keystroke-by-keystroke guide for using software as powerful as Excel in applications as varied as those encountered in CQI. Rather, our purpose is to illustrate Excel's capabilities and to stimulate readers to experiment with the software. For more detailed information about using spreadsheets for CQI, readers can consult a variety of sources.

Scoville's articles in *PC World* magazine (1992a, 1992b, 1993) discuss common CQI applications such as Pareto charts, cross-tabulations, and control charts. Zimmerman and Zimmerman's book *SPC using Lotus 1-2-3* (1992) gives detailed instructions for CQI applications using that popular spreadsheet program. Readers are also encouraged to consult the *Microsoft Excel 4.0 Users Guide* (Microsoft Corporation, 1992) for more specifics on the commands and procedures described here. Finally, readers might also explore the annual QA/QC software directory that appears each year in the March issue of *Quality Progress*, the magazine of the American Society for Quality Control. This directory lists companies that sell software modules that can be added to spreadsheet programs like Excel and others to implement various CQI tools and analyses.

To give a sense of how a single software platform for health care CQI can work in practice, we present examples of CQI team activities executed with the Microsoft Excel for Windows spreadsheet program, together with brief descriptions of how they were produced. We have selected Excel because it is perhaps the best overall choice for a single CQI platform. It is not the only candidate, nor is it the only spreadsheet program that can produce the results shown below.

What Is a Spreadsheet?

First, a brief introduction to spreadsheet software. A spreadsheet is composed of *cells*, arranged in rows and columns, into which the user places *values*—numbers and text—and *formulas*. A formula displays a calculated result, based on values that appear in other cells. Exhibit 13–A1 shows a small portion of an Excel spreadsheet. The cells in column A contain text values. Cells B1 and B2 contain numbers. Cell B4 contains values calculated using the formula visible in the right-hand box above the spreadsheet. The spreadsheet itself shows (and prints) the calculated value of the formula (8.58), not the underlying formula.

By issuing commands, the user can instruct the program to execute a variety of actions using the spreadsheet entries: for example, to change the appearance of the cells and their values, print the spreadsheet, store it on disk, sort the entries, and carry out statistical procedures. To aid in complex calculations, spreadsheet programs provide *functions*, like Excel's STDEV(), which calculates the standard deviation of a set of numbers. Excel provides over 200 analytical functions, including a wide selection of parametric and nonparametric statistics.

A spreadsheet *application* is simply an interconnected system of cell entries, with formulas to produce needed results. The formulas are, of course, the tricky part of all this. A CQI specialist or statistician might build ad hoc applications, creating formulas on the fly to explore particular sets of data. Or, with a CQI specialist's help, a software developer might set up in advance a so-called *template* application that contains text and formulas but leaves the numbers to be filled in by a staff member as the data are collected. A template application, equipped with customized commands, safeguarded with internal checks to prevent careless errors, and running on a notebook computer, can provide the front line worker with a fast, highly specialized, yet easy-to-use CQI data entry and analysis tool.

In addition to calculations, spreadsheet programs also provide a chart module that automatically creates line charts, bar charts, and the like, based on the values in a spreadsheet grid. Finally, since the spreadsheet can serve as a repository for records, it can also function as a database. Most spreadsheet programs provide explicit commands for entering, organizing, and summarizing historical records.

Exhibit 13–A1 Excel Spreadsheet. Portion of a simple Excel spreadsheet, showing text and number cell values and a formula in cell B4

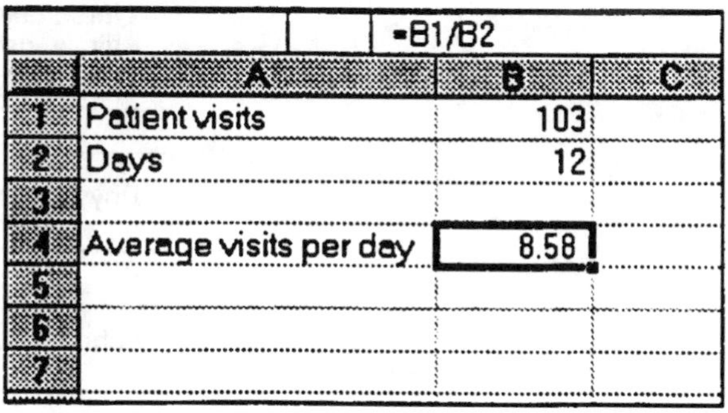

Process Flow Diagrams and Cause-and-Effect Charts

Process flow diagrams are among the most frequently used CQI tools. A process flow diagram helps the team understand the detailed steps of a process, a necessary step in pinpointing problems and formulating solutions (Wadsworth et al., 1986). The diagram shown in Figure 13–A1 shows the steps involved in a visit to a clinic monitoring patients on Coumadin therapy.

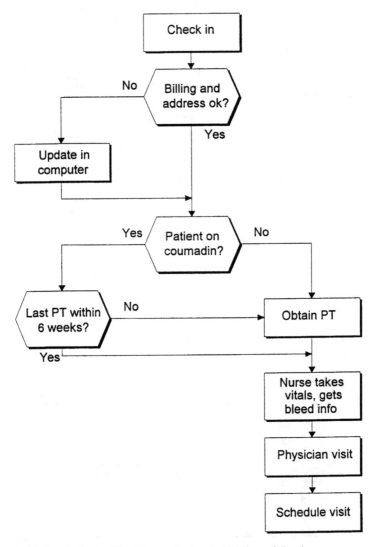

Figure 13–A1 Sample Process Flow Diagram Produced with Microsoft Excel

Since spreadsheets are conventionally used for numerical analysis, not for drawing pictures, readers will perhaps be surprised that a diagram such as Figure 13–A1 was created with a spreadsheet program. However, several members of the current generation of graphical user interface (GUI) spreadsheets contain sophisticated drawing tools that are fully adequate for preparing the diagrams commonly required for CQI. In addition to flow charts, Ishikawa or cause-and-effect diagrams can easily be produced with the same tools.

Excel features a unique drawing layer (think of it as a sheet of transparent acetate that overlays the cells of the spreadsheet) on which the user can place drawing objects such as rectangles, lines, arrows, circles, and curves. Once a basic element such as a process box has been constructed, it is quick and easy to make additional boxes by duplicating it and modifying the copies. Armed with a few techniques like these, and with just a few hours of practice, users can become quite proficient in producing process flow diagrams using the drawing layer.

Control Charts

Control charts, like the one shown in Figure 13–A2, graphically analyze the variability of a process through time (Scoville, 1993; Plsek, 1992). A control chart lets a CQI team identify the effects of *special causes* on the process. A process that operates without special causes is stable or "in control." Although a stable process produces variable results, its variations are predictable, making the process easier to manage. Special causes make a process unpredictable and thus more difficult to manage.

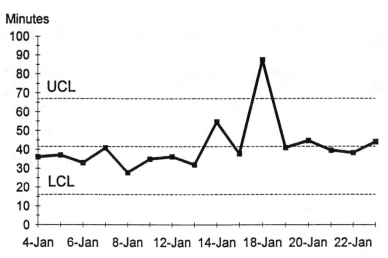

Figure 13–A2 Daily X-Bar Chart: Wait Times. This control chart was prepared with Microsoft Excel.

Consider a CQI team whose goal is to improve patient waiting times in an out-patient setting. As one of their first steps in the CQI process, the team monitored the time patients spent waiting for their regularly scheduled appointments. Each day for 16 days, the team randomly sampled six patients' records and recorded the time that elapsed from when the patients arrived to when they were escorted to an examination room, a total of 96 visits.

The control chart in Figure 13–A2 shows the mean (average) values of the daily sample (line graph), the mean of the sample means (the horizontal dashed line at 41), an upper control limit (at 67), and a lower control limit (at 16). If the process is under control, over 99 percent of sample means will fall between the control limits. The deviant point shown for January 18 indicates the presence of a special cause: the process is unstable. (The eight points in a row below the mean from January 4 to 13 is further indication of special cause.)

To produce this chart the CQI team used Excel to prepare a spreadsheet that included the 96 sample wait times and a series of formulas to calculate the sample means, the average of the sample means, and the control limits. The data and calculations for the first day, as they appear in Excel, are shown in Table 13–A1. The data values are in columns A through G, and the calculated values in columns I through M. To illustrate how Excel's statistical functions facilitate this work, the formulas in I4 through M4 are shown without detailed explanation in Table 13–A2. Rows 5 through 19 contain similar formulas (Microsoft Corporation, 1992).

Table 13–A1 C=CHART.XLS: Control Chart: x=bar. Data and formulas used to create the control chart shown in Figure 13–A2

	A	B	C	D	E	F	G	H	I	J	K	L	M
1													
2													
3	Date		Sample waiting times (min)						sd	X-bar	Mean	UCL	LCL
4	4-Jan	26	26	53	44	36	31		10.8	36.0	41.5	66.9	16.1
5	5-Jan	53	53	44	36	31	5		18.0	37.0	41.5	66.9	16.1
6	6-Jan	21	21	37	48	29	42		11.2	33.0	41.5	66.9	16.1
7	7-Jan	34	34	49	36	34	58		10.2	40.8	41.5	66.9	16.1
8	8-Jan	29	29	28	9	26	45		11.4	27.7	41.5	66.9	16.1
9	11-Jan	19	19	63	29	46	33		17.1	34.8	41.5	66.9	16.1
10	12-Jan	37	37	47	17	24	55		14.1	36.2	41.5	66.9	16.1
11	13-Jan	35	35	54	17	36	14		14.6	31.8	41.5	66.9	16.1
12	14-Jan	48	48	102	13	30	86		33.6	54.5	41.5	66.9	16.1
13	15-Jan	26	26	55	31	42	46		11.9	37.7	41.5	66.9	16.1
14	18-Jan	39	39	111	96	178	61		53.3	87.3	41.5	66.9	16.1
15	19-Jan	31	31	28	36	24	96		27.2	41.0	41.5	66.9	16.1
16	20-Jan	47	47	60	21	53	40		13.4	44.7	41.5	66.9	16.1
17	21-Jan	35	35	43	30	27	67		14.5	39.5	41.5	66.9	16.1
18	22-Jan	49	49	74	6	24	27		24.0	38.2	41.5	66.9	16.1
19	20-Jan	82	82	19	20	20	41		30.6	44.0	41.5	66.9	16.1

The formulas in columns J through M govern the lines in the chart in Figure 13–A2, which was created using Excel's new Chart Wizard. This procedure makes setting up charts feasible for even novice users. The basic line chart was modified using standard Excel features.

Database Management

Accurate data are the lifeblood of CQI. Entering, organizing, and manipulating those data are the most basic functions that any CQI software must perform. Although no spreadsheet program can replace a full-fledged relational database manager like Paradox or FoxPro, current spreadsheets enable CQI practitioners to enter, sort, and select records, transform values, and summarize data as required.

For instance, suppose a CQI team studying outpatients on coumadin therapy is interested in the relationship between patients' failure to recognize early signs of active bleeding and the frequency of serious bleeding complications. To study this, team members study patients' knowledge at each patient visit. The data entry could be done directly in Excel using its built-in data entry form, shown in Exhibit 13–A2. This form displays the data in a record-by-record format that is more compact than the normal spreadsheet view and facilitates the data entry.

Analyzing CQI data frequently involves tallying and totaling items in various categories, a task that traditionally has been difficult to perform with spreadsheet software. Excel's new Crosstab feature makes short work of it (Scoville, 1992a). In the Coumadin case study, for example, Excel's Crosstab feature was used to tally the number of patients who knew how to check for early signs of bleeds as a function of visit number. The Crosstab Wizard provides an easy-to-follow series of screens like the one shown in Exhibit 13–A3 that guide the analyst through the necessary choices.

Excel's onboard database capabilities can be augmented by Q+E, an accessory program from Pioneer Software that is included with Excel. Once installed, Q+E's commands are accessible through the regular Excel menus. Q+E plays two important roles in database management. First, it serves as a database "can

---

Table 13–A2 Excel formulas used in the spreadsheet shown in Figure 13–7 to calculate mean and control limits

Cell	Formula
I4	STDEV (B:4: G4)
J4	AVERAGE (B4: G4)
K4	AVERAGE ($J$4: $J$19)
L4	$K4 + 3* AVERAGE ($I$4: $I$19)/0.9515/SQRT (COUNT (B4: G4))
M4	$K4 − 3* AVERAGE ($I$4: $I$19)/0.9515/SQRT (COUNT (B4: G4))

Exhibit 13–A2 Data Entry Form. Excel's data entry form permits fast record-by-record entry of records.

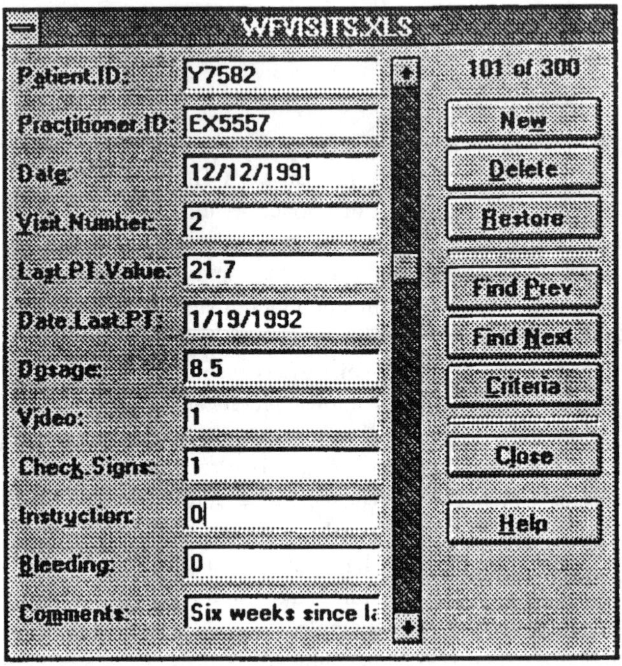

opener." That is, it can access host database systems such as DB2 or Oracle, or PC-resident databases such as Paradox or dBASE, select needed data from those tables, and put the selected records into an Excel spreadsheet for further analysis. Figure 13–A3 shows how this can be done.

Second, Q+E serves as a relational database manager for data stored in Excel tables. In a relational database, information about different *entities*, such as patients and their visits to the clinic, are stored in separate tables (i.e., separate worksheets) in order to simplify data entry and to guard against errors. Related tables share a common key field (in the current example it is patient ID) that mediates the relationship. Q+E enables one to combine records from related worksheets into a single analysis table (Figure 13–A3), matching the records by their key field values. This relational capability is especially useful when combining data downloaded from a host computer database system, such as patient records, with data entered locally into Excel in the course of a quality study.

To summarize, the single platform Excel contains sufficient database power to handle most routine CQI tasks, and its companion program, Q+E, provides a vehicle for accessing external databases.

Exhibit 13–A3 Excel's Crosstab Wizard. This provides a simple way to summarize CQI data.

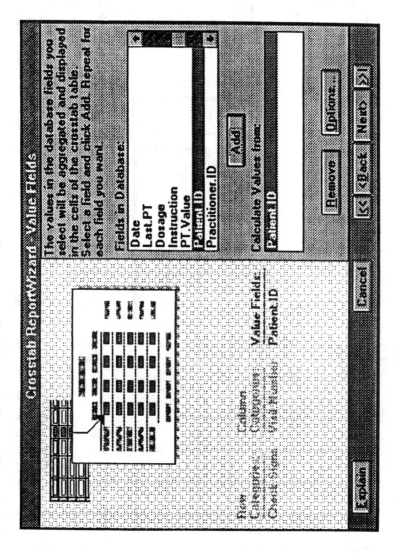

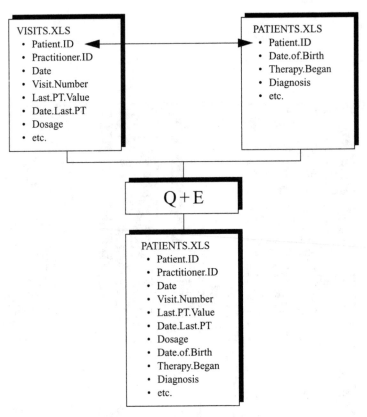

Figure 13–A3 Using Q+E. Q+E, an accessory program supplied with Excel, can combine records from related spreadsheet tables.

Pareto Charts

When CQI teams seek to solve a quality problem, they must identify its primary or root causes. In order to do this, they survey a series of problem incidents and record the cause of each one. Then they carry out a Pareto analysis. The Pareto Principle states that whenever a quality problem has multiple causes, just a few of those causes account for most of the incidents. By tallying and rank ordering the frequency of such causes, the quality team can quickly decide which ones to attack first. A Pareto chart is a histogram that displays the relative frequency of causes and quickly isolates the root causes.

At a large university hospital, quality team members used a Pareto chart to illustrate the causes for incident reports involving medications. They examined 1,062 reports and found 23 distinct causes for problems related to prescribing and dispensing drugs. Excel supports the Pareto analysis at each step: the Crosstab Wizard can be used to tally the frequencies of causes; the sorting feature arranges the causes in descending order of occurrence; formulas calculate the percentage of cases represented by each cause; and, finally, the charting tools generate the Pareto chart shown in Figure 13–A4.

Histograms

A histogram is a bar chart that plots the frequency distribution of a set of data. For instance, in the study of patient waiting times discussed above, the histogram shown in Figure 13–A5 gives a quick visual summary of the range and frequency of patient waiting times: most patients waited between 20 minutes and an hour, though waits of up to two hours were not unusual. The single 180-minute wait was an isolated event.

Excel provides two ways to prepare the values for a histogram from a set of raw waiting times. One, the Crosstab Wizard, was described above. The other, used in producing Exhibit 13–A3, is a special array formula that employs Excel's statistical function FREQUENCY(). Array formulas, a unique and very powerful feature of Excel, permit a single formula to distribute values across a range of spreadsheet cells. In this case, they permit a dynamic relationship between the data values and the histogram: as the user enters wait times into the table, the histogram changes to reflect the new values.

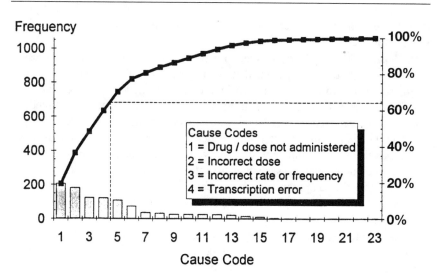

Figure 13–A4 A Pareto Chart Showing the Frequency of Incident Reports Involving Medications. Of 24 causes, the 4 described above account for almost 65 percent of the incidents.

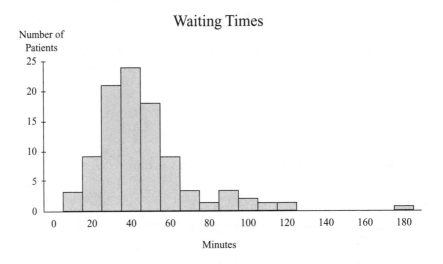

Figure 13–A5 Histogram. The data for this histogram were prepared using Excel's FREQUENCY() array function.

Scatter Diagrams and Regression Analysis

In the search for the causes of quality problems, scatter diagrams and regression analysis are powerful methods for teams to use to discern relationships between variables. Although regression analysis alone cannot conclusively prove causality, it can provide the "smoking gun" that makes a convincing case for a process intervention.

Suppose in the study of incident reports involving medications discussed above, the CQI team suggested that relying on temporary nursing personnel might contribute to the problem. To investigate that hypothesis, the team performed a retrospective study comparing on a weekly basis the number of medication error incident reports per 1,000 drug orders with the percentage of temporary FTE nursing hours. The resulting scatter diagram (Figure 13–A6) indicates a strong positive relationship between these variables. As the percentage of temporary FTE personnel increases, so does the rate of incident reports. Now this does not prove that the temporary nurses are causing medication errors, but it does suggest that further investigation into the factors surrounding the use of temporary nurses is warranted.

In most spreadsheet or charting software, scatter diagrams such as the one shown here are routine charts. But unique among general purpose spreadsheet software, Excel also provides an arsenal of statistical tools that CQI analysts can put to good use. Like the Crosstab feature, the statistical analyses are prepackaged routines that simply ask the user to indicate where the data are located,

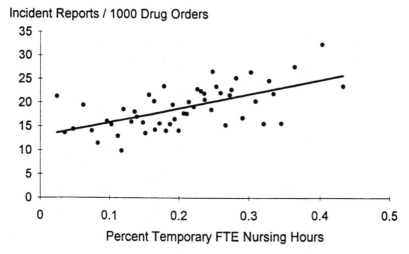

Incident Reports / 1000 Drug Orders

Figure 13–A6 Scatter Diagram. A scatter diagram with regression line generated by Excel's analysis tools.

where to put the results, and what specific operations are to be carried out. Exhibit 13–A4 shows the result of the regression analysis carried out on the incident report data. Among the other statistical procedures available in Excel are the following (Snedecor and Cochrane, 1989):

- analysis of variance
- correlation
- covariance
- descriptive statistics
- *F*-Test: two-sample for variances
- random number generation
- rank and percentile
- sampling
- *t*-test
- *z*-test

In summary, a spreadsheet program like Microsoft Excel can serve well as a single general-purpose platform for CQI analysis. It is not necessary to purchase specialized CQI software packages dedicated to the tools of quality control. We chose to illustrate the single-platform concept with Excel, but there are other good choices as well. As PC software progresses rapidly in the next few years, it is likely that these general purpose software programs will evolve to provide an even better fit with the needs of CQI practitioners.

Exhibit 13–A4 Regression Statistics. Regression statistics calculated by Excel's analysis tools provide a significance test of the relationship shown in the scatter diagram in Figure 13–A6.

Regression Statistics

Multiple R	0.616541739
R Square	0.380
Adjusted R Square	0.368
Standard Error	3.623
Observations	52

Analysis of Variance

	df	Sum of Squares	Mean Square	F	
Regression	1	402.398	402.398	30.661	1.1356E-06
Residual	50	656.199	13.124		
Total	51	1058.597			

	Coefficients	Standard Error	t Statistic	P-value	Lower 95%	Upper 95%	Lower 99%	
Intercept	12.861	1.213	10.602	1.69347E-14	10.425	15.298	9.613	1.61E+01
x1	29.731	5.369	5.537	1.07805E-06	18.946	40.515	15.353	4.41E+01

Part IV

Application

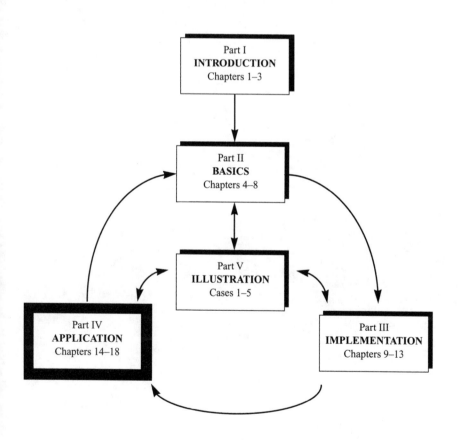

Linda S. Leininger
Russell Harris
Rudolph S. Jackson
Victor J. Strecher
Arnold D. Kaluzny

CQI in Primary Care

14

Most Americans receive health care within a primary care setting. Quality and efficiency of services are issues for primary care just as for other areas of health care (Kritchevsky and Simmons, 1991). Yet the never-ending demands of daily work are such that providers rarely have time to step back and gain perspective on the problem. Continuous quality improvement (CQI) is a potentially powerful tool for primary care providers to meet the challenges of quality and efficiency. This chapter places CQI in the context of other approaches to change in primary care practice and outlines one CQI initiative to produce change toward improved quality and efficiency of preventive care in this setting.

THE CHALLENGE OF CHANGE IN PRIMARY CARE

Medical practice must change constantly. Although there are age-old techniques that good physicians have always used, new scientific research daily adds to the evidence for or against various diagnostic and treatment approaches. The weight of evidence builds, and at some point it becomes clear that a new approach is best, that medical practice must shift to a new way of doing things. There is, for example, new and convincing evidence that screening sigmoidoscopy decreases mortality from colorectal cancer, yet most physicians have not been routinely performing this procedure.

There is another reason why medical practice must constantly change: the problems of patients change over time. Although this change is slower than the pace of medical research, the problems that patients present to physicians in the 1990s are different in important ways from patients' problems in, say, the 1960s. AIDS and the resurgence of tuberculosis, for example, necessitate new approaches to patients with cough and weight loss. A higher percentage of patients is old and has degenerative, incurable conditions, requiring very different management skills from an earlier practice with predominantly younger patients and acute medical problems. Domestic violence, while present in an earlier day, has now reached epidemic proportions in some areas.

Medical practice, however, and particularly primary care practice, is not well designed for change. Primary care is dominated by solo and small group practices and run by people without organizational experience or expertise (i.e., physicians). In general, primary care providers are so overwhelmed with the daily workload that it is impossible for them to step back and determine programmatic needs and to develop and evaluate new programs. Primary care is much less well reimbursed than other, "procedural" specialties in medicine and thus has fewer resources (e.g., personnel, computers, consultants) than other branches of medicine. Primary care, and particularly private practice (which sees the largest number of patients), has also evolved a very individualistic style of operating that makes its practitioners suspicious of external influences and of change itself.

There have been a number of attempts to change medical practice, with varying degrees of success. No approach, however, has found change simple or easy to accomplish. A recent review of 50 randomized controlled trials of continuing medical education (CME) found a direct relationship between the intensity of the intervention and the number of studies with positive outcomes (Davis et al., 1992). Traditional continuing medical education (CME) with lectures by experts, printed materials alone (Evans et al., 1986), journal articles (Haynes, 1990), and consensus statements (Kosecoff et al., 1987) generally did not have a large impact on medical practice. Several approaches, such as "academic detailing" (Soumerai and Avorn, 1990) and the influence of "opinion leaders" (Lomas et al., 1991), have been used successfully to change such simple behaviors as prescribing a specific drug or allowing a trial of vaginal birth as opposed to performing a cesarean section. These approaches need more study in other areas of medical practice to define more clearly their uses and limitations.

CQI is a new approach to change in medical practice. By CQI, we mean an approach to change in organizations that begins with collecting data about an important issue to determine to what extent there are "performance gaps," or opportunities for improvement. The organization then sets a goal to improve the outcome measured by the data and breaks down the task of achieving the goal into small, manageable steps. A plan for implementing the steps is developed and tried, and the outcome of concern is monitored to determine if improvement indeed takes place. Data from monitoring are given back to the organization regularly to allow fine tuning of the new approach and to reward those who have made changes to improve the outcome. The entire process includes all relevant members of the organization, working together to identify opportunities for improvement and new approaches to try.

To date, with few exceptions (Solberg, 1993) most experience with the CQI technique in the medical field has been within large medical institutions such as hospitals and HMOs rather than private primary care practice. Although some have been impressed with its success in large institutions, the inherent problems of change in private primary care practice noted above make it necessary to consider how to adapt this potentially powerful technique to primary care. Its promise to alter complex behavior, such as counseling for cessation of cigarette smoking, should make research in this area a high priority.

PRACTICE CHARACTERISTICS AFFECTING CQI

There are several issues to consider in the adaptation of CQI to the primary care setting. The fact that private medical practice is dominated by small practices with little management expertise and overwhelmed with daily work means that it is questionable whether practices by themselves will be able to develop the data needed to define "performance gaps" (i.e., areas where performance is not up to agreed-upon standards) and detect improvement over time. As we suggest below, developing such data may become the province of a respected second party, such as the CME department of a university or a professional association.

Although the CQI approach emphasizes change coming from within an organization, this modification of CQI envisions the practice as being initially motivated to seek change by a respected "outside" group who points out that performance is suboptimal. Clearly, the issue chosen by the "outside" group must be one, such as preventive care, understood by all to be important.

It is also doubtful that practices alone will have the time and expertise to organize practice planning groups to develop new, detailed plans that can be discussed with the rest of the staff, tried, evaluated, and fine-tuned to perform the specific function in a different way. Again, a respected second party may be needed to assist the practice in working through this process. Such second parties must be chosen carefully since the culture of many practicing physicians is to resist outside direction.

Another issue in adapting CQI to primary care practice is the lack of incentives to carry out the CQI process at all. Although hospitals and other large health care organizations are often required to complete the CQI process to remain accredited, there are no such requirements for primary care practices. Again, outside groups may be needed to reward successful change.

Finally, the medical mind set that all tests and treatments must be exactly tailored to each patient, implying that no guideline can lump people into groups of patients needing the same procedure, greatly complicates developing automatic systems of any kind. The more one can identify groups of patients who need the same procedure(s), the higher the probability that processes such as CQI can develop systems that get the job done most efficiently. Another related but complicating idea is that physicians should not advocate specific procedures, but should only provide the patient with information and options, and leave the decision to him or her. This idea again limits what office systems can accomplish.

ONE MODEL OF CQI IN PRIMARY CARE: THE NORTH CAROLINA PRESCRIBE FOR HEALTH PROJECT

The North Carolina Prescribe for Health Project (NC-PFH), funded by the National Cancer Institute, is an initiative designed to help community-based, primary care practices change how they provide preventive care for their patients. Many studies have documented that clinical preventive services are often not provided as recommended by national expert and advisory groups (Lewis, 1988). For a variety of reasons, most preventive care seems to be delivered haphazardly: some patients receive it; many don't.

One of the reasons for the difficulty in reaching higher levels of performance relates to recent changes in the paradigm of preventive care itself. Guidelines for preventive care are undergoing change. As new research shows evidence of benefit of certain procedures, these are being recommended more strongly (an example is sigmoidoscopy for colorectal cancer screening). Some tests previously considered useful are no longer recommended when they are found not to have value for screening (routine chest radiographs, for example).

The list of preventive care procedures that has been shown to reduce mortality (the ultimate goal for preventive care) is actually rather short and does not include the long battery of routine tests that has often been done in the past. The idea of an annual head-to-toe physical examination has been replaced by the concept of a periodic visit, tailored to a patient's specific risk factors. Skills, such as counseling about personal behaviors, that were seldom learned in medical school in the past are now required. The new prevention paradigm calls for a changed type of doctor-patient relationship, in which patients are encouraged to take a more active role in their own health, and patients and physicians become more like partners on a team, rather than following a hierarchical model. NC-PFH is an approach, using the principles of CQI, to help practices face and deal with these changes.

NC-PFH seeks to improve performance of preventive care services by assisting primary care practices to develop a more organized system for preventive care. In using a CQI approach to accomplish this goal, the project encourages change based on (1) data collected at baseline to document a "performance gap"; (2) plans by the practice for systematically accomplishing five "steps" in getting prevention done; and (3) feedback to the practice on how it is doing in meeting its goals for preventive care (Kaluzny et al., 1991). All members of the practice, staff as well as physicians, are involved in this process.

Primary care physician members of three sponsoring medical professional societies, the American College of Physicians, the American Academy of Family Physicians, and the National Medical Association, were randomly chosen to participate. The project is cosponsored as well by the North Carolina Area Health Education Center (AHEC) Program. These professional organizations are known for their interest in the quality and content of medical practice and have been active in formulating guidelines for preventive care. One of the important reasons for working together with professional associations in NC-PFH is that such groups may well be involved in CQI-type interventions for their member physicians in the future. Because the CQI approach includes working with members of the group as a team, the NC-PFH project works with whole practices rather than individual physicians. Making changes in practice routines is a process that involves more than the physician alone. Deciding on changes to be made and implementing these changes require the input and efforts of all members of the practice.

Baseline

The first phase of the project involved collecting baseline data on preventive care procedures recommended or performed from each of the participating practices. The data consisted of (1) reviews of randomly selected medical records of patients; (2) brief anonymous questionnaires from consecutive patients in the waiting rooms, asking about preventive care procedures done in the last year or more; and (3) questionnaires of physicians and office staff members, determining their approach to delivering preventive care. The data collection was done by members of the project staff (except for completion of physician and staff questionnaires) so as not to impose a burden on already harried office staff members. Information from medical record reviews and patient questionnaires on performance data was compiled and sent back to physicians in an easy-to-read format. Figures 14–1 and 14–2 are profiles for two different primary care practices. Figure 14–1 presents a practice in which 71 percent of the eligible patients received a mammography, 67 percent received CBE, and 85 percent received FOBT within the past year. Within the past three years, 80 percent of the eligible patients received a Pap smear, 18 percent received sigmoidoscopy, and 53 percent of smokers received smoking cessation counseling. Figure 14–2, however, presents a practice that has provided mammographies for only 20 percent of eligible patients, CBE and FOBT for 10 percent, and influenza immunization for 36 percent in the past year. During the past three years, 47 percent of the eligible patients received a Pap smear, 5 percent received a sigmoidoscopy, and 0 percent of the smokers received smoking cessation counseling. The presentation of these profiles to the respective practices provides the framework by which physicians and staff begin to assess a practice's policy regarding prevention. For example, Figure 14–1 may lead that practice to feel that although additional efforts could be directed to increasing the number of mammograms for women 50 and older, the real challenge for them is perhaps to increase sigmoidoscopies among eligible patients. The practice presented in Figure 14–2 might discern a different challenge, namely, the recognition that it is providing little preventive care and thus needs to assess its fundamental policy regarding prevention.

Half of the 62 study practices participating in NC-PFH were then chosen at random to receive a year-long period of consultation and support from NC-PFH

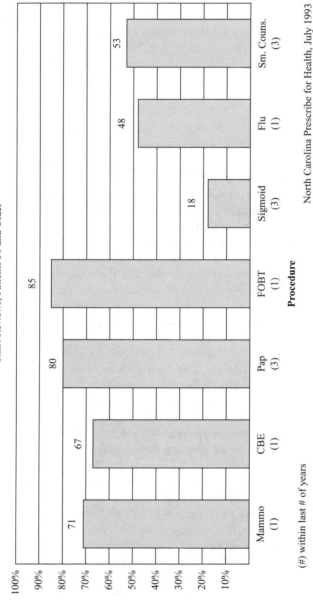

Figure 14-1 Results of Performance of Selected Preventive Care Procedures from Chart Reviews in Study Practice A.

Note: "Mammo" means mammography; "CBE" refers to clinical breast examination; "Pap" means Papanicolaou smear; "FOBT" means fecal occult blood test; "Sigmoid" refers to sigmoidoscopy; "Flu" refers to influenza immunization (for patients 65 years or older); "Sm. Couns." refers to documentation of smoking cessation counseling for patients who smoke. The number in parentheses under the name of each procedure is the number of years reviewed for that procedure.

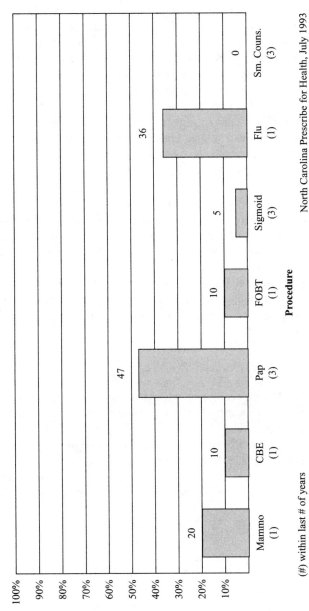

Preventive Care Performance

Chart Reviews, Patients 50 and Older

(#) within last # of years

North Carolina Prescribe for Health, July 1993

Figure 14–2 Results of Performance of Selected Preventive Care Procedures from Chart Reviews in Study Practice B.
Note: "Mammo" means mammography; "CBE" refers to clinical breast examination; "Pap" means Papanicolaou smear; "FOBT" means fecal occult blood test; "Sigmoid" refers to sigmoidoscopy; "Flu" refers to influenza immunization (for patients 65 years or older); "Sm. Couns." refers to documentation of smoking cessation counseling for patients who smoke. The number in parentheses under the name of each procedure is the number of years reviewed for that procedure.

to try new strategies for increasing preventive care in their offices. The other half of the practices received support later in the project. The intervention phase involved a series of meetings with each practice, beginning with an initial meeting with physicians and staff to review their performance results and to set goals for increasing their rates of preventive care in areas in which the practice was interested. The purpose of the meeting was to identify preventive care procedures in which there might be a "performance gap," that is, a difference between the rate at which the practice currently provided that service for eligible patients and the rate at which it would like to provide the service. The project encourages practices to focus on a short list of preventive care procedures for older adults, especially breast, cervical, and colorectal cancer screening, smoking cessation counseling, and influenza immunizations. These procedures have been shown to be effective in reducing disease-specific mortality.

Because some physicians and practices are more ready than others to put into place changes to improve screening, counseling, and immunization procedures, the content of the first meeting was adapted to fit the "stage of readiness" of the practice. For those physicians who had concerns about the effectiveness of screening tests or about the desire of their patients to receive these tests, for example, the discussion centered on these issues. Such physicians were initially at a very low "readiness to change." For other physicians who believed in the effectiveness of the procedures and were interested in learning about strategies for improving their performance of these preventive services, the discussion moved into specific ideas and examples of ways to develop and implement an office system for preventive care.

Action Steps

To deliver preventive care routinely to patients eligible for these services, practices must carry out five steps: (1) identify patients' needs for preventive care services and prompt providers about these needs; (2) recommend these services to patients; (3) perform or order the services; (4) follow up the results of the services; and (5) recall patients at the next appropriate interval. These five steps provide the framework of the office system. Many practices already had methods in place for one or two of the steps, but few were routinely addressing all five steps in a systematic way.

Subsequent meetings with the practices centered on understanding the then-current method for carrying out the steps for preventive care and then making revisions to get each step done more systematically for all eligible patients. Project team members worked with practice staff to document any systems already in place that accomplished one or more of these steps. Project members then assisted physicians and office staff together to consider various options for new ways to perform these functions, thus developing a revised system for preventive care. Practices were offered an assortment of "tools" to assist them in carrying out the functions. "Tools" included such items as flow sheets, sticky notes for charts prompting providers about procedures that are due, patient brochures detailing which preventive services the practice recommends by age and gender group, stamps and crack-and-peel labels to be used as flow sheets for charts, stickers to indicate smoking status on the charts, tickler files with cards for tracking patient needs and self-addressed postcards to recall patients, and brief patient questionnaires to identify procedures done in the past (whether in the office or elsewhere), to be used as a prompt for physicians to perform or order the procedures. Practices could select from among these tools those that best fit their needs. To the extent possible, these tools were customized to the practice's specifications.

For example, one practice decided to routinely identify a patient's needs for preventive care by having the nurse check the chart and confirm with the patient as she is doing her in-take assessment. Then she communicates this information to the physician by using a removable sticky note on the encounter page. This note (Exhibit 14–1) lists several procedures for which the patient may be eligible. The nurse simply checks the boxes for those for which the patient is due. The physician may then indicate performance or ordering of the prompted procedures by checking another box on the note and returning the note to the nurse or receptionist. The nurse gives all women patients over the age of 50 a brochure that tells them which preventive care services the practice encourages for them (Exhibit 14–2); this step is briefly documented in the chart. Patients are notified by phone of their test results. After the appropriate interval, the practice sends a reminder postcard, asking patients to call the office to set up an appointment for another preventive care visit.

Practices were encouraged to set a "start date," the date on which they would put their revised plan into action. Project staff kept in close touch with the prac-

---

Exhibit 14–1 Design of a Removable Sticky Note Used To Prompt a Provider about Preventive Services Due and To Indicate Scheduling of the Procedure

Prevention Works!

Women 50+

Due For:	Schedule:
Mammo ☐	☐
CBE ☐	☐
Pap ☐	☐
Up to Date ☐	

Exhibit 14–2 Interior of a Brochure for Patient Education about Recommendations for Preventive Care for Women Ages 50 and Over

We recommend the following for women ages 50 and over:

✓ **1**
every year

Prevention Visit
Fecal Occult Blood Test
Clinical Breast Exam

✓ **1-2**
every one - two years

Mammogram

✓ **3**
every three years

Pap Smear

✓ **5**
every five years

Sigmoidoscopy
Cholesterol Screening

✓ **10**
every ten years

Tetanus Booster

tices during this time. A month or so after the start date, an observation visit was made to each practice by project staff members to see how the system was working and to get feedback from practice staff. Observations were made in the waiting room/reception area and in the clinical area and focused on a number of items, including use of the project's office system tools, availability and use of patient education materials on preventive care, patient waiting times, and interactions among staff, physicians, and patients. These visits were scheduled for one-half day and were conducted with the consent of the practice. The observations were presented to the practice at a later follow-up meeting between practice physicians and staff and project team members. These discussions often resulted in modifications of the preventive care office system.

MONITORING

One of the most challenging aspects of the CQI intervention is to find ways to monitor the new system and to provide practices with feedback on how they are doing at increasing preventive care. As with personal attempts to change old behavior patterns and maintain new ones, the difficulty often lies not in making a change, but in keeping it going. One idea used to give practices feedback on their activities is to assist the practice in producing, at the beginning of the year, a list of all patients eligible for a certain procedure during that year. This list can often be generated by the practice billing and accounting computer system. The list then serves as a prompt to practice staff throughout the year to remind the listed patients about the procedure. They mark off the names of those patients who have received the preventive care and call or mail a postcard reminder to those who have not yet received the procedure. Sometimes computers can be used to keep track of how the practice is doing in performing preventive care.

In all, the practices in the intervention group receive support and consultation from the NC-PFH team for a period of 12 to 18 months. At the conclusion of the intervention phase, a repeat practice survey is conducted in all study practices. The repeat survey focuses on preventive care performance during the study period and allows comparisons between practices that have already received assistance and those that have not. Practices in the latter group are then offered assistance to develop office systems for preventive care in their offices. At the conclusion of the study, all practices are invited to attend a conference to discuss what was learned over the four-year period, to identify what was successful and what wasn't, and to determine strategies for diffusion of this approach to preventive care to a wider group of primary care practices.

SUMMARY

The NC-PFH project applied the principles of CQI to the challenge of improving preventive care in primary care practice. Each practice's own data, collected for them from chart reviews and patient questionnaires, was used to identify potential target areas for attention. The task of delivering preventive care was broken down into five separate steps, and each step was addressed individually. The process involved the practice as a whole, including physicians and staff, working together to solve a problem. Strategies were developed to monitor the process and to feed back to the practice the results of their efforts. The problem of lack of management expertise within practices and the reluctance to allow "outsiders" to work closely with them was overcome by the structure of the project, which was offered as a consultation, and by the sponsorship of the project by the medical professional organizations to which the physicians belonged.

THE FUTURE OF CQI IN PRIMARY CARE

Primary care medical practice will continue to face change as research continues to discover new information, as the health care system undergoes a reconfiguration, and as society demands an increasing level of quality and accountability from medical care. The application of CQI to this process of change in primary care practice holds great potential for helping physicians and their staff adapt to different ways of doing things. The challenge is to develop mechanisms for facilitating the use of CQI techniques in the thousands of individual, and very diverse, primary care practices. Medical professional organizations could play an important, ongoing role in this process by offering a service of CQI-based consultation to member physicians. Managed care organizations, health insurance companies, and professional liability carriers could offer incentives to providers for assessing the quality of care in primary care practices through the process of CQI. Finally, area health education centers and academic health centers could take a leading role in helping practices adjust to change by developing a new type of CME based on self-directed learning and set in the physician's own practice, thus enabling physicians not only to keep abreast of the ever-changing field of medicine but also to change their practice to better serve their patients.

Kit N. Simpson
Arnold D. Kaluzny
Curtis P. McLaughlin

Total Quality and the Management of Laboratories

15

The institutionwide implementation of total quality management (TQM) requires laboratory managers to be knowledgeable about the approach and involved in the implementation process. TQM is pervasive. The Joint Commission on Accreditation of Healthcare Organizations has framed its Agenda for Change in a TQM context, and the American Hospital Association has developed a guide to help hospitals design and implement TQM programs. Many consultants offer programs to educate managers and health professionals on the approach and its virtues. Some will succeed—yet many will fail. The objective of this chapter is to apply TQM within a clinical laboratory setting.

What is TQM and what is the unique contribution of laboratory managers to the TQM process? TQM is a continuous quality improvement process that goes well beyond the identification of outliers in performance. TQM aims at continuous process improvement, focusing on reducing the variation in all types of hospital processes using the scientific method and the energy and creativity of all levels of hospital personnel. It involves evaluating those processes primarily from a customer satisfaction point of view. Exhibit 15–1 outlines the principles behind TQM as perceived by Deming, one of its original architects. Westgard and Barry (1989) outline an alternative, effective paradigm for laboratory total quality based on the writings of Juran.

THE NEW PARADIGM

The implementation of TQM represents a paradigm shift for most health care organizations. The challenge is to make it work under normal hospital conditions. Success will require changes in hospital conditions:

Based on K.N. Simpson, A.D. Kaluzny, and C.P. McLaughlin, "Total quality and the management of laboratories." *Clinical Laboratory Management Review*, 5(6), November/December 1991, 448–449, 452–453, 456–458, 460, 462. Reprinted with permission, Clinical Laboratory Management Association, Inc. Copyright © 1991.

1. The objective of quality assurance must become continuous improvement rather than meeting fixed standards.
2. Multidisciplinary groups of professionals must come out of their enclaves (called silos, chimneys, or fiefdoms by some) and take collective responsibility for the patient care process.
3. Those groups must become accountable for meeting the customer's needs and expectations, with the customer being either the patient or the next user of the group's output.

Professional standards become moving targets, and the professional's task is to improve them one step at a time, one day at a time. Institutional success is then

---

Exhibit 15–1 Management Principles of TQM

TQM has two important parts:

1. It requires a paradigm shift in the organization's definition of quality from "good enough if it meets standards" to "we must work continuously to improve quality."
2. It uses a set of methods that ensures that decisions made about process improvement are based on the orderly application of scientific knowledge of how processes, numbers, and people behave.

The paradigm shift in the definition of and responsibility for the quality of an organizational product is supported by adherence to the 14 principles or points originally specified by Deming (highlighted in bold).

1. **Create constancy of purpose** by publishing to all workers "what you are about."
2. **Adopt a new philosophy,** and practice it—management and everybody.
3. **Understand the purpose of inspection:** it is for process improvement and not just to "catch" poor performers.
4. **End the practice of awarding business on the basis of the price tag:** the cheapest supplier often does not provide the best value.
5. **Improve constantly and foremost the system of production:** this means routinely changing procedures and processes to make them better.
6. **Institute training on the job**—for all workers, not just technical specialists.
7. **Institute leadership:** create leaders who see their role as teaching workers what the organization needs for them to do and who remove obstacles to good worker performance.
8. **Drive out fear:** create trust and a climate that encourages innovation.
9. **Break down barriers between departments:** we are all working toward the same goal and need to be as flexible as possible on who should do which job.
10. **Eliminate slogans, exhortations, and targets.** Improve the system: don't "drive" the workers.
11. **Eliminate quotas, management by numbers, or objectives:** instead, manage by example, leadership, and systems improvement.
12. **Remove barriers that rob people of pride of workmanship:** good work provides an intrinsic satisfaction, not the annual merit meeting.
13. **Encourage education and self-improvement for everyone:** treat people as assets to be maintained, not as expenses to be minimized.
14. **Put everyone in the organization to work to accomplish this transformation.**

measured in terms of the rate of improvement that is being made, not whether rigid standards are being met.

TQM: OLD TOOLS, NEW USES

The laboratory may seem to be an ideal place to begin implementing TQM because some TQM methods are techniques long used in laboratory quality control and management. Most laboratory workers are quite familiar with descriptive statistics, run charts, flow diagrams, checksheets, and application of the scientific method to problem analyses and planning situations. However, such familiarity can be both a blessing and a curse because it is often more difficult to get people to do "old things" in a new way than to teach them completely new methods.

In a TQM-oriented laboratory, the checksheets, run charts, and statistical tests are applied to the total production process and therefore encompass both the analytical and nonanalytical parts of laboratory work. In other words, the data collection and analysis methods (previously used in quality control to ensure the technical accuracy of the results) are applied to such quality aspects as timeliness of response to requests, turnaround time, and effective communication. Similarly, the flow charts used to examine and communicate the production process within a laboratory are extended to include nontechnical processes. The problem-solving process in a TQM-oriented laboratory is done by broad-based teams with members from all affected groups inside and outside the laboratory. Team members are trained in and use group process methods for identifying problems and generating solutions.

At this point, you may want to ask how this "TQM thing" differs from quality circles." The answer is, "in several ways." A TQM team is formed only when an opportunity for improvement (a "performance gap" or a problem) is identified as important to customers and is selected as a priority issue by management. This prevents groups of employees from spending time and other resources on issues with relatively minor potential to contribute to important organizational objectives. As another safeguard against solutions of limited practical value, the TQM team must identify the "owner" of the process and include this owner on the team. For example, the team responsible for assessing a process where the authority to make decisions is vested in physicians must include a physician representative. Representatives must have an expert understanding of the process and be actively involved in TQM group meetings. The TQM team must have expert representation from all major groups contributing to the process under study.

In a TQM-oriented laboratory, planning is not the production of documents written mainly to justify capital expenditures and budgets; it is a vigorous process used to improve communication and foster integration of the total work of the laboratory, and to link this work to the mission of the hospital. Plans are not dusty documents sitting on shelves in the offices of the medical and technical directors.

Many planning documents are publicly displayed as "storyboards" mapping problem definitions, process analyses, opportunities for process improvement, and the results of such improvements. Figure 15–1 outlines the TQM approach used by several hospitals, including examples of how TQM analytical tools might be used to study the provision of serum potassium results to emergency room customers.

TQM-oriented laboratories focus on improving customer satisfaction, but their "customers" may be defined differently from the traditional laboratory use of the word. TQM customers are individuals who use the products of your production process. Thus a customer may be a ward secretary responsible for charting routine results, a patient needing blood drawn for preadmission tests, or the anesthesiologist waiting for a STAT blood gas result. These individuals are the end users of a laboratory process and are customers who should be satisfied with the laboratory's product.

LABORATORY ISSUES

The statistical techniques of TQM will not present the same conceptual problems for clinical laboratory professionals that they do for some other medical professionals. Laboratory personnel already use them in research and in controlling laboratory operations. They are part of the scientific method of the field. The bigger challenge to laboratory specialists will be the requirement to venture out of their existing territories to participate in multidisciplinary processes and focus on issues related to customer satisfaction rather than just on test specificity, reliability, and accuracy. This will be especially challenging should group decisions favor a relaxation of standards bearing on technical quality to achieve greater customer satisfaction.

Installing TQM means learning how to manage group meetings better and understanding and respecting the objectives of other hospital functions. It requires involvement in management processes that are not under the control of the laboratory, working with other departments with less clearly defined objectives, and dealing with "real patients." It involves a new concept of supervision that is not top-down and largely procedural, but that enables and supports independent thinking and action.

TQM also involves looking outside the field for new empirically derived standards of performance (benchmarks) to emulate and may entail giving up some traditional normative standards. It involves taking initiative not to isolate the laboratory from the effects of varying demand, but to respond more directly to those variations. It may even mean disturbing a smoothly running system to see whether a new level of performance can be achieved. It means letting go of very tight controls to allow the workers to develop new and better approaches and requires accepting the fact that they are the process experts because they are closer to the work than their supervisors.

BARRIERS TO IMPLEMENTATION

The list of issues above indicates where resistance is likely to come in the laboratory. Resistance is likely to come from

1. perceived threats to professional autonomy
2. low tolerance of ambiguity in process and standards
3. difficulties in buying into organizational goals and issues
4. differing views of supervision and personal responsibility
5. concern with malpractice and quality assurance implications
6. unwillingness to accept consumer preferences and satisfaction goals
7. problems working with hospital administration and other professionals
8. lack of flexibility in planning and budgeting systems

Each of these resistance points or barriers can also be a fruitful area for personal and professional growth for both administrators and scientists. Success at overcoming them encourages further attempts to have an open, learning, and continuously improving organization.

Professional Autonomy

Health professionals have always struggled to protect their professional autonomy. Clinical pathology, with its monitoring, evaluating, and sometimes legal functions, must maintain its autonomy to fulfill its quality assurance role effectively. The fact that ancillary revenues are large and coveted by others has led to considerable bargaining power and to a perceived need to ward off "predators." More positively, the grounding of clinical chemistry and other subspecialties in hard science has conditioned laboratory personnel to value the hard data and reasoned scientific argument that applies in most areas of quality analysis. That is the value system of TQM.

Low Tolerance of Ambiguity and Fuzzy Standards

Laboratory personnel deal with physical systems in which cause and effect are logically explained. The world of services management and multidisciplinary groups requires all parties to deal with situations with a high degree of ambiguity and where standards and goals are less clear. Laboratory personnel may experience considerable frustration in such situations, but they also have an opportunity to broaden their skills in preparation for more senior management responsibilities.

Buying into Organizational Issues and Goals

Many laboratory personnel are not fully aware of the larger issues that affect their institutions. They are involved in their laboratories, but turn over the results

One TQM method uses a structured process (known as FOCUS) to identify, analyze, and design process improvements, and another known as PDCA to implement and institutionalize improvements.

Both FOCUS and PDCA are cyclical processes and provide a simple but effective "shorthand" for problem-solving and planning processes based on the scientific method. FOCUS specifies the steps to use in identifying and solving problems:

1 Find process to improve.
2 Organize team.
3 Collect information.
4. Understand variation in the process.
5. Select improvements.

PDCA reminds us to:
1 Plan and try out the change.
2 Do what it takes to implement the change.
3 Check the results.
4 Act to secure the change and to identify new problems.

The analytical tools used in FOCUS-PDCA include Ishikawa (fishbone) diagrams, flow charts, check sheets, Pareto charts, and run and control charts. The process is also carefully designed to include decision and communication tools such as brainstorming, nominal group process and consensus information to institute quality measures, and storyboards to communicate the results to others. Mentoring is a vehicle for continuous improvement of skills used in the process. An example of using TQM analytical tools to improve a laboratory's process for providing serum potassium results to their emergency room (ER) customers is shown below.

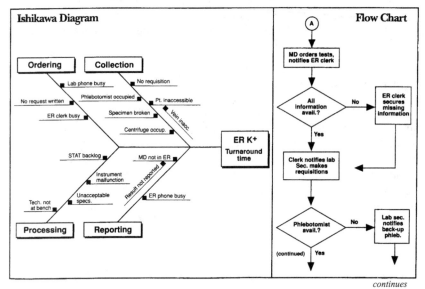

continues

Figure 15–1 A TQM Method. *Source:* Reprinted with permission of the Hospital Corporation of America. Not for further reproduction.

to clinicians to implement and have relatively little patient involvement. This presents a motivational problem inasmuch as they seldom see the good their work does. Participating in multidisciplinary groups can provide additional motivation because individuals will become more aware of the impact of their efforts. Yet initially they may be hesitant to participate because of their limited range of knowledge and reluctance to risk having that lack of knowledge exposed. TQM must be introduced in a nonthreatening manner to motivate involvement among various professional groups.

Checksheet   *continued*

Delays in production of Se K⁺ results from 1/1/91 to 1/7/91

Code/Delay Type		Mon	Tue	Wed	Thur	Fri	Sat	Sun	Total
A	Request not written by physician	I	I			I			3
B	Lab phone busy > 2 min.	I		I		II		I	5
C	Phlebotomists unavailable	III	II	III	III	II	IIII	III	20
D	Requisition not ready	II	I	I	I	I	III	II	11
E	Patient inaccessible	I	I	II	I		II	I	8
F	Vein inaccessible	I		II		I	II		6
G	Centrifuge busy	II		I		I			4
H	Specimen broken	II		I				I	4
I	STAT backlog	III			I		II	I	7
J	Tech. not at bench	II		II		I	II	I	8
K	Unacceptable specimen	I	I		II		I	II	7
L	Lab. sec. unavailable to report	III			I	I	I		6
M	ER phone not answered			I			II		3
N	MD not in ER	II		I		II		I	5
O	MD not answer page	I	I	II		II		II	8
P	Results not reported by ER sec.	II	I	II	I	III	II	II	13

Pareto Chart

Total Number of Delays — *Month of January* — Percent

Reasons for delay in production of STAT Se K⁺ for ER

C   P   D   E   J   O   Other

Control Chart

UCL = 48.08
Mean Number of Minutes
$\bar{c}$ = 31.3
LCL = 14.52

Daily mean minute turnaround Se K⁺ results for ER

M T W T F S S M T W T F S S M
Day of Week

Differing Views of Supervision and Personal Responsibility

Laboratories tend to be closely monitored and supervised. Individuals perform tasks under a watchful eye until they prove totally reliable. Standards and controls allow careful monitoring of accuracy and reliability. There is little tolerance of variability, and every individual is held responsible for his or her results. Systems are designed so that the process is under control, and errors are assumed to be the result of individual failings. It could prove difficult to convince first-line supervisors to take a more educational and supportive role and relinquish their hard-won management prerogatives. On the other hand, they have an opportunity to try out alternative management styles.

Concern for Malpractice and Quality Assurance Implications

Laboratory staff are especially aware of malpractice and quality assurance issues. They live with them all the time. They are often involved in providing information to evaluate other professionals. They have a vested interest in the quality assurance approach to quality. It will be difficult for them to accept a philosophy of continuous change and ever-shifting standards. They will be quick to see malpractice risks where clinical standards are involved. But they have considerable expertise to offer to the process and have an opportunity to make those skills appreciated by others in the hospital.

Accepting Customer Preferences and Evaluative Information

The "facts" that come from customer preferences and satisfaction reports are not the kind of hard data that scientists respect. Training will be needed to persuade scientists to accept such "soft" data. At first, they may argue that they need more "facts" even when the full interview and survey data are available. It may seem easier to discount that information than to factor it into decision making. Coming to accept the customer as the definer of quality can open up many new avenues of process evaluation and improvement.

Working with Hospital Administration and Others

TQM is a managerially driven approach. In the past, it has been easy for professionals to see administration as the enemy. There are natural friction points such as the distribution of ancillary income and the number of STAT orders allowed. Unless management spends considerable time and effort on developing communication and trust, the TQM program will be undermined by old wounds and fears. However, if that effort is successfully expended, a new and more effective set of relationships can be achieved throughout the hospital.

Lack of Flexibility in Planning and Budgeting

The pace of change that is proposed is rapid. This calls for more flexibility in planning and budgeting. Laboratories are capital-intensive operations in which system changes may require new software, layouts, and staffing patterns. Management is very likely to resist some proposals for change because of high investments already in place and the potential costs of any significant changes. Yet failing to implement work group suggestions because of rigidities in capital budgeting will undermine employee motivation.

ISSUES OF IMPLEMENTATION

How will TQM be implemented? Obviously with some difficulty. Consider two different implementation scenarios: Hospital A and Hospital B. Note that in the case of Hospital B the director of laboratories and several other managers could form the nucleus for starting the implementation process.

Hospital A had been caught up in the enthusiasm of TQM and clearly recognized that now was the time for action. TQM was an opportunity to turn their organization around and deal with a variety of problems. The effort began at the top.

The CEO held a retreat with top-level managers. They invited an external consultant to facilitate the process, with the conclusion being that TQM would be implemented within this organization. This group, in conjunction with an external consultant, published a revised mission statement and hired a vice president for TQM. That vice president took charge of this important activity and, as a member of the top management team, implemented a series of programs to redefine "the corporate culture." A series of hospitalwide training programs to enhance managerial skills to conduct the required statistical analyses and to deal with the interpersonal issues necessary to achieve the full benefits of a TQM approach were also implemented. These hospitalwide programs were further institutionalized by revising the performance appraisal system and conducting quarterly organizational assessment inventories.

Hospital B was equally impressed with the potential of TQM for dealing with a comparable set of issues of quality and cost containment but followed a slightly different approach. In this situation, top-level administrators as a group initiated a review of the organization's activities, identifying potential areas of improvement that covered a range of hospital functions. Early in their discussions, they appointed a task force composed of important mid-level managers, including nurses, physicians, dietary and laboratory personnel, and individuals from the business office. This group visited a number of other hospitals that had implemented or were in the process of implementing a TQM program.

This group provided the nucleus for developing a series of cross-functional teams directly relevant to providing patient services. For example, an operating room (OR) nursing team composed of the OR supervisor, central supply supervisor, and the head nurses of surgical floors began reviewing the specific processes involving their respective units. Another cross-functional team involved dietary and nursing floors focusing on providing food services within the organization.

Another group, which included laboratory personnel, looked at the turnaround of laboratory results with an eye to improving the hospital's capacity to serve patients and physicians. The function of these groups was to understand the work flow and to identify areas that represented problems. Each group was charged with the responsibility of resolving, or at least minimizing, problems in operating patient services.

While these task forces were ongoing within the organization, another task force was established to draft and/or refine the existing mission statement to be shared throughout the organization. Mid-level managers were given support and coaching as they began to deal with the suggestions and recommendations evolving from the cross-functional groups. Some managers were enthusiastic, others neutral, and others antagonistic. The managerial challenge was to provide support because employees' involvement and the team approach were central to the overall success of the operation. Managers were provided with mentors and their performance reviewed in terms of how well they functioned as role models for the TQM system.

As specific recommendations were made by cross-functional groups, it became increasingly apparent that existing information and performance appraisal systems were inconsistent with many recommendations. Modeling these structures became a major priority so that both systems reflected the underlying assumptions and data needs of the TQM activities. Finally, Hospital B was concerned about overall institutionalization of TQM and set up an oversight committee to monitor the program and to identify problems as they arose. The committee was composed of a cross section of individuals within the hospital, and individuals were rotated through this task force on a staggered basis, thus ensuring continuity over time.

Obviously, these two scenarios represent different approaches to implementing TQM. The first is a top-down program and, although firm empirical evidence is not available, is not likely to succeed. The program is based on the assumption that promulgating companywide programs, mission statements, and training courses will transform organizations and that employee behavior is changed by altering an organization's formal structure and incentives. As described by Beer et al.,

> This theory gets the change process exactly backward. In fact, individual behavior is powerfully shaped by the organizational roles that people play. The most effective way to change behavior, therefore, is to put people into new organizational contexts which impose new roles, responsibilities and relationships on them. This creates a situation that forces new attitudes and behaviors on people. (Beer et al., 1990, p. 159)

Regardless of whether either of these two scenarios represent your institution, a number of action steps are critical to the success of TQM implementation.

Identifying a "Performance Gap"

Perhaps the single most important factor in implementing a change process such as TQM is to highlight a perceived discrepancy between what the organization or a unit within the organization is doing and what it might or should be doing. This creates the opportunity to recognize a problem and generates the need to search for a solution. The TQM approach must then be identified as a possible solution to a recognized problem.

Emphasize Understanding the Work Process, Not Just Programmatic Change

Organizations often institute programmatic initiatives focused on changing knowledge and attitudes of personnel rather than on reshaping how work is actually performed. The task alignment facilitated by process analysis provides an opportunity to reorganize employee roles, responsibilities, and relationships to resolve specific problems. Moreover, as described in Hospital B's scenario, the flow of work can be analyzed horizontally within the organization by focusing on the substantive challenges involved in improving patient care services.

Provide Support for Personnel

TQM is a new way of doing business within the organization. Managers and personnel must provide the necessary skill training in terms of statistics and interpersonal skills and also support for staff to improve these new competencies over time through mentored practice. Developing new roles, responsibilities, and relationships requires a great deal of effort. Given the structural inertia that exists within professional organizations, it is easy to regress to well-established behavior patterns rather than to develop proficiency in the new roles, responsibilities, and relationships dictated by the TQM approach. People must be given access to training sessions, on or off site, and be encouraged to attend and to try out the concepts that they have learned in the job setting. They must be sent in sufficient critical mass from a work group to accomplish change in that workplace. Their efforts must be recognized, celebrated, and rewarded.

Monitor the Program Closely over Time

TQM is not an added function in the organization. It is multiplicative, resulting in an organizational transformation. Because TQM involves a fundamental change in what drives the organization and requires new ways of working, as well as basic cultural changes, implementation must be monitored carefully to ensure that all parts of the organization and its systems are changing together and at the desired rate.

Support the Program Behaviorally and Verbally

Management in the institution and in the laboratory must show its support of the TQM concept. This support must be verbal on numerous ceremonial occasions and also behavioral in that fact-based answers are demanded and considered; managers must follow the paradigm adopted in the TQM program in their own investigations.

CONCLUSION

TQM represents a unique opportunity for laboratory managers. As this new managerial paradigm is implemented by hospitals throughout the country, laboratory professionals and their managers can participate fully and provide leadership for their organizations. Laboratories are clearly critical actors in the Hospital B scenario. Laboratory managers need to understand the processes and operations within their own environments, but, more importantly, they need to understand the context within which the program is operating. Although the challenges are great, failure to assume responsibility is not only a missed opportunity to provide leadership but also a failure to enhance quality of laboratory services.

Arnold D. Kaluzny
Curtis P. McLaughlin
Kit N. Simpson

Applying Total Quality Management Concepts to Public Health Organizations

16

Total quality management (TQM) has arrived on the health services scene, or at least in parts of the health services system. The increasing use of TQM is an exciting development, but TQM application lags in the process of providing health services in the public sector, specifically public health agencies. TQM offers public health organizations a unique opportunity to adopt a powerful tool for strengthening management and presents a fundamental challenge to public health administrators. The objective of this chapter is to describe the potential of TQM as a major managerial innovation compared with the current management of many public health agencies and to offer guidelines to help users realize its full potential in public health applications.

STANDARDS AND ASSESSMENT

Standards in the practice of public health traditionally emphasized (1) health outcomes, (2) flexibility to allow communities to establish and quantify their own objectives, and (3) the role of government as a residual guarantor responsible for assuring that prevention services are provided through community agencies. These concepts are reflected in the American Public Health Association's *Model Standards*, published in 1985. The edition of *Model Standards* published by the American Public Health Association in 1991 links standards to meeting the health goals for the nation in the year 2000. The standards and the year 2000 objectives are an important strategic planning component, providing public health agencies with (1) a synthesis of current scientific knowledge of health promotion

Source: Adapted from Kaluzny, A.D., McLaughlin, C.P., and Simpson, K.N., "Applying Total Quality Management Concepts to Public Health Organizations," *Public Health Reports*, 107(3):257–264, May–June 1992. U.S. Department of Health and Human Resources, Public Health Service, Washington, DC.

and disease prevention, (2) statistical data on the current state of the nation's health, and (3) a prioritized list of specific health objectives.

The recent development and availability of the *Assessment Protocol for Excellence in Public Health* (APEX-PH) (1990) provides a methodology for systematically assessing departmental operations relative to meeting standards. APEX-PH gives agency leaders a clear, comprehensive, and flexible protocol for assessing organizational and community resources and needs. The workbook format helps agency leaders to meet national health promotion and disease prevention objectives at the community level. The APEX-PH protocol is a collaborative effort of the American Public Health Association, the Association of Schools of Public Health, the Association of State and Territorial Health Officers, the Centers for Disease Control, the National Association of County Health Officials, and the U.S. Conference of Local Health Officers.

The availability of the Model Standards and APEX-PH provides health agencies with a rational method to assess their potentials and goals for health outcomes. Guided by community health objectives and assessment findings, managers can formulate an agency-community health plan that can serve to direct work within programmatic areas. The health objectives that define the direction of an agency's strategy need to be broad and multidimensional.

The organizational assessment process provides a framework for developing and maintaining the capacity to carry out a community health plan. To assure that program objectives are met, health departments traditionally have depended on a system of performance standards and quality assurance (QA) methods. Although these efforts are necessary, they are not sufficient to meet the challenges now facing public health agencies. Instead of relying on traditional performance standards and QA methods, TQM offers a means to improve ongoing processes and to enhance agency performance within a changing environment.

TQM STRENGTHS

TQM focuses on work processes, applying analytical and behavioral techniques to improve those processes within an organization. For example, a group of nursing and laboratory personnel may select a process for improvement, such as untimely deliveries of laboratory test results to a prenatal clinic. Using a series of flow diagrams, they may be able to identify the steps involved in the process and the factors that may be contributing to delays. Drawing on this understanding, the group may be able to identify and try steps to improve the timeliness of the test results, monitoring the results to try to achieve continuous improvement.

In such an application, TQM presents a fundamental challenge to the use of internal performance standards to achieve public health objectives. Although the use of performance standards can be a starting point for TQM, continuous quality management goes beyond conforming to management standards. TQM includes systematic analysis of the work performed by the organization, with emphasis on the horizontal integration of services across program areas. Attention can be given, for example, to identifying and reducing variations in the work performance of interdisciplinary teams or natural work groups. Improvement is based on both outcome and process. An organization must constantly improve its problem-solving capacity, using performance standards as leverage in the improvement process. As described by some advocates, such organizations "continuously push at the margins of their expertise, trying on every front to be a bit better than before. Standards to them are ephemeral milestones on the road to perfection" (Hayes et al., 1988, p. 25).

TQM requires that change be based on the needs and desires of patients, clients, and health personnel involved in the entire work process, and possibly across programmatic areas. TQM requires meaningful participation involving all personnel levels. In particular, TQM requires rapid and thoughtful response by top management to suggestions made by participating personnel. TQM is the essence of the structured, participative philosophy behind the recommendations for using the Model Standards and APEX-PH Process to achieve community health objectives.

TQM requires that all personnel have a clear understanding of the work process and its relationship to the larger system. TQM requires using a rigorous process analysis and evaluation of all ongoing activities and the recognition and application of underlying psychosocial principles affecting people and groups within the organization. TQM requires accepting the fundamental assumption that most problems encountered in public health agencies are not the result of errors by individual persons, but of the inabilities of the system, within which all personnel must function, to perform adequately.

Whereas Model Standards and APEX-PH focus on strategic health outcome objectives and community stakeholders as the ultimate health department customers, TQM examines each link in the process used to achieve these public health goals. The customers in TQM are not only the community or clients for whom services are designed, but the many users of the agency's output, including health providers within the organization itself. The criterion is not whether the work meets some management performance standard per se, but whether the user (often a member of a different profession, or a set of personnel with the agency, or a host of other public and private health service agencies) is satisfied with the timeliness and usefulness of the service being provided by or within the public health agency. The managerial challenge is not to assure adherence to fixed standards, but to spend time and energy in facilitating and assuring continual improvement in the many interrelated processes that are the work of the department.

TRADITIONAL PERFORMANCE STANDARDS AND TQM

To illustrate the potential of TQM in public health, the following contrasts TQM with traditional management approaches that use performance standards.

The two views are not intended to be mutually exclusive, but to provide a heuristic for understanding the fundamental similarities and differences.

Traditional model	*TQM model*
Legal or professional authority	Collective or managerial responsibility
Specialized accountability	Process accountability
Administrative authority	Participation
Meeting standards	Meeting process and performance expectations
Long planning horizon	Short planning horizon
Quality assurance	Continuous improvement

Legal and Professional Authority versus Collective and Managerial Responsibility

A typical public health department represents an amalgam of legal and professional authority. Activities such as sanitation in restaurants, assurance of safe water supplies, and control of epidemics are driven by legal authority. Other activities, such as family planning and prenatal care, are medical services made available, and these processes are characterized by professional autonomy and control. Both legal and professional control processes combine to assure the enforcement of employee performance standards and are perfect candidates for improvement. For example, the process of sanitation inspection may be filled with variation and unnecessary cost and, to the extent that the process is truly understood, provides an opportunity for improving efficiency and customer satisfaction.

The TQM model focuses on the system, emphasizing collective managerial responsibility, not simply legal or professional mandates. TQM assumes that the system is the primary source of problems, and by better understanding that system, provides opportunities for improving service. TQM focuses on the work process, not on the individual worker. The objective is not to rely solely on legal or professional authority, but to challenge the interdisciplinary work group involved with the process to assume ownership of that process and take responsibility for its continuous improvement. The group most expert at improving this process is one that includes the workers currently involved in the process. In this respect, the process is conceptually compatible with providing public health services through a multidisciplinary team process.

Specialized Accountability versus Process Accountability

Public health professionals traditionally expect autonomy in performing their work. As long as there is a reasonable approximation to the standard, their autonomy is often assured. Unfortunately, intense needs for specialization, combined with professional autonomy, segment the work process. Professional groups, reinforced by specific standards, assume ownership of only part of the work process, and no single group is held accountable for the total process.

Under the performance standards approach, individual professionals seek to optimize their portion of the process, often with limited knowledge of the system within which their portion of the process works. If individual providers own parts of the process, they can improve only parts of that process. For example, nurses may try to reduce the waiting time for mothers and babies in the well-baby clinic. But since they are involved with only part of the process, albeit a significant component, any unilateral change may create problems and resistance among clerical personnel, laboratory technicians, those involved with the Special Supplemental Food Program for Women, Infants, and Children (WIC), and perhaps others who have not been involved in their effort to reduce waiting time.

TQM requires that improvement be the responsibility of all those involved in the process. Thus TQM challenges professional autonomy and demands accountability for the total work process. Accountability for the total process requires that change in the process be the responsibility of all personnel, emphasizing process improvement rather than specialized accountability.

Administrative Authority versus Participation

Under a system of performance standards, operational standards are likely to be set by some external credentialing body and implemented by administrative authority. TQM instead emphasizes interdisciplinary teams working toward the objectives set by the customers, who may be public health professionals, payers, clients, or clients' family members. By using interdisciplinary teams or groups, TQM makes workers and their front line supervisors responsible for quality instead of charging an administrator with monitoring standards.

Maintaining quality no longer consists of simply taking names and penalizing those who make errors or deviate from the standard. It means setting performance expectations that are realistic in the local setting, helping personnel to monitor their own performance, and empowering them to take corrective action. For example, funding regulations may require that a clinic be held twice a week for four hours, whereas patient preference might be that the clinic be held twice a week for three hours each time and be open on Saturday mornings for the two remaining hours. The obvious challenge is to make the health department respond and become customer driven and not merely rule driven.

Meeting Standards versus Meeting Process and Performance Expectations

The performance standards approach is applicable to a wide range of service areas. If one meets the standard, then one can divert energies and resources to meeting another standard. Standards are anonymous, are potentially compelling, and often provide powerful leverage for financing. Standards often are augmented by the larger profession, by other agencies, and by the courts. Meeting a new standard may require new resources. Since these standards are externally imposed, they transfer the onus of requesting more resources to nonagency personnel.

That is not the case with TQM. TQM requires that the agency take responsibility for its own standards and for their implementation. Anonymity is removed. The agency has to be explicit about its current record of performance and commit itself to continuous improvement. For example, state rules may require that two attempts be made to contact a patient whose Papanicolaou (Pap) smear result comes back positive. Agency personnel may decide to improve the notification process and use statistics and process analysis to challenge personnel to increase the rate of successful notification. The improvement process is, in this case, not guided by the external imposition of standards, but by the dynamic process of group effort.

Benchmarking involves comparing current activities and outcomes against the best of the competition, the idea being to develop a product or process that is better than that of the competition. The issue is not how well the agency performs a service compared with relevant organizations, but how the service is provided within other standards, compared with a given agency. Although *competition* may not be the operative term for public health departments since they have a monopoly on many of their services, public health agencies do have peer organizations upon which to base their comparisons.

The reliance on peers for the standard means that the standard changes as soon as one peer achieves a higher level of performance. One of the management lessons learned from the Japanese is that different and higher expectations do lead to better results. Benchmarks do not necessarily have to come from close peers. Indeed, the goal for reducing clinic waiting times can be a local bank or a popular restaurant rather than a neighboring clinic. This changes staff perspective from one of "we are no worse than anyone else" to one of "how good can we become?"

Long Planning Horizon versus Short Planning Horizon

TQM may help bridge the gap between strategy and performance. Model standards provide for long-term rather than short-term planning. For example, although the Model Standards Program and APEX-PH emphasize flexibility and local applicability, the process of development requires extensive consultation with external groups. This makes it difficult to relate the standards to the day-to-day concerns of the operating agency. TQM, however, is an internally oriented, from-the-bottom-up approach meant to take effect over a short period. The approach requires rapid feedback to the group making recommendations in order to support and sustain their motivation. As improvements are made, staff members initiate the search for new sources of improvement as part of the continuous improvement process.

Quality Assurance versus Continuous Improvement

Within the world of standards, QA is the vehicle for retrospectively observing deviations from a standard. QA measures have the quality of measurability and place responsibility on persons. Either standards are met or they are not met. It is easy for providers, advocates, politicians, and courts to focus on deviations and not on the standard. Improvement of the standard has great value. Improvement beyond the standard has little value, and consequently little attention is paid to trade-offs among standards.

TQM takes a different approach to quality. It requires focusing on the system as a source of error and emphasizes continuous improvement in performing an activity. TQM emphasizes the fact that improving the system is part of the job description of all personnel, not just management or designated QA personnel.

PREPARING FOR CHANGE

The ultimate success of TQM in public health depends on the ability of public health officers, administrative managers, professionals, and oversight groups to integrate the two approaches of community-defined standards for health outcomes and TQM for process improvement to achieve desired outcomes. Success will depend on their ability to meet the following challenges.

Action 1: Redefine the Role of Management

The achievement of community health outcomes through TQM requires that managers function both vertically and horizontally within the organization. Horizontally, focus must be on a work process that involves agency teams across, rather than simply within, programmatic areas. Entry-level credentials and technical knowledge will be necessary for managers, but will not be sufficient. Management must become responsible for a work process that transcends programmatic areas. That requires a common sense of mission and vision for the future, as well as skills in epidemiology, effecting organizational change, and using process analysis. Management, particularly top management, must assume direct responsibility and participate in training and skill-building activities.

Managerial change is required in the vertical relationships within an organization. Top-level managers will do less decision making, yet will be responsible for managing the development of a supportive environment and facilitating the changes required for reallocating resources as the process changes. Middle management will have responsibility for monitoring the process and authorizing the process changes that are recommended by the interdisciplinary improvement teams. First-line management will assume more decision-making authority. This authority, however, will be used in a consensual, rather than a directive, process.

Action 2: Define a Supportive Corporate Culture

Within health care, there is a tendency to look for the big breakthrough, the quick fix, and the gold standard. Although TQM occasionally produces a breakthrough, its philosophy is one of incessant change, of working with what is available, but with very high expectations. Imai (1986), for example, observes that Westerners focus on performance, whereas Easterners are concerned with both process and performance. Kilmann (1989) further suggests that change will require pervasive modifications in structure, reward systems, inservice educational philosophy, management skills, and team-building strategies.

Specifically, a health department requires a culture that supports continuous improvement in all the processes by which it implements its programs and interacts with its clients, including never-ending improvement in standards and their uses and values. This means that the workers and managers must know and accept their starting point and focus on how to improve to achieve one short-run goal, followed by another, and so on. This means that they must be willing to be evaluated on the rate of improvement rather than on whether improvement merely reached a specific level within a standard and maintained it. Clearly, the culture will have to support the flexibility and creativity required to achieve these ends over time.

Action 3: Redefine the Role of Citizen Oversight and Regulation

Public health organizations are governed by citizen oversight groups, and their mission, goals, and objectives are strongly influenced by regulatory requirements. It is important that citizen oversight groups and regulatory agencies be brought into the continuous improvement process. Oversight groups and regulatory agencies will have to be convinced of the value of a process in which one measures the current level of performance and allocates the resources needed to reach an improved level in a continuous quest for quality. They must provide the department with greater budgetary flexibility than previously, especially if a rigid line-item budget has been used. Interdisciplinary quality improvement teams quickly lose interest if improvement ideas are generated but not implemented because of rigid line-item budget adherence.

The purpose, process, and outcomes of regulation must be reexamined to assess their influence on health departments involved with TQM. Legislators, relevant public officials, citizen oversight groups, and public health managers must work closely and support experimentation in the form of carefully and continuously evaluated demonstration projects. Moreover, alliances involving industry and other health care providers already using TQM need to be developed. Such alliances must influence relevant legislative and regulatory bodies to support enabling activities.

Action 4: Map a Trajectory of Objectives

Implementing TQM requires a trajectory of changes that are expected over a period. It is not acceptable to request additional resources under the threat that failure to provide resources will reduce compliance with standard X and lose Y dollars. In fact, this approach is debilitating in the long run. It questions whether management has the initiative to set relevant objectives and take into account the unique problems faced by the organization beyond simply complying with externally imposed standards. Instead, TQM requires a series of objectives that facilitate discussion about trade-offs in time and in resources and focuses attention on reducing costs by improving the overall work process.

Action 5: Drive the Benchmarking Process from the Top

The greatest challenge will be the benchmarking process. Professionals often consider the organization at which they trained as the gold standard, and are content to emulate that approach. They do not consider daily activities in process terms and are reluctant to collect and analyze process data. They hesitate to learn from what other people are doing in very different settings. Top management must provide leadership in pointing out that, although there are differences, much can be learned from the similarities. For example, it may be difficult for public health professionals to consider emulating the way that Disneyland handles waiting lines without feeling that their profession is being demeaned, but good examples of how other types of clinics handle waiting lines are available as a comparison. Private clinics, local hospitals, and other human service organizations can be used as benchmarks.

Action 6: Create Organizational Slack

The effective implementation of TQM can be seriously hampered if there are absolutely no resources to support the improvement process. Although process improvement creates discretionary resources by reducing waste built into current work processes, initially resources may be required if the improvement process is to be credible at the onset. Since management does not know *a priori* the recommendation, the resources cannot all be budgeted, and reserve resources must be available to speed implementation. Failure to provide such resources only guarantees failure. Assuring some slack resources, or at least resource flexibility, may be the greatest challenge to the implementation of TQM in a public health agency.

Action 7: Empower the Staff to Address Problems

Many public health professionals have learned not to venture beyond their own programmatic areas. They are content to either ignore problems or assume that problems are the responsibility of others within the organization. TQM requires that professionals assume direct responsibility for identification and resolution of problems. This involves documenting processes of work, including such fundamental questions as, what are the processes, what are their objectives, and how do they really work? Moreover, it requires an understanding of how the work of one group relates to and affects the work of another and the use of this knowledge to gather and analyze data and make recommendations to improve the work process. People need to overcome status barriers. Management must provide rapid feedback on resulting proposals to improve operations. Although all of these actions require maturity in those meeting the challenge, they also require that processes be redesigned and that a learning environment be developed that is conducive to building customer and process knowledge through statistical and scientific thinking. Fortunately, both the importance of scientific thinking and the use of statistics are accepted parts of professional public health practice. The challenge will be to take these tools and apply them to internal work processes and outcomes in the health department instead of using them exclusively for problem identification and process adjustment with regard to the larger community.

Action 8: Avoid the Best Practice Syndrome

Although the use of TQM within public health requires benchmarking, it is important that public health professionals avoid adopting so-called best practice thinking. Best practice cannot exist independently of the needs of the clients and the resources of the organization. For example, in industry, competing firms often achieve successful outcomes using strikingly different approaches. One involves computers, while another does not. One relies heavily on robots, while another does not. What is common to all is that they develop innovative ways to meet the demands that their customers place on them, given the resources that they have available. Following best practice without respect to the strategic demands of the organization's environment means that the organizations get the so-called flavor of the month in terms of new concepts that guide management's search for solutions. Management techniques should never be panaceas to be applied indiscriminately. The challenge is to broaden the array of alternative approaches that managers can select from, not to select one approach to be used by everyone for everything.

Action 9: Set Realistic Time Expectations

The successful integration of TQM, Model Standards, and APEX-PH requires a realistic estimate of the time required to implement TQM and to observe its effect. The process of adapting and institutionalizing TQM, even in a small health department, will require a number of years. What is not known is whether it is best to view the organization as an entity or to start with selected work processes amenable to change within parts of the organization. The latter course takes fewer resources initially and, if it is a success, will influence the attitudes of others. However, attitudinal changes at the top are so critical that the failure to use TQM throughout the organization can severely limit more restricted efforts.

Action 10: Make Management a Model for Continuous Improvement

Since people are more impressed with actions than words, management needs to model the process for the organization. Professionals especially will be looking for discrepancies between what is advocated and what is practiced. Top management must provide the leadership and must consciously use the process as part of the overall operation. TQM is not a program to be implemented but a process to be initiated.

CONCLUSIONS

Public health organizations and public health practice face continual challenges that require a new look at how and why we organize and manage services. TQM, along with the Model Standards and the APEX-PH protocol, represent complementary methods for assuring that excellent services are provided to the community. As more health service organizations within the private sector adopt TQM concepts, the public health community needs to examine the potential of TQM within its own organizational framework.

TQM, combined with the Model Standards and the use of the APEX-PH protocol, provides an opportunity for public health professionals to transform public health practice to meet the increasingly difficult challenges we face.

Susan DesHarnais
Curtis P. McLaughlin

17

Applying and Supporting CQI in Academic Health Centers

Academic health centers (AHCs) play a central role in health care delivery. They deliver a significant portion of the nation's direct health care. They educate virtually all of the country's physicians as undergraduates and postgraduates and a significant number of other health professionals. They conduct much of the nation's basic health care research, especially clinical research. Some, such as the University of Utah (James, 1989) and the University of Michigan (Gaucher and Coffey, 1993) have also taken the lead in implementing, evaluating, and adapting total quality management (TQM) to the health care setting. Furthermore, AHCs can take a much more active role in justifying the use of continuous quality improvement (CQI), in conducting research relevant to the issues uncovered in CQI efforts, and in disseminating the results of clinical quality efforts throughout the health care system. The purpose of this chapter is to review the CQI roles that an AHC could and should play and to recommend ways that the AHC can incorporate CQI into its teaching, its research, its patient care, and its outreach. Outreach in continuing education is especially important to the dissemination of CQI.

TEACHING

A symposium announcement associated with the 13th Annual Conference of the Association of American Medical Colleges (November 12–13, 1991) stated that "the state of development of quality improvement in medical education at the present time can be characterized as embryonic. There is much to be done in the area of theory development and application. In addition, as educational institutions, medical schools have a responsibility to educate future physicians about

Source: Based on DesHarnais, S., and McLaughlin, C.P., Clinical Quality, Risk-Adjustment, and Outcome Measures in Academic Medical Centers, in *Managing in an Academic Health Care Environment*, W.F. Minogue, ed., with permission of the American College of Physician Executives, © 1992.

continuous quality improvement." The proposers of the symposium mention work at Harvard on continuous improvement applied to curriculum development and the Cleveland Asthma Project at Case Western Reserve Medical School. Their assessment appears to be correct. Interest in CQI as a model seems to be centered much more in hospital administration than in medical school teaching, possibly because hospitals, under Diagnosis-Related Groups (DRGs), have felt the impact of rising costs much more than faculty practice plans have and only they are subject to the Joint Commission on Accreditation of Healthcare Organizations' (Joint Commission) requirement of having a CQI process in place by the next accreditation visit. Furthermore, faculties are much more likely to acknowledge excellence in research and excellence in teaching than excellence in clinical care.

When To Teach CQI in the Medical Curriculum

Managers are often asking about when and how physicians should be trained in TQM. It seems unlikely that specific TQM training will be effective when added to the undergraduate medical curriculum as a discrete topic. That will just be another·session that many students will cut. The place where CQI training is most likely to be effective is in residency programs. There the learners are interacting with the hospital system with great intensity. Some residents and fellows, especially the chief residents, are coming into contact with the governance process, sitting on committees such as Pharmacy and Therapeutics. Their education should include the results of team studies in their field in order to demonstrate that CQI is legitimate clinical research, participation on teams applicable to their area of specialty, and using the residency program as a CQI project in and of itself. This is the time in their careers that they begin to see the strengths and weaknesses of their departments in systems terms. They are also sensitive to the fact that the system is very poorly designed to meet their needs and that their approach as "short-timers" affects their motivation to fight for change in the many Kafkaesque situations in which they find themselves. Using their program as an object lesson might do a lot to enhance their interest and to motivate them to devote their scarce time and energy to participating in the CQI process.

An alternative time to train physicians in AHCs is when they first begin teaching. If they have not been a chief resident, the committees and the governance structure of the school, the teaching hospital and the department are all new to them, and they are again sensitized to the system, or nonsystem as the case may be. This is a critical time to involve young physicians because once they learn how to manipulate the system, many of them detach themselves from it and thus become harder to engage in systems issues.

The University of Michigan and the University of Rochester, for example, are involving faculty in research on clinical pathways and clinical guidelines and are offering financial support for research, including faculty time, to support the development of clinical pathways, recognizing the traditional routes of motivation through professional recognition. Improvements in clinical pathways are likely to be reflected quite rapidly in the clinical behavior of new learners. However, this approach teaches little about the CQI process and philosophy and may take a long time to impact on the experienced physicians working in other settings.

Continuing Education

Those responsible for continuing medical education and Area Health Education Programs (AHECs) can contribute by making sure that the results of CQI efforts, including illustrations of the philosophy and process of CQI, are included in a broad spectrum of continuing education courses. There has been some demand for CQI training in AHEC programs, but the likelihood of reaching a wide cross section is greater when CQI outcomes are included in a variety of continuing education offerings. Therefore management must develop CQI champions in continuing education as well as in clinical practice and research.

Practice Management

Faculty practice plans under the resource based relative value scale are more likely to become involved in issues of cost and quality than in the past if they are going to fulfill their financial commitments to faculties. Initial efforts will be improved outpatient care facilities to attract patients, participation in HMOs and PPOs, outreach through satellite centers, and more aggressive marketing of services. With that, however, will have to come concerns about customer-oriented quality-of-care measures. This is not likely to happen rapidly, given the current emphasis on selecting faculty practice plan executives based on their ability to do accounting, billing, and collections. They will get involved in quality of care issues only when the dean, department chair, or medical director becomes very active in practice management and emphasizes quality improvement.

A likely reason for a teaching group to become involved in practice standards is the utilization of a quality improvement program in a competing HMO. Gottlieb et al. (1990) report the development of a number of algorithms for use by the Harvard Community Health Program (HCHP) staff and their incorporation into continuing medical education programs and into information gathering systems. They suggest that the criteria for developing algorithms should include:

- Frequency, involving commonly seen clinical conditions
- Unexplained variability in clinical practice, resource utilization, or referral patterns
- Conflict with internal resource constraints
- Apparent risk management problems

- Perceived quality of care issues with patients, clinicians, or managers
- Introduction of new technology
- Uncertainty about use or about cost implications

These appear to be the criteria that should be of interest to the faculty of a medical school as well. Yet it seems that HMOs are leading the way, presumably because the expectations of autonomy in practice activity are much less strong in a staff-model HMO such as HCHP (Madison and Konrad, 1988).

Competitive stimuli, however, can force medical school staff into quality studies. For example, the faculty of an academic family medicine department became truly interested in continuity of care only when the largest employer in the community threatened to cancel its worker's compensation/industrial medicine contract with the department because of time costs related to lack of physician continuity. There had also been many complaints about continuity of care from individual patients, but the staff became involved only when threatened with the loss of this major account. Most of the time, lost patients disappear one at a time without a ripple.

Because of the insulation of academic departments from such information through the hospital and the practice plan, improvements in care are more likely to come about when the faculty decides that the learners in the institution must experience practicing the right way. Quality will most likely come about when the faculty, as well as the teaching hospital management, decide that students (undergraduate and residents) must see exemplary practice in action. It will take medical leadership within the faculty to make that an organizational objective. In doing so, the leadership must also deal with the fact that faculty in a teaching setting are significantly less efficient than their competitors who are not teaching. As Garg et al. (1991) point out, this means facing up to some of the true costs of teaching in the clinical setting, especially in the increasingly important outpatient clinic.

Inclusion in Curriculum Development

Headrick et al. (1991) report on the four-year educational project at Case Western Reserve University School of Medicine to introduce CQI into the curriculum. It is part of an eight-week clerkship at one of a number of urban and suburban clinic sites. The application was highly constrained by time, multiple sites, and poor cost and patient information systems. The assignment given each student focused on outcomes of both costs and symptoms and then on process improvement. The strength of the reported barriers to these future physicians' learning about costs at all was amazing. The students did seem to absorb cost gathering and process improvement, but the curriculum still lacked the skills development necessary to work well in or to lead group processes.

The authors report that the Cleveland Asthma Project is one of a kind. While still rudimentary in terms of what physicians need to be leaders in process improvement, the degree to which hospitals, business leaders, and doctors are committed to CQI or TQM sends a signal to medical students about how important such efforts are. If students, residents, and physicians find indifference all around them about costs, outcome, and process of care, they will promptly forget what was taught.... The project has made us realize that good care must be provided in partnership between providers, payers, and patients. That parts of the process lie beyond the physician's office or emergency room should have come as no surprise, but we have failed to act on this knowledge. With a close ongoing partnership, perhaps we can do so in the future. (Headrick et al., 1991, p. 260)

We owe a debt of gratitude to the Case Western team for making this start, but it is damning of academic medicine if this remains the current educational state of the art in continuous improvement. As the above quote indicates, the concepts of quality, with or without continuous improvement, are going to permeate medical practice only when they permeate the medical school and its teaching settings.

Affiliation Agreements

Much that the students, residents, fellows, and faculty learn about CQI takes place in the teaching hospital, which may or may not be under a common management with the medical school. One important step that the medical school can take to enhance the CQI knowledge is to emphasize affiliations with those hospitals that have or are working on a CQI climate and culture. It would be nice if the medical school had that culture too, but it probably is more important that the training sites do. All hospitals are involved with CQI in one way or another with the impetus from the Joint Commission, but to varying degrees. The criteria that are set up for affiliations and the concerns of those site visiting and managing the affiliation relationship should reflect a bias for quality and for a CQI climate and culture. If all or most of the training sites are involved with CQI, it is only a matter of time before the medical school is too.

Cost Consciousness

Control of costs can be taught both directly and indirectly. For example, Durand et al. (1991) report that third-year medical students who are best able to organize hypotheses about patients' problems are more likely to order the appropriate diagnostic tests. The ordering of necessary tests is not affected by this factor, but the ordering of inappropriate tests is. There is, however, much more to be studied about the correlates of lower cost behaviors.

For example, Feinglass et al. (1991) report that costs go down significantly in teaching settings as autonomy in medical decision making allowed by attending physicians goes up. These authors suggest that this reflects the busy residents' inherently conservative practice style that favors moving patients out. One might also interpret it as reflecting defensive medicine directed against one's attendings. At least it indicates the large amount of variability introduced into the treatment system by lack of commonly accepted treatment processes (protocols) even within specific teaching institutions.

Multilevel and Multidisciplinary Teams

As the Cleveland Asthma Project indicates, the medical education environment has significant problems in finding ways to give medical students and residents theoretical and experiential tools to work with in the multilevel and multidisciplinary teams. One of the reported findings of that study was the insight that the process of care is much more complex than the medical teachers had assumed and that an effective outcome depends on factors outside the clinic setting as well as inside it. Hellman (1991) notes similar problems within the university in terms of bringing to bear the many relevant disciplines of the university on modern health care problems. He argues,

> Despite this impressive panoply of opportunities for better health care, the system has disturbing maldistribution with little organized preventive medicine. All these changes have vexing ethical and social policy considerations. At such times there are unique opportunities for scholarly thought and discussion involving much of the university, with the possibility that changes may be directed by such considerations. (Hellman, 1991, p. 248)

Residency and fellowship program directors should be encouraged by AHC leadership to motivate participation of their charges in CQI team efforts. They will learn a lot. It is often easy for them to opt out of CQI efforts because of existing heavy work loads and the short-term nature of their commitments. They will require the encouragement of their mentors to put in the added effort and learn the ropes of this new approach to health care quality improvement.

Practice Model Assumptions

Perhaps the most important impact of the delivery of service in AHCs is the model of practice that it develops in the minds of its learners. Many physicians tend to stay with what they learned during that period of their lives, and many values are internalized there. What are the implications of the emphasis on income generation in many teaching clinics? What is the impact of that experience on future attitudes toward process improvement? What is being learned about how variation in the treatment process is viewed and dealt with? How is process analysis to go forward in the practice setting, with its ruthless time pressures? Clearly, AHCs have to continue to address these issues. The management of AHCs has a number of possibilities, the most powerful of which is to support champions as they emerge among opinion-leading clinicians. As these people teach, practice and publish, they will attract the attention of new and old learners far faster than any program.

Fear of looking bad may be one of the barriers to CQI efforts in academic medicine. As Gaucher and Coffey (1993) point out, AHC managements often do not recognize the presence of fear in their systems. Professionals would rather define quality than measure it. However, AHCs do not necessarily have much to fear about quality. Current practice results may be favorable at AHCs as well as unfavorable. Caper (1988) shows that the conservative admission pattern of university/teaching hospitals may more than offset the higher technology and costs of such institutions. Johnson (1990) makes a similar argument concerning quality of care. He argues that teaching institutions have something to crow about. The Office of Technology Assessment's 1988 meta-study gives no indications that teaching institutions have poorer quality results than nonteaching institutions. Certainly, as Caper argues, "the time for stopping stonewalling and for taking the lead in quality issues is at hand" (p. 61).

RESEARCH

In their capacities as contract research establishments, medical schools are among those doing most of the research affecting quality in health care. Health Care Financing Administration (HCFA), National Institutes of Health (NIH), and other government health agencies understand that the way to get studies undertaken is to offer to fund them. The already extensive capacity to do clinical trials of new technology can be turned toward both prospective and retrospective studies of the older technologies that account for most of the cost of care. There is also a core of expertise available to participate actively in the development of national and specialty guidelines and a research capacity to conduct new research aimed at resolving gray areas in current theory and practice.

National Guidelines and Standards

At present, the two loci for studies of practice guidelines are: (1) the government, through the Agency for Health Care Policy and Research (AHCPR) and its Forum for Quality and Effectiveness in Health Care, and (2) medical specialty organizations.

One might well ask whether AHCs are already taking the lead in this process. Some might argue that they are. The specialty groups that are setting practice guidelines, such as the American Society of Anesthesiologists, the American College of Physicians/American Heart Association Task Force, and the American College of Obstetrics and Gynecology, include many academics. AHCs are also the loci of the AHCPR studies. However, the government's grants and contracts system emphasizes individual investigators. Institutional leadership neither seems to speak out very decisively nor provide leadership in many situations.

PORT Studies

Among key AHCPR activities have been many studies by Patient Outcomes Research Teams (PORTs), which use administrative databases, epidemiological methods, and outcome evaluations by patients and health services researchers to look at the relative effectiveness of alternative ways of diagnosing and treating high-volume conditions, including low back pain, stroke, benign prostatic hyperplasia, bedsores, urinary incontinence in adults, and depression. Medical school researchers play major roles in these large retrospective studies. Presumably, their results will be used as inputs into local consensus-building approaches and effective practice guidelines. Medical schools could and should play a major role in disseminating as well as developing such guidelines.

Consensus Conferences

Consensus conferences would seem to be the most natural of activities for academic health centers to conduct. When called together by NIH or other agencies, the renowned medical specialists from many medical centers gather and freely offer their opinions on the assigned subject. It would seem that most decisions at an AHC would come about through local, internal consensus conferences. Yet that seldom happens. There seem to be a number of factors involved:

- There is honor in being asked to a national conference, with its recognition as a noted expert as well as opportunities to network with international "peers."
- The local consensus conference would imply constraints on future behavior in a way that an extrainstitutional consensus would not.
- There is no central authority to enforce a consensus in an AHC, and the faculty would just as soon maintain their individual autonomy. Maintaining professional autonomy is a key issue in the implementation of quality programs.

A precursor to consensus conferences is development of clinical process analyses within the organization. These can stimulate recognition of the need for practice guidelines and standards. A good working description of practice guidelines is "standardized specifications for care developed by a formal process that incorporates the best scientific evidence of effectiveness with expert opinion." Such effects should show whether experienced effectiveness approaches potential effectiveness. Hopefully, any set of measures of experienced effectiveness will include components of customer satisfaction.

One of the places where the leadership of AHCs should be active is in encouraging local consensus conferences as an appropriate collegial activity carrying credit both in research and in teaching. Where there are not sufficient data to support a consensus, that should be a signal for an opportunity for high-impact clinical research.

Epidemiological/Small Area Studies

The Minnesota experience indicates that epidemiological studies based on small area data can also be the basis of research on quality (Chassin et al., 1986; Borbas et al., 1990). This can be done by individual investigators or by organized medicine in a geographic area. But the academic studies, though interesting, may not be generalizable to the rest of the medical community. Leape (1990) and Leape et al. (1991) outline a number of methodological criteria that should be applied to these retrospective studies, starting with automated insurance records.

These small area studies should not only deal with methods of treatment (technical management). They should also be applied to issues of accessibility, interpersonal process, and continuity of care. For example, Hand et al. (1991) report that the degree of compliance with technical standards (omission of hormone receptor tests and radiation therapy) varies by hospital and drops off with urban location and a higher proportion of poorly insured patients. Likewise, Lazovich et al. (1991) report that breast-conserving surgery among women with Stage I and Stage II breast cancer increases with education and income.

Implementing TQM/CQI

The quality assurance activities of the AHC can adopt a number of strategies, one of which involves adopting a research or continuous improvement attitude rather than a compliance one. This process often starts with the collection and comparison of clinical indicators, even though they deal with disease and provide little information on the processes producing the results reported (Linder, 1991). However, as Marder (1990, p. 60) argues, "indicators and practice guidelines have a symbiotic relationship. Each adds value to the other, and their development is performed simultaneously, rather than sequentially. The result is a continuing cycle of measurement and analysis leading to the knowledge necessary to

develop the tools for quality management in health care needed in the 1990s."
Work at Latter Day Saints Hospital by faculty of the University of Utah medical
school indicates great promise for the combination of carefully designed treatment protocols and computer-based expert systems in complex ICU cases where
the number of variables to be manipulated is beyond individuals' limited infor-
mation-processing capabilities (Morris, 1992).

PATIENT CARE

AHCs are the institutions that set the standard for health care quality. There are
real questions about the quality of that care. A major study indicates that 3 to 4
percent of hospital admissions suffered adverse events due to negligence or medical mismanagement (Brennan et al., 1991). This study does not report the error
rates for teaching institutions separately, but even if they are lower than the mean,
it still indicates that there is great room for improvement in the technical quality
of health care. When one adds the negative experiences of the patient while being
served and billed, there are opportunities for improvement.

As AHCs go about their work of serving numerous client publics, they have
many opportunities to educate the public and professionals about CQI, its concepts, its values, and its philosophies. The CQI story can be told in many ways as
the AHC responds to its various publics in its mission statement, in its treatment
of its constituencies and client populations, in its organization of care, in its governance processes, and in its continuing education efforts.

As Linder (1991) points out, organizations that try to influence the image of
quality through public relations and marketing are likely to end up badly. The
public's perception of quality depends on its comparison of expected quality versus experienced quality. If one works hard to convince someone that quality is
there, one is as likely to raise expectations as to bias perceptions favorably.
Therefore if the quality is in fact not raised but the expectation of it is raised, the
perception gap is being widened. Any attempt to bias that perception favorably is
likely to backfire.

On the other hand, there is merit in educating the public about how to judge
quality. This involves managing expectations by helping the public determine
what to look for and where to find it. There is a wealth of new information being
provided on outcomes that is raw data and must be interpreted. Here the public
could use some unbiased expert help. Many states are requiring the disclosure of
patient care quality indicators, patient care outcomes, and medical staff qualifica-
tions. Despite hospitals' reluctance to share this information, the data will get out
to the public and to the press. So will information from the National Practitioner
Data Bank. Both hospitals and physicians, however, will have to explain what this
means to themselves and to their patients. AHCs can take a leadership role in this
area by defining quality and by educating the public and the professionals about
this new area.

Many hospitals have statements about the importance of quality in their mission statements. Some go further in seeing to it that all employees are aware of the quality content of that mission statement and can communicate it when asked to do so. Even with these broad statements, there are differences as to operational meanings. For example, the 1991 Andersen study shows that there is still a difference of opinion between hospitals and physicians about the relative importance of cost effectiveness. The physician attributes most valued by hospitals, as seen by hospitals and by physicians, are shown in Table 17–1. After the listed attributes, the percentages fall off. Note that by far the greatest disagreement between the hospital CEOs and the physicians is over the importance of cost effectiveness. Yet cost-effective care has to become part of the expressed mission of teaching institutions unless they wish to become niche players in health care.

Cost effectiveness represents a serious threat to most academic medical centers in the early 1990s. One of our colleagues has pointed out that what the payers expect is not the most expert provider, but rather care by a qualified provider—by the least credentialed, least specialized provider who is still qualified. The academic setting operates in almost the opposite way, emphasizing the greatest possible specialization, and steers patients in that direction. Any attempt to focus on gatekeepers or generalists as the primary mode of care cuts off the financial lifeblood of the institution and with it the patient flows necessary for teaching and research. In the long run, teaching institutions are going to have to find room for care by the least qualified person who is still qualified rather than by the most qualified person who is still qualified, or they will see their patient flows dry up.

OUTREACH/ACCESS/POPULATION BASE

Lewis and Sheps (1983) argue that the alternative role is for academic health centers to take responsibility for a specific population base so that issues such as prevention and access (and hopefully cost effectiveness) are addressed. As care moves in the direction of capitation payments, most academic health centers will

Table 17–1 Physician Attributes Prized by Hospitals, as Seen by Physicians and Hospitals

Physician Attribute	% Reporting "Very Important"	
	Among Hospital CEOs	Among MDs
Clinical quality/technical competence	97	93
Relationship with patients/reputation	94	94
Cost-effectiveness in hospital practice	92	78

Source: Arthur Andersen & Co. and the American College of Healthcare Executives, *The Future of Medical Care: Physician and Hospital Relationships,* American College of Healthcare Executives, 1991.

be faced with such a choice again and again. Only then are basic issues such as prevention, perceived quality of care, and access likely to be addressed fully. Until then, the faculty is likely to continue to choose autonomy over accountability.

The AHC must have a philosophy about whether it will be responsible for a population base above and beyond that sporadically attracted by the reputation of its specialist faculty. This decision will center on the nature and purpose of the primary care delivered by the faculty. The AHC must decide whether the primary care that it delivers is the core of its undertaking or merely an appendage. Vinten-Johansen and Riska (1991) characterize the choices here and the debate over them as being over how to maintain professional autonomy between Oslerians and Flexnerians. Those value systems have to be reconciled if the institution is to pull itself together to agree on quality of care in its fullest sense. This will come out of work on a mission statement and a core set of values, should the AHC embark on a CQI process at levels above the teaching hospital.

Organization of Care

Quality is both a value and a cooperative process in an AHC. Therefore it must be reinforced by the governance processes of the institutions involved. Faculty do pay attention to quality in the tenure and promotion processes of the medical school. They must, however, also become intensively involved with it in the governance of the teaching hospital. Shortell (1985, 1990) outlines a hospital's mechanisms for involving the physician staff in its governance processes, including many quality activities such as the various peer review activities and the board of trustees. He also points out that this process has to be managed carefully to bring younger staff along in the skills necessary to maintain an effective governance process over time.

Even though Shortell emphasizes the need to integrate or bond physicians operating in a private practice, fee-for-service mode, his points are still relevant to the AHC. Physicians on a faculty must still be courted so that they are induced to buy into and conform to institutional norms, including those of quality and process analysis and change.

The introduction of cost control measures, such as DRGs, has created both new motivations for quality improvement and new areas of potential conflict as caregiving organizations move toward a single package price for services such as a normal obstetrical delivery. The medical school faculty and the hospital have a community of interest in having a safe and efficient process that attracts and satisfies patients. If obstetricians are losing patients because the care is traditional, not attractive, and costly, the hospital and the obstetricians can cooperate to develop a competitive process. But there can be other situations, such as the interaction between radiologists and the hospital administration, where the motivations of fee-for-service physician payment and DRGs put the two in an adversarial position on cost and perhaps on quality of care.

In the managed care setting, there is less apparent conflict between management and the caregivers than in a fee-for-service setting. However, pressures for productivity and reduced costs can still lead to conflict between the two. Somehow, the governance process has to allow these issues to be brought to light, discussed, and settled if the AHC is to maintain momentum in the quality arena. There are also possible conflicts within the roles of the caregivers. On one hand, the primary caregiver is expected to be an advocate and facilitator for the patient. On the other hand, the primary physician is expected to control costs by being a gatekeeper to specialists and an auditor of their performance. The governance process must address these issues squarely if the patient and the physician are to feel comfortable with the process. True early involvement should occur at the medical student or residency stage, not when one gets into practice. Instead of being sheltered from knowledge of the costs of care, including the cost of quality, students and residents should become knowledgeable about the cost issues involved as they learn about the technical alternatives.

CONCLUSION

As the producers of future physicians and other health care providers and the current producers of research, AHCs are the first line of offense in health care quality. They must assume responsibility for quality in their own operations, in their research, and in their teaching. To the extent that they continue to move cautiously in this area, they are likely to find their competitive position further eroded. The patients and payers will demand that health care be delivered in a cost-effective manner. They will remove their business from institutions that cannot deliver such care.

There are many challenges to AHCs brought about by CQI efforts. First, AHCs must make sure that their learners practice in institutions with a good quality climate and culture. They should encourage champions among their learners and faculty to undertake or participate in CQI efforts. They should support research that leads to quality improvement and reduction in unnecessary variation and waste, including setting up a modest research grants system. Their governance system and their marketing and public relations efforts should be aimed at increasing public and professional awareness of quality and of the CQI process and philosophy.

Arnold D. Kaluzny
Curtis P. McLaughlin
B. Jon Jaeger

TQM As a Managerial Innovation: Research Issues and Implications

18

Total quality management (TQM) represents a "new order of things" in the provision of health services. It requires continuous improvement in the processes that deliver care, involving interdisciplinary teams that rigorously analyze these processes, apply statistical measures to ongoing activities, and use scientific methods and psychosocial principles to reduce unnecessary variation in delivery activities. The whole emphasis on quality activities in the organization changes from identification of outliers (quality assurance) to variance reduction (continuous improvement).

TQM is a significant managerial innovation: that is, a new program or technique that represents a significant departure from the state of the art at the time it first appears, affecting the nature, location, quality, or quantity of information that is available in the decision-making process. As an innovation, it will have significant effects on the objectives, policies, and procedures of health service organizations and raise significant issues of measurement, availability of information technology, the organization of such efforts, and their impacts (Grady, et al., 1993). The purpose of this chapter is to assess some of the research issues relevant to the study of TQM as a managerial innovation. Specifically, it describes two perspectives of innovation theory relevant to the study of TQM in health service organizations and uses these perspectives to identify research issues regarding the adoption and impact of TQM within health service organizations and among work groups within these organizations.

APPROACHING THE STUDY OF TQM AS AN INNOVATION

Mohr (1982) suggests that innovation theory may be divided into two perspectives: variance and process. Variance theory assumes that certain conditions are

Source: Based on Kaluzny, A.D., McLaughlin, C.P., and Jaeger, B.J., TQM as a Managerial Innovation: Research Issues and Implications, *Health Services Management Research,* Vol. 6, No. 2, pp. 78–88, with permission of the Longman Group, © 1993.

necessary and sufficient to induce a particular phenomenon. It deals with outcomes that exist as variables and are measured as quantitative levels or amounts. For example, in the case of TQM one is concerned with impact: that is, whether the adoption of TQM makes any difference in some indicator of organizational performance. The analytical objective is to explain as much variation as possible, assuming that the unexplained variation exists because of incomplete specification. Each cause has an identifiable impact on the outcome, and its impact is not lost in interactions with other factors in the theory. Another characteristic of variance theory is that the time ordering of the contributory variables is immaterial to the outcome. Each independent contributor to the outcome is viewed as if it occurred simultaneously with all the other variables. It is essentially a cross-sectional approach and one that is consistent with most regression models.

Process theory, on the other hand, is concerned with identifying necessary conditions only. The focus is to assess the particular steps or events in the overall adoption process. Time ordering is critical for the outcome predicted in a process theory. Here the flow of causality from one variable to another requires that the intervening variables be encountered in a specific order and fashion. For example, in the case of TQM, "Did the organization identify a performance problem and identify TQM as a solution to that problem? Did problem identification and recognition of TQM precede institutionalization of TQM within the larger organization?" Process theory focuses on the rearrangement of specific elements rather than on a change in the magnitude of a particular element. Laws of chance play an important part in determining the sequencing and/or pairing of events. Process theory deals with discrete states and events and postulates that the existence of a particular endpoint connotes the occurrence of certain prior events.

The differentiation between process and variance theories of innovation is important to the study of the adoption of TQM in health service organizations. Variance theories are appropriate for analyzing the problems stemming from the basic design and ideology of the organization. Process theories serve the analysis of interactions among various elements of the organization as it adopts and adapts to TQM over time.

UNITS OF ANALYSIS

In addition to differentiating between variance and process, organizations vis-à-vis TQM can be evaluated at multiple levels. At one level, the organization as a whole is the unit of analysis. At another level, work groups and even individual staff members are the focus. Even though organizations are composed of individuals and work groups, the organization's behavior has a gestalt of its own, something more than the sum of the behaviors of its subunits. At this level, the organization interacts with other entities in its environment. For example, TQM emphasizes the interaction with customers, whose perceptions determine the parameters of quality.

At the work group level, TQM requires groups and personnel within groups to cooperate in mutual problem-solving efforts using the various statistical and behavioral approaches inherent in TQM. With the shift from intermittent to continuous improvement, the organization establishes a new climate for change in work group activities. In turn the work group sets the tone for reaction to innovation by individual professionals and support personnel. This cascading effect of change makes identification of the unit level being analyzed essential in defining the research issues related to TQM adoption and impact.

As an internally mandated change, the TQM innovation must have a locus of change within the organization. Yet at each level there is an issue of compliance or noncompliance within each work group. Since the innovation requires empowerment of all personnel affected by a problem to focus on a significant operating problem, the initial unit of adoption need not be the usual working group. One important research issue is how this process should be initiated. For example, is adoption totally dependent on the commitment of the CEO, or can a management cadre initiate the process in the absence of such commitment? The conventional wisdom is that the CEO must lead the process and all units within the organization must adopt TQM as a programmatic initiative. Yet as Beer et al. (1990) point out, more effective change may occur one work unit at a time. Thus among work groups there may be considerable variance in the level of adoption within the larger organization. Depending on the particular process selected for improvement, some units may be involved and others may choose not to participate.

RESEARCH ISSUES FOR TQM IN HEALTH CARE

There are specific research issues pertaining to each unit of analysis as one studies the change from quality assurance to continuous improvement. Impact and adoption are the two dependent variables of interest. *Impact* is the difference that the adoption of TQM makes on organizational or work group performance, whereas *adoption* is the extent to which TQM is integrated into the ongoing activities and culture of the organization. Impact includes changing professional and administrative patterns of care delivery and adjusting the organizational design to incorporate TQM processes and findings. It also involves a continuum from extreme failure to extreme success. Extreme failure involves situations where TQM not only fails to have impact but also introduces problems into the organization that make it difficult to introduce other productivity improvement schemes in the future.

Similarly, impact that far exceeds its goals and produces unanticipated benefits is considered successful. Indicators of impact on performance may include (1) increased levels of customer (including internal customer) satisfaction, (2) reduced diagnosis-specific and age-specific ratios of total hospital costs per admission over time, and (3) reduced error rates at various process stages from admission to discharge.

The designation of TQM as a managerial innovation focuses attention on adoption as a process occurring over time rather than as a single event. Although investigators studying organizational innovation do not agree on the exact number of stages in the process, they generally agree that the process involves multiple decisions and actions over a period of time. Most models begin with an awareness or knowledge stage, continue with an adoption or decision stage that includes some aspect of implementation, and conclude with an institutionalization stage that focuses on the integration of the innovation into ongoing activities.

VARIANCE THEORY AT THE ORGANIZATIONAL LEVEL

When applying the concepts of variance theory to defining research issues in the study of the adoption of TQM, consideration needs to be given to design characteristics of the organization, values and ideological orientation, and the attributes of the innovation itself. As presented in Table 18–1, the design characteristics of the health care organization should be critical predictors of the adoption/impact of TQM. Five variables—centralization, complexity, formalization, organizational slack, and information-seeking behavior—have been studied in analyzing organizational responses to innovation. Centralization and formalization and their interaction with the environment confronting the organization are important predictors of adoption. Theory suggests, for example, that in stable environments formalization and centralization may facilitate TQM adoption, whereas in unstable environments formal, complex, and centralized decision-making structures may impede adoption.

The availability of slack resources is another critical factor. Organizations with slack resources—areas where manpower and other resources can be spared to facilitate change—can more easily achieve higher levels of impact and adoption. Organizations in which resources are tightly committed to essential operations will find change more difficult. Here the generation and use of resources may involve power struggles among factions in the organization. If the adoption of TQM supports factions with a high degree of institutional influence, then adoption will be facilitated. For example, since TQM is a management innovation, it is likely to be adopted more readily in hospitals where management is the dominant group. However, if the prevailing power structure is based on some other criterion and some other group is dominant, such as physicians or trustees, adoption of TQM may encounter greater resistance. Another possible area of conflict is with the prevailing quality assurance approach. If quality assurance personnel are already on the defensive vis-à-vis the medical staff, they and the medical staff may combine to oppose TQM. If the quality assurance personnel are strong and respected, then they might be key actors in the adoption of TQM.

The basic values of elite organizational personnel vis-à-vis change are often cited as an important factor predicting change. Extending these findings, organi-

Table 18–1 Variance Theory at the Organizational Level

Theoretical Concepts	Illustrative Hypothesis/Questions	Implications
Design characteristics of the organization are critical predictors of adoption/impact of innovation.	a) Organizations with a high degree of formalization and centralization will adjust to the impact and adoption of TQM more effectively than those organizations that are less formal and decentralized.	a) The prevailing decision structure of an organization may require alterations if TQM is to have a maximal impact or successful adoption.
	b) Organizations with slack resources will adjust to TQM with greater ease than those whose resources are tightly constrained.	b) Availability of slack resources may determine the amount of conflict raised by the impact and adoption of TQM.
Values/ideological orientation of the organizational elite are critical to successful adoption of TQM.	a) Organizations with pro-change orientations will adopt TQM more successfully.	a) Symbols that reflect organizational values may require modification.
	b) Organizations that view quality as reducing process variation rather than seeking out and avoiding repetitions of outliers will adopt TQM more successfully.	b) Educational strategies to facilitate recognition of quality control as a variance reduction process must be developed and executed.
	c) Organizations that view the customer as the source of quality standards will adopt TQM more successfully.	c) The symbolic role of management is critical in facilitating organizational adjustment to these new standards for impact associated with TQM.
Attributes of an innovation in interaction with those of an organization affect the adoption/impact of TQM.	a) Organizations with congruence between the innovation and its characteristics will adopt TQM more efficiently.	a) Any generalization must take into account the interaction of organizational characteristics and the attributes of the innovation.
	b) The greater the extensiveness, longevity, and local success of TQM, the more likely the integration of clinical and nonclinical decision making.	b) Different degrees of clinical and nonclinical collaborations will exist in different organizations.

zations with a pro-change orientation will adopt TQM more successfully than those determined to maintain the status quo. The values and ideological orientation of the power elite are critical to adopting TQM; they influence decision making on resource allocation, development planning, and especially matters of symbolic significance, such as appointment of staff to decision-oriented committees. If the organization's power structure opposes change, key medical and administrative individuals are likely to support the status quo, and the mandated adoption of TQM will provoke resistance and conflict. On the other hand, in the organization where the elite favors innovation and accepts this idea of continuous improvement, promotions will go to those professionals who are willing to become TQM role models and who develop the technical skills and adopt the customer-oriented concepts of TQM. In some cases where opposition remains, the organization may have to replace those first-line supervisors who see the empowerment of workers as a threat to their position. Management's performance in its symbolic leadership role is critical as the organization adopts TQM.

An additional ideological issue is the prevailing attitude toward variations in quality. The traditional view in medicine, supported by training methods, licensure, and tort law, is that the individual professional is responsible when anything goes wrong. Therefore the primary role of supervision and quality assurance when something goes wrong has been to take names and punish those who make errors. The view of TQM presented by Deming and others is that TQM works best in a nonthreatening environment where everyone recognizes that most errors are systems problems and not individual errors. Batalden (1991), for example, and more recently, Batalden and Stoltz (1993) argue that most problems occur because the patient moves through the system from department to department, each of which is organized hierarchically and independently. Someone owns and is fiercely independent about each stage (called variously silo, smokestack, or fiefdom), but no one owns and manages the whole process that the patient experiences. TQM is most compatible with the view that the object of concern is both the technical and subjective experience of the patient, not just the technical excellence of each department. Organizations that hold this view will probably adopt TQM more effectively than others. If the organizational elites hold this view, they must develop and implement educational strategies to facilitate adoption of this viewpoint by other organizational members.

The symbolic role of management is critical in facilitating organizational adjustment to the impact and adoption of TQM. Strong leadership is essential to deal with a key aspect of TQM adoption, the maintenance of an adequate commitment during the phase-in period. Management must assume a number of important symbolic positions to facilitate implementation and ultimately institutionalization. For example, HCA requires that the hospital CEOs study TQM intensively and then teach the fundamentals to the hospital staff themselves and at most hospitals chair the periodic review of the work of the interdisciplinary improvement teams. A common storyboard is used by each team to facilitate communication and to symbolize the commonality of the approach being used. Attendance at a review meeting chaired by the CEO is a part of the indoctrination of new employees, thereby signaling management's commitment, communicating the process to the new employee, and raising expectations of participation at a future date.

Characteristics of the hospitals, along with the attributes of TQM itself, may influence its adoption effort. For example, the attributes of TQM are quite compatible with a for-profit organization with clear efficiency goals and hospitals familiar with prior process-type interventions managed from the corporate office. It remains to be seen how well large teaching hospitals with dual lines of authority (hospital and medical school departments) and loosely coupled organizational alliances fare at adoption and impact. TQM arising more out of the consensus of the elites than through a hierarchical intervention may exhibit greater effectiveness and institutionalization in such an environment, or islands of TQM excellence may appear and by their outstanding performance attract the intellectual curiosity and, finally, emulation of other units. If enough units are successful, they may coalesce into an overall TQM effort. Note, however, that the hypothesis that nonteaching hospitals will have greater success than teaching hospitals is a variance perspective, whereas the hypothetical way that teaching hospitals adopt TQM implies a process perspective.

PROCESS THEORY AT THE ORGANIZATIONAL LEVEL

Research issues related to process theories at the organizational level are shown in Table 18–2. The organization's experiences during adoption of TQM will depend on its progress through the different stages of the innovation process. The first stage of innovation is recognition. During this stage the organization identifies a performance gap, the existence of a difference between what the organization is doing and what it could be doing. During the identification stage, a plan for change is developed. Implementation is the phase during which the change occurs. Institutionalization is the last stage, during which the implemented change is accepted by personnel and integrated within the organization.

To start the process, a key event must occur, the identification of the organization's performance gap. For example, an organization must be aware that the existing definition of "quality" is not the appropriate one and that the definition must be consumer specified, or must realize that most intractable problems are related to processes that involve more than one organizational unit. That insight may come from the superior performance of a competing institution or from the belief that there has got to be a better way. It also may come about reading the many accounts in the literature of the TQM approach and its promise, or from comparing the institution as it is now with what it could be if certain processes were obtained. Finally, quality comparisons by citizens groups or by professionals utilizing more than one institution may trigger the dissatisfaction.

Table 18–2 Process Theory at the Organizational Level

Theoretical Concepts	Illustrative Hypothesis/Questions	Implications
Innovation involves a series of stages: recognition of the problem, identification of solution, implementation, and institutionalization.	a) The greater the performance gap (recognition), the more likely TQM is to be identified as a solution to a problem. b) Organizations in which TQM is implemented without recognition of a performance gap will have less successful institutionalization.	a) The organization must differentiate between long- and short-term goals. If the organization bypasses recognition of a performance gap and identification of a solution, implementation may occur, but many unanticipated problems will arise.
Innovation is a nonrecursive process.	Adoption of TQM will affect both the level and distribution of control within the organization.	New alliances and coalitions will form that may change the structure of the organization.
Design characteristics interact with the stages of innovations.	The more pervasive the performance gap, the more successful the adoption. The greater the decentralization, the greater the relationship between the recognition of a performance gap and initiation. The greater the decentralization, the less the institutionalization.	What may be functional at one stage may be dysfunctional at another.

There are several potential problems in identifying the performance gap. If there is ineffective communication between the administration and the users of the facility, some organizations may not recognize a problem or a need or an opportunity for which TQM is a possible solution. Existing measures of quality such as age- and disease-specific death rates, nosocomial infection rates, and pathology reports may be within normal ranges so that the word *quality* is not associated with the performance gap. Furthermore, TQM is not an approach that yields short-term results. It is a process aimed at influencing quality over a period of several years. If organizations do not realize that many of their problems spring from a failure to achieve many small improvements in all of their processes rather than a failure to correct glaring faults, and do not realize that most of their problems involve the interfaces between departments and functions, they have not identified the performance gap susceptible to TQM and will have a less successful adoption.

As presented in Table 18–2, innovation is a nonrecursive process. Process theory recognizes the existence of feedback loops within organizations. In this framework, organizations become learning and adaptive organisms. Adoption of TQM will affect the level and distribution of control within the organization as it moves through the innovation process. New alliances and coalitions will be created. The human resources training function in the hospital will gain importance during the implementation of the TQM process. Professional supervisors traditionally have viewed this unit as an insignificant factor in hospital affairs since they have considered all relevant training to be technical and achieved during professional education either in school or in inservice training. But this relatively impotent group may suddenly become a factor by training supervisors and staff in the statistical and behavioral techniques necessary for TQM success. Furthermore, job descriptions will be modified so that continuous improvement of all contact areas is included as an identified job task for all employees. At some point no one will be promoted who does not have a track record in continuous improvement, and skills in this area will be sought out, especially among nursing staff.

Design characteristics of the organization interact with the stages of the innovation. The more pervasive the performance gap recognized by the organization, the more successful will be the adoption of the innovation. The greater the decentralization, the greater will be the recognition of the performance gap. Thus decentralization facilitates the recognition stage of innovation. However, decentralization may have a negative impact on other stages of innovation. Decentralization makes vertical communication and control more difficult. Thus design characteristics can be functional or dysfunctional to the organization, depending on the task at hand.

VARIANCE THEORY AT THE WORK GROUP AND INDIVIDUAL LEVELS

Organizations are composed of work groups of various "shapes, sizes, and colors," and it is within and between these groups that much of the activity occurs that is critical to TQM's impact and adoption. Illustrative research issues at the work group and individual levels of the organization are shown in Table 18–3. TQM innovation research represents a unique challenge at the work group level since so many of the issues to be dealt with in TQM involve dysfunction in and among work groups. TQM requires the structuring of ad hoc groups to deal with important problems, and these groups may or may not continue to function once someone takes responsibility for the process being studied. Therefore one can study how such groups are formed, how they are trained and mentored, how they are motivated, and how they recycle themselves.

There has to be a delicate balance between strong managerial leadership and worker initiative. Management has the symbolic roles cited earlier, but personnel

Table 18–3 Variance Theory at the Work Group/Individual Levels

Theoretical Concepts	Illustrative Hypothesis/Questions	Implications
Design characteristics and their interaction with the technical basis of the tasks of the unit are critical predictors of successful adoption/impact.	Work groups with predictable technology/tasks and a highly centralized and formalized design will have a more successful adoption/impact.	A uniform strategy for adopting TQM within the organization may be inappropriate. Strategies must be targeted to the composition of the work group addressing the problem.
Organizational climate interacts with design characteristics of the work group to affect adoption/impact.	When the complexity of the work groups is high, the more supportive the climate, the more successful adoption/impact.	A supportive work group permits greater tolerance for risking TQM behavior.

in the departments involved have the relevant expertise, information, and contacts with the customers through which to gauge perceived quality. For example, Berwick (1993) tells of lying on a stretcher ready to go into an operating room and feeling slightly chilled. The transport person noticed that Berwick was cold and asked him if he would like a warm blanket. Given a positive response, he produced a blanket within 30 seconds. It obviously would have been easier for the transporter to have ignored the need, but he did not. The point is that the transport worker was in a system capable of providing warmth to a cold patient on a gurney. If the transport worker had been in a system that denied him that opportunity or criticized him for taking that initiative, he would not have done it. Management owns processes and processes support behaviors. Management has to ask for change and for initiative and personnel have to feel sufficiently empowered to respond, despite the likelihood that they will encounter problems along the way.

The identification of problem areas and the identification of process ownership will focus research on how the positions of special interest groups or coalitions shift with the issue at hand. These are usually organized around care of a specific patient population (pediatric or geriatric patients) or provision of a specific service (dietary needs, operating rooms, or medical-surgical supplies). Intradisciplinary perspectives and perceived threats to established power bases influence group interaction. Since work groups, ad hoc improvement teams, and coalitions constantly interact, strategies must be targeted to deal with changing conditions as the adoption of TQM progresses. These strategies must include specific steps to support ad hoc groups that are involved in tasks that are secondary to their usual work tasks and temporary assignments.

Individuals are also critical actors in the adoption process. Each person has his or her own set of vested interests and perceives change from an often unique point of view. Factors contributing to the individual's power to influence change include such elements as formal title and role within the organization as well as informal power and interpersonal styles. Previous experience with change, both within and outside the organization, influences a person's receptiveness to innovation and willingness to participate in facilitating change.

The design characteristics of the organization and their interaction with the technical basis of the tasks of the work group or individual are critical predictors of successful adoption and impact. Work groups with predictable tasks and a static environment, such as hospital laboratories, perform best in highly centralized and formalized structures. Work groups with complex, varied tasks and a highly dynamic environment perform better in decentralized, informal structures. For example, direct patient care professionals interact in a highly dynamic environment and with many complex tasks that must be tailored to the individual consumer (patient and practitioner).

In TQM there are also issues of familiarity with the technology. Lab personnel regularly use some of the statistical and scientific methods (run charts, frequency diagrams, flow charts) associated with TQM, but may be uncomfortable working with soft data like client perceptions and preferences. Nursing staff, on the other hand, may find the statistical techniques off-putting at first, but be highly motivated to work in group processes and on patient care issues. If the representatives of both groups are expected to address a major issue, the facilitator will have to use considerable skill to get the two comfortable with both the issue and each other's attitudes toward the techniques to be used. It is important to target the introduction of the innovation to the makeup of the work group involved. Organizational climate interacts with characteristics of the work group to affect adoption and impact. As organizations adopt TQM, they face a period of great uncertainty. Work groups with a supportive climate that meets the needs of group members will adjust to the uncertainty with less stress than others. The role and influence of the person representing the nursing team in the TQM group will have great impact on how a particular nursing staff reacts to the recommended changes. Also, if the head nurse has fostered development of open communication among staff nurses, concerns related to perceived premature discharges, for example, can be openly discussed as the ad hoc group meets, so that the nurse members can fairly represent their concerns and interests and so that the results can be interpreted as responsive, whether they mean more work or more uncertainty or not.

Attributes of TQM interact with the organizational climate and design characteristics of the work groups. Every health care unit will respond in its own way to the TQM innovation, and each work group within the organization will have a slightly different response. Such differences often give an organization strength and adaptability. The more adaptive the responses, the more likely it is that the organization will survive. What may work for one group may not work for another.

PROCESS THEORY AT THE WORK GROUP AND INDIVIDUAL LEVELS

Research issues related to process theory at the work group and individual levels are presented in Table 18–4. The interaction between the technological basis of a work unit and its design characteristics affects the rate at which a particular work group moves through the stages of innovation. An ordered process through these stages occurs, but each group may be at a different starting point initially. Some units with a heavy real-time technical demand, such as an intensive care unit, may find that work pressures do not allow time for studying issues or for recognizing a performance gap based on customer perceptions. On the other hand, some work groups may tend to lead in piloting new ideas and strategies. For example, a nursing team may already have begun to identify a performance gap related to some aspect of care, such as delays in discharge due to lack of lab orders and lab results. It may be in a better position to recognize the problem than a laboratory group that is attempting to reduce STAT requests and maintain an orderly and efficient flow of specimens through the lab. The managerial challenge is to bring these two viewpoints together and get each to understand the other's perspective before a new process acceptable to both can be developed.

The characteristics of personnel, and particularly their training, are likely to be important factors affecting the adoption process. Since TQM involves concepts and measures of quality often not included in prior professional training, educa-

---

Table 18–4 Process Theory at the Work Group/Individual Levels

Theoretical Concepts	Illustrative Hypothesis/Questions	Implications
Interaction between the technological basis of a work group and its design characteristics affects the rate at which a work group moves through the stages of adoption.	The stage of adoption that a work group is in initially will affect the rate at which the group moves through the adoption process.	Target the work groups that are most likely to be successful and focus on more resistant groups later.
Attributes of TQM affect the rate at which the work group and individual move through the adoption process.	Individual and work groups with appropriate training will affect rate of adoption over time.	Selection of the appropriate individuals to participate in a TQM work group is an important management task.
Innovation is a nonrecursive process.	Changes in the control level and distribution of personnel may occur due to TQM adoption.	Feedback strategies must be developed.

tion is likely to be a critical factor. People require a common language of quality that pertains not to unacceptable outliers, but to the reduction of variation in the desired process. Moreover, within work groups, there is a need to experiment with the notion of attaching numerical measures to things once taken for granted. Individuals need to come to understand that measuring something, following the results over time, and defining the causal process that induces variation in a measure lead to ideas and to motivation to change that process in significant ways. Where such conditions exist, work groups and individuals are likely to identify the performance gap and initiate the adoption process.

The fundamental activities of TQM may challenge the level and distribution of control within and between work units. For example, the analytical requirements of TQM may conflict with clinical training, which requires learning a set of prescribed protocols based on diagnoses and then responding to individual patient differences. Under TQM, work units and professionals reevaluate the work process and recommend and enact procedural changes. As groups and individuals learn how to make the TQM process work, it is likely that the nature of managerial control will change. For example, one of the primary causes of delays in performing certain procedures on the nursing unit may be the lack of special kits from the medical-surgical supplies department. Reporting arrangements may have to change to make the supply departments accountable for their levels of service to the clinical units. As work groups assess a wide variety of issues, it may become clear that areas of accountability and interaction could function better if existing management arrangements were modified and/or specific feedback strategies were developed.

CONCLUSIONS

There is nothing more difficult to take in hand, more perilous to conduct, or more uncertain in its success, than to take the lead in the introduction of a new order of things, because the innovator has for enemies all those who have done well under the old conditions, and luke warm defenders in those who may do well under the new.

Machiavelli, *The Prince*

As hospitals move forward against increasing competition and tighter cost containment measures, research on TQM adoption and impact at every level of the organization becomes more than an academic exercise. Some hospitals, for example, will move easily through the early stages of TQM adoption, only to find themselves unable to cope with the process of institutionalizing TQM within the organization. Other institutions will find the early stages a time of rejection by many individuals or of political turmoil over which issues can and should be addressed and which cannot. Other organizations may adapt gradually to TQM and, through changes in power configuration, new patterns of cooperation and teamwork, and new understandings of the organization and its mission, achieve institutionalization. In all cases, considerable attention will be given to the impact on cost and quality. Whether TQM is able to impact cost and/or quality may be a function of its ability to move through the various stages of the adoption process. At this point, TQM appears to be one of the few management innovations that can significantly improve hospital performance along a number of dimensions affecting both cost and quality of care. Its potential is great, yet research using both a variance and process perspective is a fundamental undertaking if TQM is to achieve its potential within health services.

Part V

Illustration

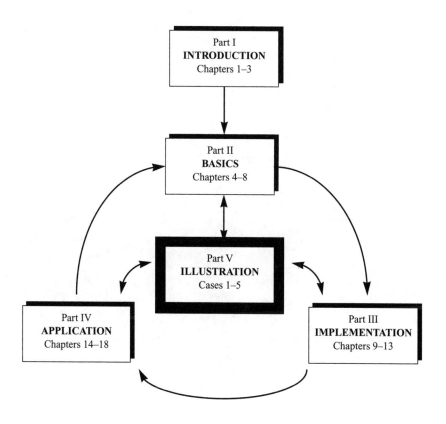

David C. Kibbe
Curtis P. McLaughlin

The Family Practice Center

Case **1**

The Family Practice Center (FPC) is the home of the 35-physician group practice of the Department of Family Medicine at the School of Medicine, University of North Carolina (UNC) at Chapel Hill. In July of 1991 the faculty was discussing the possibility of expanded evening and weekend office hours for patients. Two points of view were being expressed about faculty and patient attitudes toward continuity of care. There typically is a trade-off between offering patients (1) the convenience of being seen the same day they call in and (2) the opportunity of being seen by their own physician, i.e., continuity of care. Some staff argued that there was a trend in patient attitudes toward convenient appointment times and away from concerns about continuity with the same physician, while others disagreed.

Mr. Tony Galiani, M.B.A., the FPC manager, had recently come to Chapel Hill, North Carolina, from the Harvard Community Health Plan, where fact-based management and continuous improvement methodologies had been pioneered under Dr. Donald Berwick. At UNC, however, no system of customer satisfaction surveys had been in place at the FPC, so Tony instituted a policy of "listening to the customer." Any customer expressing dissatisfaction was referred to him by the staff and he recorded their complaints. On reviewing his records, Tony found that there had been over 200 unsolicited complaints about continuity of care between November 1, 1990, and August 1, 1991. Approximately 75 percent of the complaint records contained a reference to continuity problems. Patients' dissatisfaction about continuity could be captured by either one or both of the following patient statements: "I can't see my own (i.e., primary, usual) physician often enough when I want to," and "I don't see the same doctor often enough for the follow-up of an acute problem."

This case was prepared as a basis for classroom discussion rather than to illustrate the effective or ineffective handling of an administrative situation. Copyright © 1993 by the Kenan-Flagler Business School, University of North Carolina, Chapel Hill, NC 27599-3490. All rights reserved. Not to be reproduced without permission.

The continuity issue came to a head when another "customer," a large employer that referred its employee worker's compensation and industrial medicine cases to the FPC, threatened to withdraw from its contract on the grounds that follow-up visits were made infrequently with the same doctor who initially evaluated the patient. An employer representative stated, "We believe patients seen in your practice are out of work longer than those seen by other doctors' practices, and we believe this is due to lack of provider continuity at your facility." The message was clear: "Either fix it or lose our business." Loss of this customer would mean a significant financial loss to the practice.

FORMING A TEAM

Mr. Galiani had already discussed the possibilities of starting a total quality management (TQM) process in the Department of Family Medicine with David Kibbe, M.D., M.B.A., who was beginning a faculty development fellowship and studying quality management in medical practice. The approach they agreed on was the FOCUS-PDSA cycle, a Deming-based approach, that usually follows these steps:

- Find a process to improve.
- Organize a team that knows the process.
- Clarify current knowledge of the process and its variation.
- Understand the causes of process variation.
- Select the process improvement.
- Plan the improvement.
- Do the data collection, analysis, and improvement effort.
- Study the data for process improvement and customer outcome.
- Act to hold the gains and continue improvement.

They decided to put together the initial quality team to study the continuity problem that had now become so evident. The team was made up of seven staff volunteers with functional knowledge of the continuity problem. There were three physicians—Dr. Kibbe; Dr. Bob Gwyther, the FPC medical director; and Dr. Sam Weir—plus Mr. Galiani; Eleanor Benz, M.S.P.H., the quality assurance coordinator; and Beverly Spencer, R.N., a nursing supervisor. This group then asked Donna Harrison, M.B.A., of the University Hospital's Department of Management Engineering to act as the group's TQM/CQI consultant.

At its first meeting the team adopted as its project objective "to improve continuity of care in the Family Practice Center." Specific goals of the team included:

1. To define the problem of continuity from the patient's point of view
2. To examine in depth relevant aspects of the problem of continuity of care at the FPC using a CQI process

3. To learn and apply some of the tools and analytical methods of TQM/CQI as a means of evaluating real problems of importance to medical practice in the FPC
4. To document the effort and methods used in order to share the process with others in the FPC at the end of the project period

CONTINUITY OF CARE

Although research studies have produced conflicting results about the ability of continuity of care to improve the quality of health care outcomes, most physician observers have included continuity as one of the principles of family practice, one worth preserving.[1] In October 1991 the team surveyed the department's faculty. A large majority of the 25 surveyed agreed or strongly agreed with the statement "Continuity of care improves the quality of patient care" and all agreed or strongly agreed with "We should retain continuity of care as a principle of family practice in the FPC and teach medical students and residents its value." In the October survey of faculty preferences the majority responded that the FPC should strive to make it possible for patients to see their regular doctor some 70 percent of the time. Figure 1.1 summarizes their objectives.

"We should strive to attain a usual provider continuity level of..."

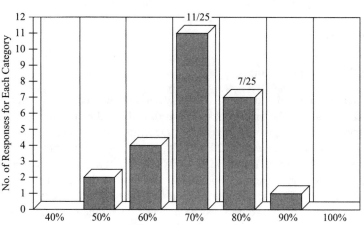

Figure 1.1 Faculty Survey on Continuity of Care, UNC Department of Family Medicine

---

[1]Continuity of care has also been identified by Ware and Snyder (1975) as one of the four main dimensions of patient satisfaction.

Next, the team decided to assess the actual degree of discontinuity in the practice. A chart audit was performed to provide information on usual provider continuity, which is simply the percentage of total visits a patient sees his or her regular physician. A random sample of 125 charts were audited for the period July 1, 1990, to June 30, 1991, and the visits were classified into three categories: health maintenance, chronic illness, and acute care. The "usual provider" was determined by noting the doctor named on the face sheet as the assigned doctor of record or, when this was not available or was inaccurate, by the chart auditor's assessment of the clinical notes as to which physician most regularly saw the patient. These results were compared with a similar audit of 265 charts performed in this practice in 1984 and published as part of an article on continuity of care in the *Journal of Family Practice* in 1985. The comparison showed that usual provider continuity had dropped significantly in the intervening period.

% Usual Provider Continuity		
Type of Visit	1984	1991
Health maintenance	86%	74%
Chronic illness	76%	61%
Acute illness	55%	29%
Overall, all visits combined	61%	45%

Therefore the team concluded that there had indeed been an actual loss of continuity in the practice that justified the perception among customers of a problem of continuity.

What the Customer Wants

The team wanted to understand what its customers wanted in terms of continuity and to establish the precedent of going directly to the customers to find out what their preferences were. Therefore in December they conducted a two-week survey of clinic users in which 229 out of the 769 visitors during the period completed the questionnaire shown in Exhibit 1.1. Given a choice between seeing their regular doctor for each visit or seeing any doctor at the time that suited them best, 79 percent of the respondents chose continuity over convenience. The respondents were further asked to choose between seeing their regular doctor with a one-week wait versus coming in when they wanted to come for a variety of situations. Seventy percent or more preferred to wait for their annual physical, for treatment of chronic conditions, for work-related physical exams, and for situations where the medicine did not seem to be working or when a hospital stay might be required. Seventy percent or more preferred immediate care by any available doctor for a painful problem, a cut or sprain, or a problem that would

Exhibit 1.1 Family Practice Center (FPC) Patient Survey

We want to improve our scheduling of doctors' appointments. Will you help us by answering the following questions? Your answers will be confidential. There is no way for anyone to know how you or any other patients answered.

Please CHECK (✔) your answers:

How long have you come to the FPC for care?
_____ less than 1 year _____ 1–2 years _____3 or more years
_____ Before today, how many times in the last 3 months have you been to the FPC?

YES	*NO*	*UNSURE*	
1. _____	_____	_____	Do you usually get a checkup or physical exam at least once a year?
2. _____	_____	_____	Do you think you should get a yearly checkup?
3. _____	_____	_____	Do you have a regular doctor at the FPC? (If no, skip to 6)
4. _____	_____	_____	Would you ever send a friend to your doctor?
5. _____	_____	_____	Have you ever thought of changing doctors?
6. _____	_____	_____	Would you like to have a regular doctor if you have none?

NONE	*SOME*	*VERY*	
_____	_____	_____	How IMPORTANT is it for you to have a regular doctor when you visit the FPC?
_____	_____	_____	How IMPORTANT is it for you to get an appointment at the times you want?

At the FPC we have different types of patients: men, women, older patients, younger patients, parents with children, single patients. We need to know how these different types of patients feel about our services and how we can meet their different needs. Would you help us by answering a few questions about yourself? Please CHECK (✔) the type that best describes you.

_____ Man	*Age:*	_____ Never married
_____ Woman	_____ 18–29 yrs.	_____ Married
Years of School:	_____ 30–39 yrs.	_____ Divorced or separated
_____ 1–6 yrs.	_____ 40–49 yrs.	_____ Widowed
_____ 7–12 yrs.	_____ 50–59 yrs.	_____ Special friend
_____ Technical School	_____ 60 or older	
_____ College		_____ Black
_____ Postgraduate		_____ White
		_____ Other

Are you now: _____ employed full time?_____ employed part time?
_____ unemployed?_____ retired?
_____ other? (describe) _____

How would you describe your health? _____ Poor _____ Average _____ Good

_____ Number of people who live with you? (Don't count yourself.)

continues

continued

To help us set a time for you to see a doctor, tell us which is more important:

(1) to see a REGULAR DOCTOR even if you must wait a week, or
(2) the TIME you need or want to come.

Read each question below and CHECK (✔) either column (1) or column (2).

(1) Regular Doctor	(2) Time	*Reasons for Seeing the Doctor*
____	____	Yearly physical exam or checkup
____	____	Physical exam for school, work, or insurance
____	____	A problem that will make you miss work today
____	____	A problem that is very painful
____	____	An injury like a cut finger or sprained ankle
____	____	Something you think may lead to a hospital stay
____	____	A problem that kept you awake all night
____	____	A problem you've had for 3 days and not getting better
____	____	A condition that needs regular visits such as high blood pressure, diabetes, arthritis, heart problems
____	____	You are having bad effects from a medicine
____	____	You think your medicine is not working
____	____	You have a problem that frightens you

In October, we added evening hours. Patients can now make appointments to see a doctor from: 8:30 a.m. to 7:00 p.m. Monday through Thursday;
                  8:30 a.m. to 5:00 p.m. on Friday;
                  8:00 a.m. to 12:00 noon Saturday.

What are YOUR BEST TIMES to come to the FPC? _____

CHECK ONLY ONE: If you HAD TO CHOOSE, would you rather
____ see your regular doctor for each visit
         OR
____ come to see any FPC doctor at a time that best suits you?

What DO YOU LIKE about the Family Practice Center? _____
_____
_____
_____

What DON'T YOU LIKE about the Family Practice Center? _____
_____
_____
_____

THANK YOU. PLEASE PUT THIS SHEET IN THE BOX ON THE COUNTER.

result in missing work. There was less agreement on preferences when the symptom was frightening or had lasted three days or more or had kept the patient awake all night, or when the medication was causing "bad effects." The team concluded that there was little difference in attitudes concerning continuity between patients and physicians, but that neither group was having its expectations for continuity met. One team member described this situation as "an unexpected problem of alignment between professional principles, patient preferences, and group practices having to do with continuity." At this point the team felt that efforts to improve continuity were justifiable and likely to improve patient and provider satisfaction.

Understanding the Causes of Process Variation

Now the basic question became, "Given that patients have complained about discontinuity, that providers are desirous of a level of continuity around 70 percent, and that the practice attained a level of continuity above 60 percent in 1984, what has caused the decline to an overall level of 45 percent, which includes the especially sharp decline in the acute illness category, from 55 percent to 29 percent?" A key concept of TQM/CQI is that any problem is likely to have multiple causes. Unfortunately, managers often waste time trying to find "magic bullets," that is, simple solutions to try to fix complex problems. TQM/CQI offers a number of methods, such as brainstorming, cause-and-effect (Ishikawa) diagrams, Pareto diagrams, and flow charts to help identify and define the various and often complex causes of a systems problem. The team used several of these approaches to better understand what had been causing discontinuity to occur. Using these methods helped the team make rapid progress in a relatively short time in determining why a patient was or was not able to see his or her physician of choice.

Although it is normal for everyone to have an opinion and to think that his or her opinion should form the basis of the solution, the TQM/CQI process requires that the team members suspend their personal judgments, especially at this stage, and simply try to enumerate as many possible causes as they can think of. During an early meeting the team brainstormed to develop a complete list of possible causes that enabled them to construct the cause-and-effect or fishbone diagram shown in Figure 1.2. That cause-and-effect diagram organized the various theories under four major headings: procedures, people, policies, and databases.

The exercise of developing the cause-and-effect chart encouraged team members to see connections between disparate parts of the process that might otherwise have been overlooked. Insights were expressed with statements like "You mean that's the way we have been doing things?" or "I didn't know you changed that procedure!" For example, during the August 21 meeting when the diagram was constructed, the team observed the following:

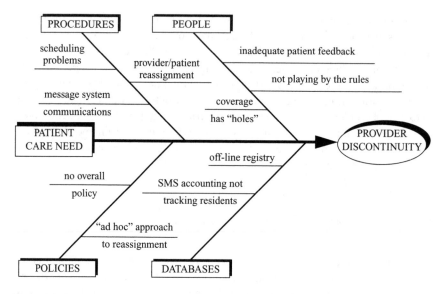

Figure 1.2 Cause-and-Effect Diagram

- Under procedures
  1. Many patients did not know who their primary doctor was because the formal reassignment of patients to residents had not taken place in July 1989 and July 1990.
  2. Medical records personnel had stopped transferring the name of the assigned physician into the chart in 1989.
  3. The patient scheduling system was not able to schedule patients into provider schedules more than one month in advance, due to persistent delays in getting out the provider schedules.
  4. The team approach by faculty and residents had been changed a year earlier when the FPC moved into a new building, reducing the level of communication between providers.
  5. The clerks handling patient call-ins for appointments did not have a written procedure to follow for making appointments.
- Under people
  1. Several faculty physicians had adjusted their schedules to allow over-booking outside the routine scheduling system, possibly in an attempt to improve continuity.
- Under policies
  1. There had not been a formal policy of promoting continuity, even though it had been a shared value. Front office staff were not aware that continuity was a priority.

- Under databases
  1. There were three databases used in the FPC to track patient information. The one that included data on physician/patient assignments was not on line and could not be readily accessed by staff when patients did not know or remember their doctor's name.

Selecting Specific Causes to Address

At the next meeting the team was asked to assess which were the most important causes of discontinuity. At this stage the usual approach is to develop a Pareto chart of the causes of the problem. This chart presents the causes in order of descending frequency, which usually illustrates the Pareto Principle that whenever a number of individual factors contribute to some overall effect, a relative few of those items account for the bulk of the effect. In most cases the causes of each adverse event are identified and the frequencies of the causes charted. In this case there were no data on the specific causes of observed discontinuity. Therefore the committee was asked to vote on the importance of eleven identified causes. The five committee members present were each allowed ten points to divide among the possible causes. The results are displayed in Figure 1.3.

Just three of the items—#1, #3, and #4—gathered 55 percent of the available points. Although #4 is a policy item ("Lack of an overall policy re: operationalizing continuity"), the first two pertained to scheduling problems. The conclusion of this exercise was that scheduling system problems were a major root cause of the discontinuity problem.

This was a surprise to several team members who thought that the assignment of patients to providers would be the area of intervention most likely to help improve continuity. Others had started out believing that the computer-assisted assignment process that matched physicians and patients would be a primary target. The dialogue around the Pareto diagram resulted in a change in some people's minds about the interactions between assignment, scheduling, and continuity. They now saw assignment, while perhaps an important issue in its own right, as having less impact on continuity than scheduling problems. Everyone involved was impressed with the efficiency of this approach. Several of the "solutions" that people brought with them to the table might have turned out to be dead ends in terms of their adverse impact on continuity.

Understanding the Scheduling System

The team decided to focus on the call-in appointment process, where most appointments were made for chronic and acute care visits. Donna Harrison assisted the team in making a flow chart of the current call-in appointment process (Figure 1.4). It was obviously a complex process in which the patient might talk to two or more FPC desk clerks or nurses before obtaining an appointment. This complexity alone might affect continuity adversely.

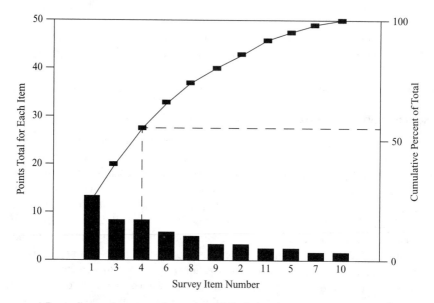

A Pareto diagram is a means of capturing and displaying the root causes, or "critical few" causes, leading to a problem, in this case provider discontinuity. The survey item numbers correspond to the following causes for provider discontinuity suggested by team members.

1. Not enough open provider appointment slots per session.
2. Not enough open appointment slots per physician, i.e., physicians not assigned enough clinic time per week.
3. Problems associated with scheduling system, e.g., too complicated, no callback system, clerks making errors.
4. Lack of an overall policy re: operationalizing continuity.
5. Conflict within the department between the goals of the residency program and those of the FPC practice.
6. An "ad hoc" approach to patient/physician assignment.
7. Problems with the process of assignment of providers to patients.
8. Not enough feedback from patients and staff when problems occur.
9. Problems due to having to use the hospital's computer database.
10. Not enough team identity in the FPC.
11. People breaking the rules and policies.

Figure 1.3 Pareto Diagram: Causes of Discontinuity, UNC Department of Family Medicine

The team meetings identified that the front desk clerks were a major influence on continuity, depending on how they would elicit patient preferences when their first choice of physician and appointment time was not available. They could offer the patient other options for times in their regular physician's schedule (continuity), or offer the patient a different physician at the desired time (convenience). Direct observation and interviews with the clerks showed that in most cases the

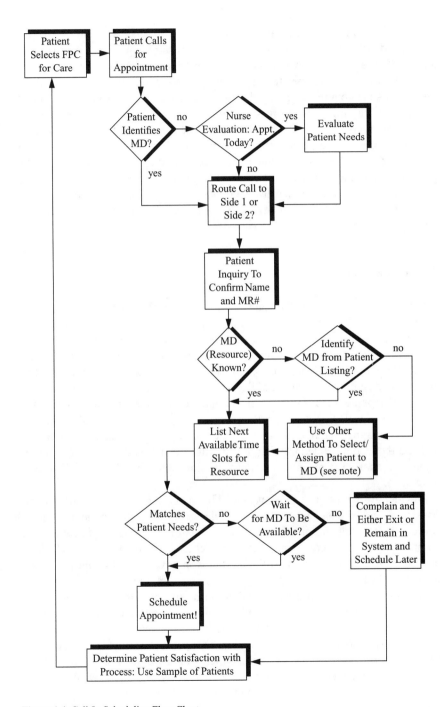

Figure 1.4 Call-In Scheduling Flow Chart

four clerks assumed that the patient wanted to see the first available doctor (urgency) and offered the patient an appointment at his or her preferred time (convenience). This systematically biased physician scheduling against continuity.

In the absence of the specific instructions from practice management to offer the patients the continuity option, the clerks took the route most convenient and less time consuming to themselves. Given the current system, it was much easier and less disruptive of their other tasks to schedule call-ins on the basis of the next available provider at a given time than it was to identify the primary physician and then try to fit the patient's time preferences into the available openings in the provider's schedule. Because the patient reassignment had not been done properly in the past three years and because there was no easy way to access the assignment information on line, on many occasions it was impossible to identify the patient's primary doctor during the course of a phone call.

Specific Recommendations

In its last three meetings the team developed specific recommendations to the department and the FPC on ways to improve provider continuity. The recommendations were grouped into five categories of potential improvement: call-in provider scheduling, provider resource planning and scheduling, provider/patient identification, information systems, and staff education and development. They called for establishing a position of Resource Scheduling Clerk that would handle all call-in appointments. All four clerks would be trained for this assignment and rotate through it. This would simplify the scheduling process, especially when the scheduler had the recommended up-to-date list of patient-physician assignments and had the recommended training in procedures that would promote continuity. Figure 1.5 shows the recommended process flow chart that the TQM/CQI team developed.

Provider availability was to be expanded by increasing the number of available physicians and leaving gaps in their schedules to see acute care patients. Since it was common to tell chronically ill patients to "call in for an appointment in three months," the team recommended that the scheduler have physician schedules available for assignment at least three months in advance so that these patients could be scheduled with their physician before they left the building.

To promote easier identification of the primary physician, the team recommended that the practice be reorganized into four groups located on specific, color-coded hallways to assist with patient/provider identification and promote provider-to-provider communication. Once that was implemented, patients were to be given the doctor's business card, which would include the names of other members of the physician's small group or "team." New patients would have labels with the doctor's name affixed to their charts and to their plastic clinic registration card.

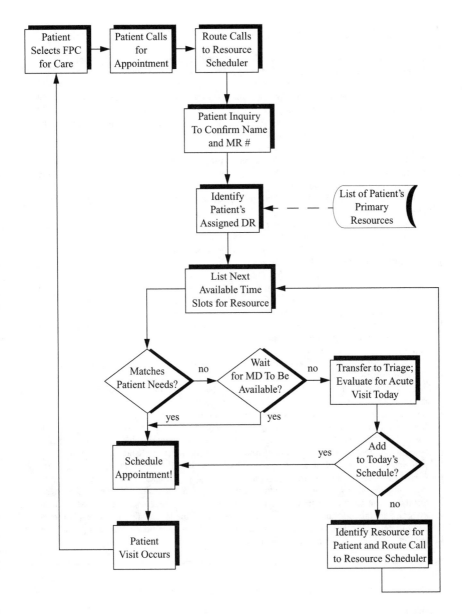

Figure 1.5 Recommended Call-In Appointment Process: Revised Flow Using Resource Scheduler

Longer term, the committee recommended a new FPC on-line information system to replace the existing three inflexible systems. They also made extensive recommendations concerning training, which are presented in Exhibit 1.2.

Exhibit 1.2 Recommendations in Staff Education and Development

Before initiating a program for staff education and development, a central question needs to be answered: Who is considered staff? In a TQM/CQI context, ALL individuals in the Department should be considered staff and should be educated on the processes at work in a TQM-oriented operation. The levels of participation will vary according to the activities performed (e.g., people involved in scheduling versus clinicians), but the commitment to improve should be equivalent. For the purposes of this discussion, the term "staff" will denote members of the Department, specifically the FPC, who are involved in nursing care, laboratory services, telecommunications, finances, and scheduling. However, it is important to recognize that the "top" of the organization needs to participate in the same training and education activities. Staff Education also needs to be Staff Reeducation for all those who have been operating under the current ineffective system.

It is recommended that all individuals receive training in the basic philosophy and methodology of TQM/CQI. In this trial program new and current members need to subscribe to the notion of providing *continuously improving and innovative* quality care to our primary customers, that is, the patients. Secondarily, in the context of the organization's "new" philosophy, the operational staff of the FPC should also receive an enlightened perspective towards the other major customers, the FPC clinicians.

Once adoption of the new FPC (or, alternatively, Departmental) philosophy occurs, everyone should recognize (and be recognized for) his or her contribution to the system, and become much more aware of the impact they have on efforts to improve the quality of our project (continuity of patient care) on a continuous basis. When problems occur in the system, each individual staff person should have a sense of investment to help identify, analyze, and resolve these problems. Similarly, staff should have the support and encouragement of upper and mid-level management of the FPC to accomplish this.

It is recommended that the education provided have as one of its main goals that each staff member form a clear understanding of his/her role, responsibilities, and specific duties associated with his or her position, and how it relates to the mission of the FPC and the Department as a whole. An active Mission Statement must be developed, adopted, and continuously reviewed to be of value to such a system. Adequate time must be set aside for detailed education (and continuous reeducation) of each staff member. New members of the Department, particularly staff members, cannot be trained by coworkers who do not have a command of the "big picture." Supervisors at all levels, who will have been oriented and trained in the TQM philosophy and methods, must take initiative to develop processes to ensure that everyone has received an adequate level of training prior to beginning work. Supervisors must also create an environment where staff can achieve their maximal potential without interference or barriers. Similarly, if facts and data are used as major factors in the management of the TQM-oriented system, then this information must be made freely available to staff for continuous improvement to occur. It cannot stop there. Education and training must be a continuous process for the FPC to improve and innovate in the future.

Implementation

Recommendations for changes, usually small and incremental changes, were discussed with key leaders, and some were implemented as early as the third month of the project. The formal recommendations were included in the team's December 1991 report that Dr. Kibbe prepared. It was 33 pages long plus appendices and was designed to explain TQM/CQI to the faculty and staff as well as provide a history of the process, present the data gathered, and justify the recommendations. Then the team presented their findings and recommendations to Departmental Grand Rounds in January 1992. The presentation was well received. Most of the questions centered on the TQM process (e.g., "Why were there no clerical personnel on the original team?") and on the implications of the team system for the providers.

The FPC went ahead with the training recommendations to raise everyone's level of awareness of the need to improve continuity. The faculty and residents were organized into small practice groups located on specific, color-coded hallways to facilitate patient-provider identification, and the call-in appointment and triage procedures were changed to simplify patient and staff decisions about whom the patient would see. The FPC is planning to adopt a computerized clinical database that will integrate the three sets of information and relate outpatient data with hospital specialty clinic data, laboratory results, and pharmacy services in the near future.

Outcomes and Holding the Gains

The last stage of the FOCUS-PDSA cycle calls for steps to hold the improvement gains and to continue to collect data that identifies the new baseline for improvement. A second chart audit on 125 randomly selected charts was conducted covering the period July 1, 1991, to June 30, 1992. The levels of continuity were up considerably from a year earlier and even above the 1984 study, as Figure 1.6 indicates. The overall continuity had increased to 74 percent from the prior year's 45 percent and was now in the range that the faculty had targeted in the TQM/CQI team's survey. Even more significantly, there were no patient complaints about continuity during the months of June, July, and August 1992.

Continuing Development

As of September 1992, there were two additional TQM/CQI teams in the FPC working on improving the timeliness of filing patient laboratory reports into patient charts and on reducing the number of charts lost or misplaced en route to and from Medical Records. These teams had already developed flow diagrams to clarify the processes involved and had collected data to obtain baseline performance figures. Faculty/resident teams now routinely included representatives from nursing, reception, and medical records in their bimonthly meetings. "Talking with data" had become much more common in committee meetings, and the tools of brainstorming, flow-charting, and cause-and-effect diagrams had become accepted tools of group work.

In conjunction with the UNC Hospitals, all employees would receive basic training in CQI methods during a half-day workshop in October, and third-year

Visit Type	1984	1991	1992	% Change, 1991–1992
Health maintenance	0.86	0.74	0.95	+28%
Chronic illness	0.71	0.61	0.84	+38%
Acute care	0.55	0.29	0.57	+97%
Overall UPC	0.61	0.45	0.74	+64%

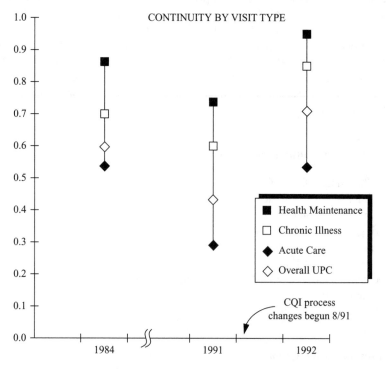

Figure 1.6 Family Practice Center: Provider Continuity Levels Pre- and Post-CQI Project Interventions. Department of Family Medicine, University of North Carolina at Chapel Hill

family practice residents would devote seven of their senior seminar sessions during the upcoming year to study of CQI in clinical settings. These sessions were being coordinated by Dr. Kibbe and would be open to residents in other specialties throughout the university.

CASE ANALYSIS

This effort has been successful in that the problematic indicator has been improved markedly. The staff have been sufficiently convinced of the value of the approach that new teams are being formed and are receiving cooperation and support. The reader will want to review that case to see why it was a success in an environment that many believe to be more difficult than most, a teaching faculty in a medical school.

Introduction

The approach used to assess and attack the continuity of care issues was one based on the experience of the National Demonstration Project and the Harvard Community Health Plan, where Mr. Galiani had previously worked. Dr. Kibbe also espoused a Deming approach like the one outlined in Chapter 2.

This case is unusual in that a single, very simple performance measure was used, namely, the proportion of the time that the patient saw the same physician on a return visit. This issue generated a number of complaints that were recorded but not acted upon until a major customer threatened to refer its industrial medicine patients to another institution. One must wonder why the rest of the complaints had gone unheeded, although with the communication gaps uncovered by the team, that problem should not be any special surprise. The achievement in terms of the improvement in continuity of care was sufficiently significant to warrant reporting in the medical literature (Kibbe et al., 1993).

Basics

The team consisted of a mixture of clinicians and administrative staff personnel with a facilitator from the hospital's management engineering department. Many of the principles on CQI teams outlined in Chapter 7 were violated. There were no clerical staff nor any residents on the team, and many of the solutions considered affected both groups. The reason for this was the educational purpose of the exercise. The team consisted of opinion leaders in the department who, once the team was successful, could provide the support for further efforts within the department involving all levels of personnel. The resistance was considered to be most likely to occur among the faculty, so they were heavily represented on the team.

Later on, the team and/or the team's staff interviewed the telephone schedulers and found out what their decision rules had been for assigning patients to available doctors and investigated the idiosyncracies of the clinic's information systems.

The team designed a special questionnaire to assess both staff and patient interest in continuity of care. This showed that the patients had a relatively sophisticated view of continuity of care contingent on the circumstances. The staff handling the telephone calls and doing the scheduling had a unidimensional approach focused on convenience rather than factoring in the type of encounter or the issue of continuity. The questionnaire was not the kind of general satisfaction questionnaire emphasized in Chapter 6, but it is another tool typical of what a team might choose to use from time to time to get baseline data for a critical analysis.

Implementation

This case shows how the leaders of a CQI process will often choose to tailor their approach with an eye toward implementation. The team was composed of individuals who might facilitate implementation as well as process analysis. Because of this weighting, additional help was obtained from the hospital's Management Engineering Department. Administrative staff also helped serve on the team, many of whose members would not spend large amounts of time on data gathering. Careful attention was paid to the types of professional autonomy and pride issues and the issues of physician time concerns and styles of decision making discussed in Chapters 9, 10, and 11. When senior medical staff members missed meetings, no attempt was made to try to make them feel guilty. The work proceeded without them. Thus they remained on board to approve the findings and sanction the implementation.

Applications

The results of the team's efforts were presented at grand rounds in the department, which gave the effort academic legitimacy in the teaching setting. Then the results were written up in article form and submitted to an academic journal. The publication of those results was intended to enhance the acceptance to CQI efforts and concepts as a part of the array of approaches relevant to academic medicine (see Chapter 17).

Curtis P. McLaughlin
Kit N. Simpson

Case **2**

Holston Valley
Hospital and Medical Center

After five years of training and team projects, Mr. Paul Bishop, Administrator of Holston Valley Hospital and Medical Center (HVHMC), was seeing the positive results of his quality management program in many ways in administrative areas, but he was still concerned about how to make more headway with the clinical use of resources.

Quality improvement had become a communitywide effort in Kingsport, a thriving industrial town of 36,365 in northeastern Tennessee. Quality management was a communitywide concern, involving employers, the chamber of commerce, the school system, the community college, and both hospitals in town. Most people agree that this concern began in 1982 with Eastman Chemical Company (Eastman), a subsidiary of Eastman Kodak employing over 11,000 at its Kingsport plants. Faced with stiff foreign competition in its markets, Eastman adopted a program that included a customer focus, employee empowerment, statistical methods, performance management, continuous improvement, education, and training management leadership. This program received an all-out push in 1985, and in 1988 Eastman was one of the nine finalists for the Malcolm Baldridge National Quality Award. Exhibit 2.1 outlines the sequence of quality events at the hospital and in the community.

Quality First

In 1986 Eastman executives were instrumental in having the Chamber of Commerce sponsor a QUALITY FIRST training session for community leaders at Northeast State Community College (then called Tri-Cities Community College).

This case was prepared as a basis for classroom discussion rather than to illustrate the effective or ineffective handling of an administrative situation. Copyright © 1992 by the Kenan-Flagler Business School, University of North Carolina, Chapel Hill, NC 27599-3490. All rights reserved. Not to be reproduced without permission.

Exhibit 2.1 Quality Events Time Line

The Community/Hospital Partnership

Community	Year	Hospital
		Quality Assurance Trained In Quality Improvement Tech.
Iowa Headquarters of Heritage Started With MFE	1991	Quality Assurance Merged With Quality Management
Area Hospitals Working Together To Sponsor Quality Management Seminar	1990	Hospital Board Instructed In MFE
Heritage HMO Started Improvement Project		Administrative Team Started Training
Kingsport Area Healthcare Improvement Process Formed	1989	
National Center For Quality Established		Hospital Introduced To Managing For Excellence
MFE Consulting Training Offered To City		MFE Consulting Training Offered To Hospital
City of Kingsport Started With MFE		The Sixth Project Team To Quality First Training
	1988	
School System Introduced To Performance Management		Admission Process Redesigned And Shortened
	1987	
Quality First Started At Northeast State Tech.		Patient Satisfaction Instrument Implemented
Kingsport Foundry Started Effort	1986	Hospital Introduced To Project Improvement
Chamber Of Commerce Researching Quality		
Customer Focus At Eastman Chemical	1982	

✸———— Holston Valley Hospital and Medical Center ————✸

Mr. Bishop and a team of Holston Valley Hospital executives attended it. The program was taught by two professors from Jackson Community College in Michigan, where the QUALITY FIRST program had been developed with assistance from the Ford Motor Company. QUALITY FIRST is a 16-week, project-focused program for teams of four or more from a firm. It emphasizes data collection and analysis, control charting, and prevention of error methods, all generally based on the precepts of W. Edwards Deming. Mr. Bishop, trained as a hospital administrator, was impressed with the approach and continued to send teams, more than 20 teams with approximately 90 participants. Documented savings at HVHMC from these team efforts included $72,000 in lower costs of linens, reductions in nurse turnover (costing $10,000–20,000 per nurse) of 6 percent, and reductions of medication delivery lead time from the pharmacy to the nursing floors from 3 to 1-1/4 hours.

The executives on that first team in August 1986 had trouble translating Deming concepts like a "single supplier" into the hospital context. Since they did not directly supervise service delivery, they took as their project the development of a patient satisfaction survey. Yet they sent four more teams that year, mostly on the basis of the reported successes of the industrial teams. Then they began to see results like the following:

- Admitting wait and processing times were reduced from 30 minutes to 5.6 minutes.
- Preadmission lab testing went from 30 percent to 75 percent.
- Length of stay dropped one day, mostly due to the efforts of the discharge planning team.

In some ways the QUALITY FIRST program was ideal for the hospital. People were gone only one day every other week for 16 weeks. The course was project oriented, so people could see the effects in the workplace.

Partnerships for Excellence

Seven major projects were completed by the end of 1988, but Mr. Bishop wanted to speed up the process. So did the city manager of Kingsport. He went to Eastman Chemical, which agreed to donate the services of Mr. David J. McClaskey, a quality management coordinator, to help adapt and use his "Managing for Excellence" training course to allow HVHMC to bring quality training "in-house." David McClaskey was an Examiner for the Malcolm Baldrige National Quality Award and helped develop the Examiner preparation course. One assistant administrator at HVHMC, Mr. Dale Richardson, received more than 100 hours of training. Then the management team and two potential in-house facilitators—a nurse and a business manager—went through the initial 80 hours of training over about seven months. During this initial run the participants found that about 30 percent of the material required modification to replace industrial illustrations with health situations. With Mr. McClaskey's cooperation they modified the material, which they now call "Partnerships for Excellence." By June 1991 the hospital was staffed with six full-time facilitators. The hospital had some 23 "natural teams," which included direct reporting relationships from the administrator through assistant administrators to department directors and to their supervisors. By June 1991 80 percent of the natural teams had completed the "Partnerships for Excellence" process, with the remainder scheduled to complete the process within eight months.

The total quality management (TQM) program consisted of four training modules. The first 80-hour module was for natural teams (groups with common supervision). It was an introduction to Deming's 14 points, Peter's "A Passion for Customers," the Red Bead Experiment, team-building exercises, listening skills, managing customer expectations, developing process measures, flow-charting, statistical thinking, and the whole QUALITY FIRST process, followed by an exercise in developing a performance management plan for the unit and planning the rollout of quality improvement in the department. There were also two modules on process teams and one on quality improvement projects, averaging 40 hours each. Process and project teams were both responsible for multifunctional issues, with the process teams intending to maintain their oversight of a process and the project teams having more of an ad hoc nature.

An example of a quality improvement project was the one concerned with nursing turnover, which had been averaging 25 percent annually. The initial task had been to define turnover, measure it, and then set a goal of reducing the rate. The target for reduction was set at 6 percent, with the new target at 19 percent. Figure 2.1 illustrates the run chart developed by the team before and after its efforts started in August 1990 with four-hour meetings every other week. The project team decided not to deal with nursing recruitment, with anyone working less than 32 hours per month, with issues of absenteeism, or with non-nursing employee turnover. Turnover was defined as the number of full- and part-time equivalents (FTEs) transferred/terminated/resigned monthly, divided by the budgeted number of full- and part-time R.N., L.P.N., nonlicensed, and clerical personnel FTEs. There was always a tension over whether to focus on total employee turnover or R.N. turnover only. There was a tangible need to benchmark HVHMC against other comparable hospitals to test the target of a 6 percent annual turnover reduction that some had presented. The costs of recruiting and training a new R.N.-level nurse had been estimated at $10,000 to $20,000.

Not all groups received the full 80 hours, since the program can be modularized, especially the process teams. A process team works together for an extended period of time to study an important patient care process. An example might be the "heart process" involving open heart and cardiac cath patients. Process teams were started most recently, require a well-trained facilitator, and generate the most conflict. Mr. Bishop noted, "We are still developing the process team framework. It is very hard for managers to stay out of the business of the process team long enough for them to produce results—we have found that we have had to limit participation of managers unless they are specifically assigned to the team." Exhibits 2.2 and 2.3 show how the roles of the natural teams and process teams have been defined to deal with the ownership role, called the role of *process steward* at HVHMC.

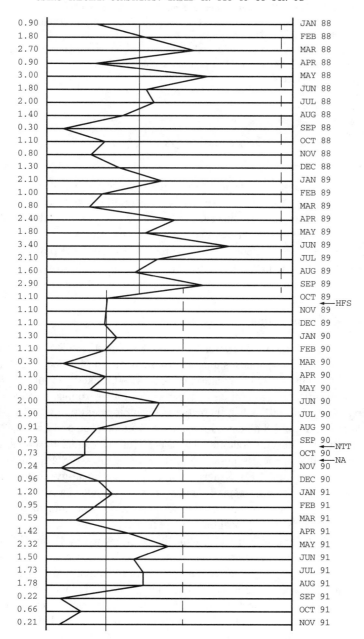

Figure 2.1 Run Chart of Nursing Turnover

Exhibit 2.2 Relationship of Process Teams and Natural Management Teams (Owners)

- Process Teams regularly report progress/accomplishments to Natural Team.
- Owner and the Process Team member communicate to all departmental employees information regarding changes to the process.
- Priorities of what to work on is discussed and negotiated with Department Natural Team.
- In determining what to work on, Process Team considers input from:
  −customers of process
  −team members
  −"Owner's Team"
- Major decisions and changes to process should be discussed with Departmental Natural Team.

—Holston Valley Hospital and Medical Center—

When a team completes the program, its members receive certificates, called licenses (implying the need for renewal), at a celebration ceremony in front of all the managers, including first-line supervisors. Often a figure from the community and/or the hospital board is asked to hand out the certificates.

HVHMC has also adopted the "Service Excellence" modules developed by the Einstein group of Philadelphia. Of the hospital's 1,800 employees, 1,500 have received this training, with the rest slated to receive it by the end of 1991.

Community Competition

The Tri-Cities area, involving Johnson City, Kingsport, and Bristol, Tennessee, and Bristol, Virginia, represents the nation's 82nd largest Metropolitan Statistical Area (MSA), with a 1990 population of 436,047. It ranked 31st out of the 281 MSAs in manufacturing earnings as a percent of total earnings in 1988. During the first quarter of 1991, when the national unemployment rate was 7.1 percent, Kingsport's rate was 3.8 percent, Johnson City's 5.6 percent, and Bristol TN-VA's 5.4 percent. It is heavily doctored. There are four substantial hospitals, two in Kingsport, and a medical school as part of East Tennessee State University in Johnson City. By mid-1991 Kingsport had 18 obstetrician-gynecologists with two more coming soon. Hospital lengths of stay, despite managed care, were above the national average. Advertising for hospitals and doctors abounds in the press, on billboards, and in local business periodicals.

Both HVHMC and Indian Path Medical Center, owned by Hospital Corporation of America (HCA), operated well below their licensed bed level. HVHMC was licensed for 540 beds, after giving up 50 beds to help bring in a for-profit rehab hospital, but operated 350 to 375 beds, having converted its wards and semiprivate rooms to all-private room status. Most community-based physicians practiced at both hospitals. Most of the physicians in the town belonged to the Kingsport Independent Practitioners' Association (IPA), which contracted to deliver services to Heritage National Healthplan (an HMO established and owned

Exhibit 2.3 Responsibilities of Process Teams*

---

1. Understand customer needs and define customer requirements.
2. Determine where the process stands in relation to customer requirements.
3. Study/analyze process:
    A. Flowcharts
    B. Discussions with people involved with process
    C. Analysis of data
    D. Benchmarks
4. Determine measures of process:
    A. Results/output measures
    A. In-process
5. Determine and list areas for improvement.
6. Feedback to Natural Unit Management Team.*
7. Work on improvement projects agreed on by Natural Unit Management Team.
8. Routinely manages the overall process by:
    A. Routinely monitoring process measures.
    B. Detecting and appropriately responding to process upsets that cannot be handled routinely within the process.
    C. Receiving and listing ideas to improve the process.

*When appropriate, the "team" can be just the process steward.

—Holston Valley Hospital and Medical Center—

---

by John Deere, initially founded to service its own employees). Sixty-two percent of Eastman Chemical Company's employees were covered under contracts with Heritage. The rest were covered by Blue Cross-Blue Shield of Tennessee under a contract that covered a wide range of services, including some preventive care. Table 2.1 provides a financial and statistical statement of operations for fiscal years ending June 30, 1988 to 1992.

HVHMC was structured with a parent holding company, Holston Valley Health Care, Inc. (HVHC); the hospital was one of three separate divisions, together with a foundation for endowment and the for-profit HVS Company, which managed a home health agency, respiratory therapy services, weight loss programs, psychiatric counseling, laundry, and other services to physicians' offices, and a number of joint ventures, including diagnostic imaging. HVHMC included a trauma center, a neonatal intensive care unit, an open-heart surgery team, and a cancer center. It was one of the larger servers of the medically indigent in the state.

Indian Path Medical Center administrative team had also participated in the same initial QUALITY FIRST training program. They also had gone through HCA's Deming-based quality management training in 1989. One project there had reduced outpatient registration wait time from 35 minutes to 5 minutes.

Community Cooperation

Despite the intense competition, Kingsport also became involved in a cooperative effort to improve the community's health. In 1988 the Midwest Business

Table 2.1 Comparative Statement of Operations

	Year Ended 6-30-88	Year Ended 6-30-89	Year Ended 6-30-90	Year Ended 6-30-91	Est. Year Ended 6-30-92
FINANCIALS ($)					
Patient serv. revenue	100,184	118,130	137,970	164,926	193,738
Revenue deductions	24,992	30,551	41,629	51,562	68,195
Other operating revenue	2,438	2,457	4,672	5,781	5,407
Net revenue	77,630	90,036	101,013	119,145	130,950
Operating expenses	74,857	86,849	97,935	113,356	129,470
Nonoperating revenue	963	768	1,922	1,867	3,271
Nonoperating expenses	512	601	130	39	58
Net nonoperating income	451	167	1,792	1,828	3,214
Net gain (loss)	3,224	3,354	4,870	7,617	4,693
STATISTICS					
Adult admissions	15,202	15,804	15,718	15,432	14,970
Adult patient days	111,803	110,459	105,498	106,304	103,368
Newborn days	4,982	4,594	4,444	4,889	4,657
Open heart cases	469	498	496	556	547
Surgical procedures	7,949	8,266	8,872	9,657	10,291
Same day service visits	5,637	5,563	5,344	6,961	7,931
Emergency room visits	52,943	55,725	56,294	57,086	58,324
Radiological procedures	75,959	77,797	78,963	81,318	84,662
CT scan procedures	6,784	7,098	7,523	8,263	8,941
Lab procedures	824,391	903,724	978,338	1,020,393	1,108,309
Cath lab procedures	2,416	2,010	2,103	2,224	2,428
MRI procedures	1,742	2,839	3,889	4,113	3,968
Length of stay	7.3	7.0	6.7	6.9	6.9
Average FTEs	1,578	1,707	1,666	1,820	2,323
FTEs/avg. occup. bed	4.3	4.7	4.7	5.0	5.3

Group on Health, after studying health purchasing and quality assessment tools, received funding from the John A. Hartford Foundation of New York to develop three demonstration sites for community cooperation to stress teamwork and reduce variation in health. Kingsport became the first demonstration site. Someone at HCA, which itself invests heavily in Deming-based quality management programs, suggested Kingsport and the request was finally brought to the attention of Mr. Rob Johnson, Manager of Benefits Coordination at Eastman. He coordinated the development of the Kingsport Area Health Improvement Project (KA-HIP), which involved representatives of the Kingsport Area Business Council on Health Care (KABACH), HVHMC, Indian Path Medical Center, Indian Path Pavilion (psychiatric), the IPA, and Heritage. After going through an intensive quality training session, the KAHIP members' representatives reviewed the health problems affecting Kingsport's population and finally selected the area of respiratory diseases as its focus. Four improvement projects were undertaken:

- reducing the number of readmissions for chronically ill respiratory patients, whom the group dubbed "frequent flyers"
- developing a more effective process for transitioning respiratory patients to nursing homes
- developing a process to encourage youth to quit/not start smoking
- determining the most appropriate means of conducting third-party utilization review

Three of the teams attended the QUALITY FIRST program with their tuition paid for by the Midwest Business Group on Health, and the four worked with an individual facilitator. In retrospect, Rob Johnson noted that this process was frustrating. "We didn't do a good job of using our project selection criteria. The projects we selected were difficult to deal with. They were too broad or aimed at a system instead of a process. Our data system wasn't effective enough to narrow the projects down to processes." Ownership was also a problem in this type of organization. "Everybody has ownership or nobody has ownership. Because KA-HIP is a community-oriented project, no one organization could claim ownership." Three of the four teams have continued to meet, and the superintendent of schools is trying to reorganize the youth and smoking team. The team working with nursing home placements has had some concrete successes, and the other teams continue to collect and interpret data.

The Heritage National HMO has also started its own quality management program in Kingsport and at its Illinois headquarters, assisted by facilitators from Eastman and HVHMC. Under the leadership of the doctors in the IPA and a team from the IPA, the HMO and the hospitals studied the resources used for postsurgical care of gall bladder removals. They found that there were about as many processes as there were physicians and developed a standard process. The net result has been to reduce the average length of stay for this procedure by two days. Dean Anderson, Operations Manager of Heritage, says, "Ultimately we hope to have improvement teams in doctor's offices. Potential improvement areas we've identified include pediatric office scheduling, lab work, and billing processes. We want to spread the quality virus and get all physicians involved. Physicians develop different practices, but through quality we hope to combine the various procedures into one formalized process."

Dr. Paul Pearlman, President of the IPA, comments, "As physicians, we have to be interested in promoting health care. Physicians have varied backgrounds, so everyone manages problems differently. What we're trying to do through KAHIP is find out why there are variations and how we can reduce them to make our processes better. It shouldn't make a difference which emergency room a person goes to. What's important is that they get quality care wherever they go." One fact that encouraged Rob Johnson was the physicians' choice of low-cost California managed care group practices as their cost and length of stay benchmark for their gallbladder study.

KAHIP has also become the task force on health for the Kingsport Tomorrow project, a communitywide program to envision Kingsport in the 21st century. Rob Johnson observed that "we're reassessing teams, poring over new data systems and targeting physicians' offices for facilitators. If we can't zero in on the problems with our present projects, then we'll discontinue them. There are a lot of resources yet to be tapped. We feel we haven't accomplished a great deal, but others looking at Kingsport and KAHIP from the outside see what we're doing here and are amazed. While it's natural for us in Kingsport to cooperate, it is not in other communities."

Community cooperation was the style in Kingsport. Eastman and the other employers wanted a happy, attractive community to attract skilled personnel to their expanding businesses. On the other hand, if health care costs had to be cut, they could and would act unilaterally. Eastman had made a study of medical admissions for low back pain and had severely restricted payments for that service. The number of admissions and their length dropped sharply, especially the admissions by primary care physicians. Eastman was aware that it could achieve the lowest health care costs by selecting a subset of physicians in the town and forming a closed-panel HMO, but Rob Johnson did not want anything that confrontational yet. "That just is not Eastman's style." Besides, he felt that it was best to work with the total system rather than minimizing Eastman's share, since cost shifting one way or another ended up saddling employers with the costs of uncompensated care throughout the community.

National Center for Quality

Another cooperative venture of the quality management community in the Tri-Cities area, building on the QUALITY FIRST program, is the National Center for Quality. This is a nonprofit corporation formed by the three chambers of commerce in 1988 that is dedicated to promoting a national interest in quality and productivity improvement. It has established a core set of courses for organizations to call on. Exhibit 2.4 shows the board membership as of January 1990. In June of 1989, Jim Wallin, Community Programs Coordinator for Eastman, was loaned to the center as its interim director. In January 1990 the board approved handing over the operation to Northeast State Technical Institute, and Al Thomas,

Exhibit 2.4 National Center for Quality: Members of the Board

R. C. Hart
Eastman Chemical Company
(Chairman of the Board)

Curtis Burnette
Aerojet Ordinance Tennessee
(President)

Will Hutsell
Eastman Chemical Company
(Vice President)

Dr. R. Wade Powers
Northeast State Technical Community
  College
(Treasurer)

D. Lynn Johnson
Eastman Chemical Company
(Secretary)

Al Thomas
National Center for Quality
(Executive Director)

Vic Dingus
Eastman Chemical Company

James R. White
Eastman Chemical Company

Paul Bishop
Holston Valley Hospital and Medical
  Center

John Andersen
First American National Bank

Bill Ring
Kingsport Foundry and Manufacturing Corp.

Don Royston
Kingsport Chamber of Commerce

Dennis Wagner
United Telephone System

Marie Williams
Greater Bristol Area Chamber of
  Commerce

Jerry Moeller
Bristol Regional Medical Center

Tim Jones
Johnson City Chamber of Commerce

Ed Fennell
City of Johnson City

Dr. James Hales
East Tennessee State University

Ann Peace
Kingsport, TN

Reneau Dubberly
Johnson City, TN

Jim Wallin
Eastman Chemical Company

Dick Wetherell
Texas Instruments

Dr. Allan Spritzer
College of Business, East Tennessee
  State University

—Holston Valley Hospital and Medical Center—

director of the QUALITY FIRST program, was asked to serve as part-time executive director of the center.

The center offers a number of courses:

- Seizing the Quality Initiative
- Leading the Quality Transformation
- Survey Techniques

- Quality and Performance Management for Educators
- Malcolm Baldridge National Quality Award
- Managing for Excellence in Healthcare

It currently has under development programs on Quality for Small Business and Quality Consultant Training. On August 5–6, 1991, the center in cooperation with the four area hospitals offered "A Competitive Healthcare and Quality Management Conference." The conference coordinator was Ms. Ether Luster, an assistant administrator at HVHMC. Paul Bishop observed, "Our psychological contract with the supporters of quality management includes our making a special effort to disseminate our story." The second conference was held April 23–24, 1992, and included such well-known presenters as Dr. Paul Batalden, Vice President of Medical Affairs at HCA, and Dr. James Roberts of the Joint Commission on Accreditation of Healthcare Organizations.

Activities at HVHMC

Paul Bishop was genuinely pleased with the hospital and the community efforts, which were attracting national recognition. For example, he had been asked to prepare and give a presentation at the 1991 Business Week Symposium of Health Care CEOs, Rockefeller Center, New York City, June 20–21, 1991, which he entitled "Innovation as a Team Sport: Solutions Through Partnership." Yet when asked about issues to be worked on, he replied, "There are hundreds of them. In health care the average time that people are satisfied with an improved service is half an hour. They immediately internalize the new achievement as the new standard and complain about how poor the service is." Over time, however, he felt that people were beginning to realize that the quality of care had genuinely improved.

His major concerns beyond day-to-day implementation were (1) how fast to change the organizational structure and the human resource infrastructure to adjust to quality management and performance management, (2) how to increase the emphasis on quality management in clinical decision making, and (3) how to get his vision of the future of this change process across to people. Early on the quality assurance (QA) effort was merged with and made subordinate to the quality management program. The existing QA staff, two medical records specialists who had been doing physician utilization review, were assigned to the new head of quality management, a former nursing supervisor. They then received quality management training. The quality management department grew rapidly with the addition of the six quality management facilitators with the titles of Quality Management Consultant. Their backgrounds included nursing supervision, clinical laboratory support, financial office support, quality management with the telephone company, undergraduate training in statistics, and medical records experience. Dale Richardson, the assistant administrator responsible for quality management, had worked as a consultant with SunHealth, a hospital consulting firm in Charlotte, North Carolina, before coming to Kingsport and still took occasional quality management assignments with them.

The performance appraisal system had been modified somewhat to include contributions to quality management, and so had the job descriptions. Yet Paul Bishop was still concerned about how fast to move away from the periodic appraisal system and toward performance management. Some senior managers who had been successful under the old style of management and believed that "the cream rises to the top" would probably resist such a move. This didn't mean that institutionalization of the concepts of quality management wasn't pretty far along. People had internalized the concepts and terms throughout the organization. A number of physicians were quite interested in some of the projects. Some people who had complained about their supervisors' passiveness were actually saying that they saw positive changes in management, while others sometimes complained about too much time spent in meetings.

The original heart process team had not been terribly successful because the individuals responsible for spearheading the process review had come from outside it. "We went to school on that one," one of the internal consultants said. "Since then the process stewards have all come from within the process. That cuts down on barriers and defensiveness." During the past year, the team and a consulting company—APM—from New York that specializes in service line development have made great strides with the heart process. The key has been in getting commitment from the physicians for improvement of the process, including cost control.

The Linen Management System

The eighth group sent to Tri-Cities Tech, for example, was a team composed of four members of nursing staff, the director of linen and laundry services, and a hospital buyer. The project assigned to them by the administrative staff was the frequent set of complaints from the nursing units about the shortage or excess of laundry delivered by the in-house laundry to the floors. The Laundry Department had tried to project the daily nursing usage on each unit, but there was little communication or coordination between the Laundry and the Nursing Units. The existing system provided no linen accountability or control and poor utilization of personnel.

When the team first met, there was little agreement on the perceived cause of this lack of coordination. Through the use of brainstorming sessions, the group reached a consensus on improving the linen distribution system. They developed the system flow chart shown in Figure 2.2. The team identified all the units involved in the process, which involved the purchase of linen, its processing by the laundry, and its distribution over two miles of hospital corridors to 22 nursing

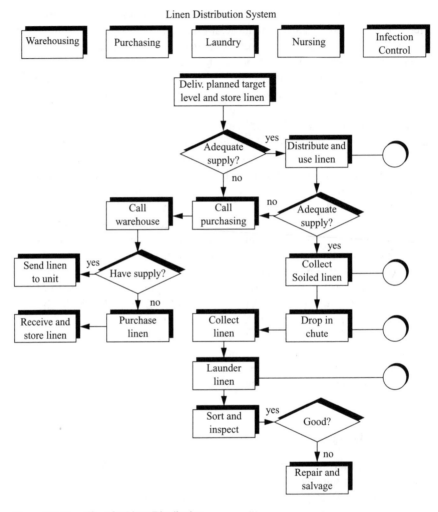

Figure 2.2 Flow Chart for Linen Distribution

unit linen closets. They then prepared the cause-and-effect (fishbone) diagram relating to inadequate linen distribution shown in Figure 2.3.

The group realized that they were still dealing with rather broad generalities
and knew little about the specifics of linen utilization. With the cooperation of the
22 nursing units, a linen inventory was conducted. On February 8, 1989, the nursing staff arrived at work to find that their first task was to count each clean piece
of linen in patient rooms and linen closets. Then for the next two days all soiled
linen was sent to the laundry in bags color coded by the unit of origin so that the
laundry could do a usage count. These counts are shown as Figures 2.4 and 2.5. A

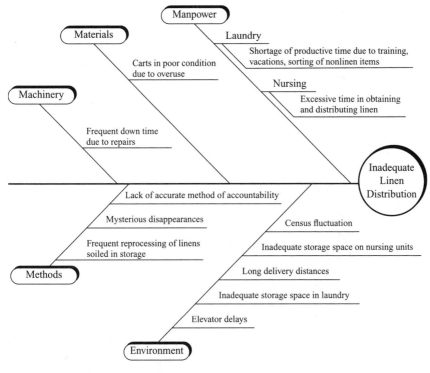

Figure 2.3 Cause-and-Effect Diagram for Linen Distribution

tour of the hospital left team members agreeing that there were adequate supplies of linens but they were distributed poorly, with too many washcloths on some units and too few on others. Crowded storage spaces did not allow enough room for storing enough pillows on most units, also leading to linen falling on the floor and needing to be reprocessed. If a unit could not store enough pillows in the linen closet, housekeeping then arranged to store some in the closets of the patient rooms.

The team then decided to conduct a pilot test of linen control on the Neuro-Orthopedics Unit. Control charts were developed based on data on usage over a 16-day period. Linen closets were rearranged and shelves labeled and marked with red tape to meet planned levels. Figure 2.6 contains an example of these control charts. Target inventory levels were set at the upper control limits on these C-charts. Since each day the closets were stocked neatly up to the specified amount, there were few shortages necessitating trips to the laundry and no excesses. The team calculated that the saving in inventory investment on the pilot floor was more than 50 percent. Extrapolated to the whole hospital, the reduction in investment was estimated at $72,000.

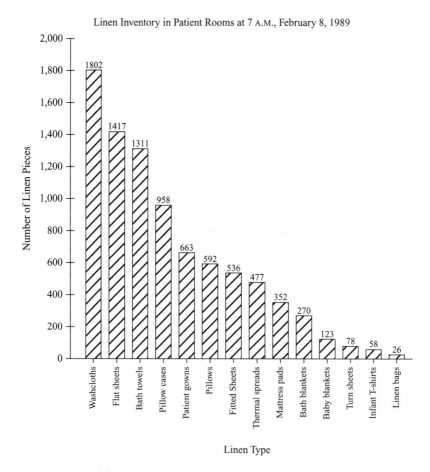

Figure 2.4 Sample Clean Linen Inventory Report

An unexpected benefit resulted from the fact that the pilot unit was going to be renovated and the new plans called for inadequate linen storage space. The team went to the architect and the hospital administration and arranged to have the storage space increased.

The team reported that there were additional savings in personnel time and energy that were difficult to quantify. They suggested that the amount of linen stored could be reduced even further if the laundry had more storage space, if laundry equipment reliability was improved, or if "mysterious disappearance of linen inventory" could be countered.

The linen team decided to stay intact to expand the approach to all nursing and ancillary departments, to expand the system to additional items such as scrub suits, and to monitor and adjust the system to changing requirements.

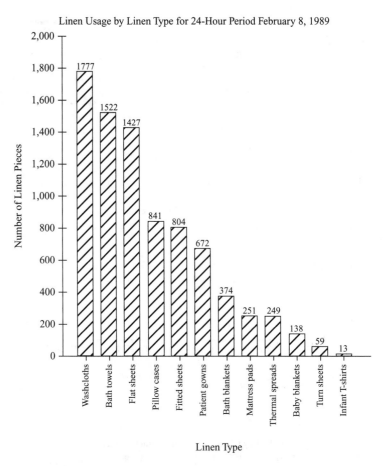

Figure 2.5 Sample Linen Usage Report

Radiology Transport Team

The Radiology Process Team attended the QUALITY FIRST Project training a little after the Linen Team. The Radiology Process Team met with the Administrative Management Team to discuss Major Improvement Opportunities (MIOs) and selected (1) Financial viability, (2) High touch, and (3) Decreased length of stay. Various subgroups were asked to develop a priority listing for improvements. The one developed by the radiology technologists is shown as Figure 2.7. Their priorities were representative, so the team went to work on processes used to transport inpatients. Patients were constantly complaining that it took too long to get back to their rooms after an exam; in some cases waits of up to two hours

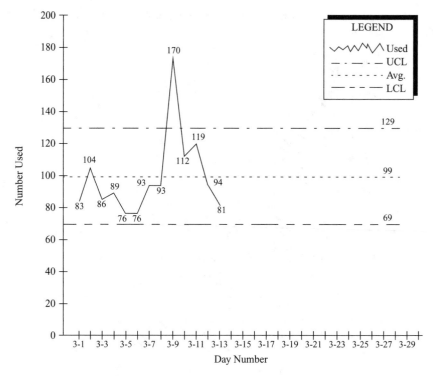

Figure 2.6 Sample Control Chart for Bath Towel Usage

Step 1: Why Choose This Improvement Project?

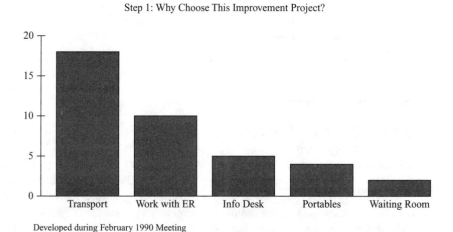

Developed during February 1990 Meeting

Figure 2.7 Radiology Improvement Projects: Priority Listing Developed by Techs

were noted. Staff members complained of delays in sending for patients. If a patient was sent for at 10 A.M., he or she might not arrive until 2 or 3 P.M. Then work flow was disrupted, schedules were delayed, and referring physicians were upset with the total wait time. These delays could hold up other tests and procedures and have a negative impact on the length of stay.

The team decided to focus on patient delays in Radiology and the wait time after a procedure was complete on an inpatient. The first piece of data collection was to determine the amount of time it would take an able-bodied transporter (orderly) to walk from the furthest point in the hospital to the Radiology Department. The transporter team member reported 15 minutes. Therefore the team set its standard for a wait for transportation as 15 to 30 minutes. A technologist team member asked each patient over a period of several days what he or she felt was a reasonable wait after a procedure. Patients appeared to consider under 10 minutes a reasonable time and 20 minutes to be the maximum. Given a focused definition of the problem, the team then decided to find the root cause. They started with a flow diagram (Figure 2.8). With the aid of their facilitator, the team then developed a cause-and-effect diagram (Figure 2.9). Based on this understanding of the process, the team conducted a survey of the transporters about the causes of the delays they encountered. They confirmed the importance of a lack of wheelchairs and stretchers, the subject of another team's analysis that was already underway.

An initial survey showed that the system was meeting the target less than 50 percent of the time. However, there were some questions about the times reported under the "honor system," so a new study was conducted using a Simplex clocking device on which the technologist clocked in when the patient was sent for and the transporter clocked in when he received the card and when he left the Radiology Department. With the new data system, the figures improved, but still were unsatisfactory 32 percent of the time.

Further study identified the fact that seven radiology transporters all worked various areas of the Imaging Section. Furthermore, they reported not to a Radiology manager, but to Dispatch Services, a source of territorial battles and attitudinal problems. The head of Dispatch Service was asked to join the team. The other team members suggested that the radiology transporters should be pooled.

At the transporters' suggestion, each transporter kept a detailed log of how time was spent, accounting for transport travel time (T.P.T.), travel to and from the patient (T.T.), and dead time (D.T.). Over half of the time was dead time, raising questions about the perceived need for more transporters (Figure 2.10).

Given the low utilization of the transporters, the team suggested to management that the seven transporters be assigned to Radiology for supervision, solving the issues of "Who is my boss?", and be retrained and upgraded to the position of Radiology Assistant so that they could perform duties such as developing film and obtaining reports. This would help solve the attitude problems since it would expand the job and increase the pay.

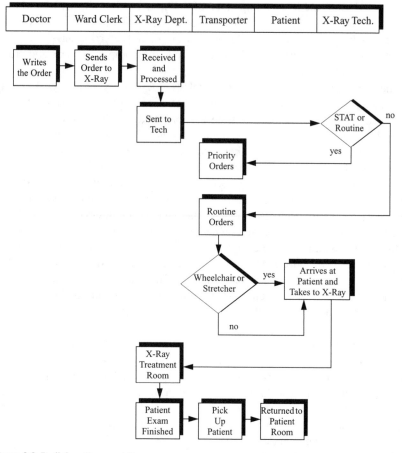

Figure 2.8 Radiology Transport Process

During the implementation phase a radio base was purchased, an area was set up for the transporters, and the six months of retraining commenced. At the time of the team presentation, Nursing Administration was putting pressure on Dispatch Services to cover weekend shifts without overtime costs. Radiology and Administration worked this out in Radiology by adding one person to be a dispatcher. The team report noted that

> In all there will be cost in a radio base, carpentry work, raise in pay, and one full-time employee. Sounds like a lot of money and not very financially viable.

> The original seven [transporters] covered shifts from 6:00 A.M. to 8 P.M., Monday through Friday, and on overtime shifts from 7:00 A.M. to

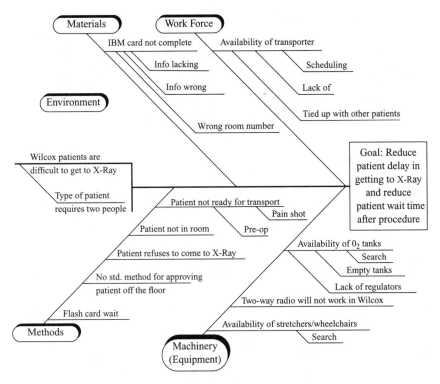

Figure 2.9 Cause-and-Effect Diagram on What Causes the Delays

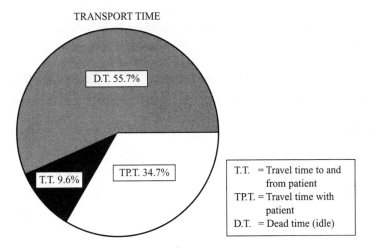

Figure 2.10 Radiology Transporter Time Breakdown (Seven-Day Average)

4 P.M. on Saturday only. Upon implementation, the shifts covered will be 5:30 A.M. to 11:00 P.M., Monday through Friday, and 7:00 A.M. to 11:00 P.M., Saturday and Sunday. At the addition of one employee, fifty-three additional hours will be added to the transportation schedule. Overtime has been reduced, the overall utilization of transportation has been increased, and we are projecting this to be at no cost. Now that is Financial Viability that even Sam Walton would be interested in.

Moving on to Clinical Quality

The hospital had recently received its initial set of SysteMetrics/McGraw-Hill IMPAQ III reports, one of the first sets sent out, providing internal resource utilization, mortality, and complications by diagnosis, by payer, and by physician. Paul Bishop saw two major issues right now: (1) how to adjust them for patient risk, and (2) how to transmit the information to the physicians in a way that would maintain the spirit of cooperation that existed, but still motivate review and action. HVHMC looked good on mortality and not as good on resource utilization. Tables 2.2 and 2.3 show some sample statistics from that report, which, except for the mortality data and average DRG weights, were based entirely on internal comparisons. The same data were available by individual physician. The variable "payer mix index" was based on the amount that the hospital was actually paid after contractual discounts and allowances, claims denials, and bad debts. Other definitions are shown in Exhibit 2.5.

In some situations Paul Bishop was not sure whether the discrepancies were due to coding errors or biases or rooted in physician behaviors. He wanted to use

---

Table 2.2 Resource Demand Information by Payer, October–December 1990

	Cases	Percent Cases	Mortality Ratio	Days Exceeding Expectation	Charges Exceeding Expectation
All cases	4,197	100		0	
Medicare		47.8	1.263	2,347	616,185
Medicaid		10.3	1.444	−1,185	−146,910
Commercial		19.1	1.091	−471	−281,633
Blue Cross		9.5	0.667	−273	−132,976
HMO		3.8	3.0	−297	−185,562
Self pay		6.7	0.667	−35	212,526
Worker's Comp.		2.8	0.5	−86	− 85,944

Table 2.3 Resource Demand Information by Product Line, October–December 1990

	Cases	Efficiency Ratio	LOS Ratio	Avg. DRG Scale	HVHMC Resource Demand Index	Payer Mix Index
Cardiac—med.	651	84.9	1.2	1.0752	0.853	66
Cardiac—surg.	162	93.5	1.1	1.0799	4.670	69
Cancer—med.	158	112.3	1.2	1.0677	0.891	64
Cancer—surg.	45	89.2	1.1	1.0044	1.125	66
Neuro—med.	222	76.8	1.0	0.9673	0.730	70
Neuro—surg.	110	96.2	1.1	0.8965	1.894	73
Renal/Uro—med.	98	102.6	1.1	0.9996	0.639	65
Renal/Uro—surg.	61	82.0	0.9	0.9169	0.673	69
Women's health	573	111.3	0.4	0.9665	0.397	67
Ortho	238	94.1	1.2	0.9580	1.229	67
Respiratory	310	82.3	1.1	1.0569	1.276	64
Medicine	530	99.2	1.3	1.0055	0.623	66
Gen. surg.	255	101.0	1.0	0.9895	1.310	69
Other surg.	265	97.5	1.2	1.1616	1.521	68
Newborn	341	153.0	0.8	1.0696	0.302	65
Psychiatry	80	70.1	1.0	1.0484	0.900	66
Ophthal.	7	89.2	0.8	0.8457	0.622	70
Trauma—med.	69	120.6	1.2	0.9907	0.535	61
Trauma—surg.	9	126.1	1.1	1.2811	1.224	62
Dental	2	84.1	0.6	1.0000	0.422	64
Substance abuse	11	73.7	0.9	1.0436	0.826	59
All cases	4,197			1.0261	1.000	66

this new information in a way that would enhance HVHMC's effectiveness and financial viability. The hospital was currently operating in the black, and he wanted it to stay that way. On the other hand, he had been careful so far to have the quality program avoid issues that might upset physicians enough to take more of their cases to competing hospitals.

Rob Johnson had suggested sharing the data with the IPA and letting them take ownership for the quality improvement process. "Our experiences with medical

Exhibit 2.5 Definitions of Terms from Systemetrics Report

The product line efficiency ratio measures the extent consumption exceeds demand. The higher the ratio, the greater the inefficiency.... Demand is set by the clinical criteria of patients, consumption is determined by charges which constitute cost to the buyer or payer.... Because the efficiency calculation is specific to each patient, and because the efficiency norm is derived from typical practice patterns of physicians utilizing services in your hospital, the ratio is a reasonable estimate of how average overall product line performance compares to average overall performance in the hospital.... In other words, to the extent average clinically adjusted charges in a product line exceed average clinically adjusted charges in the hospital, to that extent charges are inefficient either due to payer mix pricing strategy, a greater use of ancillary charges, longer lengths of stay, or some combination of these....

LOS Efficiency Ratio recognizes aggregate variation from legitimate demand for resources. It answers the question, from the buyer's point of view, that is to say, with all things considered—price, use of ancillaries, length of stay—how efficient is the hospital in a particular Product Line, DRG, payer, or at the physician level?... [It] is a unique, discrete analysis of how favorably your actual length of stay compares with the LOS you should expect, given patient clinical condition and discharge habits at your hospital compared to those in the national database.

For example, a ratio of 1.15 means that actual LOS exceeds expected LOS by 15%. More specifically, it means that discharge policy and procedures affecting the PL, coupled with physician disposition practices, result in a 15% longer length of stay in the Product Line than would be expected given overall hospital policy, procedures and practice patterns and their comparison to national norms specific to identical disease categories.

* * * * *

Once senior management has drawn conclusions about Product Line utilization and efficiency, and their effect on limited, acute resources, the next logical place to turn is to the possible improvement of net patient revenue across payers.... As with product lines, this analysis begins with an assessment of legitimate payer resource demand relative to total hospital acute demand. Number of cases is often a poor proxy for estimating resource allocation across payers. The legitimate need is not only dependent upon volume, but also in illness severity; and ultimately dependent upon resource efficiencies which would increase or lower the allocation requirement.

Mortality—a special "mortality scale" has been developed to predict mortality based on risk of death associated with the stage or progression of disease, and the effect of the interaction of comorbid conditions upon that risk. Ratios greater than 1.0 indicate the extent (percent) actual deaths exceed the national norm for the specific clinical conditions exhibited across the payer population.

backs and gallbladders show that changes in physician practice patterns show up immediately in both hospitals. Why should Paul pay all the costs of the change when Indian Path will get just as much benefit?"

CASE ANALYSIS

Eastman is convinced of the value of TQM and is trying to get all major organizations, including the town government, the schools, and the hospital to adopt it.

Given the stature of Eastman in this town, Mr. Bishop would have been foolhardy to dismiss it out of hand. But he is not just going through the motions. He is sold on the concept, and he has invested heavily in it, with a staff of four assigned to it, plus an assistant administrator who is also providing overall direction.

Introduction

One of the hospital's primary customers, the town's major employer, is sold on TQM and has helped the hospital implement an approach based on its experience. This allows the reader to think about whether there are differences between TQM and CQI. The hospital did find that the industrial training materials were relevant, but that almost half of these materials required new examples from the health care setting. Is there more difference than that?

The approach used by Eastman and by Holston Valley Hospital and Medical Center is based on the work of Deming that is reviewed in Chapter 2. The trainers at the local community college came from the auto industry milieu.

The exhibits in the case give extensive trend data on the financial and operating performance of the hospital. The reader is encouraged to analyze those data for trends and for signs of the impact of CQI on the hospital's reported results. Chapter 3 gives some examples of the types of savings that hospitals are achieving. These should be compared with the efforts undertaken and the results achieved at Holston Valley.

Basics

The techniques of TQM used by Eastman were easily adapted to this health care setting. The tools and concepts stayed the same, but many of the examples were changed to fit the CQI setting. With the company's assistance in setting up the courses at the local community college and the use of company personnel to develop the training programs, the hospital avoided extensive investments in consultants and course development. As the exhibits indicate, the seven tools as outlined in Chapters 2 and 5 were used extensively in the analyses done by the teams.

There is no evidence in the case of extensive reliance on customer satisfaction surveys of the type outlined in Chapter 6. It appears that the primary customers from the perspective of hospital management were the employers and the physicians. Management perceived that the physicians would not really want to become heavily involved in the TQM process, and the primary employer expressed an interest in dealing with clinical matters directly through the IPA and its HMO rather than through the CQI process at Holston Valley. We leave it to the reader to judge whether the hospital should have accepted that division of duties among the health care players in Kingsport.

Top management support at the level of the CEO was very strong. Mr. Bishop had made a very strong personal commitment to CQI. It is hard to tell whether this was perceived by the staff as full top management support. The role of the CEO as the head of the corporate holding company focused on financial matters would have made him relatively remote from operating personnel. Mr. Bishop took every possible occasion to "walk the talk" and emphasize the importance of this effort to his staff, including the celebrations at the weekly staff meetings and the use of outside individuals to reinforce the prominence of their efforts.

Implementation

Many of the planning approaches discussed in Chapter 9 were not evident in the case. The effort seemed to be conceived and implemented pretty much according to Mr. Bishop's conception of the TQM process. There did not seem to be any attempt to involve the hospital board or the medical staff in the planning process, nor evidence of a strong quality council or quality steering committee setting priorities for projects or setting an agenda for the expansion of the effort into more multidisciplinary areas.

The hospital staffed the implementation of CQI fully. Four full-time facilitators were trained and assigned to developing and supporting the teams. The basic training was started in teams at the community college and was experiential. Each team brought an issue from its work environment to start with. As time went on, some efforts were multidisciplinary, but were intended not to be clinical.

The implementation was limited to the administrative side of the hospital, and involvement in clinical activities was studiously avoided. This was motivated by fear that negative physician response to TQM would lead them to send more patients over to Indian Path Hospital. This is not an unrealistic concern, but it kept the hospital from reaping the clinical benefits so important to any TQM initiative. The approach to TQM at Holston Valley was well done technically. We leave it up to the reader to assess whether this effort was a success or a failure strategically.

Regardless of whether the reader agrees with the strategic thrust of this hospital's efforts, there is much to be learned about the details of reinforcing CQI at all levels of the organization. The Friday morning meeting without chairs was used quite skillfully to reinforce management's commitment to the effort. The use of the statistical tools was frequent and intense. The management understood process variation and how to begin to bring it under control and invested heavily in inculcating its administrative staff with those concepts, insights, and values. In many ways, therefore, this case makes an interesting example when studied in parallel with the West Florida Regional Medical Center case that follows.

Curtis P. McLaughlin

Case 3

West Florida Regional Medical Center (A)

West Florida Regional Medical Center (WFRMC) is an HCA-owned and operated, for-profit hospital complex on the north side of Pensacola, Florida. Licensed for 547 beds, it operated approximately 325 beds in December 1991 plus the 89-bed psychiatric Pavilion and the 58-bed Rehabilitation Institute of West Florida. The 11-story office building of the Medical Center Clinic, P.A., was attached to the hospital facility, and a new Cancer Center was under construction.

The 130 doctors practicing at the Medical Center Clinic and its satellite clinics admitted mostly to WFRMC, whereas most of the other doctors in this city of 150,000 practiced at both Sacred Heart and Baptist hospitals downtown. Competition for patients was intense, and in 1992 as many as 90 to 95 percent of patients in the hospital would be admitted subject to discounted prices, mostly Medicare for the elderly, CHAMPUS for military dependents, and Blue Cross/Blue Shield of Florida for the employed and their dependents.

The CQI effort had had some real successes over the last four years, especially in the areas where package prices for services were required. All of the management team had been trained in quality improvement techniques according to HCA's Deming-based approach, and some 25 task forces were operating. The experiment with departmental self-assessments, using the Baldridge Award criteria and an instrument developed by HCA headquarters, had spurred department heads to become further involved and begin to apply quality improvement techniques within their own work units. Yet John Kausch, the Center's CEO, and his senior leadership sensed some loss of interest among some managers, whereas others who had not bought into the idea at first were now enthusiasts.

This case was prepared as a basis for classroom discussion rather than to illustrate the effective or ineffective handling of an administrative situation. Copyright © 1992 by the Kenan-Flagler Business School, University of North Carolina, Chapel Hill, NC 27599-3490. All rights reserved. Not to be reproduced without permission.

THE HCA CQI PROCESS

John Kausch had been in the first group of HCA CEOs trained in CQI techniques in 1987 by Paul Batalden, M.D., corporate Vice President for Medical Care. John had become a member of the steering committee for HCA's overall quality effort. The HCA approach is dependent on the active and continued participation of top local management and on the Plan-Do-Check-Act (PDCA) cycle of Deming. Figure 3.1 shows that process as presented to company employees. Dr. Batalden told the case writer that he does not work with a hospital administrator until he is convinced that that individual is fully committed to the concept and is ready to lead the process at his or her own institution—a responsibility that includes being the one to teach the Quality 101 course on site to his or her own managers. John Kausch also took members of his management team to visit other quality exemplars, such as Florida Power and Light and local plants of Westinghouse and Monsanto.

In 1991 John Kausch became actively involved in the Total Quality Council of the Pensacola Area Chamber of Commerce (PATQC), when a group of Pensacola area leaders in business, government, military, education, and health care began meeting informally to share ideas in productivity and quality improvement. From this informal group emerged the PATQC under the sponsorship of the Chamber of Commerce. The vision of PATQC was "helping the Pensacola area develop into a total quality community by promoting productivity and quality in all area organizations, public and private, and by promoting economic development through aiding existing business and attracting new business development." The primary employer in Pensacola, the U.S. Navy, was using the total quality management (TQM) approach extensively, was quite satisfied with the results, and supported the Chamber of Commerce program. In fact, the first 1992 one-day seminar presented by Mr. George F. Butts, consultant and retired Chrysler Vice President for Quality and Productivity, was to be held at the Naval Air Station's Mustin Beach Officer's Club. Celanese Corporation (a Monsanto division), the largest nongovernmental employer in the area, also supported PATQC.

The CQI staffing at WFRMC was quite small, in keeping with HCA practice. The only program employee was Ms. Bette Gulsby, M.Ed., Director of Quality Improvement Resources, who served as staff and "coach" to Mr. Kausch and as a member of the quality improvement council. Figures 3.2 and 3.3 show the organization of the council and the staffing for Quality Improvement Program (QIP) support. The "mentor" was provided by headquarters staff, and in the case of WFRMC was Dr. Batalden himself. The planning process had been careful and detailed. Exhibit 3.1 shows excerpts from the planning processes used in the early years of the program.

WFRMC has been one of several HCA hospitals to work with a self-assessment tool for department heads. Exhibit 3.2 shows the cover letter sent to all department heads. Exhibit 3.3 shows the Scoring Matrix for Self-Assessment. Ex-

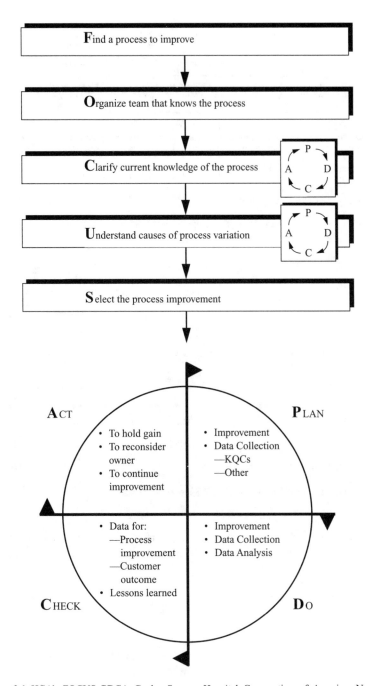

Figure 3.1 HCA's FOCUS–PDCA Cycle. *Source:* Hospital Corporation of America, Nashville, Tennessee, © 1988, 1989. Not for further reproduction.

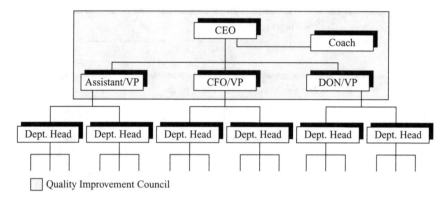

Figure 3.2 Organization Chart with Quality Improvement Council

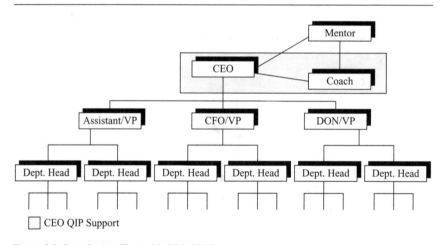

Figure 3.3 Organization Chart with CEO QIP Support

hibit 3.4 shows the Scoring Guidelines, and Exhibit 3.5 displays the five assessment categories used.

Four Examples of Teams

IV Documentation

The Nursing Department originated the IV Documentation Team in September 1990 after receiving documentation from the Pharmacy Department that over a 58-day period there had been $16,800 in lost charges related to the administration of intravenous (IV) solutions. Pharmacy attributed the loss to the nursing staff's

Exhibit 3.1 Planning Chronology for CQI

Initiation Plan—3 to 6 months, starting May 25, 1988

May 25:	Develop initial working definition of quality for WFRMC.
May 25:	Define the purpose of the Quality Improvement Council and set schedule for 2–4 P.M. every Tuesday and Thursday.
May 25:	Integrate Health Quality Trends (HQT) into continuous improvement cycle and hold initial review.
June 2:	Start several multifunctional teams with their core from those completing the Leadership Workshop with topics selected by the Quality Improvement Council using surveys, experience, and group techniques.
June 2:	Department Heads complete "CEO assessment" to identify customers and expectations, determine training needs, and identify department opportunities.
	To be discussed with assistant administrators on June 15.
June 16:	Present to QIC the Task Force report on elements and recommendations on organizational elements to guide and monitor QIP.
June 20:	Division meetings to gain consensus on Department plans and set priorities. QIC reviews and consolidates on June 21. Final assignments to Department Heads on June 22.
June 27:	Draft initial Statement of Purpose for WFRMC and present to QIC.
June 29–July 1:	Conduct first Facilitator's Training Workshop for 16.
July 1:	Task Force reports on additional QIP education and training requirements for:

> Team training and team members' handbook
> Head nurses
> Employee orientation (new and current)
> Integration of community resources (colleges and industry)
> Use of HCA network resources for Medical Staff, Board of Trustees

July 19:	Task Force report on communications program to support awareness, education, and feedback from employees, vendors, medical staff, local business, colleges and universities, and HCA.
August 1:	Complete the organization of the Quality Improvement Council.

Quality Improvement Implementation Plan to June 30, 1989

Fall:	Pilot and evaluate "Patient Comment Card System."
Oct. 21:	QIC input to draft policies/guidelines regarding: forming teams, quality responsibility, and guidelines for multifunctional teams. Brainstorm at Oct. 27 meeting, have revisions for Nov. 10 meeting, and distribute to employees by November 15.
Oct. 27:	Review proposals for communicating QIP to employees to heighten awareness and understanding, communicate on HCA and WFRMC commitments; key definitions, policies, guidelines; HQT; QIP; teams and improvements to date; responsibility and opportunities for individual employees; initiate ASAP.
Nov. 15:	Prepare statements on "On further consideration of HCA's Quality Guidelines;" discuss with department heads, hospital staff, employee orientation; use to identify barriers to QI and opportunities for QI. Develop specific action plan and discuss with QIC.

continues

continued

Dec. 1:	Identify and evaluate community sources for QI assistance—statistical and operational—including colleges, companies, and the Navy. Make recommendations.
Early Dec.:	Conduct Quality 102 course for remaining Dept. Heads. Conduct Quality 101 course for head nurses and several new Dept. Heads.
Jan. 1, 1989:	Develop and implement a suggestion program consistent with our HCA Quality Guidelines, providing quick and easy way to become involved in making suggestions/identifying situations needing improvement, providing quick feedback and recognition; and interfacing with identifying opportunities for QIP.

QIP Implementation Plan, July 1989–June 1990

Aug. 1:	Survey Department Heads to identify priorities for additional education and training.
Sept. 14–15:	Conduct a management workshop to sharpen and practice QI methods. To include practice methods; to increase management/staff confidence, comfort; to develop a model for departmental implementation; to develop process assessment/QIP implementation tool; to start Quality Team Review.
September:	Develop a standardized team orientation program to cover QI tools and group process rules.
Fall:	Expand use of HQTs and integrate into Health Quality Improvement Process (HQIP)—improve communication of results and integration of quality improvement action plans. Psychiatric Pavilion to evaluate and implement HQT recommendations from "Patient Comment Card System"—evaluate and pilot.
October:	Incorporate QIP implementation into existing management/communication structure. Establish division "steering committee functions" to guide and facilitate departmental implementation. Identify QI project for each Department Head/Assistant Administrator. Establish regular Quality Reviews into Department Manager meetings.
December:	Evaluate effectiveness of existing policies, guidelines, and practices for sanctioning, supporting, and guiding QI teams. Include Opportunity Form/ Cross Functional Team Sanctioning; Team leader and Facilitator responsibilities; Team progress monitoring/guiding; Standardized team presentation format (storyboard). Demonstrate measurable improvement through Baxter QI team.
Monthly:	Monitor and improve the suggestion program.
January:	Pilot the Clinical Process Improvement methodology.
All Year:	In all communications, written and verbal, maintain constant message regarding WFRMC commitment to HQIP; report successes of teams and suggestions; and continue to educate about principles and practices of HQIP strategy.
January:	Successfully demonstrate measurable improvement from focused QIP in one department (Medical Records).
Spring:	Expand use of HQTs and integrate into HQIP. Pilot HQT in Rehab Center. Evaluate and implement Physicians' HQT. Pilot Ambulatory Care HQT.
Summer:	Expand use of HQTs and integrate into HQIP. Human Resources—Pilot HQT. Payers—Pilot HQT.

Exhibit 3.2 Departmental Quality Improvement Assessment

In an effort to continue to monitor and implement elements of improvement and innovation within our organization, it will become more and more necessary to find methods which will describe our level of QI implementation.

The assessment or review of a quality initiative is only as good as the thought processes which have been triggered during the actual assessment. Last year (1990) the Quality Improvement Council prepared for and participated in a quality review. This exercise was extremely beneficial to the overall understanding of what was being done and the results that have been accomplished utilizing various quality techniques and tools.

The Departmental Implementation of QI has been somewhat varied throughout the organization and although the variation is certainly within the range of acceptability, it is the intent of the QIC to better understand each department's implementation road map and furthermore to provide advice/coaching on the next steps for each department.

Attached please find a scoring matrix for self-assessment. This matrix is followed by five category ratings (to be completed by each department head). The use of this type of tool reinforces the self-evaluation which is consistent with continuous improvement and meeting the vision of West Florida Regional Medical Center.

Please read and review the attachment describing the scoring instructions and then score your department category standings, relative to the approach, deployment, and effects. This information will be forwarded to Bette Gulsby by April 19, 1991, and following a preliminary assessment by the QIC, an appointment will be scheduled for your departmental review.

The review will be conducted by John Kausch and Bette Gulsby, along with your administrative director. Please take the time to review the attachments and begin your self-assessment scoring. You will be notified of the date and time of your review.

This information will be utilized for preparing for the next Department Head retreat, scheduled for May 29 and 30, 1991 at the Perdido Beach Hilton.

---

record keeping. This was the first time that the Nursing Department was aware of a problem or that the Pharmacy Department had been tracking this variable. There were other lost charges, not yet quantified, due to recording errors in the oral administration of pharmaceuticals as well.

The team formed to look at this problem found that there were some 15 possible reasons why the errors occurred, but that the primary one was that documentation of the administration of the IV solution was not entered into the Medication Administration Record (MAR). The MAR was kept at the patient bedside, and each time that a medication was administered the nurse was to enter documentation into this record.

The team had to come to understand some terms as they went along. The way that Pharmacy kept its books, anything that was sent to the floors but not billed within 48 to 72 hours was considered a "lost charge." If an inquiry was sent to the floor about the material and what happened and a correction was made, the entry was classified as "revenue recovered." Thus the core issue was not so much one of lost revenue as one of unnecessary rework in Pharmacy and on the nursing floors.

The team developed Pareto charts showing the reasons for the documentation errors. The most common ones were procedural—for example, patient moved to the operating room, or patient already discharged. Following the HCA model,

Exhibit 3.3 A Scoring Matrix for Self-Assessment

TO BE USED IN EVALUATING EXAMINATION CRITERIA

APPROACH	DEPLOYMENT (Implementation)	EFFECTS (Results)
• HQIP design includes all eight dimensions[*] • Integration across dimensions of HQIP and areas of operation	• Breadth of implementation (areas or functions) • Depth of implementation (awareness, knowledge, understanding, and applications)	• Quality of measurable results

[*]The eight dimensions of HQIP are: leadership constancy, employee mindedness, customer mindedness, process focussed, statistical thinking, PDCA driven, innovativeness, and regulatory proactiveness.

	APPROACH	DEPLOYMENT	EFFECTS
100% 80%	• World-class approach: sound, systematic, effective HQIP based, continuously evaluated, refined, and improved. • Total interaction across all functions. • Repeated cycles of innovation/improvement.	• Fully in all areas and functions. • Ingrained in the culture.	• Exceptional, world-class, superior to all competition in all areas. • Sustained (3–5 years), clearly caused by the approach.
80% 60%	• Well developed and tested, HQIP based. • Excellent integration.	• In almost all areas and functions. • Evident in the culture of all groups.	• Excellent, sustained in all areas with improving competitive advantage. • Much evidence that they are caused by the approach.
60% 40%	• Well planned, documented, sound, systematic. HQIP based, all aspects addressed. • Good integration.	• In most areas and functions. • Evident in the culture of most groups.	• Solid, with positive trends in most areas. • Some evidence that they are caused by the approach.
40% 20%	• Beginning of sound, systematic, HQIP based; not all aspects addressed. • Fair integration	• Begun in many areas and functions. • Evident in the culture of some groups.	• Some success in major areas. • Not much evidence that they are caused by the approach.
20% 0%	• Beginning of HQIP awareness. • No integration across functions.	• Beginning in some areas and functions. • Not part of the culture.	• Few or no results. • Little or no evidence that any results are caused by the approach.

Exhibit 3.4 Departmental Quality Improvement Assessment Scoring Guidelines

In order to determine your department's score in each of the five categories, please review the Scoring Matrix for self-assessment. The operational definitions for Approach, Deployment, and Effects are listed in the small boxes on the top of the scoring matrix. Each criteria is divided into percent of progress/implementation (i.e., 0%–100%). For example, you may determine that your departmental score on category 3.0 (QI Practice) is:

APPROACH	*DEPLOYMENT*	*EFFECTS*
20%	*20%*	*20%*

This means that your departmental approach has fair integration of QIP practice, your departmental deployment is evident in the culture of some of your groups, and your departmental effects are not actually evidence that they are caused by the approach.

Please remember that this is a *self-assessment* and only *you* know your departmental progress. This assessment is not a tool to generate documentation. However, if you would like to bring any particular document(s) to your review, please do so. This is only meant to provide a forum for you to showcase your progress and receive recognition and feedback on such.

Remember, review each of the self-assessment criteria of approach, deployment, and effects and become familiar with the levels or percentages described. You have three scores for each Departmental QI Assessment Category (categories 1.0–5.0).

these procedural problems were dealt with one at a time to get the accounting for unused materials right. The next step in the usual procedures was to get a run chart developed to show what was happening over time to the lost charges on IVs. Here the team determined that the best quality indicator would be the ratio of lost charges to total charges issued. At this point Pharmacy management realized that it lacked the denominator figure and that its lack of computerization led to the lack of that information. Therefore the task force was inactive for three months while Pharmacy implemented a computer system that could provide the denominator.

Ms. Debbie Koenig, Assistant Director of Nursing, who was responsible for the team, said that the next step would be to look at situations where the MAR was not at the patient bedside but perhaps up at the nursing station so that a nurse could not make the entry at the appropriate time. This was an especially bothersome rework problem because of nurses working various shifts and because occasionally an agency nurse had been on duty and was not available to consult when Pharmacy asked why documentation was not present for an IV dose of medication.

Universal Charting

There was evidence that a number of ancillary services results, "loose reports," were not getting into the patients' medical records in a timely fashion. This was irritating to physicians and could result in delays in the patient's discharge, which under DRGs meant higher costs without higher reimbursement. One employee

Exhibit 3.5 Departmental QI Assessment Categories

1.0 DEPARTMENTAL QI FRAMEWORK DEVELOPMENT

The QI Framework Development category examines how the departmental quality values have been developed, how they are applied to projects in a consistent manner, and how adoption of the values throughout the department is assessed and reinforced.
Examples of areas to address:

- Department Mission
- Departmental Quality Definition
- Departmental Employee Performance Feedback Review
- Departmental QI Plan
- QI Methods

APPROACH	DEPLOYMENT	EFFECTS
——%	——%	——%

2.0 CUSTOMER KNOWLEDGE DEVELOPMENT

The Customer Knowledge Deployment category examines how the departmental leadership has involved and utilized various facets of customer-mindedness to guide the quality effort.
Examples of areas to address:

- HQT Family of Measures (patient, employee, etc.)
- Departmental Customer Identification
- Identification of Customer Needs and Expectations
- Customer Feedback/Data Review

APPROACH	DEPLOYMENT	EFFECTS
——%	——%	——%

3.0 QUALITY IMPROVEMENT PRACTICE

The Quality Improvement Practice category examines the effectiveness of the department's efforts to develop and realize the full potential of the work force, including management, and the methods to maintain an environment conducive to full participation, quality leadership, and personal and organizational growth.
Examples of areas to address:

- Process Improvement Practice
- Meeting Skills
- QI Storyboards
- QI in Daily Work Life (individual use of QI tools, i.e., flow chart, run chart, Pareto chart)
- Practice Quality Management Guidelines
- Departmental Data Review
- Plans To Incorporate QI in Daily Clinical Operations
- Identification of Key Physician Leaders

APPROACH	DEPLOYMENT	EFFECTS
——%	——%	——%

continues

continued

4.0 QUALITY AWARENESS BUILDING

The Quality Awareness Building category examines how the department decides what quality education and training is needed by employees and how it utilizes the knowledge and skills acquired. It also examines what has been done to communicate QI to the department and how QI is addressed in departmental staff meetings.

Examples of areas to address:

- JIT Training
- Employee Orientation
- Creating Employee Awareness
- Communication of QI Results

APPROACH	DEPLOYMENT	EFFECTS
———%	———%	———%

5.0 QA/QI LINKAGE

The QA/QI Linkage category examines how the department has connected QA data and information to the QI process improvement strategy. Also examined is the utilization of QI data-gathering and decision-making tools to document and analyze data. (How the department relates the ongoing QA activities to QI process improvement activities.)

Examples of areas to address:

- QA Process Identification
- FOCUS-PDCA Process Improvement
- Regulatory/Accreditation Connection (Joint Commission)

APPROACH	DEPLOYMENT	EFFECTS
———%	———%	———%

filed a suggestion that a single system be developed to avoid people running over other people on the floor doing the "charting." A CQI team was developed and led by Ms. Debbie Wroten, Medical Records Director. The 12-member team included supervisors and directors from the Laboratory, the Pulmonary Lab, the EKG Lab, Medical Records, Radiology, and Nursing. They developed the following "Opportunity Statement":

At present six departments are utilizing nine full-time equivalents 92 hours per week for charting separate ancillary reports. Rework is created in the form of repulling of inhouse patient records creating an ever increasing demand of chart accessibility. All parties affected by this process are frustrated because the current process increases the opportunity for lost documentation, chart unavailability, increased traffic on units creating congestion, prolonged charting times, and provides for untimely availability of clinical reports for patient care. Therefore an opportunity exists to improve the current charting practice for all departments involved to allow for the efficiency, timeliness and accuracy of charting loose reports.

The team met, assessed, and flow-charted the current charting processes of the five departments involved. Key variables were defined as follows:

- Charting timeliness—number of charting times per day, consistency of charting, and reports not charted per charting round.
- Report availability— indicated by the number of telephone calls per department asking for reports not yet charted.
- Chart availability—chart is accessible at the nurses' station without interruption.
- Resource utilization—manhours and number of hours per day of charting.

Each department was asked to use a common "charting log" track for several weeks of the number of records charted, who did the charting, when it was done, the preparation time, the number of reports charted, the number of reports not charted (missed), and the personnel hours consumed in charting. The results were:

	Mean Records		Mean Hours		
Department	Per Day	Range	Per Day	Range	Comments
Medical Records	77.3	20–140	1.6	0.6–2.5	Daily
Pulmonary Lab	50.3	37–55	1.0	0.7–1.5	MWF
Clinical Lab	244.7	163–305	3.2	1.9–5.4	Daily
EKG Lab	40.2	35–48	0.8	0.1–1.0	Weekdays
Microbiology	106.9	3–197	1.4	0.1–2.2	Daily
Radiology	87.1	6–163	1.5	0.1–2.9	Daily

These data gave the team considerable insight into the nature of the problem. Not every department was picking up the materials every day. Two people could cover the whole hospital in three-quarters of an hour each or one person in 1.5 hours. The Clinical Chemistry Laboratory, Medical Records, and Radiology were making two trips per day, whereas other departments were only able to chart every other day and failed to chart over the weekends.

The processes used by all the groups were similar. The printed or typed reports had to be sorted by floors, given room numbers if missing, taken to the floors, and inserted into patient charts. If the chart was not available, they had to be held until the next round. A further problem identified was that when the clerical person assigned to these rounds was not available, a technical person, who was paid considerably more and was often in short supply, had to be sent to do the job.

A smaller team of supervisors who actually knew and owned the charting efforts in the larger departments (Medical Records, Radiology, and Clinical Chemistry) was set up to design and assess the pilot experiment. The overall team meetings were used only to brief the department heads to gain their feedback and support. A pilot experiment was run in which these three departments took turns doing the runs for each other. The results were favorable. The pilot increased timeliness and chart availability by charting four times per day on weekdays and three times per day on weekends. Report availability was improved, and there were fewer phone calls. Nursing staff, physicians, and participating departments specifically asked for the process to be continued. The hours of labor dropped from 92 weekly to less than 45, using less highly paid labor.

Therefore the team decided that the issues were important enough that they should consider setting up a separate Universal Charting Team to meet the needs of the entire hospital.

However, an unanticipated hospital census decline made impractical the possibility of requesting additional staffing, etc. Consequently the group reevaluated the possibility of continuing the arrangement developed for the pilot using the charting hours of the smaller departments on a volume basis. It was discovered that this had the effect of freeing the professional staff of the smaller departments from charting activities and a very minimal allocation of hours floated to the larger departments. It also increased the availability of charters in the larger departments for other activities.

The Payroll Department was then asked to develop a system for allocating the hours that floated from one department to another. That proved cumbersome, so the group decided to allocate charting hours on the basis of each department's volume. "In the event that one or more departments experiences a significant increase/decrease in charting needs, the group will reconvene and the hourly allocation will be adjusted."

The resulting schedule has the lab making rounds at 6 A.M. and 9 A.M. and Radiology at 4 P.M. and 9:30 P.M. Monday through Friday, and Medical Records at 6 A.M., 1 P.M., and 8 P.M. on Saturday and Sunday. Continuing statistics are kept on the process, which is shown in Exhibit 3.6. The system continues to work effectively.

Labor, Delivery, Recovery, Post-Partum (LDRP) Nursing

Competition for young families needing maternity services had become quite intense in Pensacola. WFRMC Obstetrical (OB) Services offered very traditional

Exhibit 3.6 Universal Charting Team FOCUS-PDCA Outline

F **Opportunity Statement:**

At present, six departments are utilizing 9 full-time equivalents 92 hours a week for charting separate ancillary reports. Rework is created in the form of repulling of inhouse patient records creating an ever-increasing demand of chart accessibility. All parties affected by this process are frustrated because the current process increases the opportunity for lost documentation, chart unavailability, increased traffic on units creating congestion, prolonged charting times, and provides for untimely availability of clinical reports for patient care.

Therefore an opportunity exists to improve the current charting practice for all departments involved to allow for the efficiency, timeliness, and accuracy of charting loose reports.

O Team members include:
Debbie Wroten, Medical Records Director—Leader
Bernie Grappe, Marketing Director—Facilitator
Joan Simmons, Laboratory Director
Mary Gunter, Laboratory Patient Services Coordinator
Al Clarke, Pulmonary Services Director
Carol Riley, Pulmonary Services Assistant Director
Marlene Rodrigues, EKG Supervisor
Patti Travis, EKG
Debra Wright, Medical Records Transcription Supervisor
Mike West, Radiology Director
Lori Mikesell, Radiology Transcription Supervisor
Debbie Fernandez, Head Nurse

C Assessed and flow charted current charting practices of departments.
Clarified and defined key quality characteristics of the charting process:

Charting Timeliness—number of charting times per day, consistency of charting, and reports not charted per charting round.
Report Availability—indicated by the number of telephone calls per department asking for reports not yet charted.
Chart Availability—chart is accessible at nurses' station for charting without interruption.
Resource Utilization—manhours and number of hours per day of charting.

U Gathered data on departments charting volumes and time spent on charting.

Department:

Charting Log

Date	Charting Tech vs. Clk.	Prep Time	# Reports Charted	# Reports Not Charted	Charting Time (amt)	Hour of Day	Comment

continues

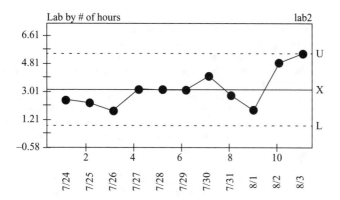

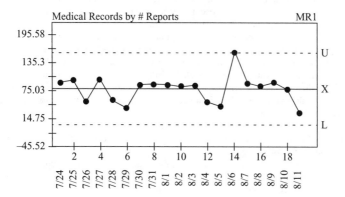

S Data gained through the pilot indicated that significant gains were available through the effort to justify proceeding with the development of a Universal Charting Team.

P The team developed a flow chart of the charting process using a universal charting team rather than previous arrangements. In order to pilot the improvement, the group decided to set up a UCT using current charters from the three major charting departments—medical records, laboratory, and radiology. The team also developed written instructions for both the charters and participating departments. A subgroup of the team actually conducted a one-day pilot before beginning extensive education to ensure that the UCT would work as planned and to be sure that the charters from each of the large departments were well versed on possible situations that might occur during the pilot.

D Piloted proposed Universal Charting Team using current charting personnel from radiology, laboratory, and medical records to chart for all departments.

C Pilot results were positive and indicated that the UCT concept offered significant advantages over the previous charting arrangements. Results were:

continues

continued

Timeliness/Chart Availability—Pilot reduced daily charting to four scheduled charting times daily for all departments. Smaller departments did not chart daily prior to pilot. The charting team also reduced the number of occasions that charters from different departments were on the nursing unit needing the same chart.

Report Availability—Telephone calls were reduced and nursing staff, physicians, and participating departments specifically asked for UCT following the pilot.

Resource Utilization—Number of manhours spent charting and preparing to chart was reduced from 92 hours weekly to less than 45 hours. The improvement also allowed the use of less expensive staff for charting.

A   The group reached consensus that the easiest configuration for the UCT would be to set up a separate UCT that would serve the needs of the entire hospital. This was to be proposed to administration by the team as the conclusion of their efforts. However, an unanticipated hospital census decline made impractical the possibility of requesting additional staffing, etc. Consequently, the group reevaluated the possibility of continuing the arrangement developed for the pilot using the charting hours to the smaller departments on a volume basis. It was discovered that this had the effect of freeing the professional staff in the smaller departments from charting responsibilities while a very minimal allocation of hours floated to the larger departments, and it increased the availability of charters in the larger departments for other activities. The payroll department was then involved in order to develop the proper mechanism and procedure for floating hours.

This modification of the previous pilot was piloted for a month with continued good results. Streamlining of the hours floating process may be necessary to place less burden on the payroll department.

Since no major changes were required following the pilot, the group has elected to adopt the piloted UCT format. Allocation of charting hours is based on a monthly review of charting volumes for each department. In the event that one or more departments experiences a significant increase/decrease in charting needs, the group will reconvene and the hourly allocation will be adjusted.

LESSONS LEARNED

Because of the size and the makeup of the team, which included a number of department heads, it was found helpful to set up a smaller team of three supervisors who actually knew and owned the charting efforts in the major departments. This group designed and assessed the initial pilot and actually piloted the pilot before bringing departmental charters into the process. As a result, overall team meetings were used primarily to brief department heads and gain their feedback and consensus.

services in 1989 in three separate units—Labor and Delivery, Nursery, and Post-Partum—and operated considerably below capacity.

A consultant was hired to evaluate the potential growth of obstetrical services, the value of current services offered by WFRMC, customers' desires, competitors' services, and opportunities for improvement. Focus group interviews with young couples (past and potential customers) indicated that they wanted safe medical care in a warm, homelike setting with the least possible number of rules. Most mothers were in their thirties, planning small families with the possibility of only one child. Fathers wanted to be "actively involved" in the birth process. The message came back, "We want to be actively involved in this experience and we want to make the decisions." The consultant challenged the staff to develop their own vision for the department based on the focus group responses, customer feedback, and trends nationally.

It became clear that there was a demand for a system in which a family-centered birth experience could occur. The system needed to revolve around the customers; not the customers following a rigid traditional routine. Customers wanted all aspects of the normal delivery to happen in the same room. The new service would allow the mother, father, and baby to remain together throughout the hospital stay, now as short as 24 hours. Friends and families would be allowed and encouraged to visit and participate as much as the new parents desired. The main goals were to be responsive to the customer's needs and to provide safe, quality medical care.

The hospital administration and the six obstetricians practicing there were eager to see obstetrical services grow. They were open to trying and supporting the new concept. The pediatricians accepted the changes, but without great enthusiasm. The anesthesiologists were opposed to the change. The OB supervisor and two of the three nursing head nurses were also opposed to any change. They wanted to continue operations in the traditional manner. When the hospital decided to adopt the new LDRP concept, it was clear that patients and families liked it but that the nursing staff, especially management, did not. The OB nursing supervisor retired, one head nurse resigned, one was terminated, and the third opted to move from her management position to a staff nurse role. Ms. Cynthia Ayres, R.N., Administrative Director, responsible for the psychiatric and cardiovascular services, was assigned to implement the LDRP transition until nursing management could be replaced.

One of the issues involved in the transition was clarification of the charge structure. Previously each unit charged separately for services and supplies. Now that the care was provided in a single central area, the old charge structure was unnecessarily complex. Duplication of charges was occurring, and some charges were being missed because no one was assuming responsibility.

Ms. Ayres decided to use the CQI process to develop a new charge process and to evaluate the costs and resource consumption of the service. Ms. Ayres had not been a strong supporter of the CQI process when it was first introduced into the organization. She had felt that the process was too slow and rigid, and that data collection was difficult and cumbersome. Several teams were organized and assigned to look at specific areas of the LDRP process.

To reach a simplified charge process, as well as a competitive price, all aspects of the process had to be analyzed. Meetings were held with the nursing and medical staff. Management of OB patient and physician preferences in terms of supplies and practices were analyzed. A number of consensus conferences were held to discuss observed variations. For example, each of the six obstetricians specified a different analgesic for pain control. All of these drugs appeared effective for pain control, but their cost per dose ranged from $10 to $75. The physicians agreed that the $10 product was acceptable since the outcome was the same.

Another standard practice was sending placentas to the pathology laboratory for analysis after every normal delivery. This involved labor time, lab charges, and a pathologist's fee for review. The total procedure cost $196. When questioned about the practice, the current medical staff did not feel it was necessary medically or the current practice nationally, but felt that they were just following the rules. Upon investigation, the team found that an incident involving a placenta had occurred 15 years ago that had led the Service Chief (since retired) to order all placentas sent to the lab. The obstetricians developed criteria for when it was medically necessary for the lab review of a placenta. This new rule decreased the number of reviews by 95 percent, resulting in cost savings to the hospital and to patients.

The team reviewed all OB charges for a one-year period. They found that in 80 percent of the normal deliveries 14 items were consistently used. The other items were due to variations in physician preferences. The teams and the physicians met and agreed which items were the basic requirements for a normal delivery. These items became the basic charges for package pricing.

The team met weekly for at least one hour for over a year. Some meetings went as long as five hours. Initially, there was a great deal of resistance and defensiveness. Everyone wanted to focus on issues that did not affect him or herself. The physicians objected that they were being forced to practice "cookbook medicine" and that the real problem was "the hospital's big markup." Hospital staff continued to provide data on actual hospital charges, resource consumption, and practice patterns. The hospital personnel continued to emphasize repeatedly that the physicians were responsible for determining care. The hospital's concern was to be consistent and decrease variation.

Another CQI team, the Documentation Team, was responsible for reviewing forms utilized previously by the three separate units. The total number of forms used had been 30. The nursing staff were documenting vital signs an average of five times each time care was provided. Through review of policies, standards, documentation, and care standards, the number of forms was reduced to 20. Nurses were now required to enter each care item only one time. The amount of time spent by nurses on documentation was reduced 50 percent, as was the cost of forms. Data entry errors were also reduced.

The excess costs that were removed were not all physician related. Many had to do with administrative and nursing policies. Many were due to old, comfortable, traditional ways of doing things. When asked why a practice was followed, the typical response was, "I don't know; that's just the way we've always done it." The OB staff is comfortable with the use of CQI. They recognize that although it requires time and effort, it does produce measurable results. The OB staff is continuing to review their practices and operations to identify opportunities to streamline services and decrease variation.

Pharmacy and Therapeutics Team

In late 1987, a CQI team was formed jointly between the hospital's Pharmacy and Therapeutics (P&T) Committee and the Pharmacy leadership. Their first topic of concern was the rapidly rising costs of inpatient drugs, especially antibiotics, which were then costing the hospital about $1.3 million per year. They decided to study the process by which antibiotics were selected and began by asking physicians how they selected antibiotics for treatment. Most of the time they ordered a culture of the organism causing the infection from the Microbiology Lab. A Microbiology Lab report would come back identifying the organism and the antibiotics to which it was sensitive and those to which it was resistant. Some physicians reported that they would look down the list until they came to an antibiotic to which the organism was sensitive and order that. That list was in alphabetical order. A study of antibiotic utilization showed a high correlation between use and alphabetical position, confirming the anecdotal reports. Therefore the team recommended to the P&T Committee that the form be changed to list the antibiotics in order of increasing cost per average daily dose. The doses used would be based on current local prescribing patterns rather than recommended dosages. The P&T Committee, which included attending physicians, approved the change and reported it in their annual report to the medical staff. Figure 3.4 shows what happened to the utilization of "expensive" antibiotics (more than $10 per dose) from 1988 to 1991. These costs were not adjusted at all for inflation in drug prices during this period. The estimated annual saving was $200,000.

Given this success, the team went on in 1989 to deal with the problem of the length of treatment with antibiotics. Inpatients did not get a prescription for ten

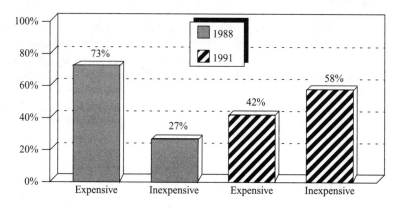

Figure 3.4 Antibiotic Utilization Ratio, Expensive:Inexpensive Doses Dispensed (expensive ≥ $10.00 per dose)

days' supply. Their IM and IV antibiotics were continued until the physician stopped the order. If a physician went away for the weekend and the patient improved, colleagues were very reluctant to alter the medication until he or she returned. The team wrestled with how to encourage the appropriate ending of the course of treatment without hassling the physicians or risking undue legal liability problems. They settled on a sticker that went into the chart at the end of three days that said that the treatment had gone on for three days at that point and that an ending date should be specified if possible. The hospital newsletter and the P&T Committee annual report noted that the physician could avoid this notice by specifying a termination date at the time of prescribing. This program seemed to be effective. Antibiotic costs again dropped, and there were no apparent quality problems introduced as measured by length of stay or by adverse events associated with the new system.

In 1990 the team began an aggressive Drug Usage Evaluation (DUE) program, hiring an assistant director of Pharmacy Clinical Services to administer it. The position had to be rigorously cost justified. DUE involved a review of cases to determine whether the selection and scheduling of powerful drugs matched the clinical picture presented. For example, if the physician prescribed one of three types of antibiotics known to represent a risk of kidney damage in 3 to 5 percent of cases, the DUE administrator ordered lab tests to study serum creatinine levels and warn the physician if they rose, indicating kidney involvement. There was a sharp decline in the adverse effects due to the use of these drugs. This program was expanded further to incorporate looking at other critical lab values and relating them to pharmacy activities beyond antibiotics: for example, use of IV solutions and potassium levels. By 1991 the unadjusted antibiotic costs for roughly the same number of admissions had dropped to less than $900,000.

Looking Ahead

One of the things that had concerned John Kausch during 1991 was the fact that implementation had varied from department to department. Although he had written in his annual CQI report that the variation had certainly been within the range of acceptability, he was still concerned about how much variation in implementation was appropriate. If maintaining enthusiasm was a concern, forcing people to conform too tightly might become a demotivator for some staff. This issue and the four mentioned at the beginning of this case study should all be addressed in the coming year.

CASE ANALYSIS

This is a hospital with a large group of physicians closely tied to it, both economically and geographically. It is also operating in an area of intense competition and tight cost controls. The fact that 90 to 95 percent of the hospital's compensation is case-based (DRGs) and not procedure-based has a profound impact on management motivation. Intense support for the CQI process provided by Dr. Batalden and his staff at corporate headquarters also affects motivation.

Introduction

The HCA approach to CQI is a Deming-based approach. The PDCA cycle is at the heart of the approach. So is the quality council, which involves all the top managers in the institution. The process is implemented one hospital at a time, whenever headquarters decides that the CEO is ready to lead the process. The process has been in place several years, and there is no question as to top management commitment on site.

The case shows some major successes in terms of savings and impacts on revenues of the type discussed in Chapter 3. The savings on antibiotics developed by the nursing-pharmacy team are substantial, over $200,000 annually, and the effort is still continuing. Similarly, the utilization of the labor and delivery facilities is up, and the same types of admissions increases were achieved by a team working in the psychiatric Pavilion (not reported in the case). Therefore the results are evident to the management and to the employees. They are also evident to the general public since the annual data reported by the Florida Cost Containment Commission, which are based on discharge summary data, show that WFRMC has become the low-priced supplier of obstetric services in the community since these changes were made.

Basics

The hospital uses standard HCA customer satisfaction surveys like those shown in Chapter 6, but these were not particularly relevant to the issues in the case. To revitalize its obstetrical business, the hospital turned to a market research firm to conduct focus groups and surveys of potential patients in the target population. Then it used a combination of management and CQI processes to develop a new approach to service delivery.

The teams used most of the seven tools of TQM as illustrated in the exhibits. They also used other tools such as market research and a sophisticated form of regression analysis to determine the relationship between alphabetical ordering of antibiotic drugs and their utilization. It was also apparent that many of the tools of epidemiology would be applicable in the continuing efforts to avoid the negative side effects of antibiotic utilization.

This case illustrates the classic planning approach outlined in Chapters 2 and 9. A detailed plan was developed, reviewed, and implemented annually, as shown in Exhibit 3.4. It was overseen by the quality council. The reader can use the information in those exhibits to gauge how much effort it takes to follow the planning guidelines established in the TQM literature. It is no small investment.

Implementation

Management decision making did not slow down because CQI teams were working on these important processes. For example, in the redesign of obstetrical processes, management studies and those of the teams went forward in parallel. The analyses done by the CQI team enlightened the decisions of management, and the information provided by management enlightened the work done by the team. The same was true of governance processes and the CQI team studying nursing and pharmacy. The P&T Committee and the CQI team worked in concert to gather data on antibiotics prescribing practices, to change laboratory reporting procedures, and to win clinician acceptance of those procedures. Other cases in this book also serve to indicate that CQI teams do not work in splendid isolation, but interact regularly with the ongoing management and governance practices of the health care organization.

In this case, it is important to note that the process changes were implemented successfully even at the expense of some clinicians. The anesthesiologists did not like the new labor and delivery setup for normal deliveries. It split their work between the high-tech delivery rooms for non-normal deliveries and the homelike rooms on the floors for normal deliveries. Yet they went along with it because it was clearly in the best interests of their customers, that is, the patients, the obstetricians, and the hospital administration. It is likely that if the process of choosing the new approach had been more participatory, they would have continued to oppose the change—probably indefinitely.

Mr. Kausch emphasizes the fact that the CQI program has had to go through a number of the transitions outlined in Chapter 11. After the first surge of enthusiasm over empowerment, and after work had taken place on the aspects of CQI that bothered people, the Quality Council had to go to work. It had to plan in detail for the next year, considering the cost and potential value of each effort. This case emphasizes the need for management to focus teams on opportunities, rather than just on problems.

Walter C. Gramley
Curtis P. McLaughlin

University Hospital and Medical Park

Case **4**

University Hospital is a full-service community hospital licensed for 130 beds, owned and operated by the Charlotte-Mecklenburg Hospital Authority (CMHA, or the Authority). It is located in the rapidly growing northeastern part of Charlotte, North Carolina, near the University of North Carolina-Charlotte and the University Research Park. It is adjacent to CMHA's 215,000 square foot Medical Park, which is fully leased to community-based practices. The first suburban Charlotte hospital, it was opened in 1985 early in the development of the University area. During its first four years the hospital lacked the population and physician base necessary to achieve a profitable activity level. However, the service area population kept growing at the rate of 5.4 percent annually, and the number of physicians admitting more than 10 patients per year grew from 10 to 43.

By 1992, approximately 40 percent of University Hospital's revenues came from outpatient services, including an accredited sleep disorder center, physical and occupation therapy, laboratory and X-ray services, a CT scan, nuclear medicine, a 24-hour emergency service, and outpatient surgery. Figure 4.1 provides an organization chart of the hospital. For inpatient services the hospital currently operates about 112 beds, five labor-delivery-recovery suites, eight operating rooms, a six-bed intensive care/cardiac care unit, and a telemetry unit. Many complex cases are referred to CMHA's Carolinas Medical Center (CMC), its 777-bed tertiary care teaching and research hospital. For example, all transplantation, cardiovascular surgery, cardiac catheterizations and angioplasties, chemotherapy, MRI procedures, and dialysis procedures in the system are done at CMC downtown.

As part of the Authority, University Hospital purchases a number of services from CMHA central operations. Purchasing and distribution are centralized by the Authority, together with Management Information Systems, Legal Services,

This case was prepared as a basis for classroom discussion rather than to illustrate the effective or ineffective handling of an administrative situation. Copyright © 1993 by the Kenan-Flagler Business School, University of North Carolina, Chapel Hill, NC 27599-3490. All rights reserved. Not to be reproduced without permission.

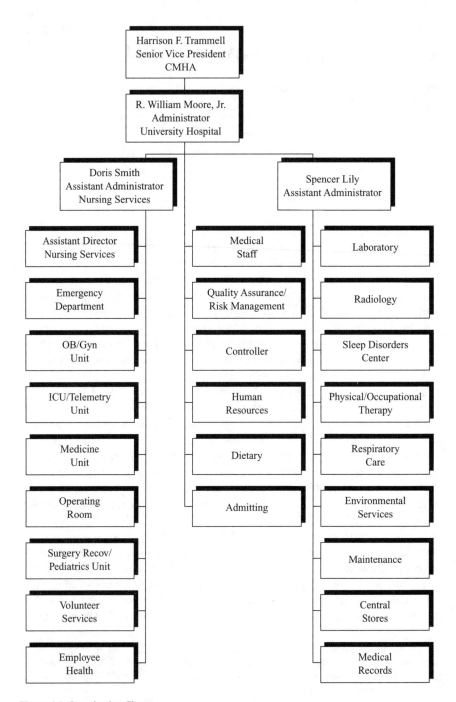

Figure 4.1 Organization Chart

Architecture and Planning, Security, Human Resources, Communications, Marketing and Public Information, and Quality/Risk Assurance Management. Specific personnel in some areas, such as Human Resources and Quality/Risk Assurance, are assigned to each facility. The purchased services allow for greater scale efficiencies, but they also represent relationships that have to be managed carefully to achieve a consistent level of quality of those services.

CHARLOTTE-MECKLENBURG HOSPITAL AUTHORITY

The Authority was created in 1943 as a "hospital authority" to finance construction and services under the North Carolina Hospitals Authorities Act. Located in Mecklenburg County, the city of Charlotte had a 1992 population of 446,000 people, while the Charlotte-Gastonia-Rock Hill (South Carolina) Southern Metropolitan Statistical Area had a population greater than 750,000. In addition to these two hospitals, the Authority maintains 11 other facilities in Mecklenburg County, including 600 nursing home beds, outreach clinics, a 115-bed rehabilitation center, an 88-bed county mental health center, and a school of nursing. It is one of the largest vertically integrated health care systems in the southeastern United States.

In 1991 the Authority received 50 percent of its funding from Medicare and Medicaid, 36 percent from private insurance, 12 percent directly from patients, and only 3 percent from other government sources, and it operated in the black. A consolidated financial statement is shown in Exhibit 4.1.

Exhibit 4.1 Financial Statement for Charlotte-Mecklenburg Hospital Authority

Revenues ($000)	
Inpatient ancillary services	$355,624
Inpatient routine services	185,374
Outpatient and emergency ancillary services	59,527
Emergency services	51,852
Outpatient services	14,092
Other operating revenue	15,566
Total	$682,035
Expenses ($000)	
Wages, salaries, benefits	$261,160
Materials and supplies	143,724
Free service, bad debts, adjustments	190,251
Depreciation	28,748
Financing costs	13,274
Funding for equipment, buildings, and new programs	44,878
Total	$682,035

CMHA was strongly supported by local business groups, with the CEOs of First Union Bank and Nation's Bank serving in 1991 as secretary and treasurer respectively of its board of commissioners. Its 1991 Annual Report strongly emphasized CMC's technological orientation as a teaching and research center that received referrals from 80 (out of 100) North Carolina and 38 South Carolina counties. The southern suburbs of Charlotte extend into South Carolina. At CMC there were 148 residents and fellows, a full-time faculty of 84, and a part-time, volunteer faculty of 600. It was designated one of the five state teaching hospitals, even though there is no medical school in the Charlotte area. It was the only hospital not located next to a medical school. Medical students were routinely assigned to rotations there from the state's medical schools. The annual report highlighted new acquisitions like a hyperbaric chamber, laser coronary ablation and radio frequency ablation, the region's only positron emission tomography (PET) scanner, digitized X-ray transmission, genetics research, helicopter and fixed wing emergency transport aircraft, and 135 publications by its faculty and staff.

BILL MOORE'S TASK

University Hospital, however, was small and did not become profitable until early 1990. The average daily census in 1991 was 63 patients. It is a nonteaching hospital. R. William Moore, Jr., M.B.A., Vice-President and Administrator, took over as administrator at University Hospital in July 1989. With an undergraduate degree in biology, Bill had risen through the ranks. He came to CMHA in 1984 from Memorial Mission Hospital in Asheville, North Carolina, to head up Environmental Services, Laundry, Security, and the Distribution Center. While in Asheville, he completed an evening M.B.A. In 1986 he was appointed administrator of the 425-bed Huntersville Oaks Nursing home, specifically to return that facility to profitability. He accomplished that in one year by focusing on cost reduction and revenue enhancement. In 1987 he assumed responsibility for CMHA's Primary Care Facilities, managing the physician practices and urgent care centers owned and operated by the Authority.

Bill Moore saw the University Hospital job as an opportunity to get back into administering an acute care hospital. The demographics of the area were favorable. The median income for northern suburban Charlotte was 50 percent higher than the average for the county. With higher incomes, low unemployment, and higher education levels, the payer mix was attractive. To target this population, the suburban hospitals aggressively sought a solid base of primary care physicians and sought to develop a "high touch" reputation as caring, quality providers of health care. Recently, the Authority had purchased or formed alliances with major physician groups around the city to further strengthen relationship ties between patients, physicians, and hospitals.

The health care environment in Charlotte can be characterized as progressive and competitive. There are three hospital groups in Charlotte: Presbyterian—642 beds, with its own acute care community hospital under construction in a high growth corridor; Mercy Hospital—330 beds, and its Mercy South with 97 beds; and CMHA. The three suburban hospitals were designed to capture market share in the phenomenal growth fringe areas and to refer the higher severity-of-illness patients to the main hospitals downtown. The latter objective allows the parent hospitals to offer comprehensive patient care to the suburban population without duplicating operating costs and with reduced capital investment.

By 1991, University Hospital had begun to realize its hoped-for potential. It had a young aggressive base of physicians, many of whom practiced exclusively at University. It was gaining market share at a rate of 2 percent per year from competing facilities. The level of activity now allowed the hospital to expand services to capture more of the market, for example, to add the telemetry unit. The number of adjusted employees per occupied bed had been managed to below national averages. University Hospital had developed a significant reputation in the university area of the city for quality and a high level of service.

Amidst the rapid growth and the positive financial performance, Bill Moore recognized the need to continue to improve the quality of service that University Hospital provided. He knew that he would concurrently have to control costs and identify high value-added elements without having a negative impact on the quality efforts. He welcomed the opportunity to develop a long-term operating strategy for the hospital, one that went beyond his earlier turnaround efforts at Huntersville Oaks and Primary Care.

Much of his efforts were driven by the changes he foresaw in the health care industry and his desire to position the hospital to meet those changes. He commented:

> How successful have we [the industry] been at managing costs? Not at all over the past ten years. If you use rate of increase as a measure, costs have continued to increase at a rate faster than the Consumer Price Index. I see this as an indication that significant changes are going to have to take place in the industry. The changes will be driven by a cost or quality. We must find a way to manage costs and offer a quality product, i.e., high value, or we will be out of business.

Bill's immediate efforts focused on two areas. First, develop stronger ties between the administration and the physicians and employees. Second, manage costs and ensure that the hospital is capturing all the revenue that it should. The extension of these efforts was to identify the correct mix of services that should be provided by the hospital. For example, shortly after his arrival, Bill arranged for the first of what would become annual retreats with the executive committee of the medical staff and other key physicians. The objective was to develop a service and marketing strategy for the hospital and to ensure physician input into that process. From his arrival he was aware that the hospital lacked a clearly defined mission that detailed the hospital's role in the community and its goals for the future. Bill believed that if a strategy could be developed for the hospital and that direction communicated to hospital employees, then real gains could be realized. He saw developing a quality improvement program as worthwhile in its own right, but also as essential in achieving this end. Furthermore, it would involve the staff in the goal-setting process.

The hospital underwent its first Joint Commission on Accreditation of Health Care Organizations' (Joint Commission) accreditation evaluation in September 1990. A new assistant administrator for nursing services, Doris Smith, R.N., introduced some management changes with the nursing staff, and the management team set out to develop a total quality management (TQM) program for University Hospital. They reviewed the activities at other hospitals and the Joint Commission's publications and talked and met again and again. They basically agreed that they would have to develop their own approach because the hospital could not afford any outside consultants.

Even before he received more intensive training in TQM, Bill set up two task forces to look at lost charges and delays in medications and treatments. The lost charges task force began work in November of 1991; the task force looking into medication delays started meeting in January of 1992. The Joint Commission evaluation feedback and comments from the physicians practicing at University had indicated that the administration of medicines was an area that presented significant opportunities for improvement. By beginning quality efforts with these task forces, Bill was consciously focusing on non–cost-saving ideas. He did not want TQM to be viewed like so many other programs over the last few years as another cost-saving gimmick pushed by management. He wanted the focus to be on *quality*, not cost.

He was comfortable with Deming's philosophy that emphasized both the scientific and the human approaches to quality. The scientific side calls for businesses to study, measure, and improve quality, employing statistical methods and planning tools; the human aspect emphasizes leadership, sound decision making, and the ability to empower and respect the work force. The Deming approach was communicated through his 14 points and through the Plan-Do-Check-Act (PDCA) steps of the Shewhart cycle. Management sets broad goals within which employees are empowered to act.

Formal TQM training began when Bill Moore attended a course on TQM at Central Piedmont Community College in Charlotte from January to March 1992. Then his two top executives, Doris Smith, R.N., and W. Spencer Lilly, M.H.A., Assistant Administrator, attended the same classes from May to June 1992. During this period the three of them developed their own localized approach which was an amalgam of W.E. Deming's approach to TQM and the Joint Commission ten-step model for monitoring and evaluation (shown in Figure 4.2 and Exhibit 4.2). The training sessions covered the following concepts: (1) customer identification, (2) quality management versus CQI, (3) the systems approach to managing, (4) Deming's 14 points, (5) the Joint Commission's ten-step

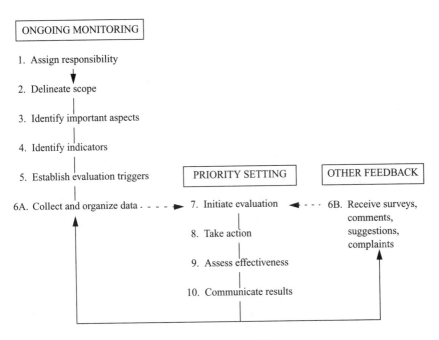

Figure 4.2 The Ten-Step Model for Monitoring and Evaluation

---

model, (6) the concept and role of brainstorming, and (7) the use of charts (Pareto diagram, flow charts, fishbone, Why Diagram, run charts, and control charts). It included a training program for department managers. The department managers met every two weeks to learn about the techniques of TQM. Bill included sessions on setting goals and objectives in the training to bring a sense of realism to the process. This allowed the managers to develop goals for the hospital while they were also developing an understanding of the TQM process. Bill, Doris, and Spencer assumed the role of a steering committee and served as facilitators that provided structure for the process. Sometimes there were role conflicts between their perceived authority status and free and open discussion, but people gradually got used to it.

The first step in the training was an exercise in customer identification aimed at developing the concept that the customer is that individual or group that receives your output. This concept included the notion that the customer is anyone that you communicate with as well, regardless of whether some exchange of services takes place. Each hospital department undertook a structured customer identification project.

After this basic training, specific teams were developed to work on problem areas. While four teams were working, the case reports on the two that had documented results were made available for the case writer.

Exhibit 4.2 Outline of the Joint Commission Ten-Step Model for Monitoring and Evaluation

Step 1. Assign responsibility
   a. Involve organization leaders
   b. Design and foster approach to continuous improvement of quality
   c. Set priorities for assessment and improvement

Step 2. Delineate scope of care and service
   a. Identify key functions and/or identify the procedures, treatments, and other activities performed in the organization

Step 3. Identify important aspects of care and service
   a. Determine the key functions, treatments, processes, and other aspects of care and service that warrant ongoing monitoring
   b. Establish priorities among the important aspects of care and service chosen

Step 4. Identify indicators
   a. Identify teams to develop indicators for the important aspects of care and service
   b. Select indicators

Step 5. Establish evaluation triggers
   a. For each indicator, the team identifies how evaluation may be triggered
   b. Select the means to trigger evaluation

Step 6. Collect and organize data
   a. Each team identifies data sources and data collection methods for the recommended indicators
   b. Design the final data-collection methodology, including those responsible for collecting, organizing, and determining whether evaluation is triggered
   c. Collect data
   d. Organize data to determine whether evaluation is required
   e. Collect data from other sources, including patient and staff surveys, comments, suggestions, and complaints

Step 7. Initiate evaluation
   a. Determine whether evaluation should be initiated
   b. Assess other feedback (for example, staff suggestions, patient-satisfaction survey results) that may contribute to priority setting for evaluation
   c. Set priorities for evaluation
   d. Teams undertake intensive evaluation

Step 8. Take actions to improve care and service
   a. Teams recommend and/or take actions

Step 9. Assess the effectiveness of actions and ensure that improvement is maintained
   a. Assess to determine whether care and service have improved
   b. If not, determine further action
   c. Repeat (a) and (b) until improvement is obtained and maintained
   d. Maintain monitoring
   e. Periodically reassess priorities for monitoring

Step 10. Communicate results to relevant individuals and groups
   a. Teams forward conclusions, actions, and results to leaders and to affected individuals, committees, departments, and services
   b. Disseminate information as necessary
   c. Leaders and others receive and disseminate comments, reactions, and information from involved individuals and groups

The Patient Charge Task Force

This task force first met in November 1991 to discuss the patient charge process. It initially focused on issues that had been discussed around the hospital for a long time: problems with late charges, lost charges, and data entry errors. These all led to audited patient bills and considerable employee time spent correcting the records.

The Patient Charge Task Force included a data entry clerk, three nursing representatives, a nurse manager, an assistant administrator, and a representative from the Central Stores Department. The committee met twice a month, but seemed to have considerable trouble in defining the problem that it was going to focus on. Finally, in April it agreed that the objective was to improve the *accuracy and timeliness* of the patient charge process.

The task force also flow-charted the charge system as shown in Exhibit 4.3. The supplies process is the responsibility of the Central Stores Department at University Hospital, which has only five employees. Most supplies come from the Distribution Center (DC), located at a central Authority warehouse. The DC is the centralized supplies buying/processing function for the entire CMHA. Even

---

Exhibit 4.3 Charge System Flow Chart

1 Set Up Process	2 Charge Process	3 Batch/Entry Process

1.1 Adequate amount of supplies available on carts
  a. Supplies stickered
  b. Supply level adequate
1.2 Charge cards prepared
  a. Cards stamped legibly
  b. Cards stamped for correct patient
  c. Cards in proper location
	2.1 Supply pulled from cart
	  a. Supply easily found
	  b. Supply available
	2.2 Stickers removed from supplies
	  a. Supplies stickered
	  b. Stickers easily removed
	2.3 Stickers placed on charge cards
	  a. Card is available
	  b. Stickers stick on cards
	  c. Stickers fit on cards
	  d. Card has room for stickers
		3.1 Charge cards replaced
		  a. "Used" cards available
		  b. "New" cards correctly prepared (1.2)
		3.2 Daily charges reconciled in storeroom
		  a. Charges are reconciled to inventory replaced by user area
		  b. Lost charge sheets completed by area and sent
		3.3 Charge cards taken to data entry
		  a. Cards batched
		  b. Put in designated area
		3.4 Charge cards entered into computer
		  a. Cards available
		  b. Cards stamped
		  c. Cards legible
		  d. Stickers legible
		  e. Sticker codes accurate

items not purchased through the DC are received and processed by the DC and then transported to University Hospital.

Most clinical departments at University Hospital, such as Nursing, Laboratories, and Radiology, work from an exchange cart system. All stocked items are received from the DC marked with bar-coded stickers on them. When an item is used, the sticker on that item is placed on a patient charge sheet. The sticker information is then fed to a bar-code reader attached to a modem, which sends the usage information to the Distribution Center to create order lists for the next day. The patient charge sheet is taken by Central Stores personnel to Data Entry personnel, who enter the patient charges based on the stickers on patient charge cards. When the exchange carts are swapped out by Central Stores for replenishment, usually daily, the usage is also recorded and reconciled against the sticker information to determine any lost charges. The expense of lost charges is charged to the unit, so it is a number that is tracked closely.

At first the task force focused primarily on the charge cards. However, they developed both a data checklist for errors concerning charge cards (Exhibit 4.4), which emphasized customer accuracy, and one for stickers and supplies errors (Exhibit 4.5). The error data on charge cards were collected over the two-week period of July 15 to July 29, 1992, and were then held until the data on stickers and supplies errors were collected, from July 29 to August 12. When the data

---

Exhibit 4.4 Patient Charge Task Force Data Checklist—Cards

Problems with Cards	*Frequency*
1. Card missing/late	
2. Card in wrong slot	
3. Card in inconvenient location	
4. Card difficult to access in Cardex	
5. Card not stamped (Addressograph)	
6. Card stamp (Addressograph) not legible	
7. Card stamped for incorrect patient	
8. Card full	
9. Card spaces too small	
10. Other (describe) _____	
_____	
_____	

Instructions

1. Please place a mark (✔) beside the above items when you encounter them.
2. Data is being collected by Nursing, Storeroom, and Business Office personnel in an effort to improve service to our customers.
3. Data will be collected from July 15, 1992 to July 29, 1992.

Exhibit 4.5 Patient Charge Task Force Data Checklist—Stickers/Supplies

---

Problems with Stickers   *Frequency*

1. No sticker on supply item
2. Sticker falls off supply item
3. Sticker falls off charge card
4. Wrong sticker on supply item
5. Multiple stickers on supply item
6. Sticker is wrong size
7. Sticker printed incorrectly/wrong information
8. Other (describe) _____
   _____
   _____

Problems with Supplies   *Frequency*

1. Supply item not available
2. Supply items in wrong location
3. Incorrect supply item level
4. Supply items counted incorrectly
5. Supply item damaged
6. Other (describe) _____
   _____
   _____

Instructions

1. Please place a mark (✔) beside the above items when you encounter them.
2. Data is being collected by Nursing, Storeroom, and Business Office personnel in an effort to improve service to our customers.
3. Data will be collected from July 29, 1992 to August 12, 1992.

---

were analyzed, the task force found that 84 percent of the errors in both categories were sticker related, mostly poor sticker printing/readability. These data were sent to the management of the Distribution Center, and that unit fixed their Addressograph machines, made a number of other equipment adjustments, and improved maintenance procedures to reduce the error rate markedly.

Six months later the group again collected the same type of data and found that the errors were quite widely distributed, which was interpreted as indicating a need for written procedures and employee training. The team then decided to develop a patient charge handbook, which was drafted by October 1992 and made available to employees in December.

Because the original stimulus was the number of audited charges and the late charges that triggered them, the committee then began to collect data on the reasons behind late charges and audited charges. This showed that the most frequent problems now were related to Pharmacy charges. The Pharmacy staff then developed its own late charge analysis, which pointed toward areas to be improved involving the communication between Pharmacy and Nursing.

Nursing/Pharmacy Task Force

When Bill Moore arrived, there was a Pharmacy/Nursing Committee that met to discuss issues surrounding the interrelationship between the nursing units and the pharmacy. Committee members consisted of the director of the pharmacy and representative staff nurses from the units. There was no consistent representation from nursing management or administration. No significant or lasting policies or procedure initiatives had resulted from this committee's work. In addition, Nursing/Pharmacy issues were discussed in the monthly nurse managers meetings and the Pharmacy and Therapeutics Committee's monthly meetings. Therefore that committee was disbanded about the end of 1991, and management continued to look for the best way to analyze processes and implement changes in this important area. It was clear that some process had to be found that would ensure that the recommendations were consistent with overall hospital goals and perceived as legitimate by the various stakeholders.

Management decided to create a new Nursing/Pharmacy Task Force in April 1992 in conjunction with the hospital's CQI efforts. The task force was chartered to evaluate systematically nursing, pharmacy, and the dispensing and administering of medications with a goal of improving medication deliveries to the patient. It consisted of the director of the pharmacy, one staff pharmacist, a nurse manager, and representatives from each nursing unit.

As he looked back over the nine months of effort by this task force, Bill Moore was generally satisfied with their efforts. The team composition had worked well. There had been problems, however, with legitimacy and achieving commitment and delegation. Eventually, much of the responsibility for the work fell on the director of Pharmacy, and Bill felt that it would have worked better if more people had been involved and taken more responsibility from the beginning.

The Nursing/Pharmacy Task Force started out looking at delays in the administration of treatments and medications. The director of Pharmacy arranged to monitor and report the delays. Figure 4.3 shows a "Why Diagram" that this team developed. This type of diagram permits systematic evaluation of the causes underlying the observed event. At the left of the exhibit is the summarized frequency distribution of these delays. The group then prioritized the delays. Since the treatment delays seemed to involve individuals from outside these two departments, the task force decided to concentrate on IV and medication delays, and they developed a cause-and-effect-type of diagram, which constitutes the right half of Figure 4.3. The data collected at each step of the process permitted the task force to apply specific solutions to the issues encountered. Equally importantly, continued collection of those data enabled follow up of the implementation and identification of places for further improvement.

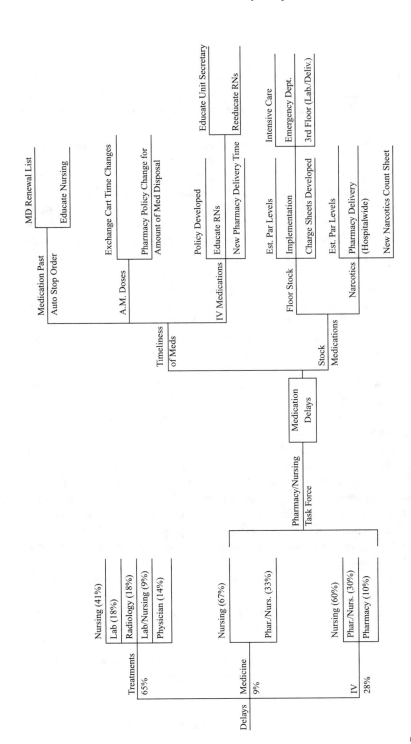

Figure 4.3 Nursing/Pharmacy Task Force: Medication Delays "Why" Diagram

Next Steps

Bill Moore was satisfied with the accomplishments of the two teams so far. He now saw two strategic decisions ahead of him. One was how to integrate the process throughout the hospital and the other was how to involve the physicians in the process.

Bill did not want to see the teams proliferate too much nor operate in an uncontrolled way or without a facilitator. "The system is very complex with very limited resources and does not lend itself to big projects." He saw the need to limit the scope by starting small and then growing. That philosophy permitted the two task forces to be a success. Yet the three top managers could not spend much more time being facilitators. Bill also recognized a risk if teams went into the study of a process without a clear understanding of how it worked or without the facilitative support of their managers. Failure to implement CQI in a manner consistent with hospital goals or without control from management was a threat to the process and a barrier to attaining a high level of participation and accomplishment. Therefore he wanted to get to the point where the department managers would act as facilitators. To do this, they would have to recognize how comprehensive TQM is and the amount of ongoing effort and hard work required. He expected that this would lead to increased acceptance and buy-in by the managers and lead to CQI's becoming part of the daily operating philosophy of the whole organization. All managers would have to undergo a major change of role from teller to teacher. How should he go about doing this?

Bill Moore also was concerned about physician involvement in this process. This appeared to be required by the Joint Commission specifications for the Hospital Quality Assessment and Improvement process. Exhibit 4.6 shows the five pages of reviewer questions that appeared in the 1992 *Accreditation Manual for Hospitals.* Although only Question QA.1.1 would apply immediately, the questions indicated what was likely to be coming within a few years. They were clearly based on a holistic concept of service. For CQI to be effective, it must incorporate all elements of customer service in the hospital. Not only is the physician a customer, but the physicians are involved in producing customer service as viewed by the patients.

Bill Moore had already raised the subject of physician involvement with the executive committee of the medical staff. That discussion had centered on developing critical paths in an effort to measure quality across the organization. This effort would be multidisciplinary and involve setting standards for a number of areas. It would rely on specific outcome measures in the operating room, Pediatrics, and Medicine. Six disease entities were identified. The executive committee did recognize the need to look into quality and agreed with the need to improve entire processes. They agreed to use other hospitals' critical paths as guides. The objective would be to reduce variation and thereby offer improved quality of service. They did report that some M.D.s believed that this would lead to

Exhibit 4.6 Reviewer Questions from the Joint Commission's *Accreditation Manual for Hospitals*

QA.1

The organization's leaders[*] set expectations, develop plans, and implement procedures to assess and improve the quality of the organization's governance, management, clinical, and support processes.

QA.1.1   The leaders undertake education concerning the approach and methods of continuous quality improvement.   1 2 3 4 5 NA

QA.1.2   The leaders set priorities for organizationwide quality improvement activities that are designed to improve patient outcomes.   1 2 3 4 5 NA

QA.1.3   The leaders allocate adequate resources for assessment and improvement of the organization's governance, managerial, clinical, and support processes, through

        QA.1.3.1   the assignment of personnel, as needed, to participate in quality improvement activities,   1 2 3 4 5 NA

        QA.1.3.2   the provision of adequate time for personnel to participate in quality improvement activities, and   1 2 3 4 5 NA

        QA.1.3.3   information systems and appropriate data management processes to facilitate the collection, management, and analysis of data needed for quality improvement.   1 2 3 4 5 NA

QA.1.4   The leaders assure that organization staff are trained in assessing and improving the processes that contribute to improved patient outcomes.   1 2 3 4 5 NA

QA.1.5   The leaders individually and jointly develop and participate in mechanisms to foster communication among individuals and among components of the organization, and to coordinate internal activities.   1 2 3 4 5 NA

QA.1.6   The leaders analyze and evaluate the effectiveness of their contributions to improving quality.   1 2 3 4 5 NA

QA.2

The organization has a written plan for assessing and improving quality that describes the objectives, organization, scope, and mechanisms for overseeing the effectiveness of monitoring, evaluation, and improvement activities. The plan includes at least the activities listed in QA.2.1 through QA.2.4.2 and described in other chapters of this Manual.   1 2 3 4 5 NA

QA.2.1   The following staff quality assessment and improvement activities are performed:

---

[*]The leaders responsible for performing the identified functions include at least the leaders of the governing body: the chief executive officer and other senior managers; the elected and appointed leaders of the medical staff and the clinical departments, and other medical staff members in hospital administrative positions; and the nursing executive and other senior nursing leaders.

    Source: Copyright © 1991 by the Joint Commission on Accreditation of Healthcare Organizations, Oakbrook Terrace, Illinois. Reprinted with permission from the 1992 *Accreditation Manual for Hospitals.*

continues

QA.2.1.1 the assessment and improvement of the quality of patient care and the clinical performance of individuals with clinical
privileges through   1 2 3 4 5 NA

QA.2.1.1.1 participation by members of each department/
service in intra- and/or interdepartmental/service monitoring
and evaluation of care; periodic review of the care; and communication of findings, conclusions, recommendations, and
actions to members of the department/service,   1 2 3 4 5 NA

QA.2.1.1.2 evaluation and improvement in the use of surgical
and other invasive procedures,   1 2 3 4 5 NA

QA.2.1.1.3 evaluation and improvement in the use of medica-
tions,   1 2 3 4 5 NA

QA.2.1.1.4 the medical record review function,   1 2 3 4 5 NA

QA.2.1.1.5 evaluation and improvement in the use of blood
and blood components, and   1 2 3 4 5 NA

QA.2.1.1.6 the pharmacy and therapeutics function   1 2 3 4 5 NA

QA.2.2   The quality of patient care, including that provided to specific age
groups, in all patient care services is monitored and evaluated.   1 2 3 4 5 NA

QA.2.2.1 The departments/services in which care is monitored
and evaluated include at least those addressed in other chapters of
this Manual, when provided.   1 2 3 4 5 NA

QA.2.2.2 The director of each department/service is responsible
for including the department's/service's activities in the monitoring and evaluation process.   1 2 3 4 5 NA

QA.2.2.2.1 The department/service participates in

QA.2.2.2.1.1 the identification of important aspects of
care relevant to the department/service,   1 2 3 4 5 NA

QA.2.2.2.1.2 the identification of indicators used to mon-
itor the quality of the important aspects of care, and   1 2 3 4 5 NA

QA.2.2.2.1.3 the evaluation of the quality of care.   1 2 3 4 5 NA

QA.2.2.3 When the hospital provides a patient care service for
which there is no designated department/service, the organization's leaders assign responsibility for implementing a monitoring
and evaluation process.   1 2 3 4 5 NA

QA.2.2.3.1 When the hospital, in its care of patients, requires
the services of another, off-site health care organization, the
monitoring and evaluation process examines the appropriate-
ness of the hospital's use of the services and the degree to
which the services aid in its care of patients.   1 2 3 4 5 NA

QA.2.3   The following hospitalwide quality assessment and improvement
activities are performed:

continues

QA.2.3.1 Infection control (see IC.1 and IC.2),   1 2 3 4 5 NA

QA.2.3.2 utilization review (see UR.1), and   1 2 3 4 5 NA

QA.2.3.3 review of accidents, injuries, patient safety, and safety
hazards (see PL.1., PL.1.3.1.2, PL.1.3.1.3, PL.1.3.1.4, and
PL.1.4.3).   1 2 3 4 5 NA

QA.2.4   Relevant results from the quality assessment activities listed in
          QA.2.1 through QA.2.3.3   1 2 3 4 5 NA

QA.2.4.1 are used primarily to study and improve processes that
affect patient care outcomes, and   1 2 3 4 5 NA

QA.2.4.2 when relevant to the performance of an individual, are
used as a component of the evaluation of individual capabilities
(see MS.2.5.5, MS.2.5.5.3, NC.2.1.1, and GB.1.14).   1 2 3 4 5 NA

QA.3
There is a planned, systematic, and ongoing process for monitoring, eval-
uating, and improving the quality of care and of key governance, mana-
gerial, and support activities that has the characteristics described in
QA.3.1 through QA.3.1.7.2.   1 2 3 4 5 NA

QA.3.1   Those aspects of care that are most important to the health and
          safety of the patients served are identified.   1 2 3 4 5 NA

QA.3.1.1 These important aspects of care are those that

QA.3.1.1.1 occur frequently or affect large numbers of pa-
tients,   1 2 3 4 5 NA

QA.3.1.1.2 place patients at risk of serious consequences or of
deprivation of substantial benefit when   1 2 3 4 5 NA

QA.3.1.1.2.1 the care is not provided correctly, or   1 2 3 4 5 NA

QA.3.1.1.2.2 the care is not provided when indicated, or   1 2 3 4 5 NA

QA.3.1.1.2.3 the care is provided when not indicated, and/
or   1 2 3 4 5 NA

QA.3.1.1.3 tend to produce problems for patients or staff.   1 2 3 4 5 NA

QA.3.1.2 Indicators are identified to monitor the quality of impor-
tant aspects of care.   1 2 3 4 5 NA

QA.3.1.2.1 The indicators are related to the quality of care
and may include clinical criteria (sometimes called "clinical
standards," "practice guidelines," or "practice parameters"). 1 2 3 4 5 NA

QA.3.1.2.1.1 These indicators are

QA.3.1.2.1.1.1 objective,   1 2 3 4 5 NA

QA.3.1.2.1.1.2 measurable, and   1 2 3 4 5 NA

QA.3.1.2.1.1.3 based on current knowledge and clini-
cal experience.   1 2 3 4 5 NA

continues

QA.3.1.3 Data are collected for each indicator.   1 2 3 4 5 NA

QA.3.1.3.1 The frequency of data collection for each indicator and the sampling of events or activities are related to

QA.3.1.3.1.1 the frequency of the event or activity monitored,   1 2 3 4 5 NA

QA.3.1.3.1.2 the significance of the event or activity monitored, and   1 2 3 4 5 NA

QA.3.1.3.1.3 the extent to which the important aspect of care monitored by the indicator has been demonstrated to be problem-free.   1 2 3 4 5 NA

QA.3.1.4 The data collected for each indicator are organized so that situations in which an evaluation of the quality of care is indicated are readily identified.   1 2 3 4 5 NA

QA.3.1.4.1 Such evaluations are prompted at a minimum by

QA.3.1.4.1.1 important single clinical events, or   1 2 3 4 5 NA

QA.3.1.4.1.2 levels or patterns/trends in care or outcomes that are at significant variance with predetermined levels and/or patterns/trends in care or outcomes.   1 2 3 4 5 NA

QA.3.1.4.2 Such evaluations may also be initiated by comparisons of the hospital's performance with that of other organizations ("benchmarking").   1 2 3 4 5 NA

QA.3.1.4.3 Such evaluations may also be initiated when there is a desire to improve overall performance.   1 2 3 4 5 NA

QA.3.1.5 When initiated, the evaluation of an important aspect of care

QA.3.1.5.1 includes a more detailed analysis of patterns/trends in the data collected on the indicators,   1 2 3 4 5 NA

QA.3.1.5.2 is designed to identify opportunities to improve, or problems in, the quality of care, and   1 2 3 4 5 NA

QA.3.1.5.3 includes review by peers when analysis of the care provided by an individual practitioner is undertaken.   1 2 3 4 5 NA

QA.3.1.6 When an important opportunity to improve, or a problem in, the quality of care is identified,

QA.3.1.6.1 action is taken to improve the care or to correct the problem, and   1 2 3 4 5 NA

QA.3.1.6.2 the effectiveness of the action taken is assessed through continued monitoring of the care.   1 2 3 4 5 NA

QA.3.1.7 The findings, conclusions, recommendations, actions taken, and results of the actions taken are

QA.3.1.7.1 documented, and   1 2 3 4 5 NA

QA.3.1.7.2 reported through established channels.   1 2 3 4 5 NA

continues

QA.4
The administration and coordination of the hospital's approach to assessing and improving quality are designed to assure that the activities described in QA.4.1 through QA.4.4 are undertaken. 1 2 3 4 5 NA

QA.4.1 Each of the quality and assessment and improvement activities outlined in QA.2 and QA.3 is performed appropriately and effectively. 1 2 3 4 5 NA

QA.4.2 Necessary information is communicated among departments/ services and/or professional disciplines when opportunities to improve patient care or problems involve more than one department/ service and/or professional discipline. 1 2 3 4 5 NA

QA.4.2.1 Information from departments/services and the findings of discrete quality assessment and improvement activities are used to detect trends, patterns, opportunities to improve, or potential problems that affect more than one department/service and/or professional discipline. 1 2 3 4 5 NA

QA.4.2.2 There are operational linkages between the risk management functions related to the clinical aspects of patient care and safety and quality assessment and improvement function. 1 2 3 4 5 NA

QA.4.2.3 Existing information from risk management activities that may be useful in identifying opportunities to improve the quality of patient care and/or resolve clinical problems is accessible to the quality assessment and improvement function. 1 2 3 4 5 NA

QA.4.3 The status of identified opportunities or problems is tracked to assure improvement or resolution. 1 2 3 4 5 NA

QA.4.4 The objectives, scope, organization, and effectiveness of the activities to assess and improve quality are evaluated at least annually and revised as necessary. 1 2 3 4 5 NA

"cookbook medicine" that would constrain their abilities to treat each patient according to his or her individual requirements. Therefore Bill Moore was concerned about how to present the approach to the medical staff overall.

Bill had already developed a model that outlined the development of critical paths. Many of the episodes in a process involved hospital personnel; other episodes were specific to physicians. Bill hoped to get M.D. input by first demonstrating that the hospital had systematically broken down each step in the process. He then wanted to outline the M.D. episodes and seek their input as to the current negative aspects of the process. By breaking down input into episodes and determining what specific areas (e.g., departments, specialties) were involved, the hospital could target the areas that needed improvement. Figure 4.4 illustrates such a path. Bill will need to determine if this is the best approach to involving all parties in the process or if there is an alternative way that could accomplish his objectives more efficiently.

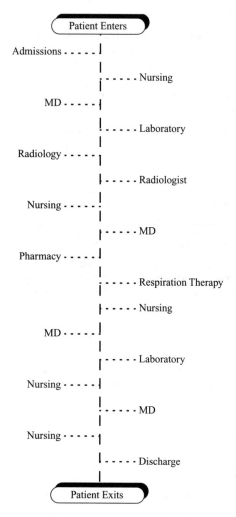

Figure 4.4 Illustration of Clinical Path

CASE ANALYSIS

The CQI approach at University Hospital is an indigenous effort, centered on the three key administrators. It was developed based on course work at a local community college, and it has worked. The investment was very small in dollars, but quite substantial in terms of administrators' time and effort. Mr. Moore's comment that many managers do not undertake or follow through on a CQI effort because it is very hard work rings true. We have heard similar responses elsewhere.

Introduction

The effort at University Hospital has proceeded slowly because of the limited size of the executive staff. It also has no funding support from the central administration, which raises interesting issues about the perceived top-down support. This is not too much of a problem here since the site CEO does strongly support the effort, but the lack of resources in a hospital losing money is a real constraint.

Basics

The basic effort of the management here is to develop a norm of teamwork (Chapter 7) and to get individuals used to decision analysis (Chapter 8). This health care organization is a relatively new part of a very large organization and Mr. Moore is now either starting or changing a culture in order to have a supportive culture at this site. He and the two other key managers also act as facilitators and curriculum developers since no funds are available for outside assistance.

Implementation

This hospital is still at the very early stages of implementation of CQI. The case reports only two major teams, but others have started subsequently. Old areas of friction are addressed anew using CQI. It is clear that for Mr. Moore CQI is as much an organization development tool as a quality tool. He is attempting to set norms for the institution as a proactive team rather than a passive receiver of direction and information from downtown.

Application

There is no discussion in the applications part of this book that focuses on the role of CQI in public hospitals. Basically, we believe that type of ownership does not play a big part in how CQI is used, nor in its relative success. We set out to develop a cross section of cases involving non-profit, for-profit, and public health care organizations, as well as both community and teaching settings. However, it is probably more difficult to get support for CQI in a public hospital because of the difficulties of budgeting for the startup of a CQI effort. This case shows how a public institution can go about adopting CQI with minimal resources. It might have been better, however, had the overall institution adopted the approach for all of its locations.

Sandra K. Evans
Ronald T. Pannesi

Case **5**

The Patient Transportation Project at University Hospitals

Sally Lloyd, Vice Chair of Nursing and Assistant Director of Operations at University Hospitals, had just received the patient transportation statistics for January 1992. She could hardly believe them—7100 transports. But how good was the system? She called Patient Transportation's new computerized number and within two minutes a transporter was dispatched! "This is quite a change from a year ago when transport response time, defined as the interval between the request for transport and the time a transporter is dispatched, averaged 26–30 minutes and the patient transport project was conceived."

The Patient Transportation Project began when University Hospitals funded a proposal to improve the delivery of inpatient transportation services. The one-year grant funded the purchase of a communications system that primarily consisted of two-way radios and a voice information system. At about this same time and prior to the arrival of the communications equipment, University Hospitals was initiating a pilot quality improvement team to work on the admission-discharge (A/D) process. This pilot program had evolved from University Hospital's participation in the National Demonstration Project on Quality Improvement in Health Care, sponsored by the John A. Hartford Foundation and the Harvard Community Health Plan.

The adage that "timing is everything" certainly proved true here. Patient transportation was one of the twelve departments/divisions invited to join the A/D continuous quality improvement (CQI) team. The introduction of the new communications technology and the application of quality improvement techniques and methods learned as participants on the A/D CQI team had propelled the operational changes in transport services. In just three months, the average transport

This case was prepared as a basis for classroom discussion rather than to illustrate the effective or ineffective handling of an administrative situation. Copyright © 1993 by the Kenan-Flagler Business School, University of North Carolina, Chapel Hill, NC 27599-3490. All rights reserved. Not to be reproduced without permission.

response time went from 30 to 15 minutes, and the response times just kept getting better even after the A/D CQI team completed its work.

UNIVERSITY HOSPITALS

University Hospitals is a 665-bed teaching and referral center whose mission as a public academic medical center is fourfold: (1) providing quality patient care, (2) educating health care professionals, (3) advancing health research, and (4) providing community service.

As a patient care resource, University Hospitals fulfills an important state and regional role by providing comprehensive services and highly specialized treatment for more than 20,000 inpatients and 500,000 outpatient visitors each year. Built in 1952, the Hospitals has continued to grow with the addition of the first Ambulatory Patient Care Facility (APCF) in 1975, two bed towers in 1975 and 1981, and the five-story Anderson wing in 1986. Most of the diagnostic and treatment facilities are concentrated in the original (1952) section of the Hospitals shown in Figure 5.1. The Hospitals' master facility plan projected an expansion of licensed beds to 702 by 1995.

The Hospitals operates its own personnel department subject to the state system of personnel management. Full-time and part-time employees numbered 4,122 in 1991, exclusive of the 510 house staff and the medical staff of 750 attending physicians, almost all of whom were faculty members of the medical school and dental school.

Patient Transportation Service

University Hospitals developed a centralized Patient Transportation Service in 1963 at the request of the Nursing Services. Six transporters were hired to escort stable patients to and from diagnostic and treatment areas throughout the hospital, thus freeing up nursing time. The transport program was managed by the director of Central Supporting Services, a department comprising patient equipment, linen room, and central sterile supply. In 1985, the transportation service became a component of the Hospitals' overall Materials Management Department. Figure 5.2 shows the organization chart after the 1982 reorganization.

Staff positions were added to the department to keep pace with the Hospitals' growth in services. The Patient Equipment supervisor provided daily supervision until 1982, when a transporter position was upgraded to a supervisor of daily operations within the service. The position was filled with the promotion of Mr. Ollie Williams, a transporter, to supervisor reporting to the supervisor of Patient Equipment. Mr. Williams started at the Hospitals in 1978 as a linen room attendant before transferring to a front door attendant position in 1980.

The Patient Transportation Service is housed in a large space on the ground floor in the original section of the Hospitals adjacent to patient equipment and

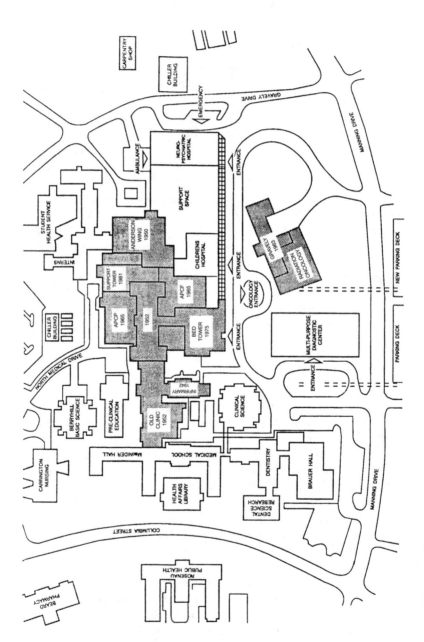

Figure 5.1 Facility Master Plan

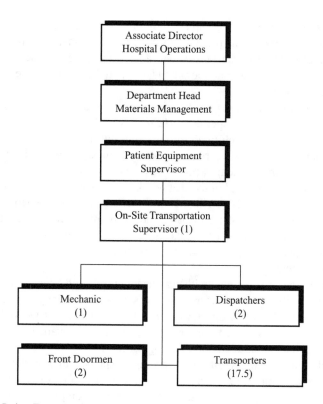

Figure 5.2 Patient Transportation Project at University Hospitals

---

storeroom activities. The space is predominantly used to store wheelchairs, stretchers, portable oxygen tanks, and equipment replacement parts. A small space at the back of the room is the staff's congregating point. The room is furnished with old chairs, a dispatcher's desk and phone, staff lockers, and a sink. Leading off this space is the transportation supervisor's small office.

The Transport Staff

At the time the project started, Patient Transportation had 23.5 full-time equivalent positions, which included 17.5 full-time and part-time transporters, a supervisor, two transporter/dispatchers, a mechanic, and two front door attendants. Of the 17.5 actual transporters, 5 were assigned Monday through Friday to Radiology according to a prior agreement. Transporters were reassigned from the central pool to cover all absences among the Radiology transporters. Transporters serviced all areas of the Hospitals except the Critical Care and Emergency Departments, operating and recovery rooms, and inpatient psychiatric units. Transporter job functions required completion of an eighth-grade education. The work force, which was predominantly African-American, included both males and females. The pay scale for transporters was among the lowest in the state's health care system. Dispatchers, front door attendants, and the mechanic were classified in higher pay grades.

Mr. Williams, the first and only Transportation Service supervisor, viewed his role as that of a day shift supervisor. He readily acknowledged that the department did not function as well in his absence, but felt there was not a lot he could do about that. He displayed a strict, authoritarian management style, and his 6'4" stature often intimidated the transporters. Mr. Williams was accused of "showing favoritism," and he freely admitted that he liked those he could "rely on to come to work and do the job." Mr. Williams interviewed, hired, scheduled, and evaluated the transporters. He rotated dispatch functions among the "better" transporters on the day shift and had two dispatchers for evenings and weekends. As higher paying positions opened up in his department, Mr. Williams typically promoted transporters.

The department was plagued with significant morale and behavioral problems. Relationships with users of transport services as well as among the transporters were often strained. The transporters, many of whom had never worked in a hospital before, were provided on-the-job training by the most available peer. Nurses, physicians, patients, and their families expressed dissatisfaction with the inconsistent and often long waits (30-minute average response times, with recorded response times as long as 129 minutes). A number of users had given up on the service and regularly performed their own transports. Complaints about discourteous service, careless transport techniques, or sloppy appearance were not uncommon. Lost transport equipment resulted in replacement costs averaging $20,000 annually.

In 1990, 16 employees from Patient Transportation agreed to participate in a hospitalwide attitude and opinion survey conducted by the Gallup Organization. Results showed that Patient Transportation's average scores for the ten dimensions measured ranked below those of all other hospital departments. Transporter attitudes toward their work environment, opportunities for professional growth and development, and organizational integration ranked among the lowest in the Hospitals (see Figure 5.3). In spite of these morale and performance problems, 11 of the employees had been with Transportation Services between 6 and 20 years. Each year, approximately one to two employees transferred to higher paying jobs and two or three resigned.

Reassigning Transport Services to the Nursing Department

The Nursing Department had over 1,400 employees in clinical, educational, and administrative positions to provide and support the delivery of patient care services across 37 inpatient units, operating and recovery rooms, and the Emer-

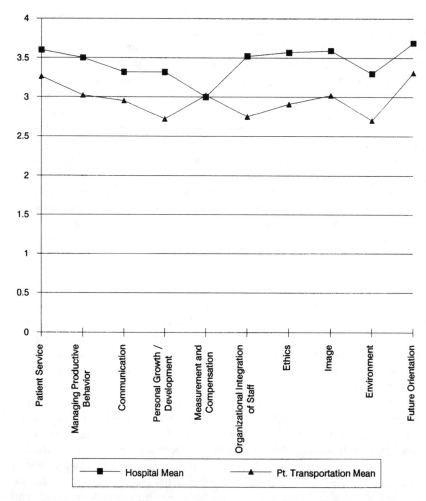

Figure 5.3 Results of Gallup Poll: Comparison Graph of Patient Transportation Department Attitudes vs. Those of Overall Hospital Staff

gency Department. The Nursing Department became administratively responsible for Transportation Services in 1989. The department's chairperson, Brenda Reynolds, and Ms. Lloyd, Vice Chair of Nursing and Assistant Director of Operations, were reluctant to take on this additional responsibility, given the nurse staffing situation at the time. The national nursing shortage was at its peak locally. Although the nursing shortage presented significant operational challenges, it also created opportunities for improvements that consumed much of nursing management's time. The Nursing Department was actively engaged in a two-year state legislative pilot project to manage licensed nurse positions and compensation separately. The pilot study had considerable potential for alleviating the Hospitals' nursing shortage and in establishing a permanent model for autonomy desired by Hospitals' executive management. Its implementation was receiving top priority among executive and middle-level nurse managers.

The transfer of administrative responsibility for Transportation Services, although unwelcome, was not entirely unexpected. Nursing, a major user of Transportation Services, had grown increasingly dissatisfied with the inefficiencies in transporting patients. Nursing management perceived these problems as stemming from employees with low self-esteem and little interest in their work.

Initially, Ms. Reynolds assumed direct line responsibility for Patient Transportation Services in order to evaluate the unit's needs. Mr. Williams continued to manage daily operations, referring personnel problems to Ms. Reynolds. Behavioral problems continued and were addressed one by one. Two employees were terminated in 1989 for performance and conduct reasons; others were moved into various stages of the Hospitals' disciplinary process.

The Project

Reynolds and Lloyd were at first caught in a reactive mode, dealing with the same problems repeatedly throughout 1989. The most significant recurring problems were user complaints about long response times. The two administrators believed that if they could shorten response times, everything else would more or less improve. They contacted the Hospitals' Management Engineering Department for assistance.

Just one morning spent observing the dispatch and transport process convinced Management Engineering and Nursing that there had to be a more efficient way of providing patient transportation services. One dispatcher with access to two phone lines handled all incoming calls. A staff member requesting service—usually a clerk on a patient care unit or in a diagnostic area—phoned in a request at the time a transport was needed, identifying to the dispatcher the patient's name, location, destination, and mode of transport. The dispatcher informed the caller that the transporter would be sent as soon as available, logged in the call, transcribed the information on a trip ticket, gave the ticket to the next available transporter on his or her return to the office, and logged in the time of dispatch. The transporter would then retrieve the requested transport equipment from the adjacent storage area. Equipment was frequently not returned to the storage area during the day, in which case the transporter would have to search throughout the Hospitals for a wheelchair or stretcher. Stretcher patients could require two transporters.

Occasionally, wrong information was communicated from the unit clerks. For example, the unit clerk might request a wheelchair when a stretcher was actually needed, or neglect to identify the need for a portable oxygen tank too. Communication errors often resulted in conflicts between clerks, nurses, and dispatchers as to who was wrong.

Benchmarking

The first action that Nursing management took was to look externally to see how other hospital transportation programs operated. Health Care Advisory Board, a national consulting group based in Washington, D.C., was contracted to conduct a survey of transport communication methods in 400+ bed teaching hospitals. The survey showed that two hospitals had improved services by equipping their transporters with two-way radios.

In pursuing the idea of two-way radios with a vendor, the administrators learned that a local community hospital's transporters were already equipped with two-way radios. A brief observation of patient transport services at the local hospital reinforced their interest. That department completed an average of 7,000 transports per month with 13 full-time equivalent transport positions. The supervisor, who also functioned as dispatcher, reassigned transporters as soon as they called in a completed transport. Space for transport equipment had been identified on each floor of the hospital, eliminating the transporter's need to return to the dispatch area between transports. One could not help noticing the teamwork displayed among the transporters. They readily responded to their peers' calls for assistance with a particular transport or with equipment search. The transporters seemed to enjoy their jobs. One transporter who had worked in another hospital's transportation department commented, "I would not do this job without walkie-talkies. It really cuts down on walking."

The supervisor also praised the system. "Before radios, I had no control over dispatch times. Now, we respond rapidly to all calls. The nurses are our greatest fans. They know we will come within a few minutes of their calls." A nursing manager said, "Before the radios, we never knew when a transporter would show up. Now, a transporter comes soon after we call. Patient transportation is the most efficient and reliable support service we have." Yet the pay was comparable to University Hospitals. The University Hospitals' administrators were sold on the system.

Soon after the site visit, they shared their findings with Mr. Williams. In discussing their observations, they emphasized the benefits to dispatchers, transporters, and users of the system. Mr. Williams, however, was not easily sold. He raised concerns that they had not considered, namely, that his dispatchers would have difficulty managing a combination of phone lines, radios, and activity logs. An automated order-entry system would resolve Mr. Williams' concerns, but this type of hospitalwide system was still in the planning stage and would not be ready for at least another three or four years.

Innovative Project Grant

Every spring, University Hospitals sponsors a competitive Innovative Project Program and awards 10 to 12 one-year grants. Projects are selected for funding based on innovation and potential for operational improvements. Nursing and Management Engineering planned to submit a proposal to fund the purchase of two-way radios; however, they needed to address Mr. Williams' concerns.

A management engineer, Ms. Karen McCall, pursued the potential of automation with various telephone companies and after a few inquiries learned of a computerized voice information system to answer all incoming calls 24 hours a day. The system's literature appeared simple enough. Users responded by touch-tone telephone to computer-activated questions concerning the transport. The system recorded and downloaded all incoming calls, transmitted messages via hard copy or computerized voice and maintained a database of activities. The UNC administrators thought that the voice information system offered definite advantages: (1) minimizing miscommunications between caller and dispatcher, (2) eliminating caller frustrations associated with delays in answering, and (3) affording the dispatcher more time to schedule transporter assignments by location and availability of equipment. Mr. Williams still wasn't convinced that the new communications system would offer any advantages. He expressed concern that transporters might lose radios, but he seemed willing to give the new system a try.

In 1990, Nursing and Management Engineering submitted a proposal to fund the purchase of two-way radios and a voice information system. The goal was to achieve measurable improvements in employee productivity. Based on the review of the transports in a one-month period, response times (defined as the interval from the time of the request to the time of the dispatch) averaged 30 minutes with a range of 26 to 33. The monthly volume of transports ranged between 4,600 and 5,300. Any time saved at the front end of a transport would increase the department's capacity for additional activity, but it was difficult to estimate how much capacity would increase, given the variability in each transport. A project to increase capacity without hiring more staff was both attractive and timely since University Hospitals forecasted increased patient volumes in 1991. The proposal was funded.

Project Implementation

Equipment delivery was anticipated in November-December 1990. In the interim, planning focused on the implementation process. It was becoming increasingly apparent that successful implementation would require on-site management support to assist Mr. Williams. Ms. Virginia Anderson, the critical care transport R.N., was the first choice. Although she had no formal management training or experience, she did have excellent people skills, teaching abilities, and first-hand knowledge of transport responsibilities and problems. She agreed to this promotion with a redefinition of responsibilities to include 40 percent time spent on management of patient transportation services. Mr. Williams appeared receptive to Ms. Anderson's appointment. In preparation for her role change, Ms. Anderson attended basic management classes offered by the Hospitals' Human Resource Development Center and a national meeting for managers of Patient Transportation Services. In January, Ms. Anderson and Mr. Williams spent a morning at the local community hospital observing the dispatcher and transporters in action.

In February 1991, the transportation staff began using the two-way radios, with the expectation that the dispatcher would schedule transporter assignments by location and availability of equipment. Transporters could now be dispatched without returning to the office. Information was put in the Hospitals' employee newsletter announcing the system's implementation. A series of unanticipated problems (equipment delivery, programming, approval of a specific telephone number, and printing publicity flyers) delayed implementation of the voice information system until August. A flyer advertising the service and phone number (6-PACE) was sent to all users (see Exhibit 5.1).

Exhibit 5.1 Flyer Advertising New Voice Response System for Patient Transportation Service Users

Now there is a fast and efficient way to order patient transportation services!

Call 6-PACE and the Voice Response System will ask you the following questions about the transport:

- patient's full name
- unit location
- transport destination
- time of appointment
- method of transport (i.e., wheelchair, stretcher or discharge cart, oxygen, IV pole)

At the end of the call, the system will play back your responses for you to verify and correct if necessary.

> The new Voice Response System is available for scheduling transport appointments 24 hours a day, 7 days a week. The transportation department is open from 7 a.m. to 7 p.m.

For "STAT" transportation requests, call 6-5252.

Linkage with the CQI Team

As efforts were underway to purchase the communications equipment, the Hospitals' director of operations announced the establishment of a cross-functional team to improve the A/D process on the medicine inpatient units. Invitations to join the team were extended to 12 departments/divisions, including Nursing and Patient Transport. The A/D team held its first meeting in October 1990.

Although the CQI process had not been introduced formally in the Hospitals, the A/D team leader, Dr. Anna Organ, served as facilitator and educated the members about the CQI process and provided just-in-time training in quality improvement techniques. The first two months were spent flow charting and collecting data on the A/D process.

The six subgroups (cross-functional teams) were formed in January 1991 to analyze specific A/D problems and processes on the Medicine service. The subgroups were expected to complete their work by May 1991 and were empowered to implement policy and procedural changes to improve the A/D process. Patient transportation was designated as one of the six subgroups. The A/D team suggested that the subgroup address the following issues: lack of priority designation for discharge orders, transporter work schedules, communications with unit clerks, and implementation of the two-way radios.

Patient Transport Subgroup Activities

Ms. Lloyd convened the patient transportation subgroup. The members represented patient transportation, medicine's clerical and nursing staff, and admitting, all departments with ownership in the process. All levels of personnel were represented, from patient transporters to nurse managers. The management engineer working on the Innovative Project also joined the team. A supervisor from Radiology joined later. The group met biweekly from January through May 1991. Although the initial charge was to focus improvement efforts on processes for discharge patients on the inpatient medicine units, the agenda was soon expanded to improving the transport services for all patients because many of the changes could not be restricted to one area of the Hospitals.

Understanding the Process

Findings from an October 1990 study of 50 discharged patients from one 25-bed medicine inpatient unit were shared with the A/D Team in December. Response times ranged from 12 to 22 minutes, and arrival times (from time of call to arrival on the unit) ranged from 21 to 31 minutes. These transport data showed a surprising improvement over data collected hospitalwide earlier in the year. The findings may have been influenced by the fact that Patient Transportation was aware of the study and may have prioritized discharge transports from the study unit. Additionally, transporters participated in the data collection. An analysis of the transport logs in January 1991 indicated that the average response time had not changed from the original average of 30 minutes measured in early 1990. The subgroup agreed to the following goals with the implementation of the two-way radios.

- For nonscheduled transports: Decrease response time from 30 minutes to 20 minutes on average.
- For scheduled transports: Achieve "on time" patient arrivals, defined as being in a range of 15 minutes before and 5 minutes after scheduled appointments.

The first few subgroup meetings were spent clarifying the process and developing the flow charts in Figure 5.4, identifying breakdowns in the system, and educating the group on the new communications system's benefits. In the group as it analyzed the process, Medicine nurses and clerks were quick to point out Patient Transportation's problems: busy phone lines, inconsistent response times, and the dispatcher's inability or unwillingness to estimate when a transporter would be available. Mr. Williams and his transporters attributed delays to time spent in search of equipment, time wasted because patients weren't ready when the transporter arrived, and incomplete or inaccurate information about the patient's mode of travel, necessitating repeat trips. Maintaining the group's focus on process was difficult, given the negative feelings that existed between transporters and nursing personnel. It seemed as though the group was going nowhere.

The next meeting's discussion focused on the Radiology transport process. Radiology transport comprised 30 to 40 percent of all patient transports Monday through Friday. The nurses and clerks were unaware that those transporters were based in Radiology and dispatched by the Radiology clerk. With the exception of diagnostic procedures requiring patient fasting or premedication, Radiology had no scheduling system. Trip tickets were prepared by the Radiology clerk and placed in a basket in no particular order. Transporters selected trip tickets randomly, retrieved transport equipment in Radiology, and then went after the patient. Following the X-ray or other procedure, the patient was handed the trip ticket and moved to a back corridor to await a transporter. Transporters were supposed to monitor this corridor closely, but patients frequently complained of long waits. Medicine nurses commented that patients scheduled for discharge were particularly inconvenienced by Radiology's lack of a scheduling system. Physicians on the Medicine service frequently ordered chest films the evening before or the morning of planned discharge. Radiology was usually unable to do the pre-discharge films until after the more complex prescheduled procedures were completed in the late morning. Patients needing routine films were fitted in as scheduling windows opened. A Radiology supervisor was invited to join the subgroup. He participated in the subgroup for the remainder of the meetings.

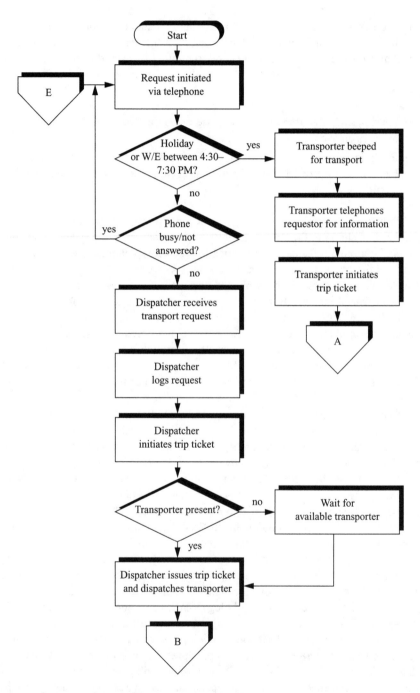

Figure 5.4 Patient Transportation Department, Original Process, 1990 *(continues)*

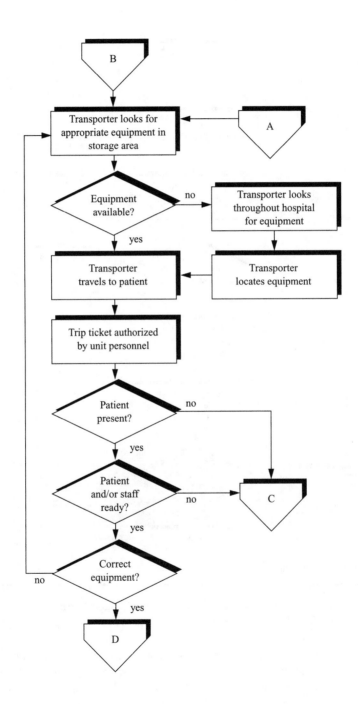

Figure 5.4 *continued*

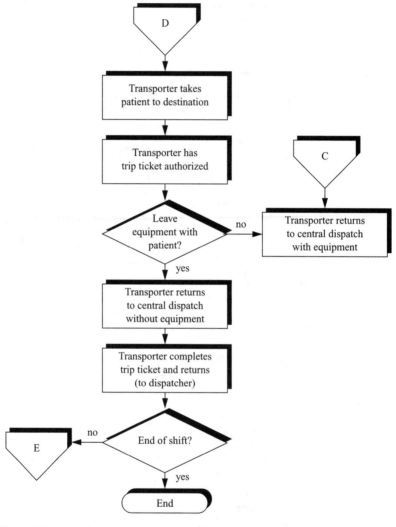

Figure 5.4 *continued*

During this discussion, Medicine nurses and clerks expressed their anger and frustration with transporter attitudes when patients were not immediately ready to leave the unit. A transporter who knew the system well responded that when they took too long getting a patient to X-ray, the Radiology staff got angry. She added, "It looks bad for us transporters." A nurse responded, "Then have X-ray call us before you come, because we don't even know the patient is scheduled to go any-where! The physicians schedule with X-ray, not with us." Mr. Williams fell back in his chair and asked, "You mean you don't have any idea we are coming?" The nurses and clerks agreed. A head nurse replied, "If we knew patients were scheduled, of course we would try to have them ready." Mr. Williams acknowledged that as long as he had been supervisor, he had thought that the nurses were aware of the scheduled tests and were just being uncooperative with the transporters. The nurses and clerks were just as surprised to learn of the transporter perceptions. Mr. Williams vowed to "set it straight" with his transporters. This realization was the first step in resolving years of friction between nursing staff and transporters. Ms. Lloyd observed, "We really lucked out! From that moment, the tone of the meetings changed. I am convinced that this air-clearing enabled the subgroup to move forward."

Opportunities for Improvement and Testing Remedies

The subgroup tackled a number of process issues over the next few months, but the work did not stop with their final meeting in May 1991. Nursing, Management Engineering, and Patient Transport continued to pursue opportunities for improving the system and the work group's performance. Along with the development of the voice information system and the two-way radios, the following steps were taken.

To Reduce Response Time. The assignment of a block of transporters to Radiology ended in May 1991 with the concurrence of Radiology. Radiology transporters had various amounts of "downtime" which they spent in Radiology's lounge. Centralization of personnel, together with the two-way radios, held potential for productivity gains while maintaining the same levels of service to Radiology.

Mr. Williams' role as supervisor was revised to include 80 percent time as dispatcher from Monday to Friday. Nursing management recognized the dispatcher role as pivotal to efficient operations and thought it especially important that Mr. Williams model the role. Based on his experiences, he and Ms. Anderson established performance standards for the off-shift dispatchers.

Transport equipment was decentralized to identified sites in the two bed towers and the Anderson wing with the intention of decreasing return trips to the dispatch area. If equipment was unavailable, the ability to stay in communication with peers was expected to facilitate an equipment search.

Work schedules were adjusted in accordance with workload rather than employee preference. Meal breaks were staggered over 2.5 hours instead of 1.5 hours. Limitations were placed on the amount of personal leave that could be taken on any given day.

To Reduce Patient Care Unit Delays. A policy was established limiting the time to five minutes that a transporter waited if a patient was not ready for transport. After five minutes, the transporter radioed the dispatcher. If another transport was waiting, the transporter was reassigned; if not, the transporter waited for the patient. On returning the patient to the unit, the transporter waited five minutes, if necessary, for assistance and then radioed the dispatcher for help. The dispatcher paged the appropriate nurse manager to intervene. Ms. Anderson met with the inpatient nurse managers and clerical supervisors to discuss the rationale for the new policy.

To Reduce Discharge Delays in Radiology. The dispatchers started placing a priority on discharge transports. The only patients that received higher priority were fasting and premedicated patients scheduled for invasive diagnostic procedures.

The patient transportation subgroup worked with Radiology's medical director and staff and physicians on inpatient Medicine units to expedite same-day requests for discharge X-rays. Radiology agreed to do these procedures weekdays between 6 and 9 P.M. and between 7 and 7:30 A.M. if transporters were available. In response, transporter schedules were adjusted slightly to expand coverage from 12 hours to 14 hours on weekdays. Radiology developed and published a scheduling system for these patients. With prenotification, nurses were expected to have patients ready for transport and to notify X-ray and Transportation of any anticipated delays (see Exhibit 5.2).

Exhibit 5.2 University Hospitals Department of Radiology

PRIORITIZATION FOR DISCHARGE RADIOLOGY ORDERS

Policy:

The department of radiology will prioritize and expedite requests for examinations on the Hospitals' patients scheduled for discharge contingent upon radiologic findings.

Procedure:

1. The physician will write the anticipated discharge order and the radiology/procedure order in the patient's chart the day before discharge.
2. For routine films (non-contrast):
    a. Unit clerk will write "pending discharge" in red ink at the top of the requisition. (Note: If the requisition exam can be performed only in the A.M. of the day of discharge, the unit clerk will write "pending discharge—perform in early A.M." in red ink at the top of the requisition.)
    b. Requisition will be sent to radiology before 5:00 P.M. of the day prior to discharge.
    c. Evening shift radiology clerk will process the requisitions for exam completion between 6:00 and 9:00 P.M., unless early A.M. is indicated.
    d. Evening shift radiology supervisor will ensure the completion of the exam prior to 9:00 P.M.
    e. If the exam is not completed during the evening shift, the evening shift radiology supervisor will discuss with the unit's charge nurse and will give the requisition to the night shift radiology supervisor with instructions to perform in the early A.M.
    f. If the exam is not completed by the radiology night shift prior to 7:30 A.M. of the day of discharge, the night shift radiology supervisor will give the requisition to the day shift radiology supervisor with instructions as to when the exam will be performed.
    g. "Discharge pending" requisitions for routine exams that cannot be sent to radiology by 5:00 P.M. on the day prior to discharge should be tubed to radiology as quickly as possible. Please call the radiology supervisor to ensure receipt of the requisition and to negotiate an expected time for the exam.

To Reduce Equipment Replacement Costs. Wheelchairs were typically left in a designated alcove off the main lobby following patient discharges. The front door attendant would access this supply of wheelchairs for arrivals needing assistance. At this end of the shift, the front door attendant returned any excess chairs to the patient transportation storage area. The alcove area could be accessed by any employee or visitor after the front door attendant left in the late afternoon. The process improvement team felt sure that they could reduce equipment loss by securing this space after hours, so a locked gate was installed.

To Improve Staff Behavior and Morale. Job descriptions and standards of performance were revised. The old standard, which expressed the expectation that there would be 18 transports per employee per eight-hour day, was replaced with a statement not focusing on numbers, but emphasizing continuing improvement and teamwork.

A dress code was established. Transporters, many of whom had been wearing T-shirts and jeans to work, were involved in the selection of the uniforms.

Ms. Anderson developed the Patient Transportation Department's first orientation program and provided classes for all employees on safety (body mechanics, falls prevention, and oxygen transport), infection control, radio communications, and guest relations. The program was piloted on the current transporters. In January 1991, Ms. Anderson initiated monthly staff meetings on day and evening shifts to keep transporters informed of new and changing events and to encourage constructive discussion of problems and possible solutions. One of the staff meetings was devoted to the review and discussion of the Gallup survey results. The staff showed no surprise with the Gallup results and comparative Hospitals data and offered few ideas for improving the situation. Updates on transportation subgroup meetings and monthly activity statistics were provided at each meeting. Year-to-date graphs showing the number of transports, average response times, and longest waits were posted in the dispatch area after each meeting.

Project Results

The radios were an immediate success. By March, the average transport response times had dropped to 15 minutes (based on a random sample of 155 weekday log entries each in January and March, 1991), and they just kept getting better (see Figure 5.5). Prioritizing discharges made little difference once the process had been improved. In July, average response times were calculated separately for weekday, weekend (7 A.M. to 3:30 P.M.) and all evening transports. The response times were five, eight, and seven minutes respectively. Figure 5.6 shows improvements made in reducing the longest waits until a transporter could be dispatched.

The volume of completed transports increased steadily during the first six months of 1991. After May, as Figure 5.7 shows, transports soared with the centralization of the transporters and with the expansion of bed capacity. Other areas

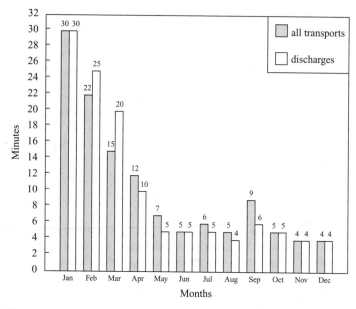

Figure 5.5 Average Transport Response Times, January through December 1991

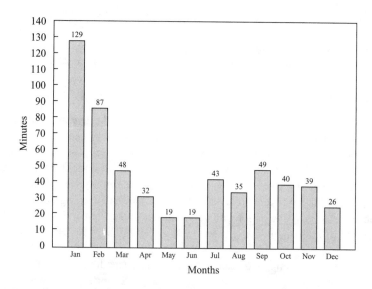

Figure 5.6 Longest Wait Times for Transport Services, January through December 1991

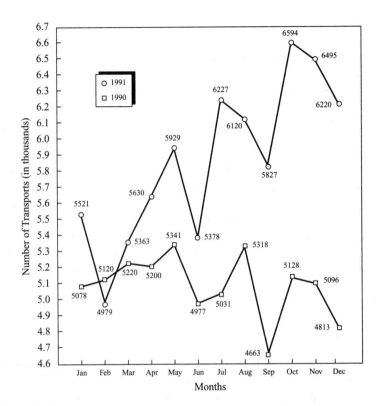

Figure 5.7 Number of Patient Transports, January through December 1990 and 1991

were asking for transport services and although the transporters were reluctant at first, services were extended to the 63-bed inpatient psychiatric unit and the post-anesthesia care unit. By the end of 1991, Radiology's Diagnostic Imaging Department suggested transferring their two full-time transporter positions to patient transportation. This added another 30 to 35 transports to each weekday shift and represented the first increase in the FTE base.

The voice information was used predominantly when the transport office was closed. Few diagnostic and treatment departments had scheduling systems in place. For the few with schedules, the system worked well. Approximately 10 to 15 transports were scheduled daily. All discharge films were accomplished the evening before or early on the morning of discharge. Transporters were dispatched 15 to 20 minutes in advance of appointments to assure "on time" patient arrivals.

Busy telephone lines were no longer a problem for callers. Stabilization of the dispatcher's role and decreased personnel activity in the dispatch area had increased dispatcher efficiency and accuracy.

The idea of decentralizing wheelchairs and stretchers throughout the hospital was a disaster! The hallway alcoves were not large enough to store more than a few wheelchairs at any one time, so equipment was rarely there when a transporter needed it. The equipment was also used by other ancillary staff and visitors. After one month of the new system, the general feeling among transporters was that dispatchers were assigning trips in such a way as to avoid frequent return trips to the dispatch area. The transporters monitored the radios and initiated peer assistance when a dispatched transporter needed equipment.

Contrary to initial concerns, no radios were lost or broken. The Fiscal Year 1993 capital budget request of $20,000 was reduced to $3,700. Transporters were keeping up with the equipment, and the secured storage area in the lobby helped reduce the loss of equipment to the public and other departments. The gate did create unanticipated problems for the Emergency Department (E.R.), which relied on this area for replenishing their supply of wheelchairs during the night. Without notifying anyone, the E.R. staff began taking wheelchairs from the dispatch area, sometimes resulting in transport start-up delays the next morning. Tensions between Mr. Williams and the E.R. aides escalated before management was aware of the problem. Giving the E.R. staff a key to the gate solved that problem.

Satisfaction Levels

Transporters and dispatchers both liked the radios. Ms. Anderson commented, "At first, it was like a new toy. Transporters talked with each other all the time—even in the presence of patients." Some transporters consistently neglected to radio in completed transports, especially when Mr. Williams was not the dispatcher. Transporter performance improved as individual behaviors were addressed and as the novelty of the radios wore off.

Patient satisfaction with transport services improved, and the number of concerns submitted to patient relations decreased, as shown in Figure 5.8. Nursing staff perceptions of transport services for clinic and inpatient areas were surveyed for the first time in October 1991. Nurses and clerks on each unit were requested to collaborate by completing one survey form per patient unit). Forty-five of the surveys shown in Exhibit 5.3 were returned, for a response rate of 88 percent. The results are shown in Figures 5.9 and 5.10.

Recognition

The Hospitals senior management council rejected an opportunity to acknowledge the transport team's accomplishments at the end of fiscal year, June 30, 1991. Salary funds were unexpectedly available to award special merit payments. Ms. Reynolds and Ms. Lloyd recommended a team award, but the idea was supported by only one other member—the CQI director. Although the transporters did not receive a monetary award, their achievements were showcased in a num-

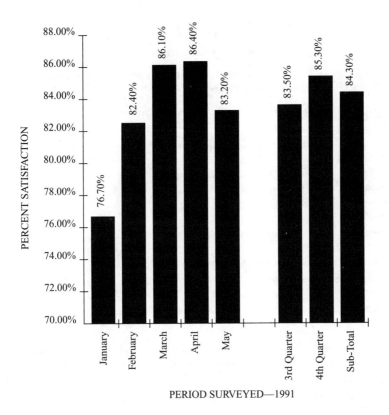

Patient Concerns	1990	1991
January	0	2
February	11	1
March	2	2
April	4	1
May	5	5
June	3	2
July	2	3
August	0	0
September	4	6
October	7	0
November	6	5
December	4	3
Totals	48	30

Figure 5.8 Patient Satisfaction with Transport Time

Exhibit 5.3 Patient Transportation Survey Form

Patient Transportation Survey

On a scale of 1 to 5 (with 5 being the highest), please express your degree of satisfaction with the performance of the Patient Transportation Department on the following parameters:

Courtesy of dispatcher when receiving patient information for transport	1 2 3 4 5
Courtesy of transporters to unit staff	1 2 3 4 5
Discretion used by transporters in discussing patient condition with unit staff	1 2 3 4 5
Patient safety precautions followed (ID bracelet checked, side rails secured on stretchers, etc.)	1 2 3 4 5
Trip ticket presented to unit staff for signature upon patient's leaving the floor	1 2 3 4 5
Patient waiting time for transport assistance Average waiting time _____	1 2 3 4 5
Courtesy and respectfulness shown to patients by transporters	1 2 3 4 5
Trip ticket presented to unit staff for signature upon patient's return to floor	1 2 3 4 5
Medical charts returned to unit desk upon patient's return from transport	1 2 3 4 5

Additional comments/suggestions: _____

_____

_____

Patient Care Unit: _____ Department # _____
(10/91)

---

ber of forums, including the CEO's meetings with all Hospitals employees. In August, Ms. Reynolds, Ms. Lloyd, and Ms. Anderson threw a surprise party for the entire staff at the change of shift. The celebration to honor the team's accomplishments since January was a great success. Other service areas became aware of the event, achieving greater visibility for the team's progress.

The Turnaround in Thinking

The original expectations for increased efficiencies were limited to the benefits that a new communications system could offer a work group stereotyped as dull and uncaring. Recently, one transporter said, when discussing a problem that she was having with an employee in another department, "You get what you expect!" The message was clear!

The turning point in the administrators' thinking happened when the CQI progress was made real through experience with the A/D project and particularly the patient transportation subgroup. Although Ms. Lloyd had studied CQI theory

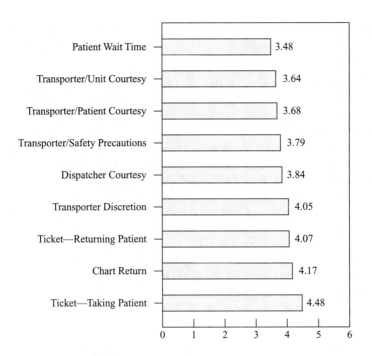

Note: Satisfaction rated on a scale of 1 to 5, with 5 being the highest score.

Figure 5.9 Patient Transportation Satisfaction Survey Results on Various Measures

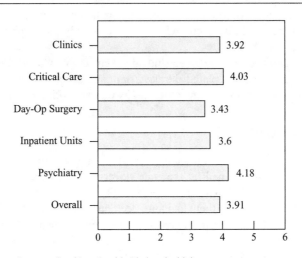

Note: Satisfaction rated on a scale of 1 to 5, with 5 being the highest score.

Figure 5.10 Patient Transportation Satisfaction Survey Results, by Department

and its application to manufacturing settings, she was skeptical about its successful translation to complex medical settings. Ms. Lloyd reflected on the experience, saying,

> As an active participant in the process, I worked closely with staff
> members at all levels to try to understand processes and the problems
> and frustrations confronting them on a daily basis. Employees became
> participants in solutions, instead of recipients of mandates. I witnessed
> their interest and pride as response times and activity levels improved.
> Their achievements in performance and staff morale are even more sur-
> prising in view of the state's FY 1991/92 salary freeze for all employ-
> ees except nurses.
>
> The CQI approach took more time than I was accustomed to spend-
> ing on operational problems. It required an unusual level of detail
> which initially tested my patience. However, my enthusiasm for the
> process grew with each small gain. I am convinced that without the
> timely introduction of CQI the Innovative Project would have been
> nothing more than an expensive band-aid.

One Problem Leads to Another

It had been almost a year since the radios were implemented and the numbers
on the charts looked good. Yet the transporters were experiencing more and more
delays on the inpatient units. Ms. Anderson's follow-up with nurse managers resulted in only brief periods of improvement. Nurses were annoyed when transporters were reassigned after five-minute delays. Patients awaiting discharge
transports and procedural areas awaiting patients often attributed the slow response times to transporters. After a year of steady gains, patient transport was
still taking the heat.

Ms. Lloyd and Ms. Anderson studied the current flow chart, Figure 5.11, again.
As Ms. Lloyd contemplated the next step, she observed, "There's no end. This
whole thing leads to so many other things we need to fix."

CASE ANALYSIS

This case centers on the changes made in the transporter system in a large
teaching hospital owned by the state government. Concern with the discharge
planning process led to the development of the transportation CQI effort. Clearly,
this was an area where there had long been unnecessary friction in the institution.
But it was an area that management had seemed reluctant to address, probably
because they had little expectation of improvement. As you have read, the effort
was quite successful.

One of the impacts of the quality movement started in response to the Japanese
quality success has been the realization that one major American quality problem

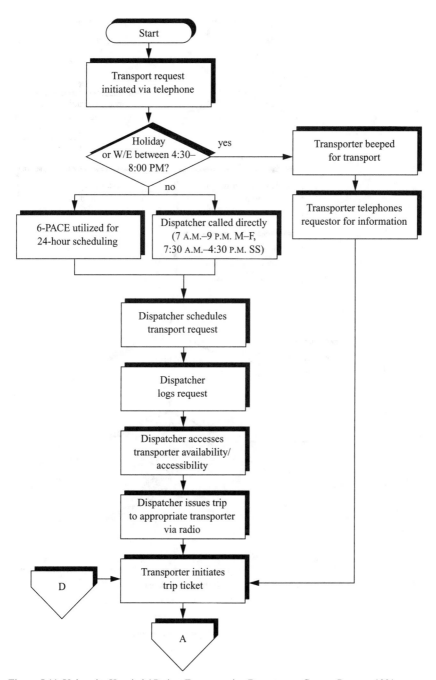

Figure 5.11 University Hospitals' Patient Transportation Department, Current Process, 1991
(continues)

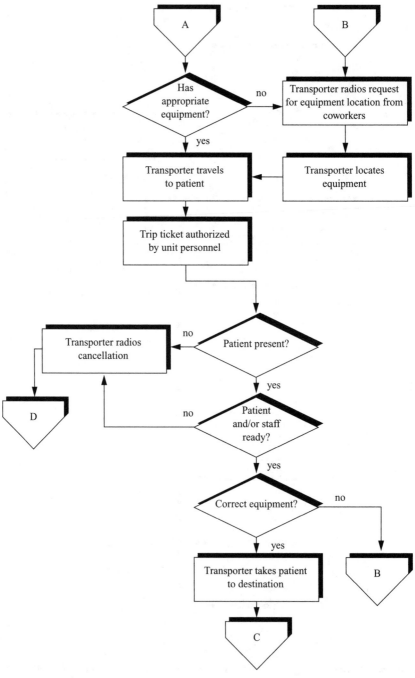

Figure 5.11 *continued*

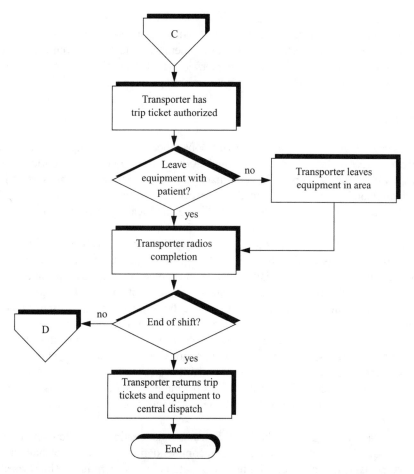

Figure 5.11 *continued*

---

was expectations that were too low, sometimes by an order of magnitude. Here management had expected little from the transporters, and they got it. This case is as much about employee empowerment as it is about quality improvement.

Introduction

CQI provided the impetus and commitment for change. Once into the change process, the teams began to address problem areas that had been left unattended. This hospital, being one of the participants in the National Demonstration Project, has had an ongoing CQI program. The discharge planning project was one of its earliest efforts. However, the decentralized nature of decision making in a large teaching hospital staffed by medical school faculty led the administration to start slowly, with a few teams to lead the way. Academics are not likely to adopt something because it has worked in the auto or chemical industries. Given their high need for professional autonomy (Chapters 9 and 11), they have to witness successful experiments such as these before accepting the concept.

Basics

This is the only case of the five in this book where benchmarking took place. A vendor suggested looking at a communications system used by transporters in a nearby community hospital. Several managers went out to look at this system in operation and were convinced that it was working well there and could work well in their institution. Demonstrations can have a significant influence on pragmatic health care professionals.

This case is a clear illustration of the stages that Chapter 10 describes for the evolution of teams. At first, the representatives of the various groups on the teams blamed the transportation delay problems on each other. This was especially true of the heated discussions about the transportation of patients to Radiology. Then, with further dialogue, people began to realize the sources of their misunderstandings, such as not knowing that the floor units had not been informed of the patient pickups. Realizing that they were poorly informed, the team members began to study the process to try to learn more about what was really happening. That was when the team truly formed. This was followed by some analyses and recommendations that resulted from the team's beginning to set norms for its own behavior and get on with performing the task at hand. The recommendations were followed.

This case also illustrates the fact that teams must continue to follow up on the results of their recommendations. The recommendation to have wheelchairs and carts available on each floor did not work out, and the system had to be revised. Likewise, unanticipated side effects were uncovered, such as issues of access to the same equipment by the emergency room staff at night. The teams must always be alert to the unintended consequences of their system changes. Not every interested party will be on every team, nor can every impact be anticipated. The concepts must be tried out, evaluated, and revised if necessary. Note that there were unintended positive consequences too. The amount spent to replace missing equipment dropped markedly with the changed system as the system came under tighter control.

Implementation

Here again we see that the efforts of management and the work of the teams interact. The organizational change that management made facilitated the changes. It unfroze the transporter system and enabled individuals to switch roles to better fit the new technology. Management provided the capital budget funds to purchase the communications system even before the CQI team came into being. Management had already benchmarked that system. However, the communicators would not have been as effective without the committee's efforts.

The committee delved into the fact that the transporters were split into two groups under separate supervision and analyzed the communications problems between the nursing stations, the transporters, and the ancillary departments. The team analysis provided the occasion for taking Mr. Williams to the community hospital to see how the system could work after he continued to raise objections to the change. Many activities can be made much less threatening when they are presented as a team project effort as opposed to management order. One cannot help wondering whether things might have gone ahead faster if a team been formed earlier and made that initial benchmarking visit, especially if it had included Mr. Williams.

The planning process cited here is unusual. Basically, those who wish to start teams need to present a proposal to management to have access to resources, including facilitators and capital budget, where necessary. Because this is a large government institution, these approval processes could take quite a bit of time. Furthermore, management was not constrained from addressing the problem while the team process was getting started. Therefore we see that management had already ordered the communicators and moved the transport service under the nursing service before the patient transport team had done its analysis. Therefore one might question what the team accomplished. Mainly, it found solutions to the issues raised by the installation of the communicators and led to the recognition of system improvements that went beyond the province of the transport service. One of these was gaining sufficient trust to merge the two sets of transporters, one in Radiology and one for the rest of the hospital. Such mergers usually improve overall productivity and service responsiveness by 15 to 25 percent due to economies of scale in covering each other's calls. The same effects have been seen elsewhere in centralized telephone customer service centers by companies such as Federal Express and American Express.

While not presented in the case, one important role of the team was to publicize the positive results. The transporters, unlike most hospital employees, had a negative image. Their performance improved, but the team served as a vehicle by which that positive effect was talked about around the hospital and by which the attitudinal changes in the transporters were responded to and reinforced. Do not ignore the importance of the CQI team as a means of disseminating, reinforcing, and rewarding positive outcomes.

Applications

This case took place in a teaching hospital, but there is no indication that the effort was associated with any of the teaching objectives of the institution. The reader should refer to Chapter 17 for some ideas about how the academic medical center might well respond to CQI and to incorporating CQI into its teaching tasks.

Chapter 15 focuses on the use of CQI in the laboratory. In this case, the Radiology Department played a major role, but it was not represented in the team effort until later. We suspect that this happens fairly often, that ancillary services are not thought of as having as much impact on processes as they really do. As health care organizations learn more about the complex and interdependent nature of their own processes, we would expect to see the ancillary departments become increasingly involved in CQI efforts.

Bibliography

Adams, D.F., et al. 1973. The complications of coronary arteriography. *Circulation* 48, no. 3:609–618.

American Public Health Association, Association of State and Territorial Health Officers, Centers for Disease Control, National Association of County Health Officials, and U.S. Conference of Local Health Officers. 1990. *Assessment protocol for excellence in public health (APEX-PH)*. Washington, D.C.: American Public Health Association.

American Public Health Association, Association of State and Territorial Health Officers, National Association of County Health Officials, U.S. Conference of Local Health Officers, and Centers for Disease Control. 1985. *Model standards: A guide for community preventive health services*. Washington, D.C.: American Public Health Association.

American Public Health Association, Association of State and Territorial Health Officers, National Association of County Health Officials, U.S. Conference of Local Health Officers, and Centers for Disease Control. 1991. *Healthy communities 2000: Model standards, guidelines for community attainment of year 2000 national health objectives*. Washington, D.C.: American Public Health Association.

Ancona, D.G. 1985. Groups in organizations: Extending laboratory models. In *Group processes and intergroup relations*, Vol. 9, *Review of personality and social psychology,* ed. C. Hendrick. Newbury Park, Calif.: Sage.

Ancona, D.G. 1990. Outward bound: Strategies for team survival in the organization. *Academy of Management Journal* 33:334–365.

Anders, G. More managed health-care systems use incentive pay to reward "best" doctors. 1992. *Wall Street Journal*, January 25, p. B1.

Andersen, A., and the American College of Healthcare Executives. 1991. *The future of medical care: Physician and hospital relationships*. Chicago: American College of Healthcare Executives.

Antman, E.M., et al. 1992. A comparison of results of meta-analysis of randomized control trials and recommendations of clinical experts: Treatments for myocardial infarction. *JAMA* 268:240–248.

Argyris, C. 1991. Teaching smart people how to learn. *Harvard Business Review* 69, no.3:99–109.

Batalden, P.B. 1991. Organizationwide quality improvement in health care. *Topics in Health Record Management* 11, no.3:1–12.

Batalden, P.B., et al. 1989. Quality improvement: The role and application of research methods. *Journal of Health Administration Education* 7:577–583.

Batalden, P.B., and E.C. Nelson. 1991. Hospital quality: Patient, physician and employee judgements. *International Journal of Health Care Quality Assurance* 3, no.4:7–17.

Batalden, P.B., and P. Stoltz. 1993. A framework for the continual improvement of health care: Building and applying professional and improvement knowledge to changes in daily work. *The Joint Commission Journal of Quality Improvement* 19, no.10:424–447.

Beach, L.R., and L.R. Burns. 1993. The Quality Improvement Strategy (QIS): A method for tying quality improvement to physician satisfaction with hospital service. Technical Report 93–7, Dept. of Management and Policy, University of Arizona, Tucson, AZ.

Beatty, M.J. 1989. Group members' decision rule orientations and consensus. *Human Communications Research* 16:279–296.

Beckhard, R. 1969. *Organization development.* Reading, Mass.: Addison-Wesley.

Beer, M., et al. 1990. Why change programs don't produce change. *Harvard Business Review* 68, no.6:158–166.

Benne, K.D., and P. Sheats. 1948. Functional roles of group members. *Journal of Social Issues* 4, no.2:41–49.

Bennett, K.J., et al. 1985. Guidelines for health technology assessment: The efficacy, effectiveness, and efficiency of neonatal intensive care. *International Journal of Technology Assessment in Health Care* 1:873–892.

Bennis, W.G., and B. Nanus. 1985. *Leaders: The strategies for taking charge.* New York: Harper and Row.

Berwick, D.M. 1989a. Continuous improvement as an ideal in healthcare. 1989. *New England Journal of Medicine* 320:53–56.

Berwick, D.M. 1989b. Health services research and quality of care. *Medical Care* 27:763–781.

Berwick, D.M. 1990. Peer review and quality management: Are they compatible? *Quality Review Bulletin* 16:246–251.

Berwick, D.M. 1991. Letter: "Peer review and quality management: Are they compatible?" *Quality Review Bulletin* 16, no.12:419–420.

Berwick, D.M. 1993. QMHC interview. *Quality Management in Health Care* 2, no.1:72–81.

Berwick, D.M., et al. 1990. *Curing health care: New strategies for quality improvement.* San Francisco: Jossey-Bass.

Bettenhausen, K.L. 1991. Five years of groups research: What we have learned and what needs to be addressed. *Journal of Management* 17:345–381.

Blades, C.A., et al. 1987. Health service efficiency: Appraising the appraisers—A critical review of economic appraisal in practice. *Social Science and Medicine* 25, no. 5:461–472.

Blum, H.L. 1974. *Planning for health: Development and application of social change theory.* New York: Human Sciences Press.

Blumberg, M. 1986. Risk-adjusting health care outcomes: A methodological review. *Medical Care Review* 43:351–393.

Bluth, E.I., et al. 1982. Improvement in "stat" laboratory turnaround time: A model continuous improvement project. *Archives of Internal Medicine* 152:837–840.

Borbas, C., et al. 1990. The Minnesota Clinical Comparison and Assessment Project. *Quality Review Bulletin* 16, no.2:87–92.

Bradford, A.R., and D.L. Cohen. 1990. *Influence without authority.* New York: Wiley.

Brennan, T.A., et al. 1991. Incidence of adverse events and negligence in hospitalized patients. *New England Journal of Medicine* 324:370–376.

Brook, R., et al. 1975. *A review of the literature on cholecystectomy: Findings, complications, utilization rates, costs, efficacy, and indications.* Santa Monica, Calif.: RAND Corp.

Burrus, W.M. 1993a. How long will CQI take to produce savings? *Quality Matters* 2, no.3:3–5.

Burrus, W.M. 1993b. Northwest Hospital counting all the way to the bank. *Quality Matters* 2, no.3: 5–7.

Buxton, M.J. 1987. Economic forces and hospital technology: A perspective from Europe. *International Journal of Technology Assessment in Health Care* 3:241–252.

Byrne, J., et al. 1993. The virtual corporation. *Business Week* no.3304:98–102.

Caper, P. 1988. Defining quality in medical care. *Health Affairs* 7, no.1:49–61.

Cattalini, D. 1993. Best practices in ambulatory surgery. *Healthcare Forum Journal* 36, no.1:28–29.

Chalmers, T.C., et al. 1987. Meta-analysis of clinical trials as a scientific discipline, I: Control of bias and comparison with large cooperative trials. *Statistics and Medicine* 6:733–744.

Chalmers, T.C., et al. 1989. Selection and evaluation of empirical research in technology assessment. *International Journal of Technology Assessment in Health Care* 5:521–536.

Chassin, M.R. 1991. Quality of care: Time to act. *JAMA* 226, no.24:3472–3473.

Chassin, M., et al. 1986. Variations in the use of medical and surgical services by the Medicare population. *New England Journal of Medicine* 314:285–290.

Chassin, M., et al. 1987. Does inappropriate use explain variation in the use of health services. *JAMA* 258, no.18:2533–2537.

Clarke, R.N., and P. Kotler. 1987. *Marketing for heathcare organizations.* Englewood Cliffs, N.J.: Prentice-Hall.

Cleary, P.D., and B.J. McNeil. 1991. Patient satisfaction as an indicator of quality of care. *Inquiry* 25, no.1:25–36.

Cohen, M.D., et al. 1972. The garbage can theory of administration. *Administrative Science Quarterly* 17:1–27.

Colditz, G.A., 1988. Measuring gain in the evaluation of medical technology: The probability of a better outcome. *International Journal of Technology Assessment in Health Care* 4:637–642.

Cooper, J.C., and J.D. Suver. 1988. Product line cost estimation: A standard cost approach. *Heathcare Financial Management* 42, no.4:60,62,64.

Cotton, P. 1991. Medical schools receive a message: Reform yourselves, then take on health care system. *JAMA* 266:2802–2804.

Counte, M.A., et al. 1992. Total Quality Management in health care organizations: An analysis of employee impacts. *Hospital and Health Services Administration,* 37:503–518.

Crosby, P.B. 1979. *Quality is free: The art of making quality certain.* New York: Mentor.

Davies, A.R., and J.E. Ware. 1988. Involving consumers in quality of care assessment. *Health Affairs* 7, no.1:33–48.

Davis, D.A., et al. 1992. Evidence for the effectiveness of CME: A review of 50 randomized controlled trials. *JAMA* 268:1111–1117.

Deber, R.B. 1992. Translating technology assessment into policy: Conceptual issues and tough choices. *International Journal of Technology Assessment in Health Care* 8:131–137.

Deming, W.E. 1986. *Out of the crisis.* Cambridge, Mass.: M.I.T. Center for Advanced Engineering Study.

Deming, W.E. 1993. *The new economics: For industry, government, education.* Cambridge, Mass.: M.I.T. Center for Advanced Engineering Study.

DesHarnais, S.I., and C.P. McLaughlin. 1992. Clinical quality, risk-adjustment, and outcome measures in academic health centers. In *Managing in an academic health care environment,* ed. W.F. Minogue, 87–113. Tampa, Fla.: American College of Physician Executives.

DesHarnais, S., et al. 1988. The risk-adjusted mortality index: A new measure of hospital performance. *Medical Care* 26:1129–1148.

DesHarnais, S., et al. 1990. Measuring hospital performance: The development and validation of risk-adjusted indexes of mortality, readmissions, and complications. *Medical Care* 28:1127–1141.

DesHarnais, S., et al. 1991. Measuring outcomes of hospital care using multiple risk adjusted indexes. *Health Services Research* 26:425–445.

Detsky, A.S., and I.G. Naglie. 1990. A clinician's guide to cost-effectiveness analysis. *Annals of Internal Medicine* 113, no.2:147–154.

Donabedian, A. 1980. The definition of quality and approaches to its assessment. In *Explorations in quality assessment and monitoring*. Vol.1;95–99. Ann Arbor, Mich.: Health Administration Press.

Donabedian, A. 1982. *The criteria and standards of quality*. Ann Arbor, Mich.: Health Administration Press.

Donabedian, A. 1986. Criteria and standards for quality assessment and monitoring. *Quality Review Bulletin*, 14, no.3:99–108.

Donabedian, A. 1990. The seven pillars of quality. *Archives of Pathology and Laboratory Medicine* 114:1115–1118.

Donabedian, A. 1993. Models of quality assurance. Leonard S. Rosenfeld Memorial Lecture, School of Public Health, University of North Carolina at Chapel Hill, February 26.

Droitcour, J., et al. 1993. A new form of meta-analysis for combining results from randomized clinical trials and medical practices databases. *International Journal of Technological Assessment in Health Care* 9:440–449.

Drummond, M.F. 1987. Economic evaluation and the rational diffusion and use of health technology. *Health Policy* 7:309–324.

Drummond, M.F., and G.L. Stoddart. 1984a. How to read clinical journals: VII. To understand an economic evaluation (Part A). *Canadian Medical Association Journal* 130:1428–1434.

Drummond, M.F., and G.L. Stoddart. 1984b. How to read clinical journals: VII. To understand an economic evaluation (Part B). *Canadian Medical Association Journal* 130:1542–1549.

Dumas, R.A. et al. 1987. Making quality control theories workable. *Training and Development Journal* 41, no.2:30–33.

Durand, R., et al. 1991. Association between third-year medical students' abilities to organize hypotheses about patients' problems and to order appropriate diagnostic tests. *Academic Medicine* 66:702–704.

Durand-Zaleski, I., and D. Jolly. 1990. Technology assessment in health care—decision makers and health care providers: What they need to know. *Health Policy* 15:37–44.

Durbin, S., et al. 1993. Integrating strategic planning and quality management in a multi-institutional system. *Quality Management in Health Care* 1, no.4:24–34.

Ebel, K.E. 1991. *Achieving excellence in business: A practical guide to the total quality transformation process*. New York: Marcel Dekker.

Eddy, D.M. 1992. *A manual for assessing health practices and designing practice policies: The explicit approach*. Philadelphia: American College of Physicians.

Ente, B.H. 1989. *Brief overview of the Joint Commission's "Agenda for Change."* Oakbrook Terrace: Joint Commission on Accreditation of Healthcare Organizations.

Evans, C.E., et al. 1986. Does a mailed continuing education program improve physician performance?: Results of a randomized trial in anti hypertensive care. *JAMA* 255:501–504.

Evans, D.B. 1990. What is cost-effectiveness analysis? *Medical Journal of Australia* 153 (Suppl.):S6–S16.

Feinberg, H.B., and H.H. Hiatt. 1979. Evaluation of medical practices: The case for technology assessment. *New England Journal of Medicine*, 301:1086–1091.

Feinglass, J., et al. 1991. The relationship of residents' autonomy and use of a teaching hospital's resources. *Academic Medicine*, 66:549–552.

Fetter, R., et al. 1989. DRG refinement with diagnosis specific comorbidities and complications: A synthesis of current approaches to patient classification. Final Report to HCFA. New Haven, Conn.: Health Systems Management Group.

Finkler, M.D., and D.D. Wirtschafter. 1991. Cost-effectiveness and obstetric services. *Medical Care* 29:951–963.

Flood, A., et al. 1982. Effectiveness in professional organizations: The impact of surgeons and surgical staff organizations on the quality of care in hospitals. *Health Services Research*, 17:341–366.

Flower, J. 1993. Benchmarking: Springboard or buzzword? *Healthcare Forum Journal*, 36, no.1:14–16.

Freund, D.A., and R.S. Dittus. 1992. Principles of pharmacoeconomic analysis of drug therapy. *PharmacoEconomics* 1, no.1:20–29.

Freidson, E. 1972. *Profession of medicine*. New York: Dodd, Mead.

Galbraith, J. 1973. *Designing complex organizations*. Reading, Mass.: Addison-Wesley.

Gardner, E.S., Jr., and C.P. McLaughlin. 1980. Forecasting: A cost containment tool for health care managers. *Health Care Management Review* 5, no.3:31–38.

Garg, M.L., et al. 1991. Primary care teaching physicians' losses of productivity and revenue at three ambulatory care centers. *Academic Medicine* 66:348–353.

Garvin, D.A. 1990. Afterword: Reflections on the future. In *Curing health care: New strategies for quality improvement*, by D.M. Berwick, A.B. Godfrey, and J. Roessner, 159–165. San Francisco: Jossey-Bass.

Gaucher, E.J., and R.J. Coffey. 1993. *Total quality in healthcare: From theory to practice*. San Francisco: Jossey-Bass.

Gill, S.L. 1987. Elements of conflict and negotiation. *Clinical Laboratory Management Review* 1: 187–192.

Gilmore, T.N. 1967. *Making a leadership change*. Boston: Little, Brown.

Gitlow, H., et al. 1989. *Tools and methods for the improvement of quality*. Homewood, Ill.: Irwin.

Glaser, J. February 1993. Chief Information Officer, Brigham and Womens Hospital, Boston, MA. Personal communication.

Godfrey, A.B. 1993. The importance of strategic quality planning and support in health care CQI activities. *Quality Matters* 2, no.2:28–29.

Gonnella, J.S. 1981. Patient case mix: Implications for medical education and hospital costs. *Journal of Medical Education* 56:610–611.

Gottlieb, L., et al. 1990. Clinical practice guidelines in an HMO: Development and implementation in a quality improvement model. *Quality Review Bulletin* 16, no.2:80–86.

Grady, M.L., et al. 1993. *Summary report: Putting research to work in quality improvement and quality assurance*. U.S. Dept. of Health and Human Services, Public Health Service, Agency for Health Care Policy and Research. AHCPR Pub. No. 93-0034, July.

Graham, N. 1990. *Quality assurance in hospitals*. Gaithersburg, Md.: Aspen Publishers.

Greer, A. 1988. The state of the art versus the state of the science. *International Journal of Technology Assessment in Health Care* 4:5–26.

Guyatt, G.H., et al. 1989. Measuring quality of life in clinical trials: A taxonomy and review. *Canadian Medical Association Journal* 140:1441–1448.

Hand, R., et al. 1991. Hospital variables associated with quality of care for breast cancer patients. *JAMA* 266:3429–3432.

Hanson, E.H. 1992. Technology assessment in a user perspective—Experiences with drug technology. *International Journal of Technology Assessment in Health Care* 8:150–165.

Harkey, J., and R.A. Vraciu. 1992. Quality of health care and financial performance: Is there a link? *Health Care Management Review* 17, no.4:55–64.

Hart, C. 1993. *Handout, Northern Telecom*—University Quality Forum, Research Triangle Park, N.C., June.

Hayes, R.H., et al. 1988. *Dynamic manufacturing.* New York: The Free Press.

Haynes, R.B. 1990. Loose connection between peer-reviewed clinical journals and clinical practice. *Annals of Internal Medicine* 113, no.9:724–728.

Headrick, L., et al. 1991. Introducing quality improvement thinking to medical students: The Cleveland Asthma Project. *Quality Review Bulletin* 17:254–260.

Hebel, J., et al. 1982. Assessment of hospital performance by use of death rates: A recent case history. *JAMA* 248:3131–3135.

Heidbreder, J.E. 1993. Benchmarking: Looking for the light—not the heat. *Healthcare Forum Journal* 36, no.1:25–27, 29.

Hellman, S. 1991. The intellectual quarantine of American medicine. *Academic Medicine* 66:245–248.

Henderson, J.C., and J.B. Thomas. 1992. Aligning business and information technology domains: Strategic planning in hospitals. *Hospital and Health Services Administration* 37, no.1:71–87.

Hirokawa, F.Y. 1988. Group communications and decision-making performance: A continued test of the functional perspective. *Human Communication Research* 14:487–515.

Hlatky, M.A., et al. 1990. Ischemic heart disease: Resource use and cost of initial coronary revascularization. Coronary angioplasty versus coronary bypass surgery. *Circulation* 82 (Suppl. IV):208–213.

Holzer, J. 1990. The advent of clinical standards for professional liability. *Quality Review Bulletin* 16, no.2:72–79.

Horn, S.D., and R.A. Horn. 1986. The computerized severity index: A new tool for case-mix management. *Journal of Medical Systems* 10:73–78.

Hornbrook, M.C. 1982. Hospital case mix: Its definition, measurement, and use: Part 1. The conceptual framework. *Medical Care Review* 39, no.1:3–5.

Huge, C. 1990. *Total quality: An executive's guide for the 1990's.* Homewood, Ill.: Irwin.

Hunter, J.E., and F.L. Schmidt. 1990. *Methods of meta-analysis: Correcting error and bias in research findings.* Newbury Park, Calif.: Sage.

Hynes, D.M., et al. 1992. Evaluating productivity in clinical research programs: The National Cancer Institute's (NCI) Community Clinical Oncology Program. *Journal of Medical Systems* 16, no.6:247–267.

Iezzoni, L.I. 1991a. Black box medical information systems: A technology needing assessment. *JAMA* 265:3006–3007.

Iezzoni, L.I. 1991b. Severity standardization and hospital quality assessment. In *Health care: Quality management for the 21st century,* ed. James Couch. Tampa, Fla.: American College of Physician Executives.

Imai, M. 1986. *Kaizen: The key to Japan's competitive success.* New York: Random House.

Jackson, S.E. 1992. Team composition in organizational settings: Issues in managing an increasingly diverse work force. In *Group Process and Productivity,* ed S. Worchel et al., 138–180. Newbury Park, Calif.: Sage.

Jaeschke, R., and D.L. Sackett. 1989. Research methods for obtaining primary evidence. *International Journal of Technology Assessment in Health Care* 5:503–519.

Jaffe, B.M. 1992. What will they think of next? *Surgical Rounds* January: 13–15.

James, B.L. 1989. *Quality management for health care delivery.* Chicago: Hospital Research and Educational Trust of the American Hospital Association.

Johnson, D.E.L. 1990. HCFA's mortality statistics boost teaching hospitals. *Health Care Strategic Management* 8, no.1:2–3.

Joint Commission on Accreditation of Healthcare Organizations. 1992. *Striving toward improvement: Six hospitals in search of quality.* Chicago: Joint Commission on Accreditation of Healthcare Organizations.

Juran, J.M. 1988. *Juran on planning for quality.* New York: The Free Press.

Kaluzny, A.D., and C.P. McLaughlin. 1992. Managing transitions: Assuring the adoption and impact of TQM. *Quality Review Bulletin* 18, no.11:380–384.

Kaluzny, A.D., et al. 1991. Prevention and early detection activities in primary care: New directions for implementation. *Cancer Detection and Prevention* 15:459–465.

Kaluzny, A.D., et al. 1992a. Applying total quality management concepts to public health organizations. *Public Health Reports* 107:257–264.

Kaluzny, A.D., et al. 1992b. Continuous quality improvement in the clinical setting: Enhancing adoption. *Quality Management in Health Care* 1, no.1:37–44.

Kaluzny, A.D., et al. 1993. TQM as managerial innovation: Research issues and implications. *Health Services Management Research* 6, no.2:78–88.

Kassirer, J.P. 1992. Clinical trials and meta-analysis: What do they do for us? *New England Journal of Medicine* 327:273–274.

Katzenbach, J.R., and D.K. Smith. 1993. *The wisdom of teams: Creating the high-performance organization.* Boston: Harvard Business School Press.

Keeler, E.B., and S. Cretin, 1983. Discounting of life-saving and other non-monetary effects. *Management Science* 29, no.3:300–306.

Kelleher, C. 1993. Relationship of physician ratings of severity of illness and difficulty of clinical management to length of stay. *Health Services Research* 27:841–842.

Kelly, J., and F. Hellinger. 1986. Physician and hospital factors associated with mortality of surgical patients. *Medical Care* 24:785–800.

Kibbe, D.C., and R.P. Scoville. 1992. Computer software for health care CQI. *Quality Management in Health Care* 1, no.4:50–58.

Kibbe, D.C., and R.P. Scoville. 1993. Tutorial: Using Microsoft Excel for CQI. *Quality Management in Health Care* 2, no.1:63–71.

Kibbe, D.C., et al. 1993. Continuous quality improvement for continuity of care. *Journal of Family Practice* 36:304–308.

Kilmann, R. 1989. *Beyond the quick fix.* San Francisco: Jossey-Bass.

King, B. 1989. *Hoshin planning: The developmental approach.* Methuen, Mass.: GOAL/QPC.

Kinnunen, J. 1990. The importance of organizational culture on development activities in a primary health care organization. *International Journal of Health Planning and Management* 5, no.1:65–71.

Knaus, W., et al. 1986. An evaluation of outcome from intensive care in major medical centers. *Annals of Internal Medicine* 104:410–418.

Kosecoff, J., et al. 1987. Effects of the National Institutes of Health Consensus Development Program on physician practice. *JAMA* 258:2708–2713.

Kritchevsky, S.B., and B.P. Simmons. 1991. Continuous quality improvement: Concepts and applications for primary care. *JAMA* 266:1817–1823.

Kume, H. 1987. *Statistical methods for quality improvement.* Tokyo: Association for Overseas Technical Scholarship.

Latham, V.M. 1987. Task type and group motivation: Implications for a behavioral approach to leadership in small groups. *Small Group Behavior* 18, no.1:56–71.

Lau, J., et al. 1992. Cumulative meta-analysis of therapeutic trials for myocardial infarction. *New England Journal of Medicine* 327:248–254.

Laupacis, A., et al. 1992. How attractive does a new technology have to be to warrant adoption and utilization? Tentative guidelines for using clinical and economic evaluations. *Canadian Medical Association Journal* 146:473–481.

Lawrence, P.R., and J.W. Lorsch. 1967. *Organization and environment.* Boston: Harvard University Press.

Lazovich, D., et al. 1991. Underutilization of breast-conserving surgery and radiation therapy among women with stage I and stage II breast cancer. *JAMA* 266:3433–3438.

Leape, L. 1987. Unnecessary surgery. *Health Services Research* 24:351–407.

Leape, L. 1990. Practice guidelines and standards: An overview. *Quality Review Bulletin* 16, no.2:42–49.

Leape, L.L., et al. 1991. The nature of adverse events in hospitalized patients: Results of the Harvard Medical Practice Study II. *New England Journal of Medicine* 324:377–384.

Lebow, J.L. 1984. Similarities and differences between mental and health care evaluation studies assessing consumer satisfaction. *Evaluation and Program Planning* 6:237–245.

Lewis, C.E. 1988. Disease prevention and health promotion practices of primary care physicians in the United States. *American Journal of Preventive Medicine* 4, no. 4(suppl.):9–16.

Lewis, I., and C. Sheps. 1983. *The sick citadel: The American academic medical center and the public interest.* Cambridge, Mass.: Oelgeschlager, Gunn and Hain.

Linder, J. 1991. Outcomes measurement: Compliance tool or strategic initiative. *Health Care Management Review* 16, no.4:21–33.

Linder, J.C. 1992. Outcomes measurement in hospitals: Can the system change the organization? *Hospital and Health Administration* 37, no.2:143–166.

Lomas, J., et al. 1991. Opinion leaders vs. audit and feedback to implement practice guidelines: Delivery after previous Cesarean section. *JAMA* 265:2202–2207.

Luce, B.R., and A. Elixhauser. 1990. Estimating costs in the economic evaluation of medical technologies. *International Journal of Technology Assessment in Health Care* 6, no.1:57–75.

Luce, B.R., and K. Simpson. 1993. Methods of cost effectiveness analysis: Areas of consensus and debate. Report prepared for Pharmaceutical Manufacturers Association through the Battelle Medical Technology Assessment and Policy Research Center. April 22.

Luft, H., and S. Hunt. 1986. Evaluating individual hospital quality through outcome statistics. *JAMA* 255:2780–2784.

Madison, D.L., and T.R. Konrad. 1988. Large medical group-practice organizations and employed physicians: A relationship in transition. *Milbank Quarterly* 66, no.2:240–282.

Marder, R.J. 1990. Relationship of clinical indicators and practice guidelines. *Quality Review Bulletin* 16, no.2:60.

Maynard, A. 1990. The design of future cost-benefit studies. *American Heart Journal* 119:761–765.

McAninch, M. 1988. Accrediting agencies and the search for quality in health care. In *Handbook of quality assurance in mental health,* ed. G. Stricker and A. Rodriguez. New York: Plenum.

McLaughlin, C.P. 1991. Negotiation as a business matter. *Carolina Journal of Pharmacy* 71, no.10:25–27.

McLaughlin, C.P. 1992. Negotiation and cooperation. *Carolina Journal of Pharmacy* 72, no.2:26–28.

McLaughlin, C.P., and A.D. Kaluzny. 1990. Total quality management in health care: Making it work. *Health Care Management Review* 15, no.3:7–14.

McMillan, J.R. 1987. Measuring customer satisfaction to improve quality of care. *Health Progress* 68 no.2:54–55,76–80.

Melum, M.M. 1990. Total quality management: Steps to success. *Hospitals* 64, no.23:42–44.

Merry, M.D. 1990. Total quality management for physicians: Translating the new paradigm. *Quality Review Bulletin* 16, no.3:101–105.

Meterko, M., et al. 1990. Patient judgments of hospital quality: Report of a pilot study. *Medical Care* 28(Suppl.9):S10–S14.

Microsoft Corporation. 1992. *Microsoft Excel users guide*. Redmond, Wash.

Mintzberg, H. 1979. *The structuring of organizations*. Englewood Cliffs, N.J.: Prentice-Hall.

Mohr, L. 1982. *Explaining organizational behavior*. San Francisco: Jossey-Bass.

Mooney, G.H. 1980. Cost-benefit analysis and medical ethics. *Journal of Medical Ethics* 6, no.4:177–179.

Morris, A.H. 1992. Protocols, ECOO2R, and the evaluation of new ARDS therapy. *Japanese Journal of Intensive Care Medicine* 16:61–63.

Moses, L., and F. Mosteller. 1968. Institutional differences in postoperative death rates: Commentary on some of the findings of the National Halothane Study. *JAMA* 203:492–494.

Mosteller, F., and E. Burdick. 1989. Current issues in health care technology assessment. *International Journal of Technology Assessment in Health Care* 5:123–136.

Myers, R. 1993. Director of Human Resources, St. Mary's Hospital, Blue Springs, MO. Personal communication.

Nelson, E.C., et al. 1991a. Gaining customer knowledge: Obtaining and using customer judgments for hospitalwide quality improvement. *Topics in Health Record Management* 11, no.3:13–26.

Nelson, E.C., et al. 1991b. The patient comment card: A system to gather patient feedback. *Quality Review Bulletin* 17, no.9:278–285.

Nelson, E.C., et al. 1992a. The physician and employee judgment system: Reliability and validity of a hospital quality measurement method. *Quality Review Bulletin* 18, no.9:284–292.

Nelson, E.C., et al. 1992b. The relationship between patient perceptions of quality and hospital financial performance. *Journal of Healthcare Marketing* 12, no.4:6–14.

Nutt, P.C. 1984. *Planning methods for health and related organizations*. New York: Wiley.

O'Guin, M.C. 1991. *The complete guide to activity based costing*. Englewood Cliffs, N.J.: Prentice-Hall.

Olmstead, R.V. 1993. Benchmarking: A method of improving health care processes by "just asking for them." *Quality Matters* 2, no.2:26–27.

Orme, C.N., and R.J. Parsons. 1992. Customer information and the quality improvement process: Developing a customer information system. *Hospital and Health Services Administration* 37, no.2:197–212.

Ouchi, W.G. 1969. A conceptual framework for the design of organizational control mechanisms. *Management Science* 19:833–845.

Pace, R.C. 1990. Personalized and depersonalized conflict in small group discussions. *Small Group Research* 21, no.1:79–96.

Palmer, R.H., et al. 1991. *Striving for quality in health care: An inquiry into policy and practice*. Ann Arbor, Mich.: Health Administration Press.

Paul-Shaheen, P. 1987. Small area analysis: A review of the North American literature. *American Journal of Health Politics, Policy and Law* 12:741–809.

Paulus, P., and D. Nagar. 1985. Environmental influences on social interaction and group development. In *Group processes and intergroup relations,* Vol.9, *Review of personality and social psychology,* ed C. Hendrick. Newbury Park, Calif.: Sage.

Peat, Marwick, Main & Co. 1988. *Setting quality standards in health care: Balancing purchaser, provider and patient expectations.* Chicago: KMPG Peat Marwick.

Peters, J.P., and S. Tseng. 1984. Managing strategic change: Moving others from awareness to action. *Hospitals and Health Services Administration* 29, no.4:7–20.

Plsek, P.E. 1991. Resource B: A primer on quality improvement tools. In *Curing health care,* ed. D.M. Berwick, A.B. Godfrey and J. Roessner, 177–219. San Francisco: Jossey-Bass.

Plsek, P.E. 1992. Tutorial: Introduction to control charts. *Quality Management in Health Care* 1, no.1:65–74.

Polit, D.F., and B.P. Hungler. 1985. *Essentials of nursing research: Methods and applications.* Philadelphia: Lippincott.

Pollack, M., et al. 1987. Accurate prediction of the outcome of pediatric intensive care: A new quantitative method. *New England Journal of Medicine* 316:134–139.

Porras, J.I., and S.J. Hoffer. 1986. Common behavior changes in successful organizational development efforts. *Journal of Applied Behavioral Science* 22:477–494.

Pritchard, R.B., and B.W. Karasick. 1973. The effects of organizational climate on managerial job performance and job satisfaction. *Organizational Behavior and Human Performance* 9:126–146.

Pugh, M. 1993. CEO of Parkview Medical Center, Pueblo, CO. Personal communication.

Reagan, P., and J. Rohrbaugh. 1990. Group decision process effectiveness: A competing values approach. *Group and Organization Studies* 15, no.1:20–43.

Reed, R., and D. Evans. 1987. The deprofessionalization of medicine: Causes, effects, and responses. *JAMA* 258:3279–3282.

Reinke, W.A., ed. 1988. *Health planning for effective management.* New York: Oxford Press.

Roemer, M.I., et al. 1968. A proposed hospital quality index: Hospital death rates adjusted for case severity. *Health Services Research* 3, no.2:96–118.

Roos, L., et al. 1985. Using computers to identify complications after surgery. *American Journal of Public Health* 75:1288–1295.

Rosselli, V.R., et al. 1989. Improved customer service boosts bottom line. *Healthcare Financial Management* 43, no.12:21–22,24–26,28.

Rubin, R.R. 1990. Can patients evaluate the quality of care? *Medical Care Review* 47:267–326.

Russell, L.B. 1992. Opportunity cost in modern medicine. *Health Affairs* 11, no.2:162–169.

Sabatini, J. 1985. Ethics and economic appraisals in health care. *Social Science and Medicine* 21, no.10:1199–1202.

Sahney, V.K., and G.L. Warden. 1991. The quest for quality and productivity in health services. *Frontiers of Health Services Management* 7, no.4:2–40.

Sahney, V.K., and G.L. Warden. 1993. The role of CQI in the strategic planning process. *Quality Management in Health Care* 1, no.4:1–11.

Sarazen, J.S. 1990. The tools of quality, Part II: Cause and effect diagrams. *Quality Progress* (July), pp.59–62.

Schweikhart, S.B., et al. 1993. Service recovery in health service organizations. *Hospital and Health Services Administration* 38, no.1:3–23.

Scoville, R. 1992a. Master class: Excel crosstabs. *PC World* 10:336.

Scoville, R. 1992b. Master class: Quality control. *PC World* 10:264.

Scoville, R. 1993. Master class: Control charts. *PC World* 11:194.

Shea, G.P., and R.A. Guzzo. 1987. Group effectiveness: What really matters? *Sloan Management Review* 28, no.2:25–31.

Shortell, S. 1985. The medical staff of the future: Replanting the Garden. *Frontiers of Health Services Management* 1, no.3:3–48.

Shortell, S. 1990. Revisiting the garden: Medicine and management in the 1990s. *Frontiers of Health Services Management* 7, no.1:3–32.

Shortell, S., et al. 1993. New versus traditional approaches to quality improvement: Implementation processes and perceived impacts. Evanston, Ill.: Northwestern University Working Paper.

Simpson, K.N., and L.B. Snyder. 1991. Informing the mammography coverage debate: Results of meta-analysis, computer modeling, and issue analysis. *International Journal of Technology Assessment in Health Care* 7:616–631.

Simpson, K.N., et al. 1991. Total quality and the management of laboratories: Implementation strategies and challenges. *Clinical Laboratory Management Review* 5:450–462.

Simpson, K.N., et al. 1992. Strategic planning for public health. *Evaluation and Program Planning* 15:383–393.

Sloan, F., et al. 1986. In-hospital mortality of surgical patients: Is there an empirical basis for standard setting. *Surgery* 99:446–454.

Snedecor, G.W., and W.G. Cochrane. 1989. *Statistical methods*. Ames, Iowa: Iowa State University Press.

Solberg, L.1993. Improving disease prevention in primary care. Washington, D.C.: AHCPR Working Paper.

Soumerai, S.B., and J. Avorn. 1990. Principles of educational outreach ("academic detailing") to improve clinical decision making. *JAMA* 263:549–556.

Starr, P. 1982. *The social transformation of American medicine*. New York: Basic Books.

Stasser, G. 1992. Pooling of unshared information during group discussion. In *Group Process and Productivity*, ed S. Worchel et al., 48–67. Newbury Park, Calif.: Sage.

Strasser, S., and R.P. Davis. 1991. *Measuring patient satisfaction for improved patient service*. Ann Arbor, Mich: Health Administration Press.

Sullivan, K.M. 1989. Comments received on Walker's odd man out approach. *American Journal of Public Health* 79:871.

Teboul, J. 1991. *Managing quality dynamics*. Englewood Cliffs, N.J.: Prentice-Hall.

Tenner, A.R., and I.J. DeToro. 1992. *Total quality management: Three steps to continuous improvement*. Reading, Mass.: Addison-Wesley.

Torrance, G.W., and D. Feeny. 1989. Utilities and quality-adjusted life years. *International Journal of Technology Assessment in Health Care* 5:559–575.

Turner, J.C., et al. 1989. Referent informational influence and group polarization. *British Journal of Social Psychology* 28:135–147.

U.S. Congress, Office of Technology Assessment. 1988. *The quality of medical care: Information for consumers*. OTA-H-386.Washington, D.C.: U.S. Government Printing Office. June.

U.S. General Accounting Office. 1992. *Cross design synthesis*. GAO/PEMD-92-18. Washington, D.C. March.

Van de Ven, A.H. 1974. *Group decision making and effectiveness: An experimental study*. Comparative Administration Research Institute of the Center for Business and Economic Research Graduate School of Business Administration Kent State University, Canton, Ohio.

Veney, J.E., and A.D. Kaluzny. 1992. *Program evaluation for health care administrators* (2nd ed.). Ann Arbor, Mich.: Health Administration Press.

Vinten-Johansen, P., and E. Riska. 1991. New Oslerians and real Flexnerians: The response to threatened professional autonomy. *International Journal of Health Services* 21:75–108.

Vladeck, B.C. 1988. Quality assurance through external controls. *Inquiry* 25:100–107.

Wadsworth, H.M., et al. 1986. *Modern methods for quality control and improvement.* New York: Wiley.

Wagner, D., et al. 1986. The case for adjusting hospital death rates for severity of illness. *Health Affairs* 5, no.2:148–153.

Walker, A.M., et al. 1988. Odd man out: A graphic approach to meta analysis. *American Journal of Public Health* 78:961–966.

Walsh, J.P., et al. 1988. Negotiated belief structures and decision performance: An empirical investigation. *Organizational Behavior and Human Decision Processes* 42:194–216.

Wanous, J.P., and M.A. Yautz. 1986. Solution diversity and the quality of group decisions. *Academy of Management Journal* 29:149–159.

Ware, J.E., and M.K. Snyder. 1975. Dimensions of patient attitudes regarding doctors and medical care services. *Medical Care* 13:669.

Watson, W.E., and L.K. Michaelsen. 1988. Group interaction behaviors that affect group performance on an intellective task. *Group and Organizational Studies* 13:495–516.

Webber, J.B., and J.P. Peters. 1983. *Strategic thinking: New frontier for hospital management.* Chicago: American Hospital Association.

Webster's New Collegiate Dictionary. 1968. G.C. Merriam & Co.

Weick, K. 1976. Educational organizations as loosely coupled systems. *Administrative Science Quarterly* 21, no.3:1–19.

Weick, K.E. 1984. Small wins: Redefining the scale of social problems. *American Psychologist* 39, no.11:40–49.

Weinstein, M.C. 1990. Principles of cost-effective resource allocation in health care organizations. *International Journal of Technology Assessment in Health Care* 6:93–103.

Weinstein, M.C., and H.V. Feinberg. 1980. *Clinical decision analysis.* Philadelphia: Saunders.

Weinstein, M.C., and W. Stason. 1977. Foundations of cost-effectiveness analysis for health and medical practices. *New England Journal of Medicine* 296:716–721.

Weinstein, M.C., and W. Stason. 1985. Cost-effectiveness of interventions to prevent or treat coronary heart disease. *Annual Review of Public Health* 6:41–63.

Wennberg, J.E. 1982. Variations in medical care among small areas. *Scientific American* 246, no.4:120–134.

Wennberg, J., and A. Gittelsohn. 1973. Small area variations in health care delivery. *Science* 182:1102–1108.

Wennberg, J.E., et al. 1987. Use of claims data systems to evaluate health care outcomes: Mortality and reoperation following prostatectomy. *JAMA* 257:933–936.

Westgard, J.O., and P.L. Barry 1989. Total quality control: Evaluation of quality management systems. *Laboratory Medicine* 20, no.6:377–384.

Williams, A. 1992. Cost-effectiveness analysis: Is it ethical? *Journal of Medical Ethics* 18, no.1:7–11.

Wilson, M.P., and C.P. McLaughlin. 1984. *Leadership and management in academic medicine.* San Francisco: Jossey-Bass.

Wilson, M.P., and C.P. McLaughlin. 1992. Strategic planning and external markets. In *Managing in an academic health care environment,* ed. W.F. Minogue, 41–60. Tampa, Fla.: American College of Physician Executives.

Wortman, P.M., and W.H. Yeaton. 1987. Using research synthesis in medical technology assessment. *International Journal of Technology Assessment in Health Care* 3:509–522.

Young, S.W., et al. 1988. Excellence in leadership through organizational development. *Nursing Administration Quarterly* 12, no.4:69–77.

Young, W.N. 1984. Incorporating severity of illness and comorbidity in case-mix measurement. *Health Care Financing Review* (Annual Suppl.) pp.23–31.

Zimmerman, S.M., and R.N. Zimmerman. 1992. *SPC using Lotus 1-2-3*. Milwaukee, Wis.: ASQC Quality Press.

Zmud, R.W., and C.P. McLaughlin. 1989. "That's not my job": Managing secondary tasks effectively. *Sloan Management Review* 30, no.2:29–36.

Zusman, J. 1991. Letter: "Peer review and quality management: Are they compatible?" *Quality Review Bulletin* 16, no.12:418–419.

Index

449